*Louisa May Alcott's*
*Fairy Tales and*
*Fantasy Stories*

24.95

# LOUISA MAY ALCOTT'S
## *Fairy Tales*
### AND
## *Fantasy Stories*

## *Edited by Daniel Shealy*

The University of Tennessee Press

KNOXVILLE

F

Library of Congress Cataloging in Publication Data
Alcott, Louisa May, 1832–1888.
    [Fairy tales and fantasy stories]
    Louisa May Alcott's fairy tales and fantasy stories / edited by Daniel
Shealy. — 1st ed.
        p.   cm.
    Includes bibliographical references.
    Summary: A scholarly collection of the fairy tales and fantasy stories of
Louisa May Alcott. A critical introduction examines the works and places
them in the context of American fantasy.
    ISBN 0-87049-752-9 (cloth : alk. paper)
    1. Fantastic fiction, American.   2. Fairy tales—United States.
[1. Fantasy.   2. Fairy tales.   3. Short stories.]   I. Shealy, Daniel.
II. Title.
PS1016.S54   1992
813'.4—dc20
[Fic]                                                      91-43144
                                                               CIP
                                                               AC

*For my parents,*
*Ruby and Ralph Shealy*

# Contents

# List of Illustrations

# Acknowledgments

I AM GRATEFUL TO THE STAFF of Harvard University Libraries (Houghton and Widner); Robin Brabham, head of Special Collections of Atkins Library at the University of North Carolina at Charlotte; and the staff at Orchard House in Concord, Massachusetts, for making available the original printings of the texts in this volume.

Sarah Elbert, Joel Myerson, Madeleine B. Stern, and Mark West offered their suggestions and expert advice while I was preparing the manuscript. I am indebted to them for their assistance. Carol Wallace Orr first brought this project to the University of Tennessee Press and gave me much help and encouragement in seeing the book through press. Wade Bruton of UNC Charlotte photographed the illustrations.

This work was supported in part by funds from the Foundation of the University of North Carolina at Charlotte and from the State of North Carolina. I also acknowledge the support of the Department of English at UNC Charlotte.

Juanita Honeycutt once again exhibited her patience and diligence in helping to prepare the typed copy for the introduction to this volume.

Finally, I am also grateful to my parents, Ruby and Ralph Shealy, and to my brothers, Roger and Clayton, for their kind support and encouragement.

# A Note on the Texts

THIS BOOK REPRINTS all of Louisa May Alcott's fantasy tales. The texts used are from the first editions of the tales' book publications. When a tale was published in both magazine and book form, the text printed here is from the first edition of the book. The bibliography provides full publication information. Several of Alcott's books were published in December of the year preceding the year listed on the copyright page. The bibliography reflects the official copyright date.

In preparing these works for publication, I have made emendations only where the text would be obviously in error or unclear without them. For example, I have corrected obvious spelling and typographical errors, inserted words and punctuation marks for clarity, and provided missing single or double quotation marks. I have let stand nineteenth-century spellings and inconsistencies in capitalization, hyphenation, and commas in series. Alcott was often careless in preparing her manuscripts for publication, and nineteenth-century compositors were not particularly careful in setting type from even the best-prepared copy; I have in general modernized or "corrected" these texts as little as possible.

# Introduction

ON CHRISTMAS DAY 1854, Louisa May Alcott presented her mother, Abigail, with a copy of her first book, *Flower Fables,* a collection of six fairy tales. Along with the volume, she included a brief letter telling her mother that into "your Christmas stocking I have put my 'first-born,' knowing that you will accept it with all its faults (for grandmothers are always kind), and look upon it merely as an earnest of what I may yet do, for, with so much to cheer me on, I hope to pass in time from fairies and fables to men and realities" (*Selected Letters* 11). Alcott would indeed go on to write of "men and realities." In less than ten years, her experiences as a Civil War nurse would be chronicled in *Hospital Sketches* (1863), and in 1868 she would publish her greatest success, *Little Women,* a landmark in children's literature and an American classic. In the following two decades, she would write many domestic novels, ensuring herself a prominent niche in the American tradition of realistic fiction, especially fiction for juveniles. Despite the enormous fame and fortune that such fiction brought to Alcott, she never left behind the fairies and fables of her younger days. Throughout her career, she continued writing fairy tales and fantasy stories, never forgetting the influence of the imagination upon impressionable readers' minds. Even with the creative output of some thirty-eight fantasy tales, this aspect of Alcott's career has largely been ignored by both the reading public and the literary scholars. More attention has been devoted to her Little Women series and her other domestic stories, and more recently to her newly discovered sensational works, or "blood-and-thunder" tales, than to her large body of fantasy literature. This book seeks to rectify that omission in the study of Alcott's canon by collecting, for the first time, all of Alcott's fairy tales and fantasy stories into one volume.

With the publication of *Flower Fables* in 1854, Alcott established herself as a pioneer in American fantasy fiction. Before the 1850s, American children had few works of American fantasy to read. During the seventeenth and eighteenth centuries, the Puritans had condemned fiction as being nothing but "lies." Children could find little exercise for the imagination in such popular American works as *The New England Primer* or John Cotton's *Spiritual Milk for Babes* or even in such British works as James Janeway's

*A Token for Children* or John Bunyan's *Pilgrim's Progress*—unless they were to imagine the blazing fires of hell or the soul's arduous journey to salvation. After 1820, as Anne Scott MacLeod has pointed out, "American preoccupation with the future of the republic and with the children who would shape that future was reflected in a greatly increased production in the United States of all forms of literature for children" (10). For the child's imagination, unfortunately, most of these works were either overtly didactic tales or informative books of science, geography, or history. The most popular of these types were Samuel Goodrich's *Peter Parley* books, works that tended to be nothing but travelogues or history lessons (often with reading quizzes at the bottom of each page), or Jacob Abbott's Rollo books, which chronicled the ongoing adventures of young Rollo, a paragon of virtue. What little fantasy literature that managed to find its way into children's hands was more than often of European origin.

By the early nineteenth century, Europe already had a rich and growing tradition in fantasy literature. Folk stories and fairy tales, of course, developed out of an oral tradition, evolving through countless tellings; however, not until the late seventeenth century were these tales finally set to paper. In 1696–97, the Frenchman Charles Perrault, or his son, published *Histoires ou Contes du Temps Passé, avec des Moralitez (Histories or Stories of Time Past, with Morals)*, whose inscription on the title page, *Contes de ma mère l'Oye (Stories of Mother Goose)* gave the volume its popular name. These eight folktales, including such classic favorites as Little Red Riding Hood, Sleeping Beauty, Cinderella, and Little Thumb, were so enormously popular that by 1729 Robert Samber had translated the work into English. By 1785, *Mother Goose Melodies* had appeared in America. Soon after the appearance of Perrault's tales, Marie Catherine d'Aulnoy published *Les Contes de Fées (The Stories of Fairies)* around 1700, literary fairy tales meant for courtly entertainment. These tales too were successful, with English translations appearing in 1707 and 1716 (Kotzin 132).

While France may have been the first to set down such fantasy tales, it was Germany that would make them known over the entire world. In 1812, the linguists Jacob and Wilhelm Grimm published *Kinder und Hausmärchen (Nursery and Household Tales)*, a superb collection of folktales they had gathered from the common folk of their native land. A second volume followed in 1815. In 1822, an introduction on the origins of the tales was included in an edition of the work, thus beginning the scholarly pursuit of collecting and studying folktales. An English edition of Grimms' tales appeared in 1823, along with the now-classic illustrations of George Cruikshank; a second volume quickly followed in 1826 (Kotzin 136, 138). Clearly, fantasy literature was beginning to gain the appreciation of readers.

Despite the success and popularity of these works, however, detractors denounced such tales as unworthy of readers' attention or harmful to the impressionable minds of children. The battle over fairy tales would rage until the late nineteenth century. Viewing the child as wiser and purer than adults, the early British Romantics, such as Wordsworth and Coleridge, championed fantasy literature, claiming that it enhanced the imagination (West 2). Of course, the opposition had their following also. Sarah Trimmer, the British editor of *The Guardian of Education,* believed that such works as *Mother Goose* would "fill the minds of children with confused notions of wonderful and supernatural events" (qtd. in Meigs 78–79). In his preface to the first English edition of Grimms' tales, Edward Taylor, the translator, noted the ongoing opposition to fairy tales:

> They are nearly discarded from the libraries of childhood. Philosophy is made the companion of the nursery: we have lisping chemists and leading-string mathematicians: this is the age of reason, not of imagination; and the loveliest dreams of fairy innocence are considered as vain and frivolous. Much might be urged against this rigid and philosophic (or rather unphilosophic) exclusion of works of fancy and fiction. Our imagination is surely as susceptible of improvement by exercise, as our judgement or our memory. (xvi)

With the help of leading Romantic writers, fairy tales and folk stories had, by 1840, become respectable as children's literature.

While the British Romantics were important in helping folktales gain respectability, the early German Romantics were crucial in the writing of original fairy tales, the "literary fairy tales" as they are called. By 1782, Johann August Musaus had used folktales in his works for adults (Kotzin 141). In *The Romantic Fairy Tale,* Marianne Thalmann examines how the origin of the Romantic fairy tales, or *Kunstmärchen,* rightfully belongs, however, to Ludwig Tieck, whose stories first appeared in 1796 (33–62).

Although the German Romantics were indeed influential in the development of the literary fairy tales, their work, for the most part, was intended for adults. As original fairy tales for children became popular, they found a wonderful creator in Denmark's Hans Christian Andersen, whose *Fairy Tales, Told for Children* was published in 1835 and translated into English in 1846. With such classic tales as "The Little Mermaid" and "The Ugly Duckling," Andersen's work became popular in Europe and America. With the appearance of Andersen's tales, the critic F. J. H. Darton claims that the literary fairy tale "had at last come into its own," and that now "it was lawful, and even praiseworthy, to invent and release fantasy and to circulate folklore itself" (247).

Without a doubt, many of these European works, including Mother Goose, Grimms' tales, and Andersen's stories, found their way into the libraries of American children and were great favorites. However, America too was soon to create its own literary folktales. The history of fantasy in American literature is filled with popular misconceptions. If one were to ask a friend to name the earliest fantasy work in America, most people would be hard-pressed to name anything before L. Frank Baum's *The Wonderful Wizard of Oz* (1900). But an enormous and wonderful outpouring of fairy tales, fables, and fantasies appeared during the nineteenth century, especially from the 1850s onward. As Mark West notes in *Before Oz*, fables began appearing in the United States around the middle of the eighteenth century, most of which were English reprints (2). However, in 1836, Samuel Goodrich published *Parley's Book of Fables*, a work that placed heavy emphasis on morals. Praising literature that was informative and educational, Goodrich, on the whole, disliked the traditional tales of Perrault and the Brothers Grimm:

> Somewhat later [after the age of ten] one of my companions lent me a volume containing the stories of Little Red Riding Hood, Puss in Boots, Blue Beard, Jack the Giant-killer, and some other of the tales of horror, commonly put into the hands of youth, as if for the express purpose of reconciling them to vice and crime. Some children, no doubt, have a ready appetite for these monstrosities, but to others they are revolting, until by repetition and familiarity, the taste is sufficiently degraded to relish them. At all events, they were shocking to me. . . . That such tales should be invented and circulated in a barbarous age, I can easily conceive. . . . But that they should be put into the hands of children, and by Christian parents, and that too in an age of light and refinement—excites in me the utmost wonder. (166, 169)

Goodrich's attitude, as Brian Attebery notes in *The Fantasy Tradition in America,* was the typical American viewpoint on fairy tales during the first half of the nineteenth century (60).

Besides *Parley's Fables,* other early nineteenth-century fantasy was also published in America. In 1848, C. B. Burkhardt published *Fairy Tales and Legends of Many Nations,* which was largely retellings of European stories. That same year, Lydia Maria Child, who wrote many didactic household works, edited *Rainbows for Children* (Attebery 63). Child's work, though allegorical at times, was also didactic, as evidenced by her own introduction to the volume: "Thus does the spirit of hopeful progress diffuse itself through all departments of literature, and even the fairy-wand points to a happier state of society" (8).

Despite these early collections of fables and fairy tales, most scholars agree that Nathaniel Hawthorne's *A Wonder Book* (1851) and *Tanglewood Tales* (1853) began the tradition of the literary fairy tale in America (Attebery 60; West 3). Both books were new versions of the ancient Greek myths, specifically reworked with a children's audience in mind. Eustace Bright, a young college student, narrates the tales, thus serving as a framing device for all the stories. The same year that *Tanglewood Tales* appeared, a friend and admirer of Hawthorne, Richard Henry Stoddard, wrote *Adventures in Fairy-Land*. In fact, Stoddard paid tribute to *A Wonder Book* in the preface to his own book, and he adopted Hawthorne's device of using a narrator to frame his works. A year later, in 1854, Louisa May Alcott would publish *Flower Fables*.

With a European tradition firmly established and an American tradition in fantasy literature beginning to form by the 1850s, where does Alcott's work fit into the tradition? Without question, Alcott's fantasy fiction belongs to the long tradition of the moral tale in America, a tradition well established by the Puritans and carried into the nineteenth century by Samuel Goodrich, Jacob Abbott, and Lydia Maria Child. The aim of most children's literature of the early nineteenth century was exemplified in the appearance, in 1827, of a major children's periodical. Established by Nathaniel Willis, *The Youth's Companion* outlined its goal to be "a small weekly journal which should entertain . . . children and insensibly instruct them; which should occupy leisure hours, and turn them to good account; which should sanction and aid parental counsel and pulpit admonition; which should, in any easy and familiar manner, warn against the ways of transgression, error and ruin, and allure to those of virtue and piety" (1). Born in 1832, Alcott was a product of the age of moral fiction. She grew up reading didactic literature, and since it dominated the literary marketplace for most of her life, it was the type of fiction she wrote. In fact, she even admitted that one of her favorite authors was Maria Edgeworth, England's most prolific writer of didactic stories and novels ("Recollections" 10). This fact, coupled with Alcott's own education by her transcendentalist father, Bronson Alcott, whose teachings stressed a strong moral fiber, influenced her own writing throughout her career, including her fantasy tales.

Alcott's fantasy stories can be placed in the didactic tradition of fantasy literature. Certainly the fables of Aesop and many of the Grimms' tales contain implicit or explicit lessons or morals. Even Charles Perrault's tales had morals attached to them at their conclusion. In his study of the fairy tale in England, Michael Kotzin notes that many Victorian writers who championed fairy tales pointed out the moral values in such stories. For example, while extolling the imaginative virtue of such tales, Thomas Carlyle also stressed their moral qualities. John Ruskin's *The King of the Golden River* (1841), Charles Dickens's *The Magic Fishbone* (1868), and Charles Kingsley's *Water Babies* (1863) all contain rather explicit morals (147). In America, the moral tradition in fantasy literature was established early in the nineteenth century with *Parley's Book of Fables*. In his preface to his work, Goodrich writes: "I am well aware that conscientious scruples are entertained by many wise and good people as to the use of fiction in juvenile books, but it appears to me that the argument commonly lies against the *abuse* and not against the use of fiction" ([5]). As already noted, Lydia Maria Child was part of this tradition. In 1844, Child published the first volume of *Flowers for Children,* which contains the short story "The Indolent Fairy," a tale similar to most of Alcott's fantasy tales, especially those of her early career. In Child's story, Papillon, a fairy "remarkable for her impatience and indolence," is ordered by the fairy queen to "go to a cavern in Ceylon, and there remain until she had fashioned a purer and more brilliant diamond than had ever rested on the brow of mortal or fairy" (130, 131). Falling asleep and dreaming of a hummingbird, which builds its nest with hard work without ever thinking of the time it takes to accomplish the task, Papillon begins to believe that honest work brings good results. Eventually, she learns that everyone appears "to be happy at their work; perhaps I can learn to be so" (137). The use of nature and the emphasis on reform clearly parallel Alcott's own work. In fact, it is quite possible that Alcott herself had read this tale since her journal indicates her familiarity with Child's work (*Journals* 68) and since Abigail Alcott, Louisa's mother, was a good friend of Child's (Cheney 41).

While Alcott's fantasy works had their didactic predecessors, they also influenced later writers, including Elizabeth Foster Wesselhoeft, wife of Alcott's longtime physician, Conrad Wesselhoeft. Writing under the name Lily F. Wesselhoeft, she would publish several fantasy books, such as *The Winds, the Woods, and the Wanderer* (1890) and *The Fairy-Folk of Blue Hill* (1895), but her didactic fantasy work *Sparrow, the Tramp* (1888), published the year of Alcott's death, acknowledges Alcott's influence upon her work: "The lamented author of 'Little Women' in her last days read with great delight the manuscript of this little story; and its publication is owing greatly to the interest which she had in it" ([5]). Thus, when Alcott's first collection of fantasy stories appeared in late 1854, her work was firmly in the moral tradition of American fiction, and it helped give shape to the didactic emphasis in the tradition of fantasy literature.

Alcott proudly noted the publication of her first book in her journal entry for 1 January 1855: "The principal event of the winter is the appearance of my book 'Flower Fables.' An edition of sixteen hundred. It has sold well and people seem to like it. I feel quite proud that the little tales that I wrote for Ellen E. when I was sixteen should now bring money and fame. . . . Miss Wealthy Stevens paid for the book, and I received $32" (*Journals* 73). Published by George W. Briggs of Boston in mid-December 1854 (although the book carries an 1855 copyright, the exact publication date was 19 December 1854), *Flower Fables* has a fascinating history.

In 1848, at the age of sixteen, Louisa Alcott taught neighborhood children, including Ralph Waldo Emerson's second child, Ellen, in the family's Hillside barn in Concord. Ellen Emerson was her audience as Alcott entertained the child with stories of a beautiful nature fairyland. Influenced by her woodland walks with her friend and neighbor Henry David Thoreau, her visits to his cabin at Walden Pond, and her readings in books such as *The Story Without an End,* Alcott fashioned a fairy world of her own (Stern 1950, 56–57). Later in life, Alcott recalled those teenage days in Concord, noting the imaginative quality of those times: "Those Concord days were the happiest of my life, for we had charming playmates in the little Emersons, Channings, Hawthornes. . . . Little pilgrims journeyed over the hills with scrip and staff, and cockle-shells in their hats; elves held their pretty revels among the pines, and 'Peter Wilkins" flying ladies came swinging down on the birch tree-tops. Lords and ladies haunted the garden and mermaids splashed in the bath-house of woven willows over the brook" ("Recollections" 12–13). Under this imaginative magical spell of a nature fairyland, the young Louisa wrote down those tales she told and presented nine-year-old Ellen with two handmade books: "The Frost King," written in a green notebook, and "The Fairy Dell," a manuscript covered with gray marbled paper and bound together with pink ribbon (Stern 1950, 58).

By 1854, Alcott had made plans to publish her tales, already having written at least three stories and several poems for such periodicals as the *Saturday Evening Gazette* and *Dodge's Literary Museum.* In a letter to her older sister, Anna, penned during the summer of 1854, Alcott noted her disappointment that the tales had not already appeared; she had, she confessed "shed my quart [of tears] . . . over the book not coming out; for that was a sad blow and I waited so long it was dreadful when my castle in the air came tumbling about my ears. Pride made me laugh in public; but I wailed in private" (*Selected Letters* 9). In November, however, arrangements were obviously secured for the publication since Bronson Alcott recorded in his journal for 17 November 1854 that he had discussed the volume with the publisher: "Today see Briggs, the publisher concerning Louisa's book 'Flower Fables' which she is printing as a child's Christmas gift" (qtd. in Stern 1990, 1850). Madeleine Stern suggests that Emerson himself may have been of help in securing Briggs as he had known the Reverend George Ware Briggs of Rhode Island, a relative of the publisher (Stern 1990, 1850). In her journal, Alcott also explains that Miss Wealthy Stevens paid for the book. It was Miss Stevens for whom Louisa had done sewing in 1852, when the Alcotts lived at 10 Pinckney Street in Boston, and she was probably the sister of William B. Stevens, who worked for a time in the Boston Globe Bank. In fact, the book's copyright notice is in William B. Stevens's name (Stern 1990, 1850–51). So with the help of friends and family, Alcott saw her "first-born" to press.

Not forgetting the role young Ellen Emerson played in the book's history, Alcott dedicated the volume to her and sent her a copy of the work, along with a short letter in December 1854: "Hoping that age has not lessened your love for the *Fairy folk* I have ventured to place your name in my little book, for your interest in their sayings & doings, first called forth these 'Flower Fables,' most of which were fancied long ago in Concord woods & fields." Expressing her dissatisfaction with the illustrations for the volume, Alcott complained to Ellen: "The pictures are not what I hoped they would be & it is very evident that the designer is not as well acquainted with fairy forms & faces as you & I are, so we must each *imagine* to suit ourselves & I hope if the fairies tell me any more stories, they will let an Elfin artist *illustrate* them" (*Selected Letters* 10–11). Ellen Emerson was, of course, flattered by such attention, and her reaction to the book was given to a friend in a letter on 21 December 1854:

> A very dignified young woman addresses you, a girl who this morning received a book *dedicated to her.* Do you understand? I am anxious that you should feel a sufficient respect for me now that I have got a book dedicated to me. It is Louisa Alcott's 'Flower Fables.' When the Alcotts lived here Louisa used to read her stories to me and I used to go wild about them, and made her write them for me. She says that 'twas I who made her publish them for I showed the written ones to Mother who liked them so much she advised Louisa to print a book. Then they were showed to some more and everyone was pleased with them. So this morning I saw a bundle on the entry table directed to me. I opened it and found the 'Flower Fables' all bound and printed very nicely with pictures, but on turning it over I saw my name in

large letters and discovered that 'twas dedicated to me! Of course I fell down in a swoon since I could not express my emotion, there being nobody in the house, and read it and looked at it from every point of view. (Emerson 82)

Was the public's reaction to the book as enthusiastic as Ellen Emerson's? George Briggs advertised the book in the 19 December 1854 *Boston Evening Transcript* as "the *most beautiful* Fairy book that has appeared for a long time, written *when in her sixteenth* year, by Louisa May Alcott, a young lady of Boston. It will be the most popular juvenile issued this season" (2). On 23 December, the *Saturday Evening Gazette,* for whom Alcott was beginning to contribute stories, reviewed the book: "Very sweet are these little legends of Fairy land, which those of our young friends, who are so fond of tales of enchantment, will, we are sure, peruse with avidity. The interest which children take in fairy tales is well known, and the infant mind is more susceptible to truths under such a guise, than in more direct tales of a moral character" (2).

It is indeed under the "guise" of enchantment that Alcott imparts her lessons in morality for young people. In this collection of six stories and three poems, Alcott creates a fairyland where the examples of love, kindness, and duty are imparted. The stories are linked by the use of fairy narrators. In the framework preceding the first selection, the Queen of the Fairies and her Maids of Honor, "far away from mortal eyes," wait for the summer moon to go down. They "'wile away the time'" by agreeing to "'tell a tale, or relate what we have done or learned this day.'" Each fairy, in turn, spins stories or recites poems.

In the first tale, "The Frost-King; or, The Power of Love," the Queen of the Fairies has long struggled to keep the cruel Frost-King from killing the flowers. After many attempts with "courtly words" and "rich gifts," the Queen is at a loss as to how to convince the cold heart of the Frost-King to have mercy on the flowers. In typical fairy-tale fashion, the weakest, Violet, agrees to undertake the challenge. While the king at first refuses, he finally agrees to make a deal with Violet. He promises never to harm the flowers of her kingdom if she will only "'go back to your own people and leave me and my Spirits to work our will on all the other flowers that bloom.'" Showing her great capacity for love, Violet refuses to let others die while those in her kingdom survive. Like many fairy-tale protagonists she is then given a difficult task to overcome: build a palace fairer than the king's icy one. Winning the love of the Frost-Spirits by speaking gentle words and teaching them "how beautiful love is," Violet finally makes the Frost-King choose: accept the flower crown of love or send "'forth your

Spirits to carry sorrow and desolation over the happy earth, and win for yourself the fear and hatred of those who would so gladly love and reverence you.'" The king, realizing his mistakes, accepts the crown of flowers, proclaiming that Violet "'has taught us that Love is mightier than fear.'"

Similar lessons of love are told in the other five tales. In "Eva's Visit to Fairy Land," little Eva is taken by fairies to their home, where she watches them at work and play, discovering that they are not "idle, wilful Spirits." On her visit, she learns to take all the "sad and discontented feelings from her heart," to let "love and patience blossom there," to show kindness and love to those who are unkind, to comfort the sick and the old, to give tender thoughts to the young and strength to the weak. By visiting fairyland, Eva finds happy "feelings in her heart" and departs "better and wiser." When such lessons are taught by fairies, the author implies, humans can remember them more easily. Love is again the theme in "Lily Bell and Thistledown." Because of the "little thorns of cruelty and selfishness that lay concealed in his gay mantle," Thistledown is unloved in fairyland. His friend, Lily Bell, is on the other hand kind, humble, and compassionate and is loved by all. Caring only for himself, Thistledown time and again causes destruction and even death. Finally, he is caught by the Brownies, who vow to punish him for his cruel deeds. Only by going on a quest alone and obtaining gifts from earth, air, and water spirits will they release him. Eventually, through the acquisition of a loving heart, Thistledown indeed redeems himself.

In "Little Bud," the quest is once more a theme, as Little Bud vows to help restore an outcast band of elves to the kingdom. Queen Dew-drop agrees, but only if the elves "'can bring hither a perfect Fairy crown, robe, and wand.'" This task, she warns, is difficult as "'none but the best and purest can form the Fairy garments.'" Unfortunately, the elves allow Little Bud to do the work, and the Queen refuses to recognize them. Little Bud, however, offers them the chance to "'dwell through the long winter in the dark, cold earth'" to watch over the flowers. She promises no payment and no help. Accomplishing this task by "seeking no reward but the knowledge of their own good deeds," the elves are readmitted to Fairy Land, thus illustrating that, if people perform good deeds out of the kindness of their hearts, they will eventually be commended.

An interesting twist on the theme of love and goodness is presented in "Little Annie's Dream," perhaps the most sophisticated of these stories. Longing to be good and patient, Annie meets a fairy who tells her she must "'learn to conquer many passions that you cherish now.'" Like the protagonist of many fairy tales, Annie is given a magic object: a flower that will produce a sweet fragrance when she has performed her duty well. However, when she is selfish, angry, unkind, or cruel, a flower-bell will sound its warning. Hearing the bell often, Annie decides to abandon trying to be a good girl. Falling asleep, she has an allegorical dream where she confronts the "shapes of Selfishness" and the "Spirits of Pride," which come from her own heart. Symbolically, they cast a shadow all around her; she soon sees a "high, dark wall" enclosing her, attempting "to shut out everything she loved." The spirits then ask her to yield up her own heart for their home, to become their slave. Through the darkness, she glimpses the pale light of the fairy flower. In her dream, the evil spirits tempt her with various ordeals, but, as the flower grows brighter, she overcomes this power. Vines and flowers soon cover the wall and, when they bloom, they break down the structure. Thus, she "worked and hoped" and eventually the evil spirits are replaced by "shining forms." The dream ends with a low voice explaining the significance of the nightmare: "'The dark, unlovely passions you have looked upon are in your heart; watch well while they are few and weak, lest they should darken your whole life, and shut out love and happiness for ever.'" Little Annie profits from her dream, "each day growing richer in the love of others, and happier in herself." Alcott is suggesting to her readers that, if they ignore the evil thoughts and bad things that they do, the dark passions will eventually rule. Only love can create a pure heart.

In the final story in *Flower Fables,* "Ripple the Water Spirit," the quest theme reappears. Here, Ripple, who lives deep in the sea, finds the drowned body of a child. Discovering the dead child's mother, Ripple hears her lament to bring back life to the little one. Ripple seeks out the Fairy Queen, who tells her that only the Fire-Spirits, which are impossible to reach, can help restore life to the child. After seeking assistance from the four seasons, Ripple finally reaches the dwelling of the Fire-Spirits; however, the vain Fire-Queen refuses help until Ripple promises to bring her jewels. When Ripple agrees, the Queen gives her part of the flame. Keeping her promise, Ripple returns and restores life to the child, and the mother rewards her with a string of pearls. Bringing the jewels to the Fire-Spirits, Ripple discovers that they all melt from the heat. Angry, the spirits vow to keep Ripple prisoner, but they finally release her when they discover the wonderful pearls. The quest is complete. Only through the help of others has Ripple been able to keep her vow. By not thinking of herself as she constantly puts her life in danger, Ripple shows the true power of love. It is this power of love that dominates *Flower Fables* and makes it such a unified book.

In her 1977 psychoanalytic biography, *Louisa May,* Martha Saxton argues that it is in *Flower Fables* that "Louisa spelled out her nightmares." Alcott's enemies, Saxton believes, are "her fears of being isolated behind a wall of sins of her own making, and the terrifying nature of some of her impulses, which she had to shut away." She goes on to say that in "each fable, the sinner repents and gains great love, and often a coveted journey home. She is received with great joy and warmth. The self-abasement produces a resolution and peace. Hard, patient, uncomplaining work always wins love . . ." (199–200). Claiming that Louisa is "spell[ing] out her nightmare," may be applying the tales too closely to Alcott's own life. Saxton is correct, however, in saying that love does triumph. What Saxton seems to ignore is that these tales were originally told by a teenager to a nine-year-old child, tales that were meant to teach morals or lessons. As MacLeod has correctly explained: "The relentless moralizing of this [nineteenth-century] literature oppresses most twentieth-century adults who read it, and some have assumed that nineteenth-century children must have been equally oppressed." She further argues that these judgments are incorrect; they are "both unhistorical and out of keeping with what we know of children and their moral attitudes." They are "unhistorical" because didacticism in nineteenth-century children's books "was not more omnipresent nor more insistent than that in most fiction . . . for adults; a fervent concern with morality was simply part of the nineteenth-century outlook. . . . And children, particularly, are not put off by strong and simplistic morality in their literature . . ." (15). Alcott's fables clearly fit into this moral tradition. Her aims were to captivate young minds with an enchanted world and to tell a good story but also to instruct them in helping to create a better self, a better world. Her own upbringing by a transcendentalist educator and her passion for Emerson's essays helped to shape her positive view of the world and to promote the idea that everyone could reform. As Emerson asks in *Nature:* "who can set bounds to the possibilities of man?" Indeed, the transcendentalists believed that only by reforming the individual, not society as a whole, could the world change. Change the individual and society will eventually change. This is the philosophy Alcott brings to her fiction. What else would one expect from the person who once signed her letters "Yours, for reforms of all kind"?

Educating and reforming children also provide the dominant tone in Alcott's second fantasy book, *The Rose Family.* In 1863, she published the realistic account of her experiences as a Civil War nurse in *Hospital Sketches.* Her publisher, James Redpath, was a noted abolitionist, and having had a moderate amount of success with the book, Alcott again turned to

Redpath with her long fairy tale *The Rose Family*. Although the book carries an 1864 copyright, it was actually published in December 1863. In her journal for that month, Alcott notes that she had intended to get the book out in time for the Christmas season, "but owing to delays it was late for the holidays & badly bound in the hurry, so the poor 'Rose Family' fared badly" (122). In her "Notes and Memoranda" for 1864, Alcott lists her royalty on *The Rose Family* as fifty dollars (*Journals* 134). Expressing her dissatisfaction with the publisher in her February 1864 journal entry, Alcott says, "Redpath does not suit me though he does his best I believe" (128).

*The Rose Family* tells how three fairy sisters—Moss, Brier, and Blush—are sent to the good fairy, Star, to cure their "troublesome faults." Each fairy child, in turn, has a chapter devoted to her adventure in overcoming her burdens. Before their experiences begin, Star gives each a talisman—a drop of water from a magic fountain, in which their mother's face will always appear. Helped by the memory of their loving mother, the three set out on separate journeys of experience. The indolent Moss becomes part of Madam Mouse's family, but she refuses to work and departs the safety of the home. Joining a revel of "night-loving insects and reptiles," she is frightened when an owl swoops down and carries away one of the revelers. As a result of her nightmarish journey, Moss learns that "there is no real pleasure in idleness." Brier, Moss's sister, is a "passionate and wilful" fairy who is placed with a family of birds, where she tempts the fledging Flutter to fly before the proper time. When Flutter falls to the ground, Brier runs away, assuming the bird is dead. On her journey, she witnesses a large black ant kill a red ant out of anger, and she wonders if she herself were any "better than the brutal black ant who had destroyed so much happiness in his blind anger." She too undergoes a nightmarish ordeal as she endures a frightening time in a swamp, where the various flowers whisper to her in the dark, tugging for her soul. Returning to the bird's nest, she has learned her lesson, only needing "to be shown how sad and unlovely her own fault looked in others, to grow glad and eager to be good."

The final chapter revolves around Blush, whose burden is vanity. In many ways this tale recalls Meg's ordeal in *Little Women*, especially in the chapter "Meg at Vanity Fair," where, upon the advice of others, she overdresses so much that Laurie is disappointed in her. Here, Blush is left in a beautiful garden, where she spends her days "arranging gay garments, looking in her glasses, and flying about to be admired by the flowers." Taking the cruel advice of the tulips, who dislike her, Blush bathes in the poisonous dew of a nightshade plant, which turns her face colorless and fades her hair. Attempting suicide (the only such attempt in Alcott's fantasy tales), she plunges into a stream, but the waves divide, and she sinks slowly to the bottom, where a water-spirit lives. The spirit gives the vain fairy important advice: "'Live for others, Blush; forget yourself, and care for the beauty of a simple earnest heart more than for loveliness of face or grace of form.'" Of course, Blush follows the advice, and in the book's conclusion all three fairies are back home, reunited with the mother, whose thoughts and love protected them by their talisman. All of these tales could have been included in *Flower Fables* as once again the power of love is demonstrated. With a specific burden to cure, each fairy finds that it is only in helping and loving others that true happiness can be discovered.

Alcott's third collection of fairy tales appeared in late 1867, published by Horace B. Fuller of Boston. In her June 1867 journal she wrote that Fuller wanted a book, and by August she had completed it (*Journals* 157). Noting that the book was out, she said in her December 1867 journal entry: "People liked it but Fuller did not make it go well for want of money" (159). *Morning Glories, and Other Stories* contained eight new tales, four poems, and a reprint of *The Rose Family*. Six of the eight tales were fantasy stories, most in same didactic vein as her earlier works.

"Shadow-Children," a unique tale in the volume, focuses on how shadows become the alter egos or consciences of several children. On midsummer day, a time of magic in fairy lore, Polly asks, "'Wouldn't it be fun to see shadows going about alone and doing things like people?'" The children's shadows then spring to life. Instead of cutting "capers" as little Ned had hoped, the shadows serve as models to the children, illustrating the proper behavior. Ned's, for instance, immediately begins to pick the peas, which Ned's mother had requested him to do. When Ned asks why the shadow is performing the job, it conveys to Ned the idea that Ned's mother does much for him so he should do what he can for her. Each shadow in turn helps the children see that being good, helping others, and doing one's duty is important. As the day ends and the children discuss the magical event, they see the shadow-mother appear on the wall, singing and watching over her shadow-children. Like the sisters' talisman in *The Rose Family,* the mother is once again the abiding force of love. Alcott, in "The Shadow-Children," stresses the importance of our "other" selves, our inner selves that tell us how we should behave, implying that we should indeed listen to these voices.

Another tale of proper behavior is "What the Swallows Did." Here, a poet mourns the loss of his wife and child, and even though he has money, friends, and the gift of writing, he cannot be comforted: "He took no notice of friends and neighbors; neither used his money for himself nor others;

found no beauty in the world, no happiness anywhere." Yearning to be free of cares like the swallows he sees, the man has essentially given up life. When the swallows hear the man's wishes, they voice their disapproval: "'If I were that man, I'd make myself useful at once.'" The birds then discuss how the man can lead a "useful" life, and after overhearing their conversation, the poet takes their advice. Using his money and his talent, he helps the poor, the sick, and the old. He becomes a changed person: "Sunshine and peace seem to reign . . . and the happiness he earned for himself, by giving it to others, flowed out in beautiful, blithe songs . . . making him friends, and bringing him honor in high places as well as low." By losing one's self, one finds one's self, Alcott reminds the reader. If people focus attention upon others, especially those in need, they forget their own troubles.

"Little Gulliver" also teaches about helping others. In the story, Davey, whose closest friend is his pet sea gull, Gulliver, lives with the lighthouse keeper, Old Dan. When Dan fails to return from town one day, Gulliver sets out to find him. However, the gull, driven by strong winds, crashes into a boat's sail and is captured by a small girl. Placed in a cage, Gulliver is finally befriended by a poor, black servant named Moppet, who promises to set the bird free: "'I don't want no tanks, birdie: I love to let you go, kase you's a slave, like I once was.'" Disheartened Moppet also reveals that "'Nobody in de world keres for me. . . . De oder chilen has folks to lub an kere for em, but Moppet's got no friends.'" As the black girl watches over Gulliver while he regains his strength to fly, she discovers Dan, whose boat had been run down by a ship in the fog. After recovering, Dan takes Moppet back to his lighthouse: "He did not mind the black skin: he only saw the loneliness of the child, the tender heart, the innocent white soul." Thus, the story ends with Dan, Davey, and Gulliver reunited and Moppet secure in the love of a family. Using several intertwining themes here, the story explores the importance of helping others in need, being independent, like Davey has to be when old Dan disappears, and overcoming prejudice, as shown when Dan adopts Moppet. In fact, this is the only Alcott fantasy story dealing with prejudice, a theme that appears in several of her adult stories.

Two other tales in *Morning Glories* also impart morals. "The Whale's Story" recounts how a proud, foolish whale turns himself into an island and is eventually killed, illustrating the Biblical idea that "pride goeth before a fall." The other didactic story, one of the more sophisticated in the book, "Fancy's Friend," is an allegory about faith and the imagination in which the characters Fact, Fiction, and Fancy struggle for dominance. In the story, Fancy visits the seashore in hopes of seeing a mermaid. When her sand drawing of a mermaid comes to life, young Fancy is delighted and begs Lorelei, as the mermaid calls herself, to follow her home. Lorelei agrees, but only on certain conditions: "'If you will promise to tell no one who and what I am, I will stay with you as long as you love and believe in me. As soon as you betray me, or lose your faith and fondness, I shall vanish. . . .'" Fancy, of course, agrees and takes the mermaid home to visit her Aunt Fiction and Uncle Fact. The ensuing struggle of whether Lorelei should stay pits the allegorical Fact, Fiction, and Fancy against each other. Fancy and Fiction want her to remain. Uncle Fact, however, insists upon reality: "'I've told my wife a dozen times that she lets Fancy read too many fairy tales and wonder-books. Her head is full of nonsense, and she is just ready to believe any ridiculous story that is told her.'" In the end, Fact wins out; however, it is not without a sense of loss for Fancy. One can clearly see how Alcott was torn here, realizing the importance of the imagination in one's life, yet also insisting upon the more practical reality.

The remaining tale, "A Strange Island," is unlike any of Alcott's previous tales. Here, no moral comes through the enchantment; instead, the emphasis is solely on the imagination. Told in the guise of a dream, a common device in Alcott's later fairy tales, the story recounts the adventures of the narrator, who finds herself on an island inhabited by characters from Mother Goose rhymes: Little Bo Peep, Little Miss Muffit, the five little piggies, Jack Sprat, old Mother Hubbard. In the end, Mother Goose, with her pointed hat, red cloak, and high-heeled shoes, arrives flying on a large goose. As she touches the ground, she is surrounded by hundreds of children, "'phantoms of all the little people who ever read and loved'" the rhymes. One can see from this tale, written in 1867, how popular Mother Goose had become in America. For a brief time, the children can forget the didactic lessons and immerse themselves in pure fantasy, a rarity in Alcott's fiction.

After the appearance of *Morning-Glories* in late 1867, four years would lapse before Alcott would print any of her fantasy works in books. But those four years were among the most important in her life. In September 1867, she recorded the following events in her journal: "Niles, partner of Roberts, asked me to write a girls [*sic*] book. Said I'd try. Fuller asked me to be the editor of 'Merry's Museum.' Said I'd try. Began at once on both new jobs, but didn't like either" (158). Though she claims to have been dissatisfied with both jobs, Alcott probably chuckled over this entry a year or two later since the latter task provided her with valuable experience and the first one changed her professional and personal life forever.

In October 1867, Horace B. Fuller, publisher of *Morning-Glories,* purchased *Merry's Museum,* one of the country's oldest children's periodicals, which had been established in 1841 by Samuel Goodrich. Agreeing to become editor for five hundred dollars a year, Alcott gained the knowledge of how a children's periodical worked, information which would certainly help her as she contributed to *The Youth's Companion, St. Nicholas,* and *Harper's Young People* in the last two decades of her career. Her output for *Merry's Museum* was enormous. From 1868 to 1871, she contributed nearly thirty poems and stories to the magazine, plus writing the column "Merry's Monthly Chat." In fact, in her debut issue, January 1868, Alcott wrote an episode that would appear a few months later in another book: the story of how four sisters give their Christmas breakfast to a needy family. The first task she had agreed to do in September 1867—to write a "girls book"—would result in *Little Women,* published in the fall of 1868. After that, there was no turning back. During the years 1868–71, Alcott, besides writing for *Merry's Museum,* would publish *Little Women* and *An Old-Fashioned Girl* and begin *Little Men.* With *Little Women* so profitable, she could not refuse to write the domestic tales the public loved. Fantasy literature would have to take a back seat in her career.

In 1871, Alcott and her publisher concocted a plan to capitalize on her newfound fame: to issue a series of short stories entitled *Aunt Jo's Scrap-Bag.* This venture would allow Alcott to make money while her literary flame was at its brightest. Not only would the series publish new tales, which she continued to write for various periodicals, but it would also provide her with an outlet to reuse her old tales. The title, of course, would take advantage of the popularity of Jo March, although Aunt Jo does not serve as a frame narrator. In her excellent study of the *Scrap-Bag* stories, Joy A. Marsella speculates on the choice of the title for the series, noting that it is one of "self-assurance and deference": "It is an act of self-assurance because Alcott (and Niles) were confident enough of her place as a major author of juvenile fiction that they were certain that short, irregular, odd-shaped 'scraps' of her writing would sell. . . . But there is a suggestion of apology too; Alcott surely knew they were not among her major works" (xv). The *Scrap-Bag* series did allow Alcott a chance to demonstrate that she could write in other genres besides the domestic tales, and it gave her the place to publish her fantasy fiction once again.

*Aunt Jo's Scrap-Bag: My Boys,* the first volume of the series, was published in January 1872. To demonstrate the enormous popularity of Alcott at this time one only has to look at the initial number of volumes printed: fifteen thousand copies (Myerson and Shealy 74). *My Boys* contained only two fantasy stories, both reprints of earlier tales. "Madam Cluck, and Her Family," originally published in the August 1869 *Merry's Museum,* is one of Alcott's most gruesome fantasy tales, with all the major characters meeting their death in violent ways. Each death is caused by the characters performing some act that points out their flaw. For example, Chanty, a bold rooster who loves to fight, meets his match and dies in a bloody battle, and Peep, who loves to eat, gobbles up too much salt, not knowing it is bad for chickens. Only little Blot's death brings real sympathy. Blot, who had been neglected by all the other chickens, is the most well behaved and affectionate of Mrs. Cluck's brood. Showing a lost kitten the way home, Blot does not return to the hen house in time and freezes to death before its door. Once again, Alcott is teaching children that if they do not overcome their faults, such as vanity, gluttony, pride, willfulness, and disobedience, they may suffer tragic consequences in their life because of them.

The second fantasy story in the collection, "A Curious Call," reprinted from the February 1869 *Merry's Museum,* is the more interesting of the two. The narrator, in what turns out to be a dream, is surprised one night by a visit from the gilted golden eagle from the Boston City Hall. The eagle then tells her about the fun that all the statues in Boston have as they come to life at night. Ending by giving the narrator some literary advice, the eagle points out subjects she should write about: "'Write some stories for the children; go and help teach them; do something, and make others do what they can to increase the Sabbath sunshine that brightens one day in the week for the poor babies who live in shady places. . . . People are so wrapped up in their own affairs they don't do half they might.'" Noting that the bird declares himself "a gentleman," Marsella argues that the eagle symbolizes the gentry values of the cultural elite and "suggests behavior that will be effective in maintaining the strength of the country. The gentlemen's behavior is highly moral and is apparently instinctive to those who possess good intentions, education, concern for others, and awareness of public issues" (21). Like many of her other fantasy works, "A Curious Call" stresses reform, the betterment of the individual and of society.

More fantasy stories followed in *Aunt Jo's Scrap-Bag. Cupid and Chow-Chow,* the third volume of the series, appeared in December 1873—in time for the holiday season. Four fantasy tales were included, along with more realistic work. Although never used, "Fairy Pinafores," had been written since January 1864, when Alcott noted in her journal that she had completed the manuscript (127). Helping the poverty-stricken and the homeless is again the theme as Cinderella's fairy godmother gathers one hundred poor children and takes them to the country, where the children sew magic pinafores. Whoever wears them will grow gentle and good. Selected from among all the children, Little Barbara takes the magical garments to the city, where she sells them out of Little Red Riding Hood's basket. Before buying the clothes, the children must kiss the penny with a kind word and friendly wish. Once Barbara has sold all the pinafores, she puts the pennies into a circle, where they sprout wings and fly away. All the rich parents and their children follow them to the fairy godmother's home; there they are so moved by the poor children that they give money to support them. Once the king hears of the magic pinafores, he too visits and feels charitable. As the story concludes, the fairy godmother tells him to "'go and make homes for all your poor. . . .'" Charity to the poor is often a theme in Alcott's fantasy stories, and it is usually the eyes and deeds of the children that open up adult hearts.

Other tales also teach lessons. While "The Moss People" is a didactic tale of how Marnie learns to be good by watching the little people in her terrarium come alive, "A Marine Merry-Making," originally included in the October 1869 *Merry's Museum,* is a satire on high society parties. The other more interesting piece is "What Fanny Heard," reprinted from the 13 May 1867 *Youth's Companion.* When Fanny complains of being bored, the objects in the house come alive, telling her of all the wonderful things she could do: play the piano, sing, sew, read. Finally, the fire spirit informs her that the house once had a child who did all those things—Fanny's mother. With the portrait of her mother looking down upon her, Fanny vows to be like her and grow into a "useful, cheerful, good woman." As in other previous tales, and in *Little Women,* the mother is the figure that gives inspiration and serves as a role model for proper behavior and a satisfying life.

In the remaining *Scrap-Bag* books, only four new fantasy stories appear. In volume four, *My Girls* (1877), "Autobiography of an Omnibus," which had originally appeared in the October 1874 *St. Nicholas,* recounts the various jobs of the omnibus, none more important than sheltering a homeless family. *Jimmy's Cruise in the Pinafore* (1879), the fifth volume in the series, includes two tales: "What Becomes of the Pins," and "Rosa's Tale." In the former, the reader learns—as the pins come alive to tell their life histories—that people, like the pins, "shape their own lives," again emphasizing how people can influence their own futures by hard work and good behavior. The latter story is narrated by Rosa, a former racehorse, who speaks "English and the peculiar dialect of the horse-country Gulliver visited." After hearing Rosa's life story, told on the night of Christmas Eve, the time when legend has it that animals can speak, her owner vows to love her forever. This talking beast tale once again expresses the idea that we all need love. Appearing in *An Old-Fashioned Thanksgiving,* published in 1882 as the sixth and last volume of the *Scrap-Bag* series, "The Dolls' Journey" is written for pure entertainment as it relates the adventures two dolls have as they are shipped from Minnesota to Maine. *An Old-Fashioned Thanksgiving* also reprints seven of the fantasy tales from *Morning-Glories,* thus making these tales available to the large audience of readers who started enjoying Alcott after *Little Women.* While fantasy literature does not dominate the *Scrap-Bag* series, it does indicate that Alcott still found it important to imbed her morals in enchantment.

Fantasy, however, does dominate two volumes of Alcott's next short story series: *Lulu's Library.* The idea for such a collection came as early as 1883, when Louisa wrote her editor Thomas Niles on 23 June: "Mrs. [Mary Mapes] Dodge begged me to consider myself mortgaged to her for tales, etc., and as I see no prospect of any time for writing books, I may be able to send her some short stories . . . and so be getting material for a new set of books like "Scrap-bag," but with a new name (*Selected Letters* 271). By the early 1880s two events had occurred that had a great impact on Alcott's career. First, her health was failing and she was unable to work for long periods of time, thus forcing her to write short stories rather than a novel, which would consume more of her energy. Second, her sister May Alcott Nieriker had died in late 1879, leaving Louisa the custody of her newborn daughter, Louisa May Neiriker, nicknamed "Lulu." These events forced Louisa to slow down her writing, to take more time to nurse her health and to raise Lulu. On 13 July 1885, Alcott again wrote Niles: "I want to know if it is too late to do it and if it is worth doing; namely to collect some of the little tales I tell Lulu and put them with the two I shall have printed the last year . . . and call it 'Lulu's Library'? I have several tiny books written down for L.; and as I can do no great work, it occurred to me that I might venture to copy these if it would do for a Christmas book for the younger set" (*Selected Letters* 290). The idea worked, of course, because it kept Alcott's name, still a popular one, before her reading public, and it allowed her to reuse stories she was writing for such magazines as *St. Nicholas.* Of the three volumes of *Lulu's Library,* two are almost entirely fantasy. Obviously, having a young, impressionable girl living with her reawakened Alcott's desire to write more tales of the imagination.

Of the twelve selections in the first volume of *Lulu's Library* (1885), seven are fantasy tales. All are didactic. For example, in "The Skipping Shoes," Kitty, a willful child who never does what people want her to do, puts on her new shoes one midsummer day and discovers that the shoes have a power of their own. They force her to run errands when she is asked and to stop when she is about to do something wrong. The magical shoes even give her the ability to talk with a cricket. By the end of the day, when the shoes lose their charms, Kitty has learned two important lessons: to run willingly when asked to perform a task and to love the creatures in nature. Another selection, "A Christmas Dream, and How It Came True," explores the theme of helping the less fortunate as Effie's dream of giving gifts to the poor is brought to reality with the aid of her mother. Helping others is also the lesson in "Rosy's Journey," as young Rosy goes on an adventurous quest to find her father. Along the way, she helps out several animals, who, in turn, end up rescuing her when she is in peril, showing that one's good deeds to others will eventually be returned.

Not only is proper behavior important for children, but, as the reader learns in "The Candy Country," so is a proper diet. When the wind carries Lily away over "rivers and hills, houses and tress," she lands in a strange land where everything is made of candy. However, after eating too much candy, she tires of it and eventually visits bread land, where she discovers healthy food. Learning to be "a good housekeeper," she goes home and grows up from a "sickly, fretful child" to a "fine, strong woman" because she eats very little candy. A healthy body, Alcott implies, is just as important as a healthy mind. Even late in her life and career, Alcott cannot escape the moral values, the positive ideals and the hope of reform that were so much a part of her younger life, of her own growth as an individual.

In mid-October 1887, less than five months before Alcott's death, *The Frost-King,* the second volume of *Lulu's Library,* was published. One of the last books Alcott worked on, it brought her career full circle. Five of the eleven tales were stories from her first book, *Flower Fables.* Thus, one of the last books published during her life (*Garland for Girls* would appear in November 1887 and the third volume of *Lulu's Library* posthumously in October 1889) was a reprint of her first one. She had returned to her nature fairyland, her "fairies and fables" (*Selected Letters* 11). Although Alcott revised the tales from *Flower Fables* by tightening up the writing and reworking some of the scenes, the themes and lessons remained the same. She even dedicated the book to her childhood friend: "To Ellen T. Emerson, one of the good fairies who still remain to us, beloved of poets, little children, and many grateful hearts" ([3]). Presenting an advance copy of the book to Emerson, she wrote: "I have ventured to dedicate this little book to you in memory of the happy old times when stories were told to you . . . & some other play mates. . . . The earlier tales you will remember in spite of some pruning of too plentiful adjectives; the later ones were told to Lulu . . ." (*Selected Letters* 320).

The new tales, those told to Lulu, are similar in style to the early *Flower Fables;* however, several stand out as being perhaps among the best of Alcott's stories. One of the most compelling is "The Flower's Story," a story within a story, which employs the fairy-tale type of the wicked stepmother. Marion, who is ill, is told the story of "The Princes and the Pansies, A Fairy Tale," by a flower that blows into her room. The two princes, Purple and Pluck, are set to inherit their father's kingdom until their stepmother locks them away. Escaping their prison, they settle down far from the kingdom, planting the magic pansy seeds given to them by their old gardener. The enchanted flowers bring comfort and happiness to all those who possess them. Giving up their plans to fight for their home, the two brothers, "Brothers of Mercy" as they are now called, dedicate their lives to helping the poor. Eventually returning to their kingdom when the father is dying, the brothers, in disguise, help their step-mother by advising her to give bread, money, and shelter to her people and to rule with justice. Repenting for her former sins, the queen decides to enter a convent while the two brothers reveal their identity and attain the throne of their kingdom. At the story's conclusion, the flower tells Marion the moral: "'Learn to rule yourself, make your own kingdom a peaceful, happy one, and find nothing too humble to teach you a lesson.'" What makes this story unique is that Alcott uses her frame story to impart the moral. The fairy tale of the two princes never explicitly reveals the lesson. Instead, it reads more like an ancient tale, making it one of the best literary fairy tales Alcott penned.

"The Fairy Spring" also resembles an old folktale rather than the overtly didactic stories of Alcott's career. In this selection, a young girl hears what the rushing brook says: follow me to the magic spring. All day she climbs the mountain, finally reaching the summit and the spring. Spending the night beside the water, she awakens and a spirit tells her to drink of the magic spring and all the pain and weariness will vanish and she will "grow healthy in body, happy in heart, and learn to see and love all the simple wholesome things." The spirit then bids the girl to go and tell the story about the healing powers of the water. Although she spreads the news, few believe her. However, the girl, her mother, a poet, and a man who has lost his family set off for the magic spring. When they return, people begin to listen and hundreds make the pilgrimage to the summit. Some even try to capitalize on the spring's power by building a resort, but the wind blows down the buildings while the water vanishes until the mountaintop is clear. Once again, the magic of the spring heals those who feel the quiet beauty of the enchanted spot. While Alcott does not reveal her moral explicitly, she implies that it is often the children who are wiser and lead the adults, an idea championed by both the British Romantics and the transcendentalists. While several of the new tales are more overtly didactic, those like "The Fairy Spring" and "The Flower's Story" seem to stand out as the more artistically satisfying since the moral is deeply embedded in the enchantment.

In *The Uses of Enchantment,* Bruno Bettelheim says, "Just because his life is often bewildering to him, the child needs even more to be given the chance to understand himself. . . . He needs . . . a moral education which subtly, and by implication only, conveys to him the advantages of moral behavior, not through abstract ethical concepts but through that which seems tangibly right" (5). In her fairy tales and fantasy stories, Louisa May Alcott recognized that need and fulfilled it. Although her work may appear too didactic to many modern readers, it must be seen as a product of its age. Being influenced by the transcendentalists, Alcott never lost the sense of self-inquiry and self-improvement that dominates much of her fantasy fiction. With her fantasy tales securely placed in the didactic tradition, Alcott's work aimed to stimulate children's imaginations, to give recognition to their problems, and to offer solutions or suggestions that would make them better individuals in a society. While Alcott's fantasy stories can make no claim to being great art, they are an important part of her canon. They may not be as ground-breaking as *Little Women* was in the history of realistic children's fiction or as surprising as her recently discovered blood-and-thunder tales, but they do demonstrate that, while she was exploring new territory with some of her work, she was also working within an existing tradition—the didactic fairy tale. Covering the entire span of her literary career, these tales, from her first book to her last one, prove she never lost the love of the "fairy folk."

# Works Cited

Alcott, Louisa May. Dedication Page. *Lulu's Library. Vol. 2. The Frost King.* Boston, Roberts Brothers, 1887.

———. *The Journals of Louisa May Alcott.* Ed. Joel Myerson and Daniel Shealy. Boston: Little, Brown, r989.

———. "Recollections of My Childhood." *Lulu's Library. Vol. 3. Recollections.* Boston: Roberts Brothers, 1889.

———. *The Selected Letters of Louisa May Alcott.* Ed. Joel Myerson and Daniel Shealy. Boston: Little, Brown, 1987.

Attebery, Brian. *The Fantasy Tradition in American Literature.* Bloomington: Indiana Univ. Press, 1980.

Bettelheim, Bruno. *The Uses of Enchantment: The Meaning and Importance of Fairy Tales.* New York: Knopf, 1976.

*Boston Evening Transcript,* 19 Dec. 1854, 2.

Cheney, Ednah Dow. *Louisa May Alcott: Her Life, Letters and Journals.* Boston: Roberts Brothers, 1889.

Child, Lydia Maria. *Flowers for Children.* New York: C. S. Francis, 1844.

———. "Preface." *Rainbows for Children.* New York: C. S. Francis and Co., 1848.

Darton, F. J. H. *Children's Books in England.* Cambridge: Cambridge Univ. Press, 1958.

Emerson, Ellen. *The Letters of Ellen Tucker Emerson.* Vol. 1. Ed. Edith E. W. Gregg, Kent: Kent State Univ. Press, 1982.

Goodrich, Samuel G. "Preface." *Parley's Book of Fables.* Hartford: White, Druier and Co., 1836.

———. *Recollections of a Lifetime.* Vol. 1. New York and Auburn: Miller, Orton, 1856.

Kotzin, Michael C. "The Fairy Tale in England, 1800–1870." *Journal of Popular Culture* 4 (Summer 1970): 130–54.

MacLeod, Anne Scott. *A Moral Tale: Children's Fiction and American Culture, 1820–1860.* Hamden, Conn.: Archon Books, 1975.

Marsella, Joy A. *The Promise of Destiny: Children and Women in the Short Stories of Louisa May Alcott.* Westport, Conn.: Greenwood, 1983.

Meigs, Cornelia, ed. *A Critical History of Children's Literature.* New York: Macmillan, 1953.

Myerson, Joel and Daniel Shealy. "The Sales of Louisa May Alcott's Books." *Harvard Library Bulletin,* new ser., 1 (Spring 1990): 47–86.

*Saturday Evening Gazette,* 23 Dec. 1854, [2].

Saxton, Martha. *Louisa May: A Modern Biography of Louisa May Alcott.* Boston: Houghton Mifflin, 1977.

Stern, Madeleine B. *Louisa May Alcott.* Norman: Univ. of Oklahoma Press, 1950.

———. "Louisa May Alcott's 'Tales for Ellen E.'" *A. B. Bookman's Weekly,* 12 Nov. 1990, 1849–60.

Taylor, Edgar. "Preface to the Original Edition." *German Popular Stories.* London, 1869.

Thalmann, Marianne. *The Romantic Fairy Tale: Seeds of Surrealism.* Trans. Mary B. Corcoran. Ann Arbor: Univ. of Michigan Press, 1964.

Wesselhoeft, Lily F. *Sparrow, the Tramp.* Boston: Roberts Brothers, 1888.

West, Mark, ed. *Before Oz: Juvenile Fantasy Stories for Nineteenth-Century America.* Hamden, Conn.: Archon Books, 1989.

Willis, Nathaniel. "Prospectus." *Youth's Companion,* 16 Apr. 1827, 1.

*Louisa May Alcott's*
*Fairy Tales and*
*Fantasy Stories*

# Flower Fables

THE SUMMER MOON shone brightly down upon the sleeping earth, while far away from mortal eyes danced the Fairy folk. Fire-flies hung in bright clusters on the dewy leaves, that waved in the cool night-wind; and the flowers stood gazing, in very wonder, at the little Elves, who lay among the fern-leaves, swung in the vine-boughs, sailed on the lake in lily cups, or danced on the mossy ground, to the music of the hare-bells, who rung out their merriest peal in honor of the night.

Under the shade of a wild rose sat the Queen and her little Maids of Honor, beside the silvery mushroom where the feast was spread.

"Now, my friends," said she, "to wile away the time till the bright moon goes down, let us each tell a tale, or relate what we have done or learned this day. I will begin with you, Sunny Lock," added she, turning to a lovely little Elf, who lay among the fragrant leaves of a primrose.

With a gay smile, "Sunny Lock" began her story.

"As I was painting the bright petals of a blue bell, it told me this tale."

# The Frost-King;
## OR, *The Power of Love*

THREE LITTLE FAIRIES sat in the fields eating their breakfast; each among the leaves of her favorite flower, Daisy, Primrose, and Violet, were happy as Elves need be.

The morning wind gently rocked them to and fro, and the sun shone warmly down upon the dewy grass, where butterflies spread their gay wings, and bees with their deep voices sung among the flowers; while the little birds hopped merrily about to peep at them.

On a silvery mushroom was spread the breakfast; little cakes of flower-dust lay on a broad green leaf, beside a crimson strawberry, which, with sugar from the violet, and cream from the yellow milkweed, made a fairy meal, and their drink was the dew from the flowers' bright leaves.

"Ah me," sighed Primrose, throwing herself languidly back, "how warm the sun grows! give me another piece of strawberry, and then I must hasten away to the shadow of the ferns. But while I eat, tell me, dear Violet, why are you all so sad? I have scarce seen a happy face since my return from Rose Land; dear friend, what means it?"

"I will tell you," replied little Violet, the tears gathering in her soft eyes. "Our good Queen is ever striving to keep the dear flowers from the power of the cruel Frost-King; many ways she tried, but all have failed. She has sent messengers to his court with costly gifts; but all have returned sick for want of sunlight, weary and sad; we have watched over them, heedless of sun or shower, but still his dark spirits do their work, and we are left to weep over our blighted blossoms. Thus have we striven, and in vain; and this night our Queen holds council for the last time. Therefore are we sad, dear Primrose, for she has toiled and cared for us, and we can do nothing to help or advise her now."

"It is indeed a cruel thing," replied her friend; "but as we cannot help it, we must suffer patiently, and not let the sorrows of others disturb our happiness. But, dear sisters, see you not how high the sun is getting? I have my locks to curl, and my robe to prepare for the evening; therefore I must be gone, or I shall be brown as a withered leaf in this warm light." So, gathering a tiny mushroom for a parasol, she flew away; Daisy soon followed, and Violet was left alone.

Then she spread the table afresh, and to it came fearlessly the busy ant and bee, gay butterfly and bird; even the poor blind mole and humble worm were not forgotten; and with gentle words she gave to all, while each learned something of their kind little teacher; and the love that made her own heart bright shone alike on all.

The ant and bee learned generosity, the butterfly and bird contentment, the mole and worm confidence in the love of others; and each went to their home better for the little time they had been with Violet.

Evening came, and with it troops of Elves to counsel their good Queen, who, seated on her mossy throne, looked anxiously upon the throng below, whose glittering wings and rustling robes gleamed like many-colored flowers.

At length she rose, and amid the deep silence spoke thus:—

"Dear children, let us not tire of a good work, hard though it be and wearisome; think of the many little hearts that in their sorrow look to us for help. What would the green earth be without its lovely flowers, and what a lonely home for us! Their beauty fills our hearts with brightness, and their love with tender thoughts. Ought we then to leave them to die uncared for and alone? They give to us their all; ought we not to toil unceasingly, that they may bloom in peace within their quiet homes? We have tried to gain the love of the stern Frost-King, but in vain; his heart is hard as his own icy land; no love can melt, no kindness bring it back to sunlight and to joy. How then may we keep our frail blossoms from his cruel spirits? Who will give us counsel? Who will be our messenger for the last time? Speak, my subjects."

Then a great murmuring arose, and many spoke, some for costlier gifts, some for war; and the fearful counselled patience and submission.

Long and eagerly they spoke, and their soft voices rose high.

Then sweet music sounded on the air, and the loud tones were hushed, as in wondering silence the Fairies waited what should come.

Through the crowd there came a little form, a wreath of pure white violets lay among the bright locks that fell so softly round the gentle face, where a deep blush glowed, as, kneeling at the throne, little Violet said:—

"Dear Queen, we have bent to the Frost-King's power, we have borne gifts unto his pride, but have we gone trustingly to him and spoken fearlessly of his evil deeds? Have we shed the soft light of unwearied love around his cold heart, and with patient tenderness shown him how bright and beautiful love can make even the darkest lot?

"Our messengers have gone fearfully, and with cold looks and courtly words offered him rich gifts, things he cared not for, and with equal pride has he sent them back.

"Then let me, the weakest of your band, go to him, trusting in the love I know lies hidden in the coldest heart.

"I will bear only a garland of our fairest flowers; these will I wind about him, and their bright faces, looking lovingly in his, will bring sweet thoughts to his dark mind, and their soft breath steal in like gentle words. Then, when he sees them fading on his breast, will he not sigh that there is no warmth there to keep them fresh and lovely? This will I do, dear Queen, and never leave his dreary home, till the sunlight falls on flowers fair as those that bloom in our own dear land."

Silently the Queen had listened, but now, rising and placing her hand on little Violet's head, she said, turning to the throng below:—

"We in our pride and power have erred, while this, the weakest and lowliest of our subjects, has from the innocence of her own pure heart counselled us more wisely than the noblest of our train. All who will aid our brave little messenger, lift your wands, that we may know who will place their trust in the Power of Love."

Every fairy wand glistened in the air, as with silvery voices they cried, "Love and little Violet."

Then down from the throne, hand in hand, came the Queen and Violet, and till the moon sank did the Fairies toil, to weave a wreath of the fairest flowers. Tenderly they gathered them, with the night-dew fresh upon their leaves, and as they wove chanted sweet spells, and whispered fairy blessings on the bright messengers whom they sent forth to die in a dreary land, that their gentle kindred might bloom unharmed.

At length it was done; and the fair flowers lay glowing in the soft starlight, while beside them stood the Fairies, singing to the music of the wind-harps:—

> "We are sending you, dear flowers,
>     Forth alone to die,
> Where your gentle sisters may not weep
>     O'er the cold graves where you lie;
> But you go to bring them fadeless life
>     In the bright homes where they dwell,
> And you softly smile that't is so,
>     As we sadly sing farewell.
> O plead with gentle words for us,

And whisper tenderly
Of generous love to that cold heart,
   And it will answer ye;
And though you fade in a dreary home,
   Yet loving hearts will tell
Of the joy and peace that you have given:
   Flowers, dear flowers, farewell!"

The morning sun looked softly down upon the broad green earth, which like a mighty altar was sending up clouds of perfume from its breast, while flowers danced gayly in the summer wind, and birds sang their morning hymn among the cool green leaves. Then high above, on shining wings, soared a little form. The sunlight rested softly on the silken hair, and the winds fanned lovingly the bright face, and brought the sweetest odors to cheer her on.

Thus went Violet through the clear air, and the earth looked smiling up to her, as, with the bright wreath folded in her arms, she flew among the soft, white clouds.

On and on she went, over hill and valley, broad rivers and rustling woods, till the warm sunlight passed away, the winds grew cold, and the air thick with falling snow. Then far below she saw the Frost-King's home. Pillars of hard, gray ice supported the high, arched roof, hung with crystal icicles. Dreary gardens lay around, filled with withered flowers and bare, drooping trees; while heavy clouds hung low in the dark sky, and a cold wind murmured sadly through the wintry air.

With a beating heart Violet folded her fading wreath more closely to her breast, and with weary wings flew onward to the dreary palace.

Here, before the closed doors, stood many forms with dark faces and harsh, discordant voices, who sternly asked the shivering little Fairy why she came to them.

Gently she answered, telling them her errand, beseeching them to let her pass ere the cold wind blighted her frail blossoms. Then they flung wide the doors, and she passed in.

Walls of ice, carved with strange figures, were around her; glittering icicles hung from the high roof, and soft, white snow covered the hard floors. On a throne hung with clouds sat the Frost-King; a crown of crystals bound his white locks, and a dark mantle wrought with delicate frost-work was folded over his cold breast.

His stern face could not stay little Violet, and on through the long hall she went, heedless of the snow that gathered on her feet, and the bleak wind that blew around her; while the King with wondering eyes looked on the golden light that played upon the dark walls as she passed.

The flowers, as if they knew their part, unfolded their bright leaves, and poured forth their sweetest perfume, as, kneeling at the throne, the brave little Fairy said,—

"O King of blight and sorrow, send me not away till I have brought back the light and joy that will make your dark home bright and beautiful again. Let me call back to the desolate gardens the fair forms that are gone, and their soft voices blessing you will bring to your breast a never failing joy. Cast by your icy crown and sceptre, and let the sunlight of love fall softly on your heart.

"Then will the earth bloom again in all its beauty, and your dim eyes will rest only on fair forms, while music shall sound through these dreary halls, and the love of grateful hearts be yours. Have pity on the gentle flower-spirits, and do not doom them to an early death, when they might bloom in fadeless beauty, making us wiser by their gentle teachings, and the earth brighter by their lovely forms. These fair flowers, with the prayers of all Fairy Land, I lay before you; O send me not away till they are answered."

And with tears falling thick and fast upon their tender leaves, Violet laid the wreath at his feet, while the golden light grew ever brighter as it fell upon the little form so humbly kneeling there.

The King's stern face grew milder as he gazed on the gentle Fairy, and the flowers seemed to look beseechingly upon him; while their fragrant voices sounded softly in his ear, telling of their dying sisters, and of the joy it gives to bring happiness to the weak and sorrowing. But he drew the dark mantle closer over his breast and answered coldly,—

"I cannot grant your prayer, little Fairy; it is my will the flowers should die. Go back to your Queen, and tell her that I cannot yield my power to please these foolish flowers."

Then Violet hung the wreath above the throne, and with weary feet went forth again, out into the cold, dark gardens, and still the golden shadows followed her, and wherever they fell, flowers bloomed and green leaves rustled.

Then came the Frost-Spirits, and beneath their cold wings the flowers died, while the Spirits bore Violet to a low, dark cell, saying as they left her, that their King was angry that she had dared to stay when he had bid her go.

So all alone she sat, and sad thoughts of her happy home came back to her, and she wept bitterly. But soon came visions of the gentle flowers dying in their forest homes, and their voices ringing in her ear, imploring her to save them. Then she wept no longer, but patiently awaited what might come.

Soon the golden light gleamed faintly through the cell, and she heard little voices calling for help, and high up among the heavy cobwebs hung poor little flies struggling to free themselves, while their cruel enemies sat in their nets, watching their pain.

With her wand the Fairy broke the bands that held them, tenderly bound up their broken wings, and healed their wounds; while they lay in the warm light, and feebly hummed their thanks to their kind deliverer.

Then she went to the ugly brown spiders, and in gentle words told them, how in Fairy Land their kindred spun all the elfin cloth, and in return the Fairies gave them food, and then how happily they lived among the cool green leaves, spinning garments for their neighbors. "And you too," said she, "shall spin for me, and I will give you better food than helpless insects. You shall live in peace, and spin your delicate threads into a mantle for the stern King; and I will weave golden threads amid the gray, that when folded over his cold heart gentle thoughts may enter in and make it their home."

And while she gayly sung, the little weavers spun their silken threads, the flies on glittering wings flew lovingly above her head, and over all the golden light shone softly down.

When the Frost-Spirits told their King, he greatly wondered, and often stole to look at the sunny little room where friends and enemies worked peacefully together. Still the light grew brighter, and floated out into the cold air, where it hung like bright clouds above the dreary gardens, whence all the Spirits' power could not drive it; and green leaves budded on the naked trees, and flowers bloomed; but the Spirits heaped snow upon them, and they bowed their heads and died.

At length the mantle was finished, and amid the gray threads shone golden ones, making it bright; and she sent it to the King, entreating him to wear it, for it would bring peace and love to dwell within his breast.

But he scornfully threw it aside, and bade his Spirits take her to a colder cell, deep in the earth; and there with harsh words they left her.

Still she sang gayly on, and the falling drops kept time so musically, that the King in his cold ice-halls wondered at the low, sweet sounds that came stealing up to him.

Thus Violet dwelt, and each day the golden light grew stronger; and from among the crevices of the rocky walls came troops of little velvet-coated moles, praying that they might listen to the sweet music, and lie in the warm light.

"We lead," said they, "a dreary life in the cold earth; the flower-roots are dead, and no soft dews descend for us to drink, no little seed or leaf can we find. Ah, good Fairy, let us be your servants: give us but a few crumbs of your daily bread, and we will do all in our power to serve you."

And Violet said, Yes; so day after day they labored to make a pathway through the frozen earth, that she might reach the roots of the withered flowers; and soon, wherever through the dark galleries she went, the soft light fell upon the roots of flowers, and they with new life spread forth in the warm ground, and forced fresh sap to the blossoms above. Brightly they bloomed and danced in the soft light, and the Frost-Spirits tried in vain to harm them, for when they came beneath the bright clouds their power to do evil left them.

From his dark castle the King looked out on the happy flowers, who nodded gayly to him, and in sweet odors strove to tell him of the good little Spirit, who toiled so faithfully below, that they might live. And when he turned from the brightness without, to his stately palace, it seemed so cold and dreary, that he folded Violet's mantle round him, and sat beneath the faded wreath upon his ice-carved throne, wondering at the strange warmth that came from it; till at length he bade his Spirits bring the little Fairy from her dismal prison.

Soon they came hastening back, and prayed him to come and see how lovely the dark cell had grown. The rough floor was spread with deep green moss, and over wall and roof grew flowery vines, filling the air with their sweet breath; while above played the clear, soft light, casting rosy shadows on the glittering drops that lay among the fragrant leaves; and beneath the vines stood Violet, casting crumbs to the downy little moles who ran fearlessly about and listened as she sang to them.

When the old King saw how much fairer she had made the dreary cell than his palace rooms, gentle thoughts within whispered him to grant her prayer, and let the little Fairy go back to her friends and home; but the Frost-Spirits breathed upon the flowers and bid him see how frail they were, and useless to a King. Then the stern, cold thoughts came back again, and he harshly bid her follow him.

With a sad farewell to her little friends she followed him, and before the throne awaited his command. When the King saw how pale and sad the gentle face had grown, how thin her robe, and weak her wings, and yet how lovingly the golden shadows fell around her and brightened as they lay

"The Frost King." From *Flower Fables,* 1855.
Courtesy of Rare Book Collection,
University of North Carolina at Charlotte.

upon the wand, which, guided by patient love, had made his once desolate home so bright, he could not be cruel to the one who had done so much for him, and in kindly tone he said,—

"Little Fairy, I offer you two things, and you may choose between them. If I will vow never more to harm the flowers you may love, will you go back to your own people and leave me and my Spirits to work our will on all the other flowers that bloom? The earth is broad, and we can find them in any land, then why should you care what happens to their kindred if your own are safe? Will you do this?"

"Ah!" answered Violet sadly, "do you not know that beneath the flowers' bright leaves there beats a little heart that loves and sorrows like our own? And can I, heedless of their beauty, doom them to pain and grief, that I might save my own dear blossoms from the cruel foes to which I leave them? Ah no! sooner would I dwell for ever in your darkest cell, than lose the love of those warm, trusting hearts."

"Then, listen," said the King, "to the task I give you. You shall raise up for me a palace fairer than this, and if you can work that miracle I will grant your prayer or lose my kingly crown. And now go forth, and begin your task; my Spirits shall not harm you, and I will wait till it is done before I blight another flower."

Then out into the gardens went Violet with a heavy heart; for she had toiled so long, her strength was nearly gone. But the flowers whispered their gratitude, and folded their leaves as if they blessed her; and when she saw the garden filled with loving friends, who strove to cheer and thank her for her care, courage and strength returned; and raising up thick clouds of mist, that hid her from the wondering flowers, alone and trustingly she began her work.

As time went by, the Frost-King feared the task had been too hard for the Fairy; sounds were heard behind the walls of mist, bright shadows seen to pass within, but the little voice was never heard. Meanwhile the golden light had faded from the garden, the flowers bowed their heads, and all was dark and cold as when the gentle Fairy came.

And to the stern King his home seemed more desolate and sad; for he missed the warm light, the happy flowers, and, more than all, the gay voice and bright face of little Violet. So he wandered through his dreary palace, wondering how he had been content to live before without sunlight and love.

And little Violet was mourned as dead in Fairy-Land, and many tears were shed, for the gentle Fairy was beloved by all, from the Queen down to the humblest flower. Sadly they watched over every bird and blossom which she had loved, and strove to be like her in kindly words and deeds. They wore cypress wreaths, and spoke of her as one whom they should never see again.

Thus they dwelt in deepest sorrow, till one day there came to them an unknown messenger, wrapped in a dark mantle, who looked with wondering eyes on the bright palace, and flower-crowned Elves, who kindly welcomed him, and brought fresh dew and rosy fruit to refresh the weary stranger. Then he told them that he came from the Frost-King, who begged the Queen and all her subjects to come and see the palace little Violet had built; for the veil of mist would soon be withdrawn, and as she could not make a fairer home than the ice-castle, the King wished her kindred near to comfort and to bear her home. And while the Elves wept, he told them how patiently she had toiled, how her fadeless love had made the dark cell bright and beautiful.

These and many other things he told them; for little violet had won the love of many of the Frost-Spirits, and even when they killed the flowers she had toiled so hard to bring to life and beauty, she spoke gentle words to them, and sought to teach them how beautiful is love. Long stayed the messenger, and deeper grew his wonder that the Fairy could have left so fair a home, to toil in the dreary palace of his cruel master, and suffer cold and weariness, to give life and joy to the weak and sorrowing. When the Elves had promised they would come, he bade farewell to happy Fairy-Land, and flew sadly home.

At last the time arrived, and out in his barren garden, under a canopy of dark clouds, sat the Frost-King before the misty wall, behind which were heard low, sweet sounds, as of rustling trees and warbling birds.

Soon through the air came many-colored troops of Elves. First the Queen, known by the silver lilies on her snowy robe and the bright crown in her hair, beside whom flew a band of Elves in crimson and gold, making sweet music on their flower-trumpets, while all around, with smiling faces and bright eyes, fluttered her loving subjects.

On they came, like a flock of brilliant butterflies, their shining wings and many-colored garments sparkling in the dim air; and soon the leafless trees were gay with living flowers, and their sweet voices filled the gardens with music. Like his subjects, the King looked on the lovely Elves, and no longer wondered that little Violet wept and longed for her home. Darker and more desolate seemed his stately home, and when the Fairies asked for flowers, he felt ashamed that he had none to give them.

At length a warm wind swept through the gardens, and the mist-clouds passed away, while in silent wonder looked the Frost-King and the Elves upon the scene before them.

Far as eye could reach were tall green trees, whose drooping boughs made graceful arches, through which the golden light shone softly, making bright shadows on the deep green moss below, where the fairest flowers waved in the cool wind, and sang, in their low, sweet voices, how beautiful is Love.

Flowering vines folded their soft leaves around the trees, making green pillars of their rough trunks. Fountains threw their bright waters to the roof, and flocks of silver-winged birds flew singing among the flowers, or brooded lovingly above their nests. Doves with gentle eyes cooed among the green leaves, snow-white clouds floated in the sunny sky, and the golden light, brighter than before, shone softly down.

Soon through the long aisles came Violet, flowers and green leaves rustling as she passed. On she went to the Frost-King's throne, bearing two crowns, one of sparkling icicles, the other of pure white lilies, and kneeling before him, said,—

"My task is done, and, thanks to the Spirits of earth and air, I have made as fair a home as Elfin hands can form. You must now decide. Will you be King of Flower-Land, and own my gentle kindred for your loving friends? Will you possess unfading peace and joy, and the grateful love of all the green earth's fragrant children? Then take this crown of flowers. But if you can find no pleasure here, go back to your own cold home, and dwell in solitude and darkness, where no ray of sunlight or of joy can enter.

"Send forth your Spirits to carry sorrow and desolation over the happy earth, and win for yourself the fear and hatred of those who would so gladly love and reverence you. Then take this glittering crown, hard and cold as your own heart will be, if you will shut out all that is bright and beautiful. Both are before you. Choose."

The old King looked at the little Fairy, and saw how lovingly the bright shadows gathered round her, as if to shield her from every harm; the timid birds nestled in her bosom, and the flowers grew fairer as she looked upon them; while her gentle friends, with tears in their bright eyes, folded their hands beseechingly, and smiled on her.

Kind thoughts came thronging to his mind, and he turned to look at the two palaces. Violet's, so fair and beautiful, with its rustling trees, calm, sunny skies, and happy birds and flowers, all created by her patient love and care. His own, so cold and dark and dreary, his empty gardens where no flowers could bloom, no green trees dwell, or gay birds sing, all desolate and dim;—and while he gazed, his own Spirits, casting off their dark mantles, knelt before him and besought him not to send them forth to blight the things the gentle Fairies loved so much. "We have served you long and faithfully," said they, "give us now our freedom, that we may learn to be beloved by the sweet flowers we have harmed so long. Grant the little Fairy's prayer; and let her go back to her own dear home. She has taught us that Love is mightier than Fear. Choose the Flower crown, and we will be the truest subjects you have ever had."

Then, amid a burst of wild, sweet music, the Frost-King placed the Flower crown on his head, and knelt to little Violet; while far and near, over the broad green earth, sounded the voices of flowers, singing their thanks to the gentle Fairy, and the summer wind was laden with perfumes, which they sent as tokens of their gratitude; and wherever she went, old trees bent down to fold their slender branches round her, flowers laid their soft faces against her own, and whispered blessings; even the humble moss bent over the little feet, and kissed them as they passed.

The old King, surrounded by the happy Fairies, sat in Violet's lovely home, and watched his icy castle melt away beneath the bright sunlight; while his Spirits, cold and gloomy no longer, danced with the Elves, and waited on their King with loving eagerness. Brighter grew the golden light, gayer sang the birds, and the harmonious voices of grateful flowers, sounding over the earth, carried new joy to all their gentle kindred.

> Brighter shone the golden shadows;
>     On the cool wind softly came
> The low, sweet tones of happy flowers,
>     Singing little Violet's name.
> 'Mong the green trees was it whispered,
>     And the bright waves bore it on
> To the lonely forest flowers,
>     Where the glad news had not gone.
>
> Thus the Frost-King lost his kingdom,
>     And his power to harm and blight.
> Violet conquered, and his cold heart
>     Warmed with music, love, and light;
> And his fair home, once so dreary,
>     Gay with lovely Elves and flowers,
> Brought a joy that never faded
>     Through the long bright summer hours.

> Thus, by Violet's magic power,
>   All dark shadows passed away,
> And o'er the home of happy flowers
>   The golden light for ever lay.
> Thus the Fairy mission ended,
>   And all Flower-Land was taught
> The "Power of Love," by gentle deeds
>   That little Violet wrought.

As Sunny Lock ceased, another little Elf came forward; and this was the tale "Silver Wing" told.

# Eva's Visit to Fairy-Land

DOWN AMONG THE GRASS and fragrant clover lay little Eva by the brook-side, watching the bright waves, as they went singing by under the drooping flowers that grew on its banks. As she was wondering where the waters went, she heard a faint, low sound, as of far-off music. She thought it was the wind, but not a leaf was stirring, and soon through the rippling water came a strange little boat.

It was a lily of the valley, whose tall stem formed the mast, while the broad leaves that rose from the roots, and drooped again till they reached the water, were filled with gay little Elves, who danced to the music of the silver lily-bells above, that rang a merry peal, and filled the air with their fragrant breath.

On came the fairy boat, till it reached a moss-grown rock; and here it stopped, while the Fairies rested beneath the violet-leaves, and sang with the dancing waves.

Eva looked with wonder on their gay faces and bright garments, and in the joy of her heart sang too, and threw crimson fruit for the little folks to feast upon.

They looked kindly on the child, and, after whispering long among themselves, two little bright-eyed Elves flew over the shining water, and, lighting on the clover-blossoms, said gently, "Little maiden, many thanks for your kindness; and our Queen bids us ask if you will go with us to Fairy-Land, and learn what we can teach you."

"Gladly would I go with you, dear Fairies," said Eva, "but I cannot sail in your little boat. See! I can hold you in my hand, and could not live among you without harming your tiny kingdom, I am so large."

Then the Elves laughed gayly, as they folded their arms about her, saying, "You are a good child, dear Eva, to fear doing harm to those weaker than yourself. You cannot hurt us now. Look in the water and see what we have done."

Eva looked into the brook, and saw a tiny child standing between the Elves. "Now I can go with you," said she, "but see, I can no longer step from the bank to yonder stone, for the brook seems now like a great river, and you have not given me wings like yours."

But the Fairies took each a hand, and flew lightly over the stream. The Queen and her subjects came to meet her, and all seemed glad to say some kindly word of welcome to the little stranger. They placed a flower-crown upon her head, laid their soft faces against her own, and soon it seemed as if the gentle Elves had always been her friends.

"Now must we go home," said the Queen, "and you shall go with us, little one."

Then there was a great bustle, as they flew about on shining wings, some laying cushions of violet leaves in the boat, others folding the Queen's veil and mantle more closely round her, lest the falling dews should chill her.

The cool waves' gentle plashing against the boat, and the sweet chime of the lily-bells, lulled little Eva to sleep, and when she woke it was in Fairy-Land. A faint, rosy light, as of the setting sun, shone on the white pillars of the Queen's palace as they passed in, and the sleeping flowers leaned gracefully on their stems, dreaming beneath their soft green curtains. All was cool and still, and the Elves glided silently about, lest they should break their slumbers. They led Eva to a bed of pure white leaves, above which drooped the fragrant petals of a crimson rose.

"You can look at the bright colors till the light fades, and then the rose will sing you to sleep," said the elves, as they folded the soft leaves about her, gently kissed her, and stole away.

Long she lay watching the bright shadows, and listening to the song of the rose, while through the long night dreams of lovely things floated like bright clouds through her mind; while the rose bent lovingly above her, and sang in the clear moonlight.

With the sun rose the Fairies, and, with Eva, hastened away to the fountain, whose cool waters were soon filled with little forms, and the air ringing with happy voices, as the Elves floated in the blue waves among the fair white lilies, or sat on the green moss, smoothing their bright locks, and wearing fresh garlands of dewy flowers. At length the Queen came forth, and her subjects gathered round her, and while the flowers bowed their heads, and the trees hushed their rustling, the Fairies sang their morning hymn to the Father of birds and blossoms, who had made the earth so fair a home for them.

Then they flew away to the gardens, and soon, high up among the tree-tops, or under the broad leaves, sat the Elves in little groups, taking their breakfast of fruit and pure fresh dew; while the bright-winged birds came fearlessly among them, pecking the same ripe berries, and dipping their little beaks in the same flower-cups, and the Fairies folded their arms lovingly about them, smoothed their soft bosoms, and gayly sang to them.

"Now, little Eva," said they, "you will see that Fairies are not idle, wilful Spirits, as mortals believe. Come, we will show you what we do."

They led her to a lovely room, through whose walls of deep green leaves the light stole softly in. Here lay many wounded insects, and harmless little creatures, whom cruel hands had hurt; and pale, drooping flowers grew beside urns of healing herbs, from whose fresh leaves came a faint, sweet perfume.

Eva wondered, but silently followed her guide, little Rose-Leaf, who with tender words passed among the delicate blossoms, pouring dew on their feeble roots, cheering them with her loving words and happy smile.

Then she went to the insects; first to a little fly who lay in a flower-leaf cradle.

"Do you suffer much, dear Gauzy-Wing?" asked the Fairy. "I will bind up your poor little leg, and Zephyr shall rock you to sleep." So she folded the cool leaves tenderly about the poor fly, bathed his wings, and brought him refreshing drink, while he hummed his thanks, and forgot his pain, as Zephyr softly sung and fanned him with her waving wings.

They passed on, and Eva saw beside each bed a Fairy, who with gentle hands and loving words soothed the suffering insects. At length they stopped beside a bee, who lay among sweet honeysuckle flowers, in a cool, still place, where the summer wind blew in, and the green leaves rustled pleasantly. Yet he seemed to find no rest, and murmured of the pain he was doomed to bear. "Why must I lie here, while my kindred are out in the pleasant fields, enjoying the sunlight and the fresh air, and cruel hands have doomed me to this dark place and bitter pain when I have done no wrong? Uncared for and forgotten, I must stay here among these poor things who think only of themselves. Come here, Rose-Leaf, and bind up my wounds, for I am far more useful than idle bird or fly."

Then said the Fairy, while she bathed the broken wing,—

"Love-Blossom, you should not murmur. We may find happiness in seeking to be patient even while we suffer. You are not forgotten or un-cared for, but others need our care more than you, and to those who take cheerfully the pain and sorrow sent, do we most gladly give our help. You need not be idle, even though lying here in darkness and sorrow; you can be taking from your heart all sad and discontented feelings, and if love and patience blossom there, you will be better for the lonely hours spent here. Look on the bed beside you; this little dove has suffered far greater pain than you, and all our care can never ease it; yet through the long days he hath lain here, not an unkind word or a repining sigh hath he uttered. Ah, Love-Blossom, the gentle bird can teach a lesson you will be wiser and better for."

Then a faint voice whispered, "Little Rose-Leaf, come quickly, or I cannot thank you as I ought for all your loving care of me."

So they passed to the bed beside the discontented bee, and here upon the softest down lay the dove, whose gentle eyes looked gratefully upon the Fairy, as she knelt beside the little couch, smoothed the soft white bosom, folded her arms about it and wept sorrowing tears, while the bird still whispered its gratitude and love.

"Dear Fairy, the fairest flowers have cheered me with their sweet breath, fresh dew and fragrant leaves have been ever ready for me, gentle hands to tend, kindly hearts to love; and for this I can only thank you and say farewell."

Then the quivering wings were still, and the patient little dove was dead; but the bee murmured no longer, and the dew from the flowers fell like tears around the quiet bed.

Sadly Rose-Leaf led Eva away, saying, "Lily-Bosom shall have a grave to-night beneath our fairest blossoms, and you shall see that gentleness and love are prized far above gold or beauty, here in Fairy-Land. Come now to the Flower Palace, and see the Fairy Court."

Beneath green arches, bright with birds and flowers, beside singing waves, went Eva into a lofty hall. The roof of pure white lilies rested on pillars of green clustering vines, while many-colored blossoms threw their bright shadows on the walls, as they danced below in the deep green moss, and their low, sweet voices sounded softly through the unlit palace, while the rustling leaves kept time.

Beside the throne stood Eva, and watched the lovely forms around her, as they stood, each little band in its own color, with glistening wings, and flower wands.

Suddenly the music grew louder and sweeter, and the Fairies knelt, and bowed their heads, as on through the crowd of loving subjects came the Queen, while the air was filled with gay voices singing to welcome her.

She placed the child beside her, saying, "Little Eva, you shall see now how the flowers on your great earth bloom so brightly. A band of loving little gardeners go daily forth from Fairy-Land, to tend and watch them, that no harm may befall the gentle spirits that dwell beneath their leaves. This is never known, for like all good it is unseen by mortal eyes, and unto only pure hearts like yours do we make known our secret. The humblest

*Eva's Visit to Fairy-Land* 21

flower that grows is visited by our messengers, and often blooms in fragrant beauty, unknown, unloved by all save Fairy friends, who seek to fill
the spirits with all sweet and gentle virtues, that they may not be useless on
the earth; for the noblest mortals stoop to learn of flowers. Now, Eglantine,
what have you to tell us of your rosy namesakes on the earth?"

From a group of Elves, whose rose-wreathed wands showed the flower
they loved, came one bearing a tiny urn, and, answering the Queen, she
said,—

"Over hill and valley they are blooming fresh and fair as summer sun
and dew can make them. No drooping stem or withered leaf tells of any evil
thought within their fragrant bosoms, and thus from the fairest of their race
have they gathered this sweet dew, as a token of their gratitude to one
whose tenderness and care have kept them pure and happy; and this, the
loveliest of their sisters, have I brought to place among the Fairy flowers
that never pass away."

Eglantine laid the urn before the Queen, and placed the fragrant rose on
the dewy moss beside the throne, while a murmur of approval went
through the hall, as each elfin wand waved to the little Fairy who had toiled
so well and faithfully, and could bring so fair a gift to their good Queen.

Then came forth an Elf bearing a withered leaf, while her many-colored
robe and the purple tulips in her hair told her name and charge.

"Dear Queen," she sadly said, "I would gladly bring as pleasant tidings
as my sister, but, alas! my flowers are proud and wilful, and when I went to
gather my little gift of colored leaves for royal garments, they bade me
bring this withered blossom, and tell you they would serve no longer one
who will not make them Queen over all the other flowers. They would
yield neither dew nor honey, but proudly closed their leaves and bid me
go."

"Your task has been too hard for you," said the Queen kindly, as she
placed the drooping flower in the urn Eglantine had given, "you will see
how this dew from a sweet, pure heart will give new life and loveliness
even to this poor faded one. So can you, dear Rainbow, by loving words
and gentle teachings, bring back lost purity and peace to those whom pride
and selfishness have blighted. Go once again to the proud flowers, and tell
them when they are queen of their own hearts they will ask no fairer kingdom. Watch more tenderly than ever over them, see that they lack neither
dew nor air, speak lovingly to them, and let no unkind word or deed of
theirs anger you. Let them see by your patient love and care how much
fairer they might be, and when next you come, you will be laden with gifts
from humble, loving flowers."

Thus they told what they had done, and received from their Queen some gentle chiding or loving word of praise.

"You will be weary of this," said little Rose-Leaf to Eva; "come now and see where we are taught to read the tales written on flower-leaves, and the sweet language of the birds, and all that can make a Fairy heart wiser and better."

Then into a cheerful place they went, where were many groups of flowers, among whose leaves sat the child Elves, and learned from their flower-books all that Fairy hands had written there. Some studied how to watch the tender buds, when to spread them to the sunlight, and when to shelter them from rain; how to guard the ripening seeds, and when to lay them in the warm earth or send them on the summer wind to far off hills and valleys, where other Fairy hands would tend and cherish them, till a sisterhood of happy flowers sprang up to beautify and gladden the lonely spot where they had fallen. Others learned to heal the wounded insects, whose frail limbs a breeze could shatter, and who, were it not for Fairy hands, would die ere half their happy summer life had gone. Some learned how by pleasant dreams to cheer and comfort mortal hearts, by whispered words of love to save from evil deeds those who had gone astray, to fill young hearts with gentle thoughts and pure affections, that no sin might mar the beauty of the human flower; while others, like mortal children, learned the Fairy alphabet. Thus the Elves made loving friends by care and love, and no evil thing could harm them, for those they helped to cherish and protect ever watched to shield and save them.

Eva nodded to the gay little ones, as they peeped from among the leaves at the stranger, and then she listened to the Fairy lessons. Several tiny Elves stood on a broad leaf while the teacher sat among the petals of a flower that bent beside them, and asked questions that none but Fairies would care to know.

"Twinkle, if there lay nine seeds within a flower-cup and the wind bore five away, how many would the blossom have?"

"Four," replied the little one.

"Rosebud, if a Cowslip opens three leaves in one day and four the next, how many rosy leaves will there be when the whole flower has bloomed?"

"Seven," sang the gay little Elf.

"Harebell, if a silkworm spin one yard of Fairy cloth in an hour, how many will it spin in a day?"

"Twelve," said the Fairy child.

"Primrose, where lies Violet Island?"

"In the Lake of Ripples."

"Lilla, you may bound Rose Land."

"On the north by Ferndale, south by Sunny Wave River, east by the hill of Morning Clouds, and west by the Evening Star."

"Now, little ones," said the teacher, "you may go to your painting, that our visitor may see how we repair the flowers that earthly hands have injured."

Then Eva saw how, on large, white leaves, the Fairies learned to imitate the lovely colors, and with tiny brushes to brighten the blush on the anemone's cheek, to deepen the blue of the violet's eye, and add new light to the golden cowslip.

"You have stayed long enough," said the Elves at length, "we have many things to show you. Come now and see what is our dearest work."

So Eva said farewell to the child Elves, and hastened with little Rose-Leaf to the gates. Here she saw many bands of Fairies, folded in dark mantles that mortals might not know them, who, with the child among them, flew away over hill and valley. Some went to the cottages amid the hills, some to the sea-side to watch above the humble fisher folks; but little Rose-Leaf and many others went into the noisy city.

Eva wondered within herself what good the tiny Elves could do in this great place; but she soon learned, for the Fairy band went among the poor and friendless, bringing pleasant dreams to the sick and old, sweet, tender thoughts of love and gentleness to the young, strength to the weak, and patient cheerfulness to the poor and lonely.

Then the child wondered no longer, but deeper grew her love for the tender-hearted Elves, who left their own happy home to cheer and comfort those who never knew what hands had clothed and fed them, what hearts had given of their own joy, and brought such happiness to theirs.

Long they stayed, and many a lesson little Eva learned; but when she begged them to go back, they still led her on, saying, "Our work is not yet done; shall we leave so many sad hearts when we may cheer them, so many dark homes that we may brighten? We must stay yet longer, little Eva, and you may learn yet more."

Then they went into a dark and lonely room, and here they found a pale, sad-eyed child, who wept bitter tears over a faded flower.

"Ah," sighed the little one, "it was my only friend, and I cherished it with all my lone heart's love; 't was all that made my sad life happy; and it is gone."

Tenderly the child fastened the drooping stem, and placed it where the one faint ray of sunlight stole into the dreary room.

"Do you see," said the Elves, "through this simple flower will we keep the child pure and stainless amid the sin and sorrow around her. The love of this shall lead her on through temptation and through grief, and she shall be a spirit of joy and consolation to the sinful and the sorrowing."

And with busy love toiled the Elves amid the withered leaves, and new strength was given to the flower; while, as day by day the friendless child watched the growing buds, deeper grew her love for the unseen friends who had given her one thing to cherish in her lonely home; sweet, gentle thoughts filled her heart as she bent above it, and the blossom's fragrant breath was to her a whispered voice of all fair and lovely things; and as the flower taught her, so she taught others.

The loving Elves brought her sweet dreams by night, and happy thoughts by day, and as she grew in childlike beauty, pure and patient amid poverty and sorrow, the sinful were rebuked, sorrowing hearts grew light, and the weak and selfish forgot their idle fears, when they saw her trustingly live on with none to aid or comfort her. The love she bore the tender flower kept her own heart innocent and bright, and the pure human flower was a lesson to those who looked upon it; and soon the gloomy house was bright with happy hearts, that learned of the gentle child to bear poverty and grief as she had done, to forgive those who brought care and wrong to them, and to seek for happiness in humble deeds of charity and love.

"Our work is done," whispered the Elves, and with blessings on the two fair flowers, they flew away to other homes;—to a blind old man who dwelt alone with none to love him, till through long years of darkness and of silent sorrow the heart within had grown dim and cold. No sunlight could enter at the darkened eyes, and none were near to whisper gentle words, to cheer and comfort.

Thus he dwelt forgotten and alone, seeking to give no joy to others, possessing none himself. Life was dark and sad till the untiring Elves came to his dreary home, bringing sunlight and love. They whispered sweet words of comfort,—how, if the darkened eyes could find no light without, within there might be never-failing happiness; gentle feelings and sweet, loving thoughts could make the heart fair, if the gloomy, selfish sorrow were but cast away, and all would be bright and beautiful.

They brought light-hearted children, who gathered round him, making the desolate home fair with their young faces, and his sad heart gay with their sweet, childish voices. The love they bore he could not cast away, sunlight stole in, the dark thoughts passed away, and the earth was a pleasant home to him.

Thus their little hands led him back to peace and happiness, flowers bloomed beside his door, and their fragrant breath brought happy thoughts of pleasant valleys and green hills; birds sang to him, and their sweet voices woke the music in his own soul, that never failed to calm and comfort. Happy sounds were heard in his once lonely home, and bright faces gathered round his knee, and listened tenderly while he strove to tell them all the good that gentleness and love had done for him.

Still the Elves watched near, and brighter grew the heart as kindly thoughts and tender feelings entered in, and made it their home; and when the old man fell asleep, above his grave little feet trod lightly, and loving hands laid fragrant flowers.

Then went the Elves into the dreary prison-houses, where sad hearts pined in lonely sorrow for the joy and freedom they had lost. To these came the loving band with tender words, telling of the peace they yet might win by patient striving and repentant tears, thus waking in their bosoms all the holy feelings and sweet affections that had slept so long.

They told pleasant tales, and sang their sweetest songs to cheer and gladden, while the dim cells grew bright with the sunlight, and fragrant with the flowers the loving Elves had brought, and by their gentle teachings those sad, despairing hearts were filled with patient hope and earnest longing to win back their lost innocence and joy.

Thus to all who needed help or comfort went the faithful Fairies; and when at length they turned towards Fairy-Land, many were the grateful, happy hearts they left behind.

Then through the summer sky, above the blossoming earth, they journeyed home, happier for the joy they had given, wiser for the good they had done.

All Fairy-Land was dressed in flowers, and the soft wind went singing by, laden with their fragrant breath. Sweet music sounded through the air, and troops of Elves in their gayest robes hastened to the palace where the feast was spread.

Soon the bright hall was filled with smiling faces and fair forms, and little Eva, as she stood beside the Queen, thought she had never seen a sight so lovely.

The many-colored shadows of the fairest flowers played on the pure white walls, and fountains sparkled in the sunlight, making music as the cool waves rose and fell, while to and fro, with waving wings and joyous voices, went the smiling Elves, bearing fruit and honey, or fragrant garlands for each other's hair.

Long they feasted, gayly they sang, and Eva, dancing merrily among them, longed to be an Elf that she might dwell for ever in so fair a home.

At length the music ceased, and the Queen said, as she laid her hand on little Eva's shining hair:—

"Dear child, to-morrow we must bear you home, for, much as we long to keep you, it were wrong to bring such sorrow to your loving earthly friends; therefore we will guide you to the brook-side, and there say farewell till you come again to visit us. Nay, do not weep, dear Rose-Leaf; you shall watch over little Eva's flowers, and when she looks at them she will think of you. Come now and lead her to the Fairy garden, and show her what we think our fairest sight. Weep no more, but strive to make her last hours with us happy as you can."

With gentle caresses and most tender words the loving Elves gathered about the child, and, with Rose-Leaf by her side, they led her through the palace, and along green, winding paths, till Eva saw what seemed a wall of flowers rising before her, while the air was filled with the most fragrant odors, and the low, sweet music as of singing blossoms.

"Where have you brought me, and what mean these lovely sounds?" asked Eva.

"Look here, and you shall see," said Rose-Leaf, as she bent aside the vines, "but listen silently or you cannot hear."

Then Eva, looking through the drooping vines, beheld a garden filled with the loveliest flowers; fair as were all the blossoms she had seen in Fairy-Land, none were so beautiful as these. The rose glowed with a deeper crimson, the lily's soft leaves were more purely white, the crocus and humble cowslip shone like sunlight, and the violet was blue as the sky that smiled above it.

"How beautiful they are," whispered Eva, "but, dear Rose-Leaf, why do you keep them here, and why call you this your fairest sight?"

"Look again, and I will tell you," answered the Fairy.

Eva looked, and saw from every flower a tiny form come forth to welcome the Elves, who all, save Rose-Leaf, had flown above the wall, and were now scattering dew upon the flowers' bright leaves and talking gayly with the Spirits, who gathered around them, and seemed full of joy that they had come. The child saw that each one wore the colors of the flower that was its home. Delicate and graceful were the little forms, bright the silken hair that fell about each lovely face; and Eva heard the low, sweet murmur of their silvery voices and the rustle of their wings. She gazed in silent wonder, forgetting she knew not who they were, till the Fairy said,—

"These are the spirits of the flowers, and this the Fairy Home where those whose hearts were pure and loving on the earth come to bloom in fadeless beauty here, when their earthly life is past. The humblest flower that blooms has a home with us, for outward beauty is a worthless thing if all be not fair and sweet within. Do you see yonder lovely spirit singing with my sister Moonlight? a clover blossom was her home, and she dwelt unknown, unloved; yet patient and content, bearing cheerfully the sorrows sent her. We watched and saw how fair and sweet the humble flower grew, and then gladly bore her here, to blossom with the lily and the rose. The flowers' lives are often short, for cruel hands destroy them; therefore is it our greatest joy to bring them hither, where no careless foot or wintry wind can harm them, where they bloom in quiet beauty, repaying our care by their love and sweetest perfumes."

"I will never break another flower," cried Eva; "but let me go to them, dear Fairy; I would gladly know the lovely spirits, and ask forgiveness for the sorrow I have caused. May I not go in?"

"Nay, dear Eva, you are a mortal child, and cannot enter here; but I will tell them of the kind little maiden who has learned to love them, and they will remember you when you are gone. Come now, for you have seen enough, and we must be away."

On a rosy morning cloud, surrounded by the loving Elves, went Eva through the sunny sky. The fresh wind bore them gently on, and soon they stood again beside the brook, whose waves danced brightly as if to welcome them.

"Now, ere we say farewell," said the Queen, as they gathered nearer to the child, "tell me, dear Eva, what among all our Fairy gifts will make you happiest, and it shall be yours."

"You good little Fairies," said Eva, folding them in her arms, for she was no longer the tiny child she had been in Fairy-Land, "you dear good little Elves, what can I ask of you, who have done so much to make me happy, and taught me so many good and gentle lessons, the memory of which will never pass away? I can only ask of you the power to be as pure and gentle as yourselves, as tender and loving to the weak and sorrowing, as untiring in kindly deeds to all. Grant me this gift, and you shall see that little Eva has not forgotten what you have taught her."

"The power shall be yours," said the Elves, and laid their soft hands on her head; we will watch over you in dreams, and when you would have tidings of us, ask the flowers in your garden, and they will tell you all you would know. Farewell. Remember Fairy-Land and all your loving friends."

They clung about her tenderly, and little Rose-Leaf placed a flower crown on her head, whispering softly, "When you would come to us again, stand by the brook-side and wave this in the air, and we will gladly take you to our home again. Farewell, dear Eva. Think of your little Rose-Leaf when among the flowers."

Long Eva watched their shining wings, and listened to the music of their voices as they flew singing home, and when at length the last little form had vanished among the clouds, she saw that all around her where the Elves had been, the fairest flowers had sprung up, and the lonely brook-side was a blooming garden.

Thus she stood among the waving blossoms, with the Fairy garland in her hair, and happy feelings in her heart, better and wiser for her visit to Fairy-Land.

# Lily-Bell and Thistledown

ONCE UPON A TIME, two little Fairies went out into the world, to seek their fortune. Thistledown was as gay and gallant a little Elf as ever spread a wing. His purple mantle, and doublet of green, were embroidered with the brightest threads, and the plume in his cap came always from the wing of the gayest butterfly.

But he was not loved in Fairy-Land, for, like the flower whose name and colors he wore, though fair to look upon, many were the little thorns of cruelty and selfishness that lay concealed by his gay mantle. Many a gentle flower and harmless bird died by his hand, for he cared for himself alone, and whatever gave him pleasure must be his, though happy hearts were rendered sad, and peaceful homes destroyed.

Such was Thistledown; but far different was his little friend, Lily-Bell. Kind, compassionate, and loving, wherever her gentle face was seen, joy and gratitude were found; no suffering flower or insect, that did not love and bless the kindly Fairy; and thus all Elf-Land looked upon her as a friend.

Nor did this make her vain and heedless of others; she humbly dwelt among them, seeking to do all the good she might; and many a houseless bird and hungry insect that Thistledown had harmed did she feed and shelter, and in return no evil could befall her, for so many friends were all about her, seeking to repay her tenderness and love by their watchful care.

She would not now have left Fairy-Land, but to help and counsel her wild companion, Thistledown, who, discontented with his quiet home, *would* seek his fortune in the great world, and she feared he would suffer from his own faults, for others would not always be as gentle and forgiving as his kindred. So the kind little Fairy left her home and friends to go with him; and thus, side by side, they flew beneath the bright summer sky.

On and on, over hill and valley, they went, chasing the gay butterflies, or listening to the bees, as they flew from flower to flower like busy little housewives, singing as they worked; till at last they reached a pleasant garden, filled with flowers and green, old trees.

"See," cried Thistledown, "what a lovely home is here; let us rest among the cool leaves, and hear the flowers sing, for I am sadly tired and hungry."

So into the quiet garden they went, and the winds gayly welcomed them, while the flowers nodded on their stems, offering their bright leaves for the Elves to rest upon, and fresh, sweet honey to refresh them.

"Now, dear Thistle, do not harm these friendly blossoms," said Lily-Bell; "see how kindly they spread their leaves, and offer us their dew. It would be very wrong in you to repay their care with cruelty and pain. You will be tender for my sake, dear Thistle."

Then she went among the flowers, and they bent lovingly before her, and laid their soft leaves against her little face, that she might see how glad they were to welcome one so good and gentle, and kindly offered their dew and honey to the weary little Fairy, who sat among their fragrant petals and looked smilingly on the happy blossoms, who, with their soft, low voices, sang her to sleep.

While Lily-Bell lay dreaming among the rose-leaves, Thistledown went wandering through the garden. First he robbed the bees of their honey, and rudely shook the little flowers, that he might get the dew they had gathered to bathe their buds in. Then he chased the bright winged flies, and wounded them with the sharp thorn he carried for a sword; he broke the spider's shining webs, lamed the birds, and soon wherever he passed lay wounded insects and drooping flowers; while the winds carried the tidings over the garden, and bird and blossom looked upon him as an evil spirit, and fled away or closed their leaves, lest he should harm them.

Thus he went, leaving sorrow and pain behind him, till he came to the roses where Lily-Bell lay sleeping. There, weary of his cruel sport, he stayed to rest beneath a graceful rose-tree, where grew one blooming flower and a tiny bud.

"Why are you so slow in blooming, little one? You are too old to be rocked in your green cradle longer, and should be out among your sister flowers," said Thistle, as he lay idly in the shadow of the tree.

"My little bud is not yet strong enough to venture forth," replied the rose, as she bent fondly over it; "the sunlight and the rain would blight her tender form, were she to blossom now, but soon she will be fit to bear them; till then she is content to rest beside her mother, and to wait."

"You silly flower," said Thistledown, "see how quickly I will make you bloom! your waiting is all useless." And speaking thus, he pulled rudely apart the folded leaves, and laid them open to the sun and air; while the rose mother implored the cruel Fairy to leave her little bud untouched.

"It is my first, my only one," said she, "and I have watched over it with such care, hoping it would soon bloom beside me; and now you have destroyed it. How could you harm the little helpless one, that never did aught to injure you?" And while her tears fell like summer rain, she drooped in grief above the little bud, and sadly watched it fading in the sunlight; but Thistledown, heedless of the sorrow he had given, spread his wings and flew away.

Soon the sky grew dark, and heavy drops began to fall. Then Thistle hastened to the lily, for her cup was deep, and the white leaves fell like curtains over the fragrant bed; he was a dainty little Elf, and could not sleep among the clovers and bright buttercups. But when he asked the flower to unfold her leaves and take him in, she turned her pale, soft face away, and answered sadly, "I must shield my little drooping sisters whom you have harmed, and cannot let you in."

Then Thistledown was very angry, and turned to find shelter among the stately roses; but they showed their sharp thorns, and, while their rosy faces glowed with anger, told him to begone, or they would repay him for the wrong he had done their gentle kindred.

He would have stayed to harm them, but the rain fell fast, and he hurried away, saying, "The tulips will take me in, for I have praised their beauty, and they are vain and foolish flowers."

But when he came, all wet and cold, praying for shelter among their thick leaves, they only laughed, and said scornfully, "We know you, and will not let you in, for you are false and cruel, and will only bring us sorrow. You need not come to us for another mantle, when the rain has spoilt your fine one; and do not stay here, or we will do you harm."

Then they waved their broad leaves stormily, and scattered the heavy drops on his dripping garments.

"Now must I go to the humble daisies and blue violets," said Thistle, "they will be glad to let in so fine a Fairy, and I shall die in this cold wind and rain."

So away he flew, as fast as his heavy wings would bear him, to the daisies; but they nodded their heads wisely, and closed their leaves yet closer, saying sharply,—

"Go away with yourself, and do not imagine we will open our leaves to you, and spoil our seeds by letting in the rain. It serves you rightly; to gain our love and confidence, and repay it by such cruelty! You will find no shelter here for one whose careless hand wounded our little friend Violet, and broke the truest heart that ever beat in a flower's breast. We are very angry with you, wicked Fairy; go away and hide yourself.

"Ah," cried the shivering Elf, "where can I find shelter? I will go to the violets: they will forgive and take me in."

But the daisies had spoken truly; the gentle little flower was dead, and her blue-eyed sisters were weeping bitterly over her faded leaves.

"Now I have no friends," sighed poor Thistledown, "and must die of cold. Ah, if I had but minded Lily-Bell, I might now be dreaming beneath some flower's leaves."

"Others can forgive and love, beside Lily-Bell and Violet," said a faint, sweet voice; "I have no little bud to shelter now, and you can enter here." It was the rose mother that spoke, and thistle saw how pale the bright leaves had grown, and how the slender stem was bowed. Grieved, ashamed, and wondering at the flower's forgiving words, he laid his weary head on the bosom he had filled with sorrow, and the fragrant leaves were folded carefully about him.

But he could find no rest. The rose strove to comfort him; but when she fancied he was sleeping, thoughts of her lost bud stole in, and the little heart beat so sadly where he lay, that no sleep came; while the bitter tears he had caused to flow fell more coldly on him than the rain without. Then he heard the other flowers whispering among themselves of his cruelty, and the sorrow he had brought to their happy home; and many wondered how the rose, who had suffered most, could yet forgive and shelter him.

"Never could I forgive one who had robbed me of my children. I could bow my head and die, but could give no happiness to one who had taken all my own," said Hyacinth, bending fondly over the little ones that blossomed by her side.

"Dear Violet is not the only one who will leave us," sobbed little Mignonette; "the rose mother will fade like her little bud, and we shall lose our gentlest teacher. Her last lesson is forgiveness; let us show our love for her, and the gentle stranger Lily-Bell, by allowing no unkind word or thought of him who has brought us all this grief."

The angry words were hushed, and through the long night nothing was heard but the dropping of the rain, and the low sighs of the rose.

Soon the sunlight came again, and with it Lily-Bell seeking for Thistledown; but he was ashamed, and stole away.

When the flowers told their sorrow to kind-hearted Lily-Bell, she wept bitterly at the pain her friend had given, and with loving words strove to comfort those whom he had grieved; with gentle care she healed the wounded birds, and watched above the flowers he had harmed, bringing each day dew and sunlight to refresh and strengthen, till all were well again; and though sorrowing for their dead friends, still they forgave Thistle for the sake of her who had done so much for them. Thus, erelong, buds fairer than that she had lost lay on the rose mother's breast, and for all she had suffered she was well repaid by the love of Lily-Bell and her sister flowers.

And when bird, bee, and blossom were strong and fair again, the gentle Fairy said farewell, and flew away to seek her friend, leaving behind many grateful hearts, who owed their joy and life to her.

Meanwhile, over hill and dale went Thistledown, and for a time was kind and gentle to every living thing. He missed sadly the little friend who had left her happy home to watch over him, but he was too proud to own his fault, and so went on, hoping she would find him.

One day he fell asleep, and when he woke the sun had set, and the dew began to fall; the flower-cups were closed, and he had nowhere to go, till a friendly little bee, belated by his heavy load of honey, bid the weary Fairy come with him.

"Help me to bear my honey home, and you can stay with us to-night," he kindly said.

So Thistle gladly went with him, and soon they came to a pleasant garden, where among the fairest flowers stood the hive, covered with vines and overhung with blossoming trees. Glow-worms stood at the door to light them home, and as they passed in, the Fairy thought how charming it must be to dwell in such a lovely place. The floor of wax was pure and white as marble, while the walls were formed of golden honey-comb, and the air was fragrant with the breath of flowers.

"You cannot see our Queen to-night," said the little bee, "but I will show you to a bed where you can rest."

And he led the tired Fairy to a little cell, where on a bed of flower-leaves he folded his wings and fell asleep.

As the first ray of sunlight stole in, he was awakened by sweet music. It was the morning song of the bees.

> "Awake! awake! for the earliest gleam
>     Of golden sunlight shines
> On the rippling waves, that brightly flow
>     Beneath the flowering vines.
> Awake! awake! for the low, sweet chant
>     Of the wild-birds' morning hymn
> Comes floating by on the fragrant air,
>     Through the forest cool and dim;
>         Then spread each wing,
>         And work, and sing,
> Through the long, bright sunny hours;
>         O'er the pleasant earth

We journey forth,
For a day among the flowers.

"Awake! awake! for the summer wind
   Hath bidden the blossoms unclose,
Hath opened the violet's soft blue eye,
   And wakened the sleeping rose.
And lightly they wave on their slender stems
   Fragrant, and fresh, and fair,
Waiting for us, as we singing come
   To gather our honey-dew there.
     Then spread each wing,
     And work, and sing,
Through the long, bright sunny hours;
     O'er the pleasant earth
     We journey forth,
For a day among the flowers."

Soon his friend came to bid him rise, as the Queen desired to speak with him. So, with his purple mantle thrown gracefully over his shoulder, and his little cap held respectfully in his hand, he followed Nimble-Wing to the great hall, where the Queen was being served by her little pages. Some bore her fresh dew and honey, some fanned her with fragrant flower-leaves, while others scattered the sweetest perfumes on the air.

"Little Fairy," said the Queen, "you are welcome to my palace; and we will gladly have you stay with us, if you will obey our laws. We do not spend the pleasant summer days in idleness and pleasure, but each one labors for the happiness and good of all. If our home is beautiful, we have made it so by industry; and here, as one large, loving family, we dwell; no sorrow, care, or discord can enter in, while all obey the voice of her who seeks to be a wise and gentle Queen to them. If you will stay with us, we will teach you many things. Order, patience, industry, who can teach so well as they who are the emblems of these virtues?

"Our laws are few and simple. You must each day gather your share of honey, see that your cell is sweet and fresh, as you yourself must be; rise with the sun, and with *him* to sleep. You must harm no flower in doing your work, nor take more than your just share of honey; for they so kindly give us food, it were most cruel to treat them with aught save gentleness and gratitude. Now will you stay with us, and learn what even mortals seek to know, that labor brings true happiness?"

And Thistle said he would stay and dwell with them; for he was tired of wandering alone, and thought he might live here till Lily-Bell should come, or till he was weary of the kind-hearted bees. Then they took away his gay garments, and dressed him like themselves, in the black velvet cloak with golden bands across his breast.

"Now come with us," they said. So forth into the green fields they went, and made their breakfast among the dewy flowers; and then till the sun set they flew from bud to blossom, singing as they went; and Thistle for a while was happier than when breaking flowers and harming gentle birds.

But he soon grew tired of working all day in the sun, and longed to be free again. He could find no pleasure with the industrious bees, and sighed to be away with his idle friends, the butterflies; so while the others worked he slept or played, and then, in haste to get his share, he tore the flowers, and took all they had saved for their own food. Nor was this all; he told such pleasant tales of the life he led before he came to live with them, that many grew unhappy and discontented, and they who had before wished no greater joy than the love and praise of their kind Queen, now disobeyed and blamed her for all she had done for them.

Long she bore with their unkind words and deeds; and when at length she found it was the ungrateful Fairy who had wrought this trouble in her quiet kingdom, she strove, with sweet, forgiving words, to show him all the wrong he had done; but he would not listen, and still went on destroying the happiness of those who had done so much for him.

Then, when she saw that no kindness could touch his heart, she said:—

"Thistledown, we took you in, a friendless stranger, fed and clothed you, and made our home as pleasant to you as we could; and in return for all our care, you have brought discontent and trouble to my subjects, grief and care to me. I cannot let my peaceful kingdom be disturbed by you; therefore go and seek another home. You may find other friends, but none will love you more than we, had you been worthy of it; so farewell." And the doors of the once happy home he had disturbed were closed behind him.

Then he was very angry, and determined to bring some great sorrow on the good Queen. So he sought out the idle, wilful bees, whom he had first made discontented, bidding them follow him, and win the honey the Queen had stored up for the winter.

"Let us feast and make merry in the pleasant summer-time," said Thistle; "winter is far off, why should we waste these lovely days, toiling to lay up the food we might enjoy now. Come, we will take what we have made, and think no more of what the Queen has said."

So while the industrious bees were out among the flowers, he led the droves to the hive, and took possession of the honey, destroying and laying waste the home of the kind bees; then, fearing that in their grief and anger they might harm him, Thistle flew away to seek new friends.

After many wanderings, he came at length to a great forest, and here beside a still lake he stayed to rest. Delicate wood-flowers grew near him in the deep green moss, with drooping heads, as if they listened to the soft wind singing among the pines. Bright-eyed birds peeped at him from their nests, and many-colored insects danced above the cool, still lake.

"This is a pleasant place," said Thistle; "it shall be my home for a while. Come hither, blue dragon-fly, I would gladly make a friend of you, for I am all alone."

The dragon-fly folded his shining wings beside the Elf, listened to the tale he told, promised to befriend the lonely one, and strove to make the forest a happy home to him.

So here dwelt Thistle, and many kind friends gathered round him, for he spoke gently to them, and they knew nothing of the cruel deeds he had done; and for a while he was happy and content. But at length he grew weary of the gentle birds, and wild-flowers, and sought new pleasure in destroying the beauty he was tired of; and soon the friends who had so kindly welcomed him looked upon him as an evil spirit, and shrunk away as he approached.

At length his friend the dragon-fly besought him to leave the quiet home he had disturbed. Then Thistle was very angry, and while the dragon-fly was sleeping among the flowers that hung over the lake, he led an ugly spider to the spot, and bade him weave his nets about the sleeping insect, and bind him fast. The cruel spider gladly obeyed the ungrateful Fairy; and soon the poor fly could move neither leg nor wing. Then Thistle flew away through the wood, leaving sorrow and trouble behind him.

He had not journeyed far before he grew weary, and lay down to rest. Long he slept, and when he awoke, and tried to rise, his hands and wings were bound; while beside him stood two strange little figures, with dark faces and garments, that rustled like withered leaves; who cried to him, as he struggled to get free,—

"Lie still, you naughty Fairy, you are in the Brownies' power, and shall be well punished for your cruelty ere we let you go."

So poor Thistle lay sorrowfully, wondering what would come of it, and wishing Lily-Bell would come to help and comfort him; but he had left her, and she could not help him now.

Soon a troop of Brownies came rustling through the air, and gathered round him, while one who wore an acorn-cup on his head, and was their King, said, as he stood beside the trembling Fairy,—

"You have done many cruel things, and caused much sorrow to happy hearts; now you are in my power, and I shall keep you prisoner till you have repented. You cannot dwell on the earth without harming the fair things given you to enjoy, so you shall live alone in solitude and darkness, till you have learned to find happiness in gentle deeds, and forget yourself in giving joy to others. When you have learned this, I will set you free."

Then the Brownies bore him to a high, dark rock, and, entering a little door, led him to a small cell, dimly lighted by a crevice through which came a single gleam of sunlight; and there, through long, long days, poor Thistle sat alone, and gazed with wistful eyes at the little opening, longing to be out on the green earth. No one came to him, but the silent Brownies who brought his daily food; and with bitter tears he wept for Lily-Bell, mourning his cruelty and selfishness, seeking to do some kindly deed that might atone for his wrong-doing.

A little vine that grew outside his prison rock came creeping up, and looked in through the crevice, as if to cheer the lonely Fairy, who welcomed it most gladly, and daily sprinkled its soft leaves with his small share of water, that the little vine might live, even if it darkened more and more his dim cell.

The watchful Brownies saw this kind deed, and brought him fresh flowers, and many things, which Thistle gratefully received, though he never knew it was his kindness to the vine that gained for him these pleasures.

Thus did poor Thistle strive to be more gentle and unselfish, and grew daily happier and better.

Now while Thistledown was a captive in the lonely cell, Lily-Bell was seeking him far and wide, and sadly traced him by the sorrowing hearts he had left behind.

She healed the drooping flowers, cheered the Queen Bee's grief, brought back her discontented subjects, restored the home to peace and order, and left them blessing her.

Thus she journeyed on, till she reached the forest where Thistledown had lost his freedom. She unbound the starving dragon-fly, and tended the wounded birds; but though all learned to love her, none could tell where the Brownies had borne her friend, till a little wind came whispering by, and told her that a sweet voice had been heard, singing Fairy songs, deep in a mossgrown rock.

Then Lily-Bell went seeking through the forest, listening for the voice.

Long she looked and listened in vain; when one day, as she was wandering through a lonely dell, she heard a faint, low sound of music, and soon a distant voice mournfully singing,—

> "Bright shines the summer sun,
>    Soft is the summer air;
> Gayly the wood-birds sing,
>    Flowers are blooming fair.
> "But, deep in the dark, cold rock,
>    Sadly I dwell,
> Longing for thee, dear friend,
>    Lily-Bell! Lily-Bell!"

"Thistle, dear Thistle, where are you?" joyfully cried Lily-Bell, as she flew from rock to rock. But the voice was still, and she would have looked in vain, had she not seen a little vine, whose green leaves fluttering to and fro seemed beckoning her to come; and as she stood among its flowers she sang,—

> "Through sunlight and summer air
>    I have sought for thee long,
> Guided by birds and flowers,
>    And now by thy song.
>
> "Thistledown! Thistledown!
>    O'er hill and dell
> Hither to comfort thee
>    Comes Lily-Bell."

Then from the vine-leaves two little arms were stretched out to her, and Thistledown was found. So Lily-Bell made her home in the shadow of the vine, and brought such joy to Thistle, that his lonely cell seemed pleasanter to him than all the world beside; and he grew daily more like his gentle friend. But it did not last long, for one day she did not come. He watched and waited long, for the little face that used to peep smiling in through the vine-leaves. He called and beckoned through the narrow opening, but no Lily-Bell answered; and he wept sadly as he thought of all she had done for him, and that now he could not go to seek and help her, for he had lost his freedom by his own cruel and wicked deeds.

At last he besought the silent Brownie earnestly to tell him whither she had gone.

"O let me go to her," prayed Thistle; "if she is in sorrow, I will comfort her, and show my gratitude for all she has done for me: dear Brownie, set me free, and when she is found I will come and be your prisoner again. I will bear and suffer any danger for her sake."

"Lily-Bell is safe," replied the Brownie; "come, you shall learn the trial that awaits you."

Then he led the wondering Fairy from his prison, to a group of tall, drooping ferns, beneath whose shade a large white lily had been placed, forming a little tent, within which, on a couch of thick green moss, lay Lily-Bell in a deep sleep; the sunlight stole softly in, and all was cool and still.

"You cannot wake her," said the Brownie, as Thistle folded his arms tenderly about her. "It is a magic slumber, and she will not wake till you shall bring hither gifts from the Earth, Air, and Water Spirits. 'T is a long and weary task, for you have made no friends to help you, and will have to seek for them alone. This is the trial we shall give you; and if your love for Lily-Bell be strong enough to keep you from all cruelty and selfishness, and make you kind and loving as you should be, she will awake to welcome you, and love you still more fondly than before."

Then Thistle, with a last look on the little friend he loved so well, set forth alone to his long task.

The home of the Earth Spirits was the first to find, and no one would tell him where to look. So far and wide he wandered, through gloomy forests and among lonely hills, with none to cheer him when sad and weary, none to guide him on his way.

On he went, thinking of Lily-Bell, and for her sake bearing all; for in his quiet prison many gentle feelings and kindly thoughts had sprung up in his heart, and he now strove to be friends with all, and win for himself the love and confidence of those whom once he sought to harm and cruelly destroy.

But few believed him; for they remembered his false promises and evil deeds, and would not trust him now; so poor Thistle found few to love or care for him.

Long he wandered, and carefully he sought; but could not find the Earth Spirits' home. And when at length he reached the pleasant garden where he and Lily-Bell first parted, he said within himself,—

"Here I will stay awhile, and try to win by kindly deeds the flowers' forgiveness for the pain and sorrow I brought them long ago; and they may learn to love and trust me. So, even if I never find the Spirits, I shall be worthier Lily-Bell's affection if I strive to atone for the wrong I have done."

Then he went among the flowers, but they closed their leaves, and

"Lily-Bell and Thistledown."
From *Lulu's Library, Vol. 2: The Frost-King*, 1887.

shrank away, trembling with fear; while the birds fled to hide among the leaves as he passed.

This grieved poor Thistle, and he longed to tell them how changed he had become; but they would not listen. So he tried to show, by quiet deeds of kindness, that he meant no harm to them; and soon the kind-hearted birds pitied the lonely Fairy, and when he came near sang cheering songs, and dropped ripe berries in his path, for he no longer broke their eggs, or hurt their little ones.

And when the flowers saw this, and found the once cruel Elf now watering and tending little buds, feeding hungry insects, and helping the busy ants to bear their heavy loads, they shared the pity of the birds, and longed to trust him; but they dared not yet.

He came one day, while wandering through the garden, to the little rose he had once harmed so sadly. Many buds now bloomed beside her, and her soft face glowed with motherly pride, as she bent fondly over them. But when Thistle came, he saw with sorrow how she bade them close their green curtains, and conceal themselves beneath the leaves, for there was danger near; and, drooping still more closely over them, she seemed to wait with trembling fear the cruel Fairy's coming.

But no rude hand tore her little ones away, no unkind words were spoken; but a soft shower of dew fell lightly on them, and Thistle, bending tenderly above them, said,—

"Dear flower, forgive the sorrow I once brought you, and trust me now for Lily-Bell's sake. Her gentleness has changed my cruelty to kindness, and I would gladly repay all for the harm I have done; but none will love and trust me now."

Then the little rose looked up, and while the dew-drops shone like happy tears upon her leaves, she said,—

"I *will* love and trust you, Thistle, for you are indeed much changed. Make your home among us, and my sister flowers will soon learn to love you as you deserve. Not for sweet Lily-Bell's sake, but for your own, will I become your friend; for you are kind and gentle now, and worthy of our love. Look up, my little ones, there is no danger near; look up, and welcome Thistle to our home."

Then the little buds raised their rosy faces, danced again upon their stems, and nodded kindly at Thistle, who smiled on them through happy tears, and kissed the sweet, forgiving rose, who loved and trusted him when most forlorn and friendless.

But the other flowers wondered among themselves, and Hyacinth said,—

"If Rose-Leaf is his friend, surely we may be; yet still I fear he may soon grow weary of this gentleness, and be again the wicked Fairy he once was, and we shall suffer for our kindness to him now."

"Ah, do not doubt him!" cried warm-hearted little Mignonette; "surely some good spirit has changed the wicked Thistle into this good little Elf. See how tenderly he lifts aside the leaves that overshadow pale Harebell, and listen now how softly he sings as he rocks little Eglantine to sleep. He has done many friendly things, though none save Rose-Leaf has been kind to him, and he is very sad. Last night when I awoke to draw my curtains closer, he sat weeping in the moonlight, so bitterly, I longed to speak a kindly word to him. Dear sisters, let us trust him."

And they all said little Mignonette was right; and, spreading wide their leaves, they bade him come, and drink their dew, and lie among the fragrant petals, striving to cheer his sorrow. Thistle told them all, and, after much whispering together, they said,—

"Yes, we will help you to find the Earth Spirits, for you are striving to be good, and for love of Lily-Bell we will do much for you."

So they called a little bright-eyed mole, and said, "Downy-Back, we have given you a pleasant home among our roots, and you are a grateful little friend; so will you guide dear Thistle to the Earth Spirits' home?"

Downy-Back said, "Yes," and Thistle, thanking the kindly flowers, followed his little guide, through long, dark galleries, deeper and deeper into the ground; while a glow-worm flew before to light the way. On they went, and after a while, reached a path lit up by bright jewels hung upon the walls. Here Downy-Back, and Glimmer, the glow-worm, left him, saying,—

"We can lead you no farther; you must now go on alone, and the music of the Spirits will guide you to their home."

Then they went quickly up the winding path, and Thistle, guided by the sweet music, went on alone.

He soon reached a lovely spot, whose golden halls were bright with jewels, which sparkled brightly, and threw many-colored shadows on the shining garments of the little Spirits, who danced below the melody of soft, silvery bells.

Long Thistle stood watching the brilliant forms that flashed and sparkled round him; but he missed the flowers and the sunlight, and rejoiced that he was not an Earth Spirit.

At last they spied him out, and, gladly welcoming him, bade him join in their dance. But Thistledown was too sad for that, and when he told them all his story they no longer urged, but sought to comfort him; and one whom they called little Sparkle (for her crown and robe shone with the brightest diamonds, said): "You will have to work for us, ere you can win a gift to show the Brownies; do you see those golden bells that make such music, as we wave them to and fro? We worked long and hard ere they were won, and you can win one of those, if you will do the task we give you."

And Thistle said, "No task will be too hard for me to do for dear Lily-Bell's sake."

Then they led him to a strange, dark place, lit up with torches; where troops of Spirits flew busily to and fro, among damp rocks, and through dark galleries that led far down into the earth. "What do they here?" asked Thistle.

"I will tell," replied little Sparkle, "for I once worked here myself. Some of them watch above the flower-roots, and keep them fresh and strong; others gather the clear drops that trickle from the damp rocks, and form a little spring, which, growing ever larger, rises to the light above, and gushes forth in some green field or lonely forest; where the wild-birds come to drink, and wood-flowers spread their thirsty leaves above the clear, cool waves, as they go dancing away, carrying joy and freshness wherever they go. Others shape the bright jewels into lovely forms, and make the good-luck pennies which we give to mortals whom we love. And here you must toil till the golden flower is won."

Then Thistle went among the Spirits, and joined in their tasks; he tended the flower-roots, gathered the water drops, and formed the good-luck pennies. Long and hard he worked, and was often sad and weary, often tempted by unkind and selfish thoughts; but he thought of Lily-Bell, and strove to be kind and loving as she had been; and soon the Spirits learned to love the patient Fairy, who had left his home to toil among them for the sake of his gentle friend.

At length came little Sparkle to him, saying, "You have done enough; come now, and dance and feast with us, for the golden flower is won."

But Thistle could not stay, for half his task was not yet done; and he longed for sunlight and Lily-Bell. So, taking a kind farewell, he hastened through the torch-lit path up to the light again; and, spreading his wings, flew over hill and dale till he reached the forest where Lily-Bell lay sleeping.

It was early morning, and the rosy light shone brightly through the lily-leaves upon her, as Thistle entered, and laid his first gift at the Brownie King's feet.

"You have done well," said he, "we hear good tidings of you from bird and flower, and you are truly seeking to repair the evil you have done. Take now one look at your little friend, and then go forth to seek from the Air Spirits your second gift."

Then Thistle said farewell again to Lily-Bell, and flew far and wide among the clouds, seeking the Air Spirits; but though he wandered till his weary wings could bear him no longer, it was in vain. So, faint and sad, he lay down to rest on a broad vine-leaf, that fluttered gently in the wind; and as he lay, he saw beneath him the home of the kind bees whom he had so disturbed, and Lily-Bell had helped and comforted.

"I will seek to win their pardon, and show them that I am no longer the cruel Fairy who so harmed them," thought Thistle, "and when they become again my friends, I will ask their help to find the Air Spirits; and if I deserve it, they will gladly aid me on my way."

So he flew down into the field below, and hastened busily from flower to flower, till he had filled a tiny blue-bell with sweet, fresh honey. Then he stole softly to the hive, and, placing it near the door, concealed himself to watch. Soon his friend Nimble-Wing came flying home, and when he spied the little cup, he hummed with joy, and called his companions around him.

"Surely, some good Elf has placed it here for us," said they; "let us bear it to our Queen; it is so fresh and fragrant it will be a fit gift for her"; and they joyfully took it in, little dreaming who had placed it there.

So each day Thistle filled a flower-cup, and laid it at the door; and each day the bees wondered more and more, for many strange things happened. The field-flowers told of the good spirit who watched above them, and the birds sang of the same kind little Elf bringing soft moss for their nests, and food for their hungry young ones; while all around the hive had grown fairer since the Fairy came.

But the bees never saw him, for he feared he had not yet done enough to win forgiveness and friendship; so he lived alone among the vines, daily bringing them honey, and doing some kindly action.

At length, as he lay sleeping in a flower-bell, a little bee came wandering by, and knew him for the wicked Thistle; so he called his friends, and, as they flew murmuring around him, he awoke.

"What shall we do to you, naughty Elf?" said they. "You are in our power, and we will sting you if you are not still."

"Let us close the flower-leaves around him and leave him here to starve," cried one, who had not yet forgotten all the sorrow Thistle had caused them long ago.

"No, no, that were very cruel, dear Buzz," said little Hum; "let us take him to our Queen, and she will tell us how to show our anger for the wicked deeds he did. See how bitterly he weeps; be kind to him, he will not harm us more."

"You good little Hum!" cried a kind-hearted robin who had hopped near to listen to the bees. "Dear friends, do you not know that this is the good Fairy who has dwelt so quietly among us, watching over bird and blossom, giving joy to all he helps? It is *he* who brings the honey-cup each day to you, and then goes silently away, that you may never know who works so faithfully for you. Be kind to him, for if he has done wrong, he has repented of it, as you may see."

"Can this be naughty Thistle?" said Nimble-Wing.

"Yes, it is I," said Thistle, "but no longer cruel and unkind. I have tried to win your love by patient industry. Ah, trust me now, and you shall see I am not naughty Thistle any more."

Then the wondering bees led him to their Queen, and when he had told his tale, and begged their forgiveness, it was gladly given; and all strove to show him that he *was* loved and trusted. Then he asked if they could tell him where the Air Spirits dwelt, for he must not forget dear Lily-Bell; and to his great joy the Queen said, "Yes," and bade little Hum guide Thistle to Cloud-Land.

Little Hum joyfully obeyed; and Thistle followed him, as he flew higher and higher among the soft clouds, till in the distance they saw a radiant light.

"There is their home, and I must leave you now, dear Thistle," said the little bee; and, bidding him farewell, he flew singing back; while Thistle, following the light, soon found himself in the Air Spirits' home.

The sky was gold and purple like an autumn sunset, and long walls of brilliant clouds lay round him. A rosy light shone through the silver mist, on gleaming columns and the rainbow roof; soft, fragrant winds went whispering by, and airy little forms were flitting to and fro.

Long Thistle wondered at the beauty round him; and then he went among the shining Spirits, told his tale, and asked a gift.

But they answered like the Earth Spirits. "You must serve us first, and then we will gladly give you a robe of sunlight like our own."

And then they told him how they wafted flower-seeds over the earth, to beautify and brighten lonely spots; how they watched above the blossoms by day, and scattered dews at night, brought sunlight into darkened places, and soft winds to refresh and cheer.

"These are the things we do," said they, "and you must aid us for a time."

And Thistle gladly went with the lovely spirits; by day he joined the sunlight and the breeze in their silent work; by night, with Star-Light and her sister spirits, he flew over the moon-lit earth, dropping cool dew upon the folded flowers, and bringing happy dreams to sleeping mortals. Many a kind deed was done, many a gentle word was spoken; and each day lighter grew his heart, and stronger his power of giving joy to others.

At length Star-Light bade him work no more, and gladly gave him the gift he had won. Then his second task was done, and he flew gayly back to the green earth and slumbering Lily-Bell.

The silvery moonlight shone upon her, as he came to give his second gift; and the Brownie spoke more kindly than before.

"One more trial, Thistle, and she will awake. Go bravely forth and win your last and hardest gift."

Then with a light heart Thistle journeyed away to the brooks and rivers, seeking the Water Spirits. But he looked in vain; till, wandering through the forest where the Brownies took him captive, he stopped beside the quiet lake.

As he stood here he heard a sound of pain, and, looking in the tall grass at his side, he saw the dragon-fly whose kindness he once repayed by pain and sorrow, and who now lay suffering and alone.

Thistle bent tenderly beside him, saying, "Dear Flutter, do not fear me. I will gladly ease your pain, if you will let me; I am your friend, and long to show you how I grieve for all the wrong I did you, when you were so kind to me. Forgive, and let me help and comfort you."

Then he bound up the broken wing, and spoke so tenderly that Flutter doubted him no longer, and was his friend again.

Day by day did Thistle watch beside him, making little beds of cool, fresh moss for him to rest upon, fanning him when he slept, and singing sweet songs to cheer him when awake. And often when poor Flutter longed to be dancing once again over the blue waves, the Fairy bore him in his arms to the lake, and on a broad leaf, with a green flag for a sail, they floated on the still water; while the dragon-fly's companions flew about them, playing merry games.

At length the broken wing was well, and Thistle said he must again seek the Water Spirits. "I can tell you where to find them," said Flutter; "you must follow yonder little brook, and it will lead you to the sea, where the Spirits dwell. I would gladly do more for you, dear Thistle, but I cannot, for they live deep beneath the waves. You will find some kind friend to aid you on your way; and so farewell."

Thistle followed the little brook, as it flowed through field and valley, growing ever larger, till it reached the sea. Here the wind blew freshly, and the great waves rolled and broke at Thistle's feet, as he stood upon the shore, watching the billows dancing and sparkling in the sun.

"How shall I find the Spirits in this great sea, with none to help or guide me? Yet it is my last task, and for Lily-Bell's sake I must not fear or falter now," said Thistle. So he flew hither and thither over the sea, looking through the waves. Soon he saw, far below, the branches of the coral tree.

"They must be here," thought he, and, folding his wings, he plunged into the deep, cold sea. But he saw only fearful monsters and dark shapes that gathered round him; and, trembling with fear, he struggled up again.

The great waves tossed him to and fro, and cast him bruised and faint upon the shore. Here he lay weeping bitterly, till a voice beside him said, "Poor little Elf, what has befallen you? These rough waves are not fit play-mates for so delicate a thing as you. Tell me your sorrow, and I will comfort you."

And Thistle, looking up, saw a white sea-bird at his side, who tried with friendly words to cheer him. So he told all his wanderings, and how he sought the Sea Spirits.

"Surely, if bee and blossom do their part to help you, birds should aid you too," said the Seabird. "I will call my friend, the Nautilus, and he will bear you safely to the Coral Palace where the Spirits dwell." So, spreading his great wings, he flew away, and soon Thistle saw a little boat come dancing over the waves, and wait beside the shore for him.

In he sprang. Nautilus raised his little sail to the wind, and the light boat glided swiftly over the blue sea. At last Thistle cried, "I see lovely arches far below; let me go, it is the Spirits' home."

"Nay, close your eyes, and trust to me. I will bear you safely down," said Nautilus.

So Thistle closed his eyes, and listened to the murmur of the sea, as they sank slowly through the waves. The soft sound lulled him to sleep, and when he awoke the boat was gone, and he stood among the Water Spirits, in their strange and lovely home.

Lofty arches of snow-white coral bent above him, and the walls of brightly tinted shells were wreathed with lovely sea-flowers, and the sunlight shining on the waves cast silvery shadows on the ground, where sparkling stones glowed in the sand. A cool, fresh wind swept through the waving garlands of bright sea-moss, and the distant murmur of dashing waves came softly on the air. Soon troops of graceful Spirits flitted by, and when they found the wondering Elf, they gathered round him, bringing pearl-shells heaped with precious stones, and all the rare, strange gifts that lie beneath the sea. But Thistle wished for none of these, and when his tale was told, the kindly Spirits pitied him; and little Pearl sighed, as she told him of the long and weary task he must perform, ere he could win a crown of snow-white pearls like those they wore. But Thistle had gained strength and courage in his wanderings, and did not falter now, when they led him to a place among the coral-workers, and told him he must labor here, till the spreading branches reached the light and air, through the waves that danced above.

With a patient hope that he might yet be worthy of Lily-Bell, the Fairy left the lovely spirits and their pleasant home, to toil among the coral-builders, where all was strange and dim. Long, long, he worked; but still the waves rolled far above them, and his task was not yet done; and many bitter tears poor Thistle shed, and sadly he pined for air and sunlight, the voice of birds, and breath of flowers. Often, folded in the magic garments which the Spirits gave him, that he might pass unharmed among the fearful creatures dwelling there, he rose to the surface of the sea, and, gliding through the waves, gazed longingly upon the hills, now looking blue and dim so far away, or watched the flocks of summer birds, journeying to a warmer land; and they brought sad memories of green old forests, and sunny fields, to the lonely little Fairy floating on the great, wild sea.

Day after day went by, and slowly Thistle's task drew towards an end. Busily toiled the coral-workers, but more busily toiled he; insect and Spirit daily wondered more and more, at the industry and patience of the silent little Elf, who had a friendly word for all, though he never joined them in their sport.

Higher and higher grew the coral-boughs, and lighter grew the Fairy's heart, while thoughts of dear Lily-Bell cheered him on, as day by day he steadily toiled; and when at length the sun shone on his work, and it was done, he stayed but to take the garland he had won, and to thank the good Spirits for their love and care. Then up through the cold, blue waves he swiftly glided, and, shaking the bright drops from his wings, soared singing up to the sunny sky.

On through the fragrant air went Thistle, looking with glad face upon the fair, fresh earth below, where flowers looked smiling up, and green trees bowed their graceful heads as if to welcome him. Soon the forest where Lily-Bell lay sleeping rose before him, and as he passed along the cool, dim wood-paths, never had they seemed so fair.

But when he came where his little friend had slept, it was no longer the dark, silent spot where he last saw her. Garlands hung from every tree, and the fairest flowers filled the air with their sweet breath. Bird's gay voices echoed far and wide, and the little brook went singing by, beneath the arching ferns that bent above it; green leaves rustled in the summer wind, and the air was full of music. But the fairest sight was Lily-Bell, as she lay on the couch of velvet moss that Fairy hands had spread. The golden flower lay beside her, and the glittering robe was folded round her little form. The warmest sunlight fell upon her, and the softest breezes lifted her shining hair.

Happy tears fell fast, as Thistle folded his arms around her, crying, "O Lily-Bell, dear Lily-Bell, awake! I have been true to you, and now my task is done."

Then, with a smile, Lily-Bell awoke, and looked with wondering eyes upon the beauty that had risen round her.

"Dear Thistle, what mean these fair things, and why are we in this lovely place?"

"Listen, Lily-Bell," said the Brownie King, as he appeared beside her. And then he told all that Thistle had done to show his love for her; how he had wandered far and wide to seek the Fairy gifts, and toiled long and hard to win them; how he had been loving, true, and tender, when most lonely and forsaken.

"Bird, bee, and blossom have forgiven him, and none is more loved and trusted now by all, than the once cruel Thistle," said the King, as he bent down to the happy Elf, who bowed low before him.

"You have learned the beauty of a gentle, kindly heart, dear Thistle; and you are now worthy to become the friend of her for whom you have done so much. Place the crown upon her head, for she is Queen of all the Forest Fairies now."

And as the crown shone on the head that Lily-Bell bent down on Thistle's breast, the forest seemed alive with little forms, who sprang from flower and leaf, and gathered round her, bringing gifts for their new Queen.

"If I am Queen, then you are King, dear Thistle," said the Fairy. "Take the crown, and I will have a wreath of flowers. You have toiled and suffered for my sake, and you alone should rule over these little Elves whose love you have won."

"Keep your crown, Lily-Bell, for yonder come the Spirits with their gifts to Thistle," said the Brownie. And, as he pointed with his wand, out from among the mossy roots of an old tree came trooping the Earth Spirits, their flower-bells ringing softly as they came, and their jewelled garments glittering in the sun. On to where Thistledown stood beneath the shadow of the flowers, with Lily-Bell beside him, went the Spirits; and then forth sprang little Sparkle, waving a golden flower, whose silvery music filled the air. "Dear Thistle," said the shining Spirit, "what you toiled so faithfully to win for another, let us offer now as a token of our love for you."

As she ceased, down through the air came floating bands of lovely Air Spirits, bringing a shining robe, and they too told their love for the gentle Fairy who had dwelt with them.

Then softly on the breeze came distant music, growing ever nearer, till over the rippling waves came the singing Water Spirits, in their boats of many-colored shells; and as they placed their glittering crown on Thistle's head, loud rang the flowers, and joyously sang the birds, while all the Forest Fairies cried, with silvery voices, "Lily-Bell and Thistledown! Long live our King and Queen!"

"Have you a tale for us too, dear Violet-Eye?" said the Queen, as Zephyr ceased. The little Elf thus named looked from among the flower-leaves where she sat, and with a smile replied, "As I was weaving garlands in the field, I heard a primrose tell this tale to her friend Golden-Rod."

# Little Bud

IN A GREAT FOREST, high up among the green boughs, lived Bird Brown-Breast, and his bright-eyed little mate. They were now very happy; their home was done, the four blue eggs lay in the soft nest, and the little wife sat still and patient on them, while the husband sang, and told her charming tales, and brought her sweet berries and little worms.

Things went smoothly on, till one day she found in the nest a little white egg, with a golden band about it.

"My friend," cried she, "come and see! Where can this fine egg have come from? My four are here, and this also; what think you of it?"

The husband shook his head gravely, and said, "Be not alarmed, my love; it is doubtless some good Fairy who has given us this, and we shall find some gift within; do not let us touch it, but do you sit carefully upon it, and we shall see in time what has been sent us."

So they said nothing about it, and soon their home had four little chirping children; and then the white egg opened, and, behold, a little maiden lay singing within. Then how amazed were they, and how they welcomed her, as she lay warm beneath the mother's wing, and how the young birds did love her.

Great joy was in the forest, and proud were the parents of their family, and still more of the little one who had come to them; while all the neighbors flocked in, to see Dame Brown-Breast's little child. And the tiny maiden talked to them, and sang so merrily, that they could have listened for ever. Soon she was the joy of the whole forest, dancing from tree to tree, making every nest her home, and none were ever so welcome as little Bud; and so they lived right merrily in the green old forest.

The father now had much to do to supply his family with food, and choice morsels did he bring little Bud. The wild fruits were her food, the fresh dew in the flower-cups her drink, while the green leaves served her for little robes; and thus she found garments in the flowers of the field, and a happy home with Mother Brown-Breast; and all in the wood, from the stately trees to the little mosses in the turf, were friends to the merry child.

And each day she taught the young birds sweet songs, and as their gay music rang through the old forest, the stern, dark pines ceased their solemn waving, that they might hear the soft sounds stealing through the dim

"Little Bud." From *Lulu's Library,*
*Vol. 2: The Frost-King,* 1887.

wood-paths, and mortal children came to listen, saying softly, "Hear the flowers sing, and touch them not, for the Fairies are here."

Then came a band of sad little Elves to Bud, praying that they might hear the sweet music; and when she took them by the hand, and spoke gently to them, they wept and said sadly, when she asked them whence they came,—

"We dwelt once in Fairy-Land, and O how happy were we then! But alas! we were not worthy of so fair a home, and were sent forth into the cold world. Look at our robes, they are like the withered leaves; our wings are dim, our crowns are gone, and we lead sad, lonely lives in this dark forest. Let us stay with you; your gay music sounds like Fairy songs, and you have such a friendly way with you, and speak so gently to us. It is good to be near one so lovely and so kind; and you can tell us how we may again become fair and innocent. Say we may stay with you, kind little maiden."

And Bud said, "Yes," and they stayed; but her kind little heart was grieved that they wept so sadly, and all she could say could not make them happy; till at last she said,—

"Do not weep, and I will go to Queen Dew-Drop, and beseech her to let you come back. I will tell her that you are repentant, and will do anything to gain her love again; that you are sad, and long to be forgiven. This will I say, and more, and trust she will grant my prayer."

"She will not say no to you, dear Bud," said the poor little Fairies; "she will love you as we do, and if we can but come again to our lost home, we cannot give you thanks enough. Go, Bud, and if there be power in Fairy gifts, you shall be as happy as our hearts' best love can make you."

The tidings of Bud's departure flew through the forest, and all her friends came to say farewell, as with the morning sun she would go; and each brought some little gift, for the land of Fairies was far away, and she must journey long.

"Nay, you shall not go on your feet, my child," said Mother Brown-Breast; "your friend Golden-Wing shall carry you. Call him hither, that I may seat you rightly, for if you should fall off my heart would break."

Then up came Golden-Wing, and Bud was safely seated on the cushion of violet-leaves; and it was really charming to see her merry little face, peeping from under the broad brim of her cowslip hat, as her butterfly steed stood waving his bright wings in the sunlight. Then came the bee with his yellow honey-bags, which he begged she would take, and the little brown spider that lived under the great leaves brought a veil for her hat, and besought her to wear it, lest the sun should shine too brightly; while the ant came bringing a tiny strawberry, lest she should miss her favorite fruit. The mother gave her good advice, and the papa stood with his head on one side, and his round eyes twinkling with delight, to think that his little Bud was going to Fairy-Land.

Then they all sang gayly together, till she passed out of sight over the hills, and they saw her no more.

And now Bud left the old forest far behind her. Golden-Wing bore her swiftly along, and she looked down on the green mountains, and the peasant's cottages, that stood among over-shadowing trees; and the earth looked bright with its broad, blue rivers winding through soft meadows, the singing birds, and flowers, who kept their bright eyes ever on the sky.

And she sang gayly as they floated in the clean air, while her friend kept time with his waving wings, and ever as they went along all grew fairer; and thus they came to Fairy-Land.

As Bud passed through the gates, she no longer wondered that the exiled Fairies wept and sorrowed for the lovely home they had lost. Bright clouds floated in the sunny sky, casting a rainbow light on the Fairy palaces below, where the Elves were dancing; while the low, sweet voices of the singing flowers sounded softly through the fragrant air, and mingled with the music of the rippling waves, as they flowed on beneath the blossoming vines that drooped above them.

All was bright and beautiful; but kind little Bud would not linger, for the forms of the weeping Fairies were before her; and though the blossoms nodded gayly on their stems to welcome her, and the soft winds kissed her cheek, she would not stay, but on to the Flower Palace she went, into a pleasant hall whose walls were formed of crimson roses, amid whose leaves sat little Elves, making sweet music on their harps.

When they saw Bud, they gathered around her, and led her through the flower-wreathed arches to a group of the most beautiful Fairies, who were gathered about a stately lily, in whose fragrant cup sat one whose purple robe and glittering crown told she was their Queen.

Bud knelt before her, and, while tears streamed down her little face, she told her errand, and pleaded earnestly that the exiled Fairies might be forgiven, and not be left to pine far from their friends and kindred. And as she prayed, many wept with her; and when she ceased, and waited for her answer, many knelt beside her, praying forgiveness for the unhappy Elves.

With tearful eyes, Queen Dew-Drop replied,—

"Little maiden, your prayer has softened my heart. They shall not be left sorrowing and alone, nor shall you go back without a kindly word to cheer and comfort them. We will pardon their fault, and when they can bring hither a perfect Fairy crown, robe, and wand, they shall be again received as children of their loving Queen. The task is hard, for none but the best and purest can form the Fairy garments; yet with patience they may yet restore their robes to their former brightness. Farewell, good little maiden; come with them, for but for you they would have dwelt for ever without the walls of Fairy-Land."

"Good speed to you, and farewell," cried they all, as, with loving messages to their poor friends, they bore her to the gates.

Day after day toiled little Bud, cheering the Fairies, who, angry and disappointed, would not listen to her gentle words, but turned away and sat alone weeping. They grieved her kind heart with many cruel words; but patiently she bore with them, and when they told her they could never perform so hard a task, and must dwell for ever in the dark forest, she answered gently, that the snow-white lily must be planted, and watered with repentant tears, before the robe of innocence could be won; that the sun of love must shine in their hearts, before the light could return to their dim crowns, and deeds of kindness must be performed, ere the power would come again to their now useless wands.

Then they planted the lilies; but they soon drooped and died, and no light came to their crowns. They did no gentle deeds, but cared only for themselves; and when they found their labor was in vain, they tried no longer, but sat weeping. Bud, with ceaseless toil and patient care, tended the lilies, which bloomed brightly, the crowns grew bright, and in her hands the wands had power over birds and blossoms, for she was striving to give happiness to others, forgetful of herself. And the idle Fairies, with thankful words, took the garments from her, and then with Bud went forth to Fairy-Land, and stood with beating hearts before the gates; where crowds of Fairy friends came forth to welcome them.

But when Queen Dew-Drop touched them with her wand, as they passed in, the light faded from their crowns, their robes became like withered leaves, and their wands were powerless.

Amid the tears of all the Fairies, the Queen led them to the gates, and said,—

"Farewell! It is not in my power to aid you; innocence and love are not within your hearts, and were it not for this untiring little maiden, who has toiled while you have wept, you never would have entered your lost home. Go and strive again, for till all is once more fair and pure, I cannot call you mine."

"Farewell!" sang the weeping Fairies, as the gates closed on their outcast friends; who, humbled and broken-hearted, gathered around Bud; and she, with cheering words, guided them back to the forest.

Time passed on, and the Fairies had done nothing to gain their lovely home again. They wept no longer, but watched little Bud, as she daily tended the flowers, restoring their strength and beauty, or with gentle words flew from nest to nest, teaching the little birds to live happily together; and wherever she went blessings fell, and loving hearts were filled with gratitude.

Then, one by one, the Elves secretly did some little work of kindness, and found a quiet joy come back to repay them. Flowers looked lovingly up as they passed, birds sang to cheer them when sad thoughts made them weep. And soon little Bud found out their gentle deeds, and her friendly words gave them new strength. So day after day they followed her, and like a band of guardian spirits they flew far and wide, carrying with them joy and peace.

And not only birds and flowers blessed them, but human beings also; for with tender hands they guided little children from danger, and kept their young hearts free from evil thoughts; they whispered soothing words to the sick, and brought sweet odors and fair flowers to their lonely rooms. They sent lovely visions to the old and blind, to make their hearts young and bright with happy thoughts.

But most tenderly did they watch over the poor and sorrowing, and many a poor mother blessed the unseen hands that laid food before her hungry little ones, and folded warm garments round their naked limbs. Many a poor man wondered at the fair flowers that sprang up in his little garden-plot, cheering him with their bright forms, and making his dreary home fair with their loveliness, and looked at his once barren field, where now waved the golden corn, turning its broad leaves to the warm sun, and promising a store of golden ears to give him food; while the care-worn face grew bright, and the troubled heart filled with gratitude towards the invisible spirits who had brought him such joy.

Thus time passed on, and though the exiled Fairies longed often for their home, still, knowing they did not deserve it, they toiled on, hoping one day to see the friends they had lost; while the joy of their own hearts made their life full of happiness.

One day came little Bud to them, saying,—

"Listen, dear friends. I have a hard task to offer you. It is a great sacrifice for you light-loving Fairies to dwell through the long winter in the dark, cold earth, watching over the flower-roots, to keep them free from the little grubs and worms that seek to harm them. But in the sunny Spring when they bloom again, their love and gratitude will give you happy homes among their bright leaves.

"It is a wearisome task, and I can give you no reward for all your tender care, but the blessings of the gentle flowers you will have saved from death. Gladly would I aid you; but my winged friends are preparing for their journey to warmer lands, and I must help them teach their little ones to fly, and see them safely on their way. Then, through the winter, must I seek the dwellings of the poor and suffering, comfort the sick and lonely, and give hope and courage to those who in their poverty are led astray. These things must I do; but when the flowers bloom again I will be with you, to welcome back our friends from over the sea."

Then, with tears, the Fairies answered, "Ah, good little Bud, you have taken the hardest task yourself, and who will repay you for all your deeds of tenderness and mercy in the great world? Should evil befall you, our hearts would break. We will labor trustingly in the earth, and thoughts of you shall cheer us on; for without you we had been worthless beings, and never known the joy that kindly actions bring. Yes, dear Bud, we will gladly toil among the roots, that the fair flowers may wear their gayest robes to welcome you.

Then deep in the earth the Fairies dwelt, and no frost or snow could harm the blossoms they tended. Every little seed was laid in the soft earth, watered, and watched. Tender roots were folded in withered leaves, that no chilling drops might reach them; and safely dreamed the flowers, till summer winds should call them forth; while lighter grew each Fairy heart, as every gentle deed was tenderly performed.

At length the snow was gone, and they heard little voices calling them to come up; but patiently they worked, till seed and root were green and strong. Then, with eager feet, they hastened to the earth above, where, over hill and valley, bright flowers and budding trees smiled in the warm sunlight, blossoms bent lovingly before them, and rang their colored bells, till the fragrant air was full of music; while the stately trees waved their great arms above them, and scattered soft leaves at their feet.

Then came the merry birds, making the wood alive with their gay voices, calling to one another, as they flew among the vines, building their little homes. Long waited the Elves, and at last she came with Father Brown-Breast.

Happy days passed; and summer flowers were in their fullest beauty, when Bud bade the Fairies come with her.

Mounted on bright-winged butterflies, they flew over forest and meadow, till with joyful eyes they saw the flower-crowned walls of Fairy-Land.

Before the gates they stood, and soon troops of loving Elves came forth to meet them. And on through the sunny gardens they went, into the Lily Hall, where, among the golden stamens of a graceful flower, sat the Queen; while on the broad, green leaves around it stood the bright-eyed little maids of honor.

Then, amid the deep silence, little Bud, leading the Fairies to the throne, said,—

"Dear Queen, I here bring back your subjects, wiser for their sorrow, better for their hard trial; and now might any Queen be proud of them, and bow to learn from them that giving joy and peace to others brings it four-fold to us, bearing a double happiness in the blessings to those we help. Through the dreary months, when they might have dwelt among fair Southern flowers, beneath a smiling sky, they toiled in the dark and silent earth, filling the hearts of the gentle Flower Spirits with grateful love, seeking no reward but the knowledge of their own good deeds, and the joy they always bring. This they have done unmurmuringly and alone; and now, far and wide, flower blessings fall upon them, and the summer winds bear the glad tidings unto those who droop in sorrow, and new joy and strength it brings, as they look longingly for the friends whose gentle care hath brought such happiness to their fair kindred.

"Are they not worthy of your love, dear Queen? Have they not won their lovely home? Say they are pardoned, and you have gained the love of hearts pure as the snow-white robes now folded over them."

As Bud ceased, she touched the wondering Fairies with her wand, and the dark faded garments fell away; and beneath, the robes of lily-leaves glittered pure and spotless in the sunlight. Then, while happy tears fell, Queen Dew-Drop placed the bright crowns on the bowed heads of the kneeling Fairies, and laid before them the wands their own good deeds had rendered powerful.

They turned to thank little Bud for all her patient love, but she was gone; and high above, in the clear air, they saw the little form journeying back to the quiet forest.

She needed no reward but the joy she had given. The Fairy hearts were pure again, and her work was done; yet all Fairy-Land had learned a lesson from gentle little Bud.

# Little Annie's Dream;
## OR, The Fairy Flower

IN A LARGE AND pleasant garden sat little Annie all alone, and she seemed very sad, for drops that were not dew fell fast upon the flowers beside her, who looked wonderingly up, and bent still nearer, as if they longed to cheer and comfort her. The warm wind lifted up her shining hair and softly kissed her cheek, while the sunbeams, looking most kindly in her face, made little rainbows in her tears, and lingered lovingly about her. But Annie paid no heed to sun, or wind, or flower; still the bright tears fell, and she forgot all but her sorrow.

"Little Annie, tell me why you weep," said a low voice in her ear; and, looking up, the child beheld a little figure standing on a vine-leaf at her side; a lovely face smiled on her, from amid bright locks of hair, and shining wings were folded on a white and glittering robe, that fluttered in the wind.

"Who are you, lovely little thing?" cried Annie, smiling through her tears.

"I am a Fairy, little child, and am come to help and comfort you; now tell me why you weep, and let me be your friend," replied the spirit, as she smiled more kindly still on Annie's wondering face.

"And are you really, then, a little Elf, such as I read of in my fairy books? Do you ride on butterflies, sleep in flower-cups, and live among the clouds?"

"Yes, all these things I do, and many stranger still, that all your fairy books can never tell; but now, dear Annie," said the Fairy, bending nearer, "tell my why I found no sunshine on your face; why are these great drops shining on the flowers, and why do you sit alone when *bird* and *bee* are calling you to play?"

"Ah, you will not love me any more if I should tell you all," said Annie, while the tears began to fall again; "I am not happy, for I am not good; how shall I learn to be a patient, gentle child? good little Fairy, will you teach me how?"

"Gladly will I aid you, Annie, and if you truly wish to be a happy child, you first must learn to conquer many passions that you cherish now, and make your heart a home for gentle feelings and happy thoughts; the task is hard, but I will give this fairy flower to help and counsel you. Bend hither, that I may place it in your breast; no hand can take it hence, till I unsay the spell that holds it there."

As thus she spoke, the Elf took from her bosom a graceful flower, whose snow-white leaves shone with a strange, soft light. "This is a fairy flower," said the Elf, "invisible to every eye save yours; now listen while I tell its power, Annie. When your heart is filled with loving thoughts, when some kindly deed has been done, some duty well performed, then from the flower there will arise the sweetest, softest fragrance, to reward and gladden you. But when an unkind word is on your lips, when a selfish, angry feeling rises in your heart, or an unkind, cruel deed is to be done, then will you hear the soft, low chime of the flower-bell; listen to its warning, let the word remain unspoken, the deed undone, and in the quiet joy of your own heart, and the magic perfume of your bosom flower, you will find a sweet reward."

"O kind and generous Fairy, how can I ever thank you for this lovely gift!" cried Annie. "I will be true, and listen to my little bell whenever it may ring. But shall I never see *you* more? Ah! if you would only stay with me, I should indeed be good."

"I cannot stay now, little Annie," said the Elf, "but when another Spring comes round, I shall be here again, to see how well the fairy gift has done its work. And now farewell, dear child; be faithful to yourself, and the magic flower will never fade."

Then the gentle Fairy folded her little arms around Annie's neck, laid a soft kiss on her cheek, and, spreading wide her shining wings, flew singing up among the white clouds floating in the sky.

And little Annie sat among her flowers, and watched with wondering joy the fairy blossom shining on her breast.

The pleasant days of Spring and Summer passed away, and in little Annie's garden Autumn flowers were blooming everywhere, with each day's sun and dew growing still more beautiful and bright; but the fairy flower, that should have been the loveliest of all, hung pale and drooping on little Annie's bosom; its fragrance seemed quite gone, and the clear, low music of its warning chime rang often in her ear.

When first the Fairy placed it there, she had been pleased with her new gift, and for a while obeyed the fairy bell, and often tried to win some fragrance from the flower, by kind and pleasant words and actions; then, as the Fairy said, she found a sweet reward in the strange, soft perfume of the magic blossom, as it shone upon her breast; but selfish thoughts would come to tempt her, she would yield, and unkind words fell from her lips;

and then the flower drooped pale and scentless, the fairy bell rang mournfully, Annie would forget her better resolutions, and be again a selfish, wilful little child.

At last she tried no longer, but grew angry with the faithful flower, and would have torn it from her breast; but the fairy spell still held it fast, and all her angry words but made it ring a louder, sadder peal. Then she paid no heed to the silvery music sounding in her ear, and each day grew still more unhappy, discontented, and unkind; so, when the Autumn days came round, she was no better for the gentle Fairy's gift, and longed for Spring, that it might be returned; for now the constant echo of the mournful music made her very sad.

One sunny morning, when the fresh, cool winds were blowing, and not a cloud was in the sky, little Annie walked among her flowers, looking carefully into each, hoping thus to find the Fairy, who alone could take the magic blossom from her breast. But she lifted up their drooping leaves, peeped into their dewy cups in vain; no little Elf lay hidden there, and she turned sadly from them all, saying, "I will go out into the fields and woods, and seek her there. I will not listen to this tiresome music more, nor wear this withered flower longer." So out into the fields she went, where the long grass rustled as she passed, and timid birds looked at her from their nests; where lovely wild-flowers nodded in the wind, and opened wide their fragrant leaves, to welcome in the murmuring bees, while butterflies, like winged flowers, danced and glittered in the sun.

Little Annie looked, searched, and asked them all if any one could tell her of the Fairy whom she sought; but the birds looked wonderingly at her with their soft, bright eyes, and still sang on; the flowers nodded wisely on their stems, but did not speak, while butterfly and bee buzzed and fluttered away, one far too busy, the other too idle, to stay and tell her what she asked.

Then she went through broad fields of yellow grain, that waved around her like a golden forest; here crickets chirped, grasshoppers leaped, and busy ants worked, but they could not tell her what she longed to know.

"Now will I go among the hills," said Annie, "she may be there." So up and down the green hill-sides went her little feet; long she searched and vainly she called; but still no Fairy came. Then by the river-side she went, and asked the gay dragon-flies, and the cool white lilies, if the Fairy had been there; but the blue waves rippled on the white sand at her feet, and no voice answered her.

Then into the forest little Annie went; and as she passed along the dim, cool paths, the wood-flowers smiled up in her face, gay squirrels peeped at her, as they swung amid the vines, and doves cooed softly as she wandered by; but none could answer her. So, weary with her long and useless search, she sat amid the ferns, and feasted on the rosy strawberries that grew beside her, watching meanwhile the crimson evening clouds that glowed around the setting sun.

The night-wind rustled through the boughs, rocking the flowers to sleep; the wild birds sang their evening hymns, and all within the wood grew calm and still; paler and paler grew the purple light, lower and lower drooped little Annie's head, the tall ferns bent to shield her from the dew, the whispering pines sang a soft lullaby; and when the Autumn moon rose up, her silver light shone on the child, where, pillowed on green moss, she lay asleep amid the wood-flowers in the dim old forest.

And all night long beside her stood the Fairy she had sought, and by elfin spell and charm sent to the sleeping child this dream.

Little Annie dreamed she sat in her own garden, as she had often sat before, with angry feelings in her heart, and unkind words upon her lips. The magic flower was ringing its soft warning, but she paid no heed to anything, save her own troubled thoughts; thus she sat, when suddenly a low voice whispered in her ear,—

"Little Annie, look and see the evil things that you are cherishing; I will clothe in fitting shapes the thoughts and feelings that now dwell within your heart, and you shall see how great their power becomes, unless you banish them for ever."

Then Annie saw, with fear and wonder, that the angry words she uttered changed to dark, unlovely forms, each showing plainly from what fault or passion it had sprung. Some of the shapes had scowling faces and bright, fiery eyes; these were the spirits of Anger. Others, with sullen, anxious looks, seemed gathering up all they could reach, and Annie saw that the more they gained, the less they seemed to have; and these she knew were shapes of Selfishness. Spirits of Pride were there, who folded their shadowy garments round them, and turned scornfully away from all the rest. These and many others little Annie saw, which had come from her own heart, and taken form before her eyes.

When first she saw them, they were small and weak; but as she looked they seemed to grow and gather strength, and each gained a strange power over her. She could not drive them from her sight, and they grew ever stronger, darker, and more unlovely to her eyes. They seemed to cast black shadows over all around, to dim the sunshine, blight the flowers, and drive away all bright and lovely things; while rising slowly round her Annie saw a high, dark wall, that seemed to shut out everything she loved; she dared not move, or speak, but, with a strange fear at her heart, sat watching the dim shapes that hovered round her.

Higher and higher rose the shadowy wall, slowly the flowers near her died, lingeringly the sunlight faded; but at last they both were gone, and left her all alone behind the gloomy wall. Then the spirits gathered round her, whispering strange things in her ear, bidding her obey, for by her own will she had yielded up her heart to be their home, and she was now their slave. Then she could hear no more, but, sinking down among the withered flowers, wept sad and bitter tears, for her lost liberty and joy; then through the gloom there shown a faint, soft light, and on her breast she saw her fairy flower, upon whose snow-white leaves her tears lay shining.

Clearer and brighter grew the radiant light, till the evil spirits turned away to the dark shadow of the wall, and left the child alone.

The light and perfume of the flower seemed to bring new strength to Annie, and she rose up, saying, as she bent to kiss the blossom on her breast, "Dear flower, help and guide me now, and I will listen to your voice, and cheerfully obey my faithful fairy bell."

Then in her dream she felt how hard the spirits tried to tempt and trouble her, and how, but for her flower, they would have led her back, and made all dark and dreary as before. Long and hard she struggled, and tears often fell; but after each new trial, brighter shone her magic flower, and sweeter grew its breath, while the spirits lost still more their power to tempt her. Meanwhile, green, flowering vines crept up the high, dark wall, and hid its roughness from her sight; and over these she watched most tenderly, for soon, wherever green leaves and flowers bloomed, the wall beneath grew weak, and fell apart. Thus little Annie worked and hoped, till one by one the evil spirits fled away, and in their place came shining forms, with gentle eyes and smiling lips, who gathered round her with such loving words, and brought such strength and joy to Annie's heart, that nothing evil dared to enter in; while slowly sank the gloomy wall, and, over wreaths of fragrant flowers, she passed out into the pleasant world again, the fairy gift no longer pale and drooping, but now shining like a star upon her breast.

Then the low voice spoke again in Annie's sleeping ear, saying, "The dark, unlovely passions you have looked upon are in your heart; watch well while they are few and weak, lest they should darken your whole life, and shut out love and happiness for ever. Remember well the lesson of the dream, dear child, and let the shining spirits make your heart their home."

And with that voice sounding in her ear, little Annie woke to find it was a dream; but like other dreams it did not pass away; and as she sat alone, bathed in the rosy morning light, and watched the forest waken into life, she thought of the strange forms she had seen, and, looking down upon the flower on her breast, she silently resolved to strive, as she had striven in her dream, to bring back light and beauty to its faded leaves, by being what the Fairy hoped to render her, a patient, gentle little child. And as the thought came to her mind, the flower raised its drooping head, and, looking up into the earnest little face bent over it, seemed by its fragrant breath to answer Annie's silent thought, and strengthen her for what might come.

Meanwhile the forest was astir, birds sang their gay good-morrows from tree to tree, while leaf and flower turned to greet the sun, who rose up smiling on the world; and so beneath the forest boughs and through the dewy fields went little Annie home, better and wiser for her dream.

Autumn flowers were dead and gone, yellow leaves lay rustling on the ground, bleak winds went whistling through the naked trees, and cold, white Winter snow fell softly down; yet now, when all without looked dark and dreary, on little Annie's breast the fairy flower bloomed more beautiful than ever. The memory of her forest dream had never passed away, and through trial and temptation she had been true, and kept her resolution still unbroken; seldom now did the warning bell sound in her ear, and seldom did the flower's fragrance cease to float about her, or the fairy light to brighten all whereon it fell.

So, through the long, cold Winter, little Annie dwelt like a sunbeam in her home, each day growing richer in the love of others, and happier in herself; often was she tempted, but, remembering her dream, she listened only to the music of the fairy bell, and the unkind thought or feeling fled away, the smiling spirits of gentleness and love nestled in her heart, and all was bright again.

So better and happier grew the child, fairer and sweeter grew the flower, till Spring came smiling over the earth, and woke the flowers, set free the streams, and welcomed back the birds; then daily did the happy child sit among her flowers, longing for the gentle Elf to come again, that she might tell her gratitude for all the magic gift had done.

At length, one day, as she sat singing in the sunny nook where all her fairest flowers bloomed, weary with gazing at the far-off sky for the little form she hoped would come, she bent to look with joyful love upon her bosom flower; and as she looked, its folded leaves spread wide apart, and, rising slowly from the deep white cup, appeared the smiling face of the lovely Elf whose coming she had waited for so long.

"Dear Annie, look for me no longer; I am here on your own breast, for you have learned to love my gift, and it has done its work most faithfully and well," the Fairy said, as she looked into the happy child's bright face, and laid her little arms most tenderly about her neck.

"And now have I brought another gift from Fairy-Land, as a fit reward for you, dear child," she said, when Annie had told all her gratitude and love; then, touching the child with her shining wand, the Fairy bid her look and listen silently.

And suddenly the world seemed changed to Annie; for the air was filled with strange, sweet sounds, and all around her floated lovely forms. In every flower sat little smiling Elves, singing gayly as they rocked amid the leaves. On every breeze, bright, airy spirits came floating by; some fanned her cheek with their cool breath, and waved her long hair to and fro, while others rang the flower-bells, and made a pleasant rustling among the leaves. In the fountain, where the water danced and sparkled in the sun, astride of every drop she saw merry little spirits, who plashed and floated in the clear, cool waves, and sang as gayly as the flowers, on whom they scattered glittering dew. The tall trees, as their branches rustled in the wind, sang a low, dreamy song, while the waving grass was filled with little voices she had never heard before. Butterflies whispered lovely tales in her ear, and birds sang cheerful songs in a sweet language she had never understood before. Earth and air seemed filled with beauty and with music she had never dreamed of until now.

"O tell me what it means, dear Fairy! is it another and a lovelier dream, or is the earth in truth so beautiful as this?" she cried, looking with wondering joy upon the Elf, who lay upon the flower in her breast.

"Yes, it is true, dear child," replied the Fairy, "and few are the mortals to whom we give this lovely gift; what to you is now so full of music and of light, to others is but a pleasant summer world; they never know the language of butterfly or bird or flower, and they are blind to all that I have given you the power to see. These fair things are your friends and playmates now, and they will teach you many pleasant lessons, and give you many happy hours; while the garden where you once sat, weeping sad and bitter tears, is now brightened by your own happiness, filled with loving friends by your own kindly thoughts and feelings; and thus rendered a pleasant summer home for the gentle, happy child, whose bosom flower will never fade. And now, dear Annie, I must go; but every Springtime, with the earliest flowers, will I come again to visit you, and bring some fairy gift. Guard well the magic flower, that I may find all fair and bright when next I come."

Then, with a kind farewell, the gentle Fairy floated upward through the sunny air, smiling down upon the child, until she vanished in the soft, white clouds, and little Annie stood alone in her enchanted garden, where all was brightened with the radiant light, and fragrant with the perfume of her fairy flower.

When Moonlight ceased, Summer-Wind laid down her rose-leaf fan, and, leaning back in her acorn cup, told this tale of

# Ripple, the Water-Spirit

DOWN IN THE DEEP blue sea lived Ripple, a happy little Water-Spirit; all day long she danced beneath the coral arches, made garlands of bright ocean flowers, or floated on the great waves that sparkled in the sunlight; but the pastime that she loved best was lying in the many-colored shells upon the shore, listening to the low, murmuring music the waves had taught them long ago; and here for hours the little Spirit lay watching the sea and sky, while singing gayly to herself.

But when tempests rose, she hastened down below the stormy billows, to where all was calm and still, and her sister Spirits waited till it should be fair again, listening sadly, meanwhile, to the cries of those whom the wild waves wrecked and cast into the angry sea, and who soon came floating down, pale and cold, to the Spirits' pleasant home; then they wept pitying tears above the lifeless forms, and laid them in quiet graves, where flowers bloomed, and jewels sparkled in the sand.

This was Ripple's only grief, and she often thought of those who sorrowed for the friends they loved, who now slept far down in the dim and silent coral caves, and gladly would she have saved the lives of those who lay around her; but the great ocean was far mightier than all the tender-hearted Spirits dwelling in its bosom. Thus she could only weep for them, and lay them down to sleep where no cruel waves could harm them more.

One day, when a fearful storm raged far and wide, and the Spirits saw great billows rolling like heavy clouds above their heads, and heard the wild winds sounding far away, down through the foaming waves a little child came floating to their home; its eyes were closed as if in sleep, the long hair fell like sea-weed round its pale, cold face, and the little hands still clasped the shells they had been gathering on the beach, when the great waves swept it into the troubled sea.

With tender tears the Spirits laid the little form to rest upon its bed of flowers, and, singing mournful songs, as if to make its sleep more calm and deep, watched long and lovingly above it, till the storm had died away, and all was still again.

While Ripple sang above the little child, through the distant roar of winds and waves she heard a wild, sorrowing voice, that seemed to call for help. Long she listened, thinking it was but the echo of their own plaintive song, but high above the music still sounded the sad, wailing cry. Then, stealing silently away, she glided up through foam and spray, till, through the parting clouds, the sunlight shone upon her from the tranquil sky; and, guided by the mournful sound, she floated on, till, close before her on the beach, she saw a woman stretching forth her arms, and with a sad, imploring voice praying the restless sea to give her back the little child it had so cruelly borne away. But the waves dashed foaming up among the bare rocks at her feet, mingling their cold spray with her tears, and gave no answer to her prayer.

When Ripple saw the mother's grief, she longed to comfort her; so, bending tenderly beside her, where she knelt upon the shore, the little Spirit told her how her child lay softly sleeping, far down in a lovely place, where sorrowing tears were shed, and gentle hands laid garlands over him. But all in vain she whispered kindly words; the weeping mother only cried,—

"Dear Spirit, can you use no charm or spell to make the waves bring back my child, as full of life and strength as when they swept him from my side? O give me back my little child, or let me lie beside him in the bosom of the cruel sea."

"Most gladly will I help you if I can, though I have little power to use; then grieve no more, for I will search both earth and sea, to find some friend who can bring back all you have lost. Watch daily on the shore, and if I do not come again, then you will know my search has been in vain. Farewell, poor mother, you shall see your little child again, if Fairy power can win him back." And with these cheering words Ripple sprang into the sea; while, smiling through her tears, the woman watched the gentle Spirit, till her bright crown vanished in the waves.

When Ripple reached her home, she hastened to the palace of the Queen, and told her of the little child, the sorrowing mother, and the promise she had made.

"Good little Ripple," said the Queen, when she had told her all, "your promise never can be kept; there is no power below the sea to work this charm, and you can never reach the Fire-Spirits' home, to win from them a flame to warm the little body into life. I pity the poor mother, and would most gladly help her; but alas! I am a Spirit like yourself, and cannot serve you as I long to do."

"Ah, dear Queen! if you had seen her sorrow, you too would seek to keep the promise I have made. I cannot let her watch for *me* in vain, till I have done my best: then tell me where the Fire-Spirits dwell, and I will ask of them the flame that shall give life to the little child and such great happiness to the sad, lonely mother: tell me the path, and let me go."

"It is far, far away, high up above the sun, where no Spirit ever dared to venture yet," replied the Queen. "I cannot show the path, for it is through the air. Dear Ripple, do not go, for you can never reach that distant place: some harm most surely will befall; and then how shall we live, without our dearest, gentlest Spirit? Stay here with us in your own pleasant home, and think no more of this, for I can never let you go."

But Ripple would not break the promise she had made, and besought so earnestly, and with such pleading words, that the Queen at last with sorrow gave consent, and Ripple joyfully prepared to go. She, with her sister Spirits, built up a tomb of delicate, bright-colored shells, wherein the child might lie, till she should come to wake him into life; then, praying them to watch most faithfully above it, she said farewell, and floated bravely forth, on her long, unknown journey, far away.

"I will search the broad earth till I find a path up to the sun, or some kind friend who will carry me; for, alas! I have no wings, and cannot glide through the blue air as through the sea," said Ripple to herself, as she went dancing over the waves, which bore her swiftly onward towards a distant shore.

Long she journeyed through the pathless ocean, with no friends to cheer her, save the white sea-birds who went sweeping by, and only stayed to dip their wide wings at her side, and then flew silently away. Sometimes great ships sailed by, and then with longing eyes did the little Spirit gaze up at the faces that looked down upon the sea; for often they were kind and pleasant ones, and she gladly would have called to them and asked them to be friends. But they would never understand the strange, sweet language that she spoke, or even see the lovely face that smiled at them above the waves; her blue, transparent garments were but water to their eyes, and the pearl chains in her hair but foam and sparkling spray; so, hoping that the sea would be most gentle with them, silently she floated on her way, and left them far behind.

At length green hills were seen, and the waves gladly bore the little Spirit on, till, rippling gently over soft white sand, they left her on the pleasant shore.

"Ah, what a lovely place it is!" said Ripple, as she passed through sunny valleys, where flowers began to bloom, and young leaves rustled on the trees.

"Why are you all so gay, dear birds?" she asked, as their cheerful voices sounded far and near; "is there a festival over the earth, that all is so beautiful and bright?"

"Do you not know that Spring is coming? The warm winds whispered it days ago, and we are learning the sweetest songs, to welcome her when she shall come," sang the lark, soaring away as the music gushed from his little throat.

"And shall I see her, Violet, as she journeys over the earth?" asked Ripple again.

"Yes, you will meet her soon, for the sunlight told me she was near; tell her we long to see her again, and are waiting to welcome her back," said the blue flower, dancing for joy on her stem, as she nodded and smiled on the Spirit.

"I will ask Spring where the Fire-Spirits dwell; she travels over the earth each year, and surely can show me the way," thought Ripple, as she went journeying on.

Soon she saw Spring come smiling over the earth; sunbeams and breezes floated before, and then, with her white garments covered with flowers, with wreaths in her hair, and dew-drops and seeds falling fast from her hands, the beautiful season came singing by.

"Dear Spring, will you listen, and help a poor little Spirit, who seeks far and wide for the Fire-Spirits' home?" cried Ripple; and then told why she was there, and begged her to tell what she sought.

"The Fire-Spirits' home is far, far away, and I cannot guide you there; but Summer is coming behind me," said Spring, "and she may know better than I. But I will give you a breeze to help you on your way; it will never tire nor fail, but bear you easily over land and sea. Farewell, little Spirit! I would gladly do more, but voices are calling me far and wide, and I cannot stay."

"Many thanks, kind Spring!" cried Ripple, as she floated away on the breeze; "give a kindly word to the mother who waits on the shore, and tell her I have not forgotten my vow, but hope soon to see her again."

Then Spring flew on with her sunshine and flowers, and Ripple went swiftly over hill and vale, till she came to the land where Summer was dwelling. Here the sun shone warmly down on the early fruit, the winds blew freshly over fields of fragrant hay, and rustled with a pleasant sound among the green leaves in the forests; heavy dews fell softly down at night,and long, bright days brought strength and beauty to the blossoming earth.

"Now I must seek for Summer," said Ripple, as she sailed slowly through the sunny sky.

"I am here, what would you with me, little Spirit?" said a musical voice in her ear; and, floating by her side, she saw a graceful form, with green robes fluttering in the air, whose pleasant face looked kindly on her, from beneath a crown of golden sunbeams that cast a warm, bright glow on all beneath.

Then Ripple told her tale, and asked where she should go; but Summer answered,—

"I can tell no more than my young sister Spring where you may find the Spirits that you seek; but I too, like her, will give a gift to aid you. Take this sunbeam from my crown; it will cheer and brighten the most gloomy path through which you pass. Farewell! I shall carry tidings of you to the watcher by the sea, if in my journey round the world I find her there."

And Summer, giving her the sunbeam, passed away over the distant hills, leaving all green and bright behind her.

So Ripple journeyed on again, till the earth below her shone with yellow harvests waving in the sun, and the air was filled with cheerful voices, as the reapers sang among the fields or in the pleasant vineyards, where purple fruit hung gleaming through the leaves; while the sky above was cloudless, and the changing forest-trees shone like a many-colored garland, over hill and plain; and here, along the ripening corn-fields, with bright wreaths of crimson leaves and golden wheat-ears in her hair and on her purple mantle, stately Autumn passed, with a happy smile on her calm face, as she went scattering generous gifts from her full arms.

But when the wandering Spirit came to her, and asked for what she sought, this season, like the others, could not tell her where to go; so, giving her a yellow leaf, Autumn said, as she passed on,—

"Ask Winter, little Ripple, when you come to his cold home; he knows the Fire-Spirits well, for when he comes they fly to the earth, to warm and comfort those dwelling there; and perhaps he can tell you where they are. So take this gift of mine, and when you meet his chilly winds, fold it about you, and sit warm beneath its shelter, till you come to sunlight again. I will carry comfort to the patient woman, as my sisters have already done, and tell her you are faithful still."

Then on went the never-tiring Breeze, over forest, hill, and field, till the sky grew dark, and bleak winds whistled by. Then Ripple, folded in the soft, warm leaf, looked sadly down on the earth, that seemed to lie so desolate and still beneath its shroud of snow, and thought how bitter cold the leaves and flowers must be; for the little Water-Spirit did not know that Winter spread a soft white covering above their beds, that they might safely sleep below till Spring should waken them again. So she went sorrowfully on, till Winter, riding on the strong North-Wind, came rushing by, with a sparkling ice-crown in his streaming hair, while from beneath his crimson cloak, where glittering frost-work shone like silver threads, he scattered snow-flakes far and wide.

"What do you seek with me, fair little Spirit, that you come so bravely here amid my ice and snow? Do not fear me; I am warm at heart, though rude and cold without," said Winter, looking kindly on her, while a bright smile shone like sunlight on his pleasant face, as it glowed and glistened in the frosty air.

When Ripple told him why she had come, he pointed upward, where the sunlight dimly shone through the heavy clouds, saying,—

"Far off there, beside the sun, is the Fire-Spirits' home; and the only path is up, through cloud and mist. It is a long, strange path, for a lonely little Spirit to be going; the Fairies are wild, wilful things, and in their play may harm and trouble you. Come back with me, and do not go this dangerous journey to the sky. I'll gladly bear you home again, if you will come."

But Ripple said, "I cannot turn back now, when I am nearly there. The Spirits surely will not harm me, when I tell them why I am come; and if I win the flame, I shall be the happiest Spirit in the sea, for my promise will be kept, and the poor mother happy once again. So farewell, Winter! Speak to her gently, and tell her to hope still, for I shall surely come."

"Adieu, little Ripple! May good angels watch above you! Journey bravely on, and take this snow-flake that will never melt, as *my* gift," Winter cried, as the North-Wind bore him on, leaving a cloud of falling snow behind.

"Now, dear Breeze," said Ripple, "fly straight upward through the air, until we reach the place we have so long been seeking; Sunbeam shall go before to light the way, Yellow-leaf shall shelter me from heat and rain, while Snow-flake shall lie here beside me till it comes of use. So farewell to the pleasant earth, until we come again. And now away, up to the sun!"

When Ripple first began her airy journey, all was dark and dreary; heavy clouds lay piled like hills around her, and a cold mist filled the air; but the Sunbeam, like a star, lit up the way, the leaf lay warmly round her, and the tireless wind went swiftly on. Higher and higher they floated up, still darker and darker grew the air, closer the damp mist gathered, while the black clouds rolled and tossed, like great waves, to and fro.

"Ah!" sighed the weary little Spirit, "shall I never see the light again, or feel the warm winds on my cheek? It is a dreary way indeed, and but for the Seasons' gifts I should have perished long ago; but the heavy clouds *must* pass away at last, and all be fair again. So hasten on, good Breeze, and bring me quickly to my journey's end."

Soon the cold vapors vanished from her path, and sunshine shone upon her pleasantly; so she went gayly on, till she came up among the stars, where many new, strange sights were to be seen. With wondering eyes she looked upon the bright worlds that once seemed dim and distant, when she gazed upon them from the sea; but now they moved around her, some shining with a softly radiant light, some circled with bright, many-colored rings, while others burned with a red, angry glare. Ripple would have gladly stayed to watch them longer, for she fancied low, sweet voices called her, and lovely faces seemed to look upon her as she passed; but higher up still, nearer to the sun, she saw a far-off light, that glittered like a brilliant crimson star, and seemed to cast a rosy glow along the sky.

"The Fire-Spirits surely must be there, and I must stay no longer here," said Ripple. So steadily she floated on, till straight before her lay a broad, bright path, that led up to a golden arch, beyond which she could see shapes flitting to and fro. As she drew near, brighter glowed the sky, hotter and hotter grew the air, till Ripple's leaf-cloak shrivelled up, and could no longer shield her from the heat; then she unfolded the white snow-flake, and, gladly wrapping the soft, cool mantle round her, entered through the shining arch.

Through the red mist that floated all around her, she could see high walls of changing light, where orange, blue, and violet flames went flickering to and fro, making graceful figures as they danced and glowed; and underneath these rainbow arches, little Spirits glided, far and near, wearing crowns of fire, beneath which flashed their wild, bright eyes; and as they spoke, sparks dropped quickly from their lips, and Ripple saw with wonder, through their garments of transparent light, that in each Fairy's breast there burned a steady flame, that never wavered or went out.

As thus she stood, the Spirits gathered round her, and their hot breath would have scorched her, but she drew the snow-cloak closer round her, saying,—

"Take me to your Queen, that I may tell her why I am here, and ask for what I seek."

So, through long halls of many-colored fire, they led her to a Spirit fairer than the rest, whose crown of flames waved to and fro like golden plumes, while, underneath her violet robe, the light within her breast glowed bright and strong.

"This is our Queen," the Spirits said, bending low before her, as she turned her gleaming eyes upon the stranger they had brought.

Then Ripple told how she had wandered round the world in search of them, how the Seasons had most kindly helped her on, by giving Sunbeam, Breeze, Leaf, and Flake; and how, through many dangers, she had come at last to ask of them the magic flame that could give life to the little child again.

When she had told her tale, the spirits whispered earnestly among themselves, while sparks fell thick and fast with every word; at length the Fire-Queen said aloud,—

"We cannot give the flame you ask, for each of us must take a part of it from our own breasts; and this we will not do, for the brighter our bosom-fire burns, the lovelier we are. So do not ask us for this thing; but any other gift we will most gladly give, for we feel kindly towards you, and will serve you if we may."

But Ripple asked no other boon, and, weeping sadly, begged them not to send her back without the gift she had come so far to gain.

"O dear, warm-hearted Spirits! give me each a little light from your own breasts, and surely they will glow the brighter for this kindly deed; and I will thankfully repay it if I can." As thus she spoke, the Queen, who had spied out a chain of jewels Ripple wore upon her neck, replied,—

"If you will give me those bright, sparkling stones, I will bestow on you a part of my own flame; for we have no such lovely things to wear about our necks, and I desire much to have them. Will you give it me for what I offer, little Spirit?"

Joyfully Ripple gave her the chain; but, as soon as it touched her hand, the jewels melted like snow, and fell in bright drops to the ground; at this the Queen's eyes flashed, and the Spirits gathered angrily about poor Ripple, who looked sadly at the broken chain, and thought in vain what she could give, to win the thing she longed so earnestly for.

"I have many fairer gems than these, in my home below the sea; and I will bring all I can gather far and wide, if you will grant my prayer, and give me what I seek," she said, turning gently to the fiery Spirits, who were hovering fiercely round her.

"You must bring us each a jewel that will never vanish from our hands as these have done," they said, "and we will each give of our fire; and when the child is brought to life, you must bring hither all the jewels you can gather from the depths of the sea, that we may try them here among the flames; but if they melt away like these, then we shall keep you prisoner, till you give us back the light we lend. If you consent to this, then take our gift, and journey home again; but fail not to return, or we shall seek you out."

And Ripple said she would consent, though she knew not if the jewels could be found; still, thinking of the promise she had made, she forgot all else, and told the Spirits what they asked most surely should be done. So each one gave a little of the fire from their breasts, and placed the flame in a crystal vase, through which it shone and glittered like a star.

Then, bidding her remember all she had promised them, they led her to the golden arch, and said farewell.

So, down along the shining path, through mist and cloud, she travelled back; till, far below, she saw the broad blue sea she left so long ago.

Gladly she plunged into the clear, cool waves, and floated back to her pleasant home; where the Spirits gathered joyfully about her, listening with tears and smiles, as she told all her many wanderings, and showed the crystal vase that she had brought.

"Now come," said they, "and finish the good work you have so bravely carried on." So to the quiet tomb they went, where, like a marble image, cold and still, the little child was lying. Then Ripple placed the flame upon his breast, and watched it gleam and sparkle there, while light came slowly back into the once dim eyes, a rosy glow shone over the pale face, and breath stole through the parted lips; still brighter and warmer burned the magic fire, until the child awoke from his long sleep, and looked in smiling wonder at the faces bending over him.

Then Ripple sang for joy, and, with her sister Spirits, robed the child in graceful garments, woven of bright sea-weed, while in his shining hair they wreathed long garlands of their fairest flowers, and on his little arms hung chains of brilliant shells.

"Now come with us, dear child," said Ripple; "we will bear you safely up into the sunlight and the pleasant air; for this is not your home, and yonder, on the shore, there waits a loving friend for you."

So up they went, through foam and spray, till on the beach, where the fresh winds played among her falling hair, and the waves broke sparkling at her feet, the lonely woman still stood, gazing wistfully across the sea. Suddenly, upon a great blue billow that came rolling in, she saw the Water-Spirits smiling on her; and high aloft, in their white gleaming arms, her child stretched forth his hands to welcome her; while the little voice she so longed to hear again cried gayly,—

"See, dear mother, I am come; and look what lovely things the gentle Spirits gave, that I might seem more beautiful to you."

Then gently the great wave broke, and rolled back to the sea, leaving Ripple on the shore, and the child clasped in his mother's arms.

"O faithful little Spirit! I would gladly give some precious gift to show my gratitude for this kind deed; but I have nothing save this chain of little pearls: they are the tears I shed, and the sea has changed them thus, that I might offer them to you," the happy mother said, when her first joy was passed, and Ripple turned to go.

"Yes, I will gladly wear your gift, and look upon it as my fairest ornament," the Water-Spirit said; and with the pearls upon her breast, she left the shore, where the child was playing gayly to and fro, and the mother's glad smile shone upon her, till she sang beneath the waves.

And now another task was to be done; her promise to the Fire-Spirits must be kept. So far and wide she searched among the caverns of the sea, and gathered all the brightest jewels shining there; and then upon her faithful Breeze once more went journeying through the sky.

The Spirits gladly welcomed her, and led her to the Queen, before whom she poured out the sparkling gems she had gathered with such toil and care; but when the Spirits tried to form them into crowns, they trickled from their hands like colored drops of dew, and Ripple saw with fear and sorrow how they melted one by one away, till none of all the many she had brought remained. Then the Fire-Spirits looked upon her angrily, and when she begged them to be merciful, and let her try once more, saying,—

"Do not keep me prisoner here. I cannot breathe the flames that give you life, and but for this snow-mantle I too should melt away, and vanish like the jewels in your hands. O dear Spirits, give me some other task, but let me go from this warm place, where all is strange and fearful to a Spirit of the sea."

They would not listen; and drew nearer, saying, while bright sparks showered from their lips, "We will not let you go, for you have promised to be ours if the gems you brought proved worthless; so fling away this cold white cloak, and bathe with us in the fire fountains, and help us bring back to our bosom flames the light we gave you for the child."

Then Ripple sank down on the burning floor, and felt that her life was nearly done; for she well knew the hot air of the fire-palace would be death to her. The Spirits gathered round, and began to lift her mantle off; but underneath they saw the pearl chain, shining with a clear, soft light, that only glowed more brightly when they laid their hands upon it.

"O give us this!" cried they; "it is far lovelier than all the rest, and does not melt away like them; and see how brilliantly it glitters in our hands. If we may but have this, all will be well, and you are once more free."

And Ripple, safe again beneath her snowflake, gladly gave the chain to them; and told them how the pearls they now placed proudly on their breasts were formed of tears, which but for them might still be flowing. Then the Spirits smiled most kindly on her, and would have put their arms about her, and have kissed her cheek, but she drew back, telling them that every touch of theirs was like a wound to her.

"Then, if we may not tell our pleasure so, we will show it in a different way, and give you a pleasant journey home. Come out with us," the Spirits said, "and see the bright path we have made for you." So they led her to the lofty gate, and here, from sky to earth, a lovely rainbow arched its radiant colors in the sun.

"This is indeed a pleasant road," said Ripple. "Thank you, friendly Spirits, for your care; and now farewell. I would gladly stay yet longer, but we cannot dwell together, and I am longing sadly for my own cool home. Now Sunbeam, Breeze, Leaf, and Flake, fly back to the Seasons whence you came, and tell them that, thanks to their kind gifts, Ripple's work at last is done."

Then down along the shining pathway spread before her, the happy little Spirit glided to the sea.

"Thanks, dear Summer-Wind," said the Queen; "we will remember the lessons you have each taught us, and when next we meet in Fern Dale, you shall tell us more. And now, dear Trip, call them from the lake, for the moon is sinking fast, and we must hasten home."

The Elves gathered about their Queen, and while the rustling leaves were still, and the flowers' sweet voices mingled with their own, they sang this

FAIRY SONG

The moonlight fades from flower and tree,
    And the stars dim one by one;
The tale is told, the song is sung,
    And the Fairy feast is done.
The night-wind rocks the sleeping flowers,
    And sings to them, soft and low.
The early birds erelong will wake:
    'T is time for the Elves to go.

O'er the sleeping earth we silently pass,
  Unseen by mortal eye,
And send sweet dreams, as we lightly float
  Through the quiet moonlit sky;—
For the stars' soft eyes alone may see,
  And the flowers alone may know,
The feasts we hold, the tales we tell:
  So 't is time for the Elves to go.

From bird, and blossom, and bee,
  We learn the lessons they teach;
And seek, by kindly deeds, to win
  A loving friend in each.
And though unseen on earth we dwell,
  Sweet voices whisper low,
And gentle hearts most joyously greet
  The Elves where'er they go.

When next we meet in the Fairy dell,
  May the silver moon's soft light
Shine then on faces gay as now,
  And Elfin hearts as light.
Now spread each wing, for the eastern sky
  With sunlight soon will glow.
The morning star shall light us home:
  Farewell! for the Elves must go.

As the music ceased, with a soft, rustling sound the Elves spread their shining wings, and flew silently over the sleeping earth; the flowers closed their bright eyes, the little winds were still, for the feast was over, and the Fairy lessons ended.

THE END.

# The Rose Family

## CHAPTER ONE

ONCE UPON A TIME there lived in Fairyland a family who, as is the custom, bore the name of the flower which was their care. There was the papa, the mamma, and four little daughters, Blush, Brier, Moss, and Eglantine,— or Tina, as her playmates called her, for she was a baby-elf still lying in her green cradle, and had not yet learned to use her gauzy little wings as her sisters did. Their home was in a rose-tree, among whose flowers they found all that elves could need. In some they slept with the petals drooping like crimson curtains over them to shield from wind and rain; in others they laid their gossamer garments, making them fresh and fragrant with the perfume of the leaves between which they were folded. On the slender branches hung their harps,—*we* call them cobwebs, and hear no sound, but to the delicate senses of the fairy folk there came airy melodies as the wind swept by. A broad-leaved plantain grew at the rose-tree's root, and there they spread their dainty meals;—little loaves of flower-dust and honey, fresh dew in red-brimmed moss-cups, a single berry prettily sliced on a lesser leaf, and eaten in acorn-cups, with cream from the milk-weed, and sugar from the red-clover blossom, whose deep cells the bees can never wholly rifle.

Papa Rose went daily to Court, for he was connected with the royal families of York and Lancaster, and, being a wise and virtuous elf, was the Queen's prime minister. The mamma, whom her neighbors called "bonny little madam," as she came from Scotland, remained at home among the roses, for, like mortal mothers, she had many duties to perform that home might be always beautiful to those she loved. Blush, Brier, and Moss, after a morning romp with Tina, flew away to the fairy school, where they learned all manner of pleasant things which human children never know; such as the history of flowers, the language of insects, the large utterance of trees, and the sweet gossip of the wind. All day each was busied with some useful task; for elves are not foolish little gad-abouts, as we have been taught to think them, but people very like ourselves in the cares and troubles that come to them, only infinitely smaller than we, with microscopic joys and afflictions to match. Thus the Rose family helped rule the kingdom, kept house, studied, and played all day, and at night enjoyed themselves together like mortal families till the evening red faded and the dew began to fall.

So lived the Roses, till the watchful mother saw that a little fault had sprung up, like a harmful weed, in the garden of small virtues which she had planted in the natures of her elder daughters. Moss was gentle and kind, but sadly indolent, and as fond of play as the idlest butterfly that ever flew; Brier, though a merry, generous-hearted elf, was passionate and wilful; while little Blush, the fairest of them all, was vain of the bloom on her delicate cheek, the blue of her smiling eyes, the gold of her shining hair, and the grace of her airy shape. Long did the mother try to cure these troublesome faults, and earnestly did the little ones promise to be good— O, very good!—when she spoke to them. But though they wept and sighed, resolved and promised, they did not heartily *try;* so nothing came of it. At last the papa said to their troubled mamma, as they sat talking in the moonlight of the naughty little daughters sleeping all about them: "My love, there is no way left but to send them to the good fairy, Star, who is gentle and wise, and will make them what we desire."

"Yes, it shall be as you say, dear friend," replied Madam Rose, hiding her face in a cobweb handkerchief, for it was very hard to part with all three. But being a most excellent mamma, and remembering how wisely and well the learned Star had taught many a small sinner, she agreed to the papa's decision without a bit of scolding or fuss, though she wept so bitterly all night that the rose where she slept was wet as with rain.

Next morning, when the young elves woke and learned what was to happen, great was the lamentation, and their papa had to carry them sobbing from their mother's arms into the car, drawn by a span of white butterflies, which waited to take them away. Till they were out of sight they waved their cowslip hats, looking backward through their tears to the pleasant home they left behind; for on the topmost twig still stood the dear mamma, lifting Tina in her arms that she might kiss her little hand to them, and in her baby voice re-echo their farewells.

The wise Star lived on an enchanted island, weaving wonderful spells, helping the moon rule the sea, the dew to do its silent work, the wind to carry winged seeds to desolate spots, and sending sun or shower to help them thrive. The pupils sent her were taught by love, not fear, and none had proved too wild or wilful for her gentle rule.

"How beautiful!" cried the young Roses, as they alighted near the lake upon whose bosom floated the fairy palace underneath a rainbow arch. The island was encircled with a garland of white lilies, blue water-weeds, and cardinal-flowers that glowed among the reeds like spires of flame. Dragon-flies with gleaming bodies darted to and fro, gold and silver fish glittered underneath the ripples as they kissed the shore, all the air was cool and still, and over palace, lake, and island a sunny silence seemed to brood, as if some spell secured to Star the studious calm she loved.

Ringing a harebell, whose chime echoed far across the lake, Papa Rose seated his little daughters in a great white lily, having embraced them tenderly, and, setting the flower afloat, watched it till it anchored at the palace-steps. He had sent a message by the earliest breeze that blew, for in Fairyland the winds are postmen; so Star knew who was coming, and why they were sent. Twinkling off the drops that filled his eyes as the three little figures vanished, Papa Rose turned toward home, feeling as many human fathers have felt when they have left their children behind them.

The elves found Star waiting for them, and loved her even before she spoke. A most benignant-looking spirit she seemed, clothed in mist, with a clearly shining star upon her forehead and a winning smile upon her lips. With one glance of her magically gifted eye, she saw into the hearts before her, felt how best to teach them, and began her lesson without more delay. Calling them about her, she said, as she caressed them with the friendliest look: "My little elves, I have such faith in the love you bear your mother, that I shall use no other spell, and trust to that alone. You left her weeping at your loss; yet it is in your power to change her tears to smiles, and make home happy, by remembering what I tell you now. Each is to work alone, with no help but the talisman I give, and the desire to become what we would have you. In each of these three drops of water from this magic fountain you will always see your mother's face as in a glass. Let no naughtiness dim their brightness, no selfish thought or unkind feeling bring a shadow to the face you love, but so live that it may always smile; and when this is done, your lesson is learned, your separation ended. Fear nothing, but drink, and whenever you may wake hold fast your talisman and heartily begin your task."

Wondering, yet obedient, the three received the shining drops, drank of the golden water, and sank into a deep and dreamless sleep.


CHAPTER TWO


WHEN MOSS AWOKE, she found herself in a sunshiny meadow, where daisies and buttercups nodded in the grass, blithe winds blew, birds sang, and butterflies, like winged flowers, fluttered everywhere. Here, among the roots of an ancient oak, with a mossy threshold, and vines overhanging her door, lived Madam Mouse, with her three little sons, Squeak, Nibble, and Scamper. She was the kindest and best of Quakerish mice, and hers would have been the happiest home in the field, if the excellent father-mouse had not laid asleep in a neighboring grove, with a drooping fern at his head and a cheerful dandelion at his feet. It was to this household that Moss was welcomed on her awakening. Squeak, Nibble, and Scamper opened their beady eyes wide with delight on seeing the beautiful elf, and their mother gave a feast in honor of the guest; for fairies make famous whatever family they visit.

"Now listen to me, dearest child, while I tell you about our neighbors here," said Madam Mouse, as they sat together under the vine, while the little ones played hide-and-seek in the grass, and the sun set over the hill. "Up above there lives Skip, the squirrel, and a merry fellow he is, though he has neither wife nor family to keep him brisk and jolly. But who knows what may fall out, and who can tell why the acorns that grow on the tree where Miss Nimble Whisk lives are so much sweeter than ours? Yes, yes, I fancy we shall have a wedding this year. Next, under the brakes, lives Spin, the spider, as quiet and busy an insect as ever wove a web. Then among the buttercups there at your side Chirp the cricket, keeps house with his noisy wife and daughters, who sing half the night, when they should be asleep. Down by the rock, where the columbines grow, Lightheart, the lark, has her nest. We are a gay neighborhood, that you may believe; for when our work is done, we dance and sing in the twilight, or ramble over the field in search of adventures."

"And what am I to do here, where all are so busy?" asked lazy Moss, fearing some task was in store for her.

"You must help each one in their work, for you will find no pleasure with us unless you daily do some healthful task to keep you happy and show you the beauty of industry. Fie! do not pout and toss your head in that disrespectful manner, else I shall send you away to stay with neighbor Toad, who has grown so stout through indolence that she can only sit blinking all day in the sun; and that would not be so pleasant, I fancy, for she lives in a hole, and might gobble you up if no worm or fly was at hand. Think well of what I tell you, and please your worthy parents by doing what they desire. Now come away to bed; we must be up with the sun, for on Saturday all good housewives have much to do."

Thinking her hostess a very prosy mouse, and resolving to enjoy herself in her own way, Moss followed Nibble into a tidy little chamber hollowed out among the gnarled roots of the oak, carpeted with moss, hung with deep-red leaves, and furnished with a sumptuous thistle-down bed, in which the elf soon fell asleep to the lullaby a mosquito sang outside the cobweb curtains gathered round her.

She was awakened by the young mice dancing over her bed, tapping her cheek with their little paws, and lifting her hair to peep at her blooming face, for they thought her very lovely.

"Go away and leave me in peace! I am very tired, and shall not rise yet," she cried, as they unfurled her wings and tried to make her follow them.

"Mamma will give you no breakfast if you do not come when we call; she is very punctual, and has waited five minutes already."

"I shall come when I like; so drop the curtain and let me alone," was all Moss answered, settling her tiny nightcap and drawing the mullein-leaf blanket more cosily over her shoulders.

"Oh! oh! what a lazy thing! Come and tell mamma that she says she won't," cried the mice, frisking away through the winding galleries, squeaking shrilly as they ran.

"Bless me, what a stir they make," thought Moss, and, instead of getting up, lay dreaming about it till the sun was high. Then she went to seek her breakfast, but not a morsel remained, and she would have fared ill had she not found a cluster of strawberries, on which she made a dainty meal. As she ate she looked about her, thinking what a busy place she was in, for Skip was at work in the oak, Spin wove away at his leafy loom, Lightheart was singing her morning song in the clouds, Chirp was hopping over the field to his work, and, close by, Scamper and Squeak were pulling an oak-leaf laden with seeds, their little tails twined about the stem, and were trotting stoutly along, while Nibble ran behind to steady the load. All were up and at work, the air was filled with a busy hum, and the meadow seemed like a great hive full of industrious bees. Moss alone was idle, and, though ashamed of her indolence, it was too pleasant, swaying to and fro on a tall fern, basking in the sun, and listening to the song of the grass as it waved in the wind, to rise and labor with the rest; so till noon she lay dreaming the dreams that fairies love.

When the sun grew hot, she gladly hastened to the cool oak chambers, eager to eat and drink of the good things she had seen stored there; for Madam Mouse was a thrifty housewife. But, as before, the table was cleared; Nibble was eating the last berry, Scamper and Squeak were washing their faces, as their tidy mother had taught them to do, and she was giving a thirsty bee the only drop of honey that remained.

"Am I to have no dinner?" asked Moss, knowing that she deserved none, yet hoping to get a great deal, as lazy people are apt to do.

With a pert whisk of the tail Squeak cried out: "Ah, ha! did n't we tell you mamma would not feed a lazy elf? When you are good, she will give whatever you ask, and you will be plump and happy like us."

"Hush!" said his mother, "or I must put your little tail in the crack, that a pinch or two may teach you to govern your tongue, my son. No, Moss, you will find no food here unless you obey me, for I cannot take care of an indolent elf, who has no desire to do her duty and earn her bread, like the rest of us."

"I shall not work," said Moss, sullenly.

"Then go and live in your own idle fashion till you tire of it; then come back, and I'll show you a surer way to be happy and good."

"I shall find my own too pleasant for that, I fancy," answered Moss, getting naughtier and naughtier the more she gave way to her dislike for industry.

The little mice were so astonished at her daring to speak in that way to their mamma, that they tumbled down in a heap, and, passing by them with a saucy nod, Moss flew away to the river-side, where a hospitable lizard gave her some dinner, and entertained her till one of the baby lizards fell into a ditch and broke his leg. Fearing that she should be asked to stay and watch with him, Moss slipped away, and, sitting in a river-lily, laughed and sung with the water-beetles and the merry west-wind till the motion of the waves lulled her to sleep.

A dew-drop falling on her face roused her, and, looking up, she found the moon in the sky, and herself on the bank, where the breeze had laid her when the lilies wished to draw their curtains. The night was mild, the stars friendly eyes watched over her, and she felt no fear; so, pillowing her head on a daisy, and pulling a thick leaf over her, she thought to herself, "This is as fine a bed as one need desire, and I shall not soon go back to tiresome Madam Mouse while I get on so well alone."

As she spoke, a sudden gust blew away her coverlet, a bat caught her up as he swept by, and, before she could recover from her fright, bore her away to his nest, in an ivy-covered wall.

"I am cousin to the Mouse family, therefore it is quite proper that you pay me a visit; but as I am a bachelor, and my house is not such as best pleases young ladies, I shall take you to Neighbor Moth's ball, close by. Give me your hand, and remember that, though I present my friends Monsieur Firefly and Professor Beetle, you must dance with me first."

So said the bat, in his disagreeable voice, as he clung to the wall with his leathery wings. Moss was mortally afraid of him, had no desire to go to a ball, and was ready to cry with dismay at the troubles she had brought on herself; but Flit would take no denial, and skimmed away with her so fast that her poor little wings ached with the flight.

In a dell not far away Moss saw lights glancing, heard music sounding, and presently found herself in the midst of a party of night-loving insects and reptiles. Not a respectable ball in the least, for the wildest merriment prevailed. Mosquitoes, dorbugs, and frogs piped, drummed, and trumpeted like mad; katydids in green gauze, and grasshoppers from the opera, flew about in a most indecorous manner; fireflies whisked sober millers here and there, till their gowns were burnt and torn; glowworms and long-legged spiders flirted sadly under the mushrooms; and Lady Moth was as giddy as the rest, for a dissipated butterfly in scarlet and gold was there, and such an honor had not been done her balls for an age.

Pretty Moss made a great stir when Flit presented her; Major Butterfly left Lady Moth to fold his bright wings at her side; Monsieur Firefly was charmed with her grace; and Professor Beetle, forgetting his mourning suit, droned compliments into her ear, and danced till his horny eyes swam dizzily in his head. Moss was dragged to and fro till she was ready to faint with weariness and fear; but the nimble-footed spiders bid her dance on, the music played faster and faster, the friendly moon went down, and often did poor Moss long to be safe in her cosey bed in the oaken chamber, with kind Madam Mouse to watch over her sleep.

Suddenly, just when the revel was gayest, an owl darted into their midst, and bore Flit struggling away. In an instant the music stopped, the dancers vanished, and the dell was deserted by all but Moss, who, trembling with affright, crept into an empty snail-shell, and lay shivering there till dawn.

When daylight came, she timidly stole out, and flew away to rest in the sunshine among the purple morning-glories that half covered a cottage-wall. Believing that her troubles were over, she slept sweetly till she woke to find herself a prisoner in the flower, which, closing with the heat, now held her fast. Vainly she called for help, and beat upon the walls, which narrowed rapidly, while the sun shone hotter and hotter, and the air grew more close each moment. "Now I must die," she thought, "and never see my home again. O dear mamma! forgive me, and good by!" Clasping her hands together on her little bosom in despair, she felt the long-neglected talisman, and eagerly drew it out for a last look at the face she never thought to see again. Very sadly it looked back at her, and the reproachful tenderness that filled the loving eyes so wrung her heart with sorrow and remorse, that, with a bitter cry, she sank down, and lay there like one dead.

A breath of fresh air, sweeping through her prison, recalled her to life; and the first sound she heard was a cheerful voice that said: "It is no bee caught in the morning-glory cup, but the loveliest fairy ever seen. She is not dead, grandmother, for she moves her tiny wings. What can I do for you, dear little creature? I am so large, I fear to hurt you with the gentlest touch. Lie here, and get your breath again, but do not be afraid of me, because I love your race, and often hear wonder-stories of you from the humming-birds that live among my flowers."

Lifting her dim eyes, Moss saw a child's pitying face above her; but she could only smile her thanks and kiss the small hand where she lay. Placing the elf on a vine-leaf that fluttered in the wind, the child went back to her wheel, for no bee was busier than she; and as she spun, she sang like any bird, because the blind old grandmother, knitting in the sun, loved to hear her cheery voice above the music of the wheel.

> "O flower at my window,
>     Why blossom you so fair,
> With your green and purple cup
>     Upturned to sun and air?
> 'I bloom, blithesome Bessie,
>     To cheer your childish heart;
> The world is full of labor,
>     And this shall be my part.'
>         Whirl, busy wheel, faster,
>             Spin, little thread, spin;
>         The sun shines fair without,
>             And we are gay within.
>
> "O robin in the tree-top,
>     With sunshine on your breast,
> Why brood you so patiently
>     Above your hidden nest?
> 'I brood, blithesome Bessie,
>     And sing my humble song,
> That the world may have more music
>     From my little ones erelong.'
>         Whirl, busy wheel, faster
>             Spin, little thread, spin,
>         The sun shines fair without,
>             And we are gay within.
>
> "O balmy wind of summer,
>     O silver-singing brook,
> Why rustle through the branches?
>     Why shimmer in your nook?

'I flutter, blithesome Bessie,
    Like a blessing far and wide;
I scatter bloom and verdure
    Where'er my footsteps glide,'
        Whirl, busy wheel, faster,
            Spin, little thread, spin,
        The sun shines fair without,
            And we are gay within.

"O brook and breeze and blossom,
    And robin on the tree,
You make a joy of duty,
    A pride of industry;
Teach me to work as blithely,
    With a willing hand and heart:
The world is full of labor,
    And I must do my part.
        Whirl, busy wheel, faster,
            Spin, little thread, spin,
        The sun shines fair without,
            And we are gay within."

"Yes," sighed the elf, as she listened, "it is as Madam Mouse said,—there is no real pleasure in idleness. I will no longer think of selfish ease alone, but try to gather resolution from all I have suffered, and begin my task for love of dear mamma."

So anxious was she to be gone, that, scarcely staying to thank the friendly child, Moss hurried away, fearing some fresh misfortune would befall her unless she fell to work at once. With many tears she owned her fault, asking to be made a diligent and happy elf. Madam Mouse received her kindly, and did not lecture her, for all she said was, "Now you are my good child again, and I am pleased with you."

"What shall I do first?" asked Moss, springing out of bed when the little mice called her next morning at dawn.

"Come and welcome the sun with me, for I bear him good-morrows from all in the field," said the lark, as she rose from her nest.

"Are you never tired of this long flight?" asked the elf, as they floated up through rosy clouds to the blue above.

"No, for I can never fly high enough, nor pour forth my happiness loud enough, I am so weak and small. But though I never reach the sun, I carry back with me blithe memories of things above here to gladden my whole day." And with a gush of unspeakable joy falling from her little throat,

Lightheart soared far out of sight, then dropped into her nest, leaving musical echoes behind.

"Ah! that was fine! and I'll go again to-morrow," cried Moss. "What next, Mother Mouse?"

"Come to the river and bring up water for the day," said Nibble, always interested in the eating and drinking part of the housekeeping.

Away they all raced, eager to see which would fill their green pitcher first, for they used the leaves of a plant called Forefathers' Cup, and Mrs. Mouse had rows of them in her cool cellar, as we keep wine-casks in our own.

The more Moss did, the more she liked it, and all day long she worked like a busy ant, helping Skip store acorns, shaking down ripe grains from the wheat-ears for madam's small harvesting, tripping over the field with Chirp to see the sick and poor; for he was a minister, as all might see by his black coat and the charitable zeal with which he hurried to and fro, preaching a cheerful sermon as he worked. At night she went with Spin to spread his webs on the grass, that the dew might fall and the moon shine on them till they were bleached to a silvery whiteness, and thus made fit for fairy cloth.

Thus working with each of her friends, little Moss soon learned many a useful thing, and for every trial and temptation found a solace in her fairy talisman. All in the field loved her and tried to make her happy; for they saw how patiently she tried to do well, and how eagerly she longed to see her home again.

Mamma Mouse had many a gay feast in her pleasant rooms; for when rain fell without, Flash the firefly and Glimmer the glowworm lent their light; Skip came down to crack nuts and jokes, Spin told stories as endless as his webs, Chirp sang psalms as heartily as Martin Luther, whom he very much resembled, being lively, stout, and zealous, while Moss and the young mice played games and romped till their heads spun around.

So the summer days passed in the

"Books and work and healthful play"

manner which is best for all of us; and when at length the face in the magic-mirror always smiled upon her, Moss knew her task was done, and joyfully waited her summons home.

CHAPTER THREE

WHEN BRIER AWOKE from her long sleep, she looked with wondering eyes about her, for she was no longer in the fairy palace, but alone in a deep forest. Squirrels skipped from tree to tree, birds came fearlessly to bathe in the clear pool at her feet, wood-flowers nodded on their stems, and all the air was filled with the pleasant murmur of the pines. At first Brier only wondered how she came there, then she called her sisters loud and long; and when nothing but a naughty echo mimicked her, she grew very angry and threw herself down weeping and fretting because she was sent away to live alone in the great wood.

As she lay sobbing, with her cheek against the grass, a soft voice said beside her: "Little Brier, do not weep so passionately; you are not to stay alone, for the forest is full of friends who will gladly try to make it pleasant for you. Come with me; I have a softer bed and little feast prepared for you above there."

Brier looked up to find a mild-eyed dove waving its white wings beside her, as it cooed these gentle words; and, before the fairy could answer, came other little voices from the tree above her head, calling: "Come up! come up, mamma! and bring the wonderful elf. We cannot fly and we cannot wait; come soon, else we shall fall out with trying to see."

With that Brier heard a flapping of wings, a rustling of leaves, and saw two small heads peering over the edge of a nest, with eyes full of eager delight. Up flew the mother dove and up flew Brier to where little Flutter and Coo lay in their downy cradle, and the gentle papa sat by with a ripe berry in his bill to offer the guest.

"Here she is," said the dove. "You must try to make your home very happy to dear Brier, for she has left a far lovelier one to stay with us a little. Be very tender with her, that she may not grieve for her sisters, and may look back with pleasure on her visit here."

"O, that we will, mamma, if she will only be our little friend, and love us as we love her," cried the young doves, putting up their bills to kiss her; and hopping joyfully on their unsteady pink legs.

"Now, my darlings," said the mother, after they had supped and talked quite gayly for a while, "papa and I must go and see neighbor Linnet, for she is very ill, and we are afraid little Twitter may suffer for food. Therefore we will leave you to play together, and soon be back again."

The doves flew away, and presently their comfortable cooing sounded through the wood. Brier was her gentlest self now; so she told Flutter and Coo her merriest tales, taught them elfin games, and danced on a leaf before them till they quite stared with wonder. As the sun set they said, "Good night"; for these birds never fretted when bed-time came, never cried to have the lamp left, nor had any fear of goblins, but tucked their little heads under their wings and fell asleep without troubling mamma by a single pout. Brier often did all these naughty things, but she never told the doves so, only sat in the twilight on a bending bough, and sang them a fairy

LULLABY

"Now the day is done,
    Now the shepherd sun
Drives his white flocks from the sky;
    Now the flowers rest
    On their mother's breast,
Hushed by her low lullaby.

"Now the glowworms glance,
    Now the fireflies dance,
Under fern-boughs green and high;
    And the western breeze
    To the forest trees
Chants a tuneful lullaby.

"Now 'mid shadows deep
    Falls blessed sleep,
Like dew from the summer sky;
    And the whole earth dreams,
    In the moon's soft beams,
While night breathes a lullaby.

"Now, birdlings, rest,
    In your wind-rocked nest,
Unscared by the owl's shrill cry;
    For with folded wings
    Little Brier swings,
And singeth your lullaby."

In this gentle family lived the elf, and for a time all went well, for those about her were so lovely in their manners, so unselfish, kind, and patient, she had no cause for anger, wilfulness, or discontent, but seemed to be a perfect fairy, and was much beloved by all in the wood. By and by she began to get tired of this quiet life, to forget to look often at her bosom monitor, and cross feelings soon brought unkind words. The doves grieved over this and tried to help her, but the little fault was not easy to be cured, and nothing but trying very hard, very patiently on Brier's own part, could ever change it.

One day, when Papa Dove was gone to market in a distant barley-field, and Mamma was rocking Twitter Linnet to sleep, Flutter and Coo sat coseyly in the nest watching the dragon-flies play among the water-weeds below.

"Ah, if we could only fly, what merry games we would have down there! It seems as if I could not stay up here another day, I so long to see a little of the world, which looks so fine from this high place," sighed Flutter.

"Yes," answered Coo; "I, too, long to use my wings, for they seem large and strong enough. But mamma will not teach us yet, so we must wait till she thinks best. I hope it will be soon, for at night I dream of such far flights into the sky that I wake feeling as if I should spring out of the nest for joy."

"We shall not have to wait long, little sister," said Flutter, "for last night, when I woke to stretch my legs a bit, I heard papa say that, as soon as Neighbor Linnet was on the wing again, our flying lessons would begin; and that will be soon, I fancy, for she sat on a sunny twig a whole hour to-day."

"I can teach you to fly without waiting at all," said Brier, looking out from the leaf behind which she had gone to sulk. "Hop forth to the edge of the nest, spread your wings, give a small leap, and all will go well with you."

"Mamma bade us wait for her, and I am afraid some mischief will happen if we disobey," answered Coo, as Brier unfurled her shining wings and smiled again.

"Might we not try?" asked Flutter, eagerly. "I long so to sit on the moss by the pool, and peck a seed or a bug or two for myself. Let us just fly down, and surprise mamma by sitting all in a row on that pretty green mound. I think we might without harm."

"I dare not, because we promised. It is such a long, long way, and we might easily fall on the stones. Do not go, Flutter; do not tempt her, dear Brier. Just think, if she break a leg or a wing, how sad it will be!"

"I'm not afraid!" cried Flutter, hopping out of the nest. "Come hither, Brier, and show me how to use these fine wings of mine as gracefully as you do your own."

"See now, I spread them thus, lift up my feet, and float away like a thistle-down"; and away went Brier, high over the tree-tops, then down in airy circles, till she rippled with her little foot the surface of the pool.

"Yes, yes, that looks very charming, but is not so easy as one might suppose," said Flutter, skipping timidly up and down with much flapping of her half-grown wings. "I cannot lift this heavy body of mine, for I am a sadly fat bird, though I never knew it till now. Can you not help one a bit, dear Brier?"

"I shall not help you at all, if you do not obey me at once," answered the elf, with a frown. "You said you were not afraid, but I do not believe it; else you would soar boldly away, and not stand twittering and trembling here. Come and help me, Coo; if you fly first, she will be ashamed not to follow, and then we will have gay times in the air."

"No, I cannot, and it is not kind of you to take poor Flutter away, for we cannot fly at once, as you fairies do. Come back, sister, and let us play safely here. O, do! it is so wrong to disobey mamma."

But Flutter and Brier would not listen to good little Coo, and still stayed out on the bough. The elf floated and flew, soared up and swooped down, but the timid bird could not gain courage to follow. Then Brier grew angry, and saying, "I shall wait no longer, fly away at once, you foolish thing!" she thrust her off the branch. Poor Flutter spread her feeble wings, but they could not uphold her, and, with a cry of affright, she fell heavily to the ground, and lay quite still, as if she were dead.

Coo, forgetting her fear, flew to the edge of the nest, and called her mother in a louder tone than had ever passed her little bill before, while Brier bent over the motionless dove, and tried to recall it to life. But the soft eyes were closed, the white bosom ruffled and bruised.

"Oh! what shall I do?" cried the terrified elf. "I never meant to hurt her like this, and how shall I make her better before the mamma comes back?"

"Go and hide yourself in the darkest nook of the wood, and never hope to be forgiven for a thing like this. Go away before her mother comes, for this sight will surely break her heart," chirped a wren, hastening down from her nest near by.

"Yes indeed, you had best fly away at once, for now not even a gnat will be friends with you, but all of us will fear you, for you are not what we thought you; so go away, and leave us in peace, naughty Brier!"

A dragon-fly spoke, and all about her, from pool and grass, and trees and air, echoed voices, calling, "Go away, go away, naughty Brier!"

"I will go away to my own lovely home, for I hate this gloomy forest, and I will never come among you again, unkind and uncivil creatures that you are!" cried Brier, forgetting everything in her passion; and, without another look at Flutter, another word to Coo, she darted away with a whirr like that of an angry humming-bird, when he finds no honey in a flower.

A long way flew Brier, till her wings were tired and her breath quite gone, she went so fast; then she paused in a lonely part of the wood, and sat down on a pebble to rest. She would not think yet, for she was still in a naughty mood, and when one begins to remember the unkind things one has done, one begins to get sorry for them, and longs to be forgiven. In order that she might forget the sad accident which she had caused, the elf hummed a song as she sat; but it sounded harsh and out of tune, because she was so herself; so she stopped singing, and amused herself by watching an ant village near by. Very busy were the inhabitants of Emmetville, running up and down the streets; some with loads of food, some with grains of sand from their underground houses, others doing errands which none but ants would have to do. Being a fairy, Brier could understand their language, and heard them singing and talking as they worked, and very funny were some of the songs and sayings. Close by her seat rose a neat little mound, and one most industrious ant was tugging away with load after load of sand from within; up he would come with a big grain, lay it nicely outside, take a breath of fresh air, and hurry back again in such haste that he often tumbled head over heels down his little hole. Brier liked this busy one, for he sang as he worked, and had a very pleasant expression of countenance. As he paused to settle a large grain of yellow sand on the top of the mound, as an ornament to the front door, Brier said: "Mr. Emmet, why are you in such haste? and why do you never stop to rest or talk with your neighbor?"

The ant made her a little bow, and answered, gayly: "I am about to be married, and wish to get my house in fine order as soon as I can; therefore I work with all my might, and sing meanwhile, for I am the happiest fellow in all the town, and shall have a grand wedding to-morrow. Ha! ha! Come and see us then, if you will."

With that he gave a little skip for joy, lost his footing, and rolled down the mound, laughing as he went, till he fell against a big black ant, who was walking by in a very stately manner. When the red ant came tumbling over his back, he grew dreadfully angry, and cried out in a rough voice: "What! what! is this the way you play tricks on respectable persons, you unmannerly mite? Wait a bit, and see what comes of such pranks."

"Indeed, indeed, sir, it was only an accident, and upon my word it shall never happen again," began the red ant, very humbly, as he gathered himself up with a great many bows.

But the black ant was in such a towering rage he would not listen, nor understand, but fell upon poor little Mr. Emmet, and beat and bit and dragged him here and there most unmercifully. Brier besought him to let go, and all the ant people came running to see, but dared not help, because the black ant was far bigger and stronger than they, and belonged to a very fierce tribe, which had destroyed their village more than once. So they ran away again as fast as they came; and when the black fellow had vented his rage, he went on his way, leaving the Emmet quite dead on the ground. Brier was very much grieved and shocked at such a display of temper, and cried over the departed ant very tenderly, as she laid him in the little house he would not want any more. She set up the handsome yellow grain as a monument, and sent a message to the unhappy ant-bride, telling how it happened, for she could not go to see her,—no, that would be altogether too sad.

Then she sorrowfully went on her way, thinking of poor Flutter, wondering if she, too, were dead, and feeling as if she herself were no better than the brutal black ant who had destroyed so much happiness in his blind anger. Full of these dismal feelings, she flew aimlessly here and there till nightfall; then, homesick, cold, and weary, she crept into a pine-tree, longing to be safe again between downy Flutter and Coo, with Mamma Dove's sheltering wings folded over her head. As she sat sighing and shivering in the gloomy tree, there arose a great noise below her, and, peeping down, she saw a badly built nest, full of young crowlets, all fighting for a bit of carrion their father had just given them. Such shrill cawing and pecking and beating of wings Brier had never seen. Each crowlet wanted all, and none would stop to settle the matter amicably, but all fought and screamed till feathers flew, the nest rocked, and more than one eye was nearly pecked out. None succeeded in getting the morsel, for in the skirmish it fell to the ground and was lost. A crow near by flew down, gobbled it up, and gave them a scolding for being so silly.

All this frightened Brier so much, that when the crowlets fell to reproaching each other, and began a fresh quarrel, she flew away as if some fearful thing was after her, and never stopped till a wide marsh lay before her. It was quite dark now, and a heavy dew began to fall; but the elf had nowhere to go, and sat weeping underneath a dilapidated mushroom, wondering what would become of her. Presently a brilliant light came dancing over the marsh, and a voice cried out: "Come hither! come hither! I will show you a safe, warm place. Trust to me, and follow."

Gladly Brier obeyed, and hastened after the friendly light, which flitted hither and thither, now gleaming brightly, now flickering like a dim candle in the wind. The tired fairy followed till her wings gave out, and she was forced to ask if they were not nearly at the journey's end. Then the false light vanished with a mocking laugh, and Brier fluttered down upon the damp moss, where she lay faint with weariness and fear. The tempting Will-o'-the-wisp danced round her again, evil-eyed snakes looked out from their coverts, strange plants nodded in their sleep, noisome vapors filled the air, and hoarse-voiced frogs came hopping up to touch the shuddering elf with their clammy fingers, and bid her come and play with them among the green pools of the fen.

"O go away, and leave me to die in peace!" cried Brier. "Do not hurt me, for I am a lost, unhappy elf, who has no friend in the wide world to save her now."

"Do not fear, poor little creature! for we will befriend you, though we are but small and weak," whispered sweet voices from the moss. "Lie here and rest till morning; nothing shall harm you, for we will guard your sleep, and send you happy dreams."

"Who are you?" asked Brier, already soothed by the gentle tones and fragrant breath that surrounded her. "May I trust you? I have been once deceived, and am very miserable."

"Yes, we know that, and we pity you; now rest your weary little head in the shadow of our leaves, and tell us how we can best comfort you."

Brier felt the soft touch of some flowery sprite as a drop of honey came upon her lips, and her head was pillowed on some gentle bosom. So friendly were the words, the acts, of these unknown beings, she was touched and won at once. Lying there, she presently began to weep repentant tears, and sobbed out: "Ah, the only comfort I can know is to be able to undo the naughty thing which I have done. Can you show me how I shall make the doves forgive and love me as they did?"

"Dear little Brier, there is but one way to reach what you desire," whispered the sweet voices in her ear. "Go humbly back and ask to be forgiven; then show that your penitence is sincere by keeping a careful guard upon tongue and temper. It needs but little knowledge to tell us that gentleness wins its way everywhere, and patient is the sweetest virtue which mortal, elf, or flower can possess."

"Do not listen to these weak and foolish words," cried other voices above Brier's head, while a bitter odor filled the air. "Look up and listen to us, for we will show a better way to be happy. Do not go back nor humble yourself to any one. Go on and look for pleasure everywhere; for life was not given to be wasted in uprooting harmless little passions such as yours. Heed our words, and ask no pardon of the silly doves, who will but despite you for your weak submission."

"It is a brave, a beautiful thing to say, 'Forgive me, I have done wrong; I will amend,'" breathed the other voices from the moss. "O listen to us, and conquer the small passions while you may, lest they become your masters, and rule you like a slave. Go back, dear elf, and with a single word wipe out the bitterness of your regret, atone for the unkind deed, and let it be a lesson that shall serve you all your life."

Wondering and perplexed lay Brier, listening to the unseen spirits that warned and tempted her. First she thought to obey the selfish ones, and try to be good no longer, because it was so hard. But the unhappy hours she had spent, the sad sights she had seen, the fright, the weariness, and want she had suffered, showed her that happiness would not come without self-control. Next she bent to hearken to the gentler voices, and tender thoughts began to come, good resolutions sprung up, and meek desires seemed to comfort her as she received and welcomed them. Then for the first time did she see a faint light glimmering on the moss; she thought it was a glow-worm, and put out her tiny hands to warm them at his lamp; but no worm, no firefly, nor even a stray moonbeam did she find. As she moved, the golden shadow followed, and soon she found that it was shining brightest on her own breast. It was the talisman, and as she drew it out, through all the gloom her mother's face smiled on her with the look that always softened little Brier's heart, and helped her to repent even in her naughtiest hours. It did so then; for, laying down her wet cheek on the dear face in the magic drop, she cried out, through her tears: "O dear mamma! I will be good, I will be good! Speak no more to me, bad spirits, for I must not listen; and you, friendly voices, whisper your wise warnings in my ear, that I may do my duty, may be forgiven for my fault, and be again a gentle little Brier."

As the words left her lips, her heavy eyelids closed, a warm wind breathed across her lips like a good-night kiss, and through the clouds the moon shone out like a motherly face watching over the lonely elf all night long.

When she woke, her first thought was to see who the good and evil counsellors had been. A tall, flame-colored marsh-lily rang its bells about her; its leaves stained with dark spots, its bitter breath filling all the air. Turning from the savage-looking flower, with its noisy jangle, she found beside her a cluster of white violets blooming freshly even in that unlovely spot, and lifting their meek faces to the light with an innocent serenity that rebuked her as no words of theirs had done. She kissed and thanked them gratefully, and flew away a wiser, better elf for that night in the dreary fen.

Flutter Dove lay on her bed of feathers in the shadow of the ferns, for every bird in the wood had helped to make it soft for her: even the baby-birds had plucked a billful of down from their breasts or a cherished feather from among the few their little tails possessed. The bruised wing was still folded, but the ruffled bosom was white and smooth as ever, and Flutter's eyes shone again as she cooed to Twitter Linnet who sat beside her, or looked up to answer her sister, who stood on the bough above showering sweet names and merry songs upon her, for Coo could not come down to play with her. Mamma Dove tripped about on her rosy feet, bringing seeds, worms, or water from the pool where the Papa was making bubbles shine and ripples flow, while he bathed his wings and dipped his head quite out of sight.

Suddenly a weary little figure stood before them; its robe was soiled and torn, its tiny feet bleeding, its face stained with tears, and very sad. At first they did not know it, till, kneeling beside Flutter, it said, very humbly: "It is I, bad, passionate Brier. I have learned a lesson, and will try most patiently to be all that you would have me. Will you forgive and take me back again?"

Then Flutter waved her one wing for joy, and Coo nearly fell off the bough in her delight, the kind mother-bird folded the penitent elf beneath her wings, and the father came hurrying from the pool to bid her be assured that they forgave and loved her better than before.

"Now that is right beautiful! But I fear I could not so soon have pardoned such a thing, and been so glad to welcome that Brier Rose back," said neighbor Wren to Glance the dragon-fly, as they watched the doves.

"Yes indeed, it would be a fine matter if all in the wood followed their generous example, and learned to be as charitable to the faults of others. I for one will say a friendly word to the elf, for I was very sharp with her when Flutter fell, and have been somewhat troubled at heart ever since."

As he spoke Glance darted away to bid his neighbors greet Brier without reproof or coldness, while Madam Wren sent her daughter Jenny to see if she could be of use to Madam Dove. Cock Robin soon followed with the ripest berry he could find, and all in the forest were kind to the elf, for the sake of the doves who had suffered most, but forgave so readily.

Poor Brier had not thought to be so tenderly received, and it did her more good than a hundred scoldings. Every one was so kind, it almost broke her heart to remember all the ungentle things she had said and done to them; and when Papa Dove had brought her new garments from Silverthread the spider, when mamma had bathed and bound up her wounded feet, and little Coo had gathered her cosily into the nest, she put her arms about her neck and fell asleep, resolving to be the very opposite of all she had been, till the past was quite forgotten and the good Star fully satisfied.

She kept her promise; for, like many a child, she only needed to be shown how sad and unlovely her own fault looked in others, to grow glad and eager to be good. Often quick words rose to her lips and anger burned in her heart, for it takes many efforts, many failures, to make a real success; but when the gust of passion had passed by, she asked pardon, and tried still harder to subdue her bosom sin. Whenever she found herself getting very bad, she thought of the dead ant, the quarrelsome crowlets, the night in the fen, and all the misery she had brought upon herself. That helped her, and with each day the face in the talisman shone clearer and smiled sweeter on the now gentle-tempered Brier.

CHAPTER FOUR

BLUSH OPENED HER EYES in a garden, and looked delightedly about her, thinking within herself, "I cannot fail to be happy in such a blooming place as this; I will choose the finest flower for my palace, and live here like a queen."

All through the garden she went, but was not satisfied till she came to the Crown-imperial. It had no perfume, but was dressed in scarlet and gold, and in each cup there lay a drop which was not dew, but a part of the flower, and these Blush made her mirrors. Here she lived and soon found friends among the tulips growing close by. Her days she spent in arranging gay garments, looking in her glasses, and flying about to be admired by the flowers, many of whom flattered the vain elf, that she might stay with them, for fairies are dearly beloved by flowers. The wiser blossoms warned her of her folly in thus wasting her life, and none pitied her more sincerely than Mignonette, who lived in a sunny corner among the pansies and blue larkspurs. She often ventured to remind Blush that time was going and nothing had been done; but the elf only looked scornfully down on the sad-colored plant, bade her take care of herself, and floated away to the tulips, who clad her in purple and gold.

One morning a busy breeze came through the garden, proclaiming that a messenger from Fairyland was on his way, and bidding them prepare to greet him. Then every flower spread her colored leaves, opened her cells, and put on her dew-drop ornaments, till each glittered in the sun. Soon they saw the Honey-king approaching, for he had been to Elf-land with his tribute of sweets to the Queen, and brought her message back.

"See!" cried the Rose, "see his velvet cloak, the golden bands on his breast, the gleam of his wings, and hear his deep voice as he sings on his way. Ah, if he would but come to me, I should be the happiest flower that ever bloomed."

On came the royal bee humming as he flew, and each flower trembled with expectation as they watched and waited. He hovered above the rose a moment, but Mignonette's breath was sweeter than hers. Away to the sad-colored blossom he flew, and, standing beside her, delivered his message.

"I am bidden to tell you that the elves are coming to choose one among you to be the summer queen; and when autumn comes, and they return to lay you in your winter beds, if she has ruled wisely and well, they will bear her away to bloom in Fairyland forever."

When the flowers heard this, great were the rejoicings, for this was the highest honor that could be done them, and each hoped to gain it. The sun shone and the dew fell alike on all, and they who used these good gifts aright grew daily in strength and beauty. Now Blush had nothing to do with the matter, and should have helped the flowers instead of thinking only of herself. But she was so vain she hoped to be chosen the queen, both because of her beauty and her birth, and all day long she flew busily here and there, preparing the finest suit, that she might outshine all about her. This was not kind, and the plants disliked her more and more, for she took away their dew to bathe in, broke off their fairest leaves for her robes, powdered her hair with their golden pollen, and gave them no peace for their own affairs.

"Can you not tell me how I may wash away all traces of the sun from my face? It is not as fair as it used to be, and will soon be as brown as ugly Minnie's, if I cannot freshen its bloom."

She spoke to the tulips, who had ceased to be her friends when they found she was trying to outdo them in splendor; but they hid their dislike under smiling faces, and replied: "Down by the wall yonder grows a plant with violet flowers; go and bathe in their dew, pretty Blush, and see how fair you'll become."

If Blush had studied fairy lore instead of her own lovely face, she would have known that the violet flowers grew on the deadly nightshade, which would only blight and destroy. But she knew nothing of it, and, hastening away, bathed in the poisonous dew, then flew home, and to sleep, that she might be fresh for the morrow.

With the first peep of day Blush was before her mirror, to see if the change had been wrought. But she started with dismay, for a colorless face, with dim eyes, white lips, and faded hair, looked back at her. She thought the morning mist had blurred her glass, and tried another, but in each it was the same, and then she saw the cruel loss which had befallen her. Full of grief and indignation, she flew to reproach the tulips, but they answered, scornfully: "Foolish thing! when we told you to bathe in the flowers yonder, we meant the purple jessamine, not the evil nightshade. We thought an elf who gave herself such airs knew everything, and think you justly punished for your vanity. Now that you are not fit to be seen, you had better hide yourself till the elves are gone,"—and the cruel tulips turned laughing away.

Poor little Blush knew they spoke falsely, and went sadly away to hide herself behind a burdock-leaf that grew near the fountain in a lonely corner, for she wished to see, yet not be seen.

With the first rays of the sun came the fairy troop, some on rosy clouds, some on the morning wind, some on their own fleet wings. Each flower heart beat fast as the shining band alighted and passed along the blooming terraces. On it went by the stately Lily, who grew pale with grief when she saw that the wands were not lowered before her, and with an imploring voice she cried: "Are not my leaves stainless as snow? Am I not stately and fair? Why am I not chosen queen?"

But the elves replied, as they pointed to a cluster of heart's-ease, dying for want of sun and air in the shadow of Lily's broad leaves: "In your white bosom lies a haughty heart, careless of all things but itself. We cannot crown you till you have learned the beauty of humility."

Blushing with anger, the Rose demanded, as they passed her by: "Do you not see me? Am I not the queen of flowers, royal and sweet? Give me the crown: it is my right."

But soft hands put the thorny branches back, and the elfin voices whispered: "Passion makes no flower fair, however royal be its birth. Rule yourself, wilful Rose, then you may wisely govern others."

Now when neither of the rival beauties were chosen, no other plant dared speak, but waited in wondering silence while the elves passed all the flowers that possessed a single charm, until they reached the nook where Mignonette was rocking a baby butterfly to sleep upon her breast. Here every wand fell, and amid an astonished hush the fairies proclaimed *her* the summer queen.

Now when Blush saw this she could not bear it; the thought that the ugly brown flower, whom she had despised, was to reign over all the garden, to have a court, ministers, and maids of honor, to be visited by ambassadors from other courts, to receive gifts, and in the autumn to be carried in state to Fairyland, was too much for the disappointed elf, because with vanity comes envy, and she could not endure that any one should be more praised or honored than herself. As all the fairy harps began to tinkle, the flower-bells to ring, and the coronation festival opened with great splendor, Blush cried out: "I will not stay to see this; if I cannot be lovely, I will die and be forgotten"; and, flying up to the fountain's brim, she plunged deep into the cold, dark water dashing there. She hoped to die at once, for fairies do not receive their magic wands till they are grown, and many things have power to hurt them before that time. But to her great surprise, the waves divided without harming or even wetting her a drop, and she sank safely to the bottom, where lived a solitary water-sprite, who looked much amazed when the elf came floating into her blue chamber, as she sat in a shell singing the song the fountain repeated to the flowers above.

The sprite was very kind to Blush, and glad to have a friend, for she was very lonely; and they fell to talking quite as if they had known one another a long time.

"I cannot understand why I was not drowned in coming hither," said the elf, when she had told her troubles.

"You must have some fairy charm about you, and that made the water harmless," answered the sprite.

Then Blush remembered her talisman, and looked at it, longing to feel her mother's arms about her, and hear her gentle voice comforting her sorrow. Like Moss and Brier, she had forgotten to look often at it and be guided by its smiles or tears. Now it was a most consoling thought, that, though she was so plain, her mother would still love her, still wait and hope to see her, and have no reproach for her if she were only good. Now it seemed time to begin her task, and, having no beauty to fill her little head with vain fancies, her heart woke up from its long sleep and bade her live for better things.

"Kind sprite, can you help me to be humble, generous, and truly useful? I desire to do well, but I have spent my days in foolish play, and now I cannot tell how it is best to cure my vanity," she said, with tears in her dim eyes.

"Live for others, Blush; forget yourself, and care for the beauty of a simple, earnest heart more than for loveliness of face or grace of form. Nothing can change or take this charm away; and I will help you to obtain it if you really care for it."

"I do, I do; try me, and see if I am not sincere."

The sprite believed her, and till twilight fell amused the elf in her own charming manner,—teaching her to understand the liquid music of the waves, the strange language of the fishes, that glided to and fro above them like golden birds in a blue sky; telling her sweet stories of a water-spirit's life in river, lake, and sea; rocking her in a rosy shell; feeding her on delicate food; and leading her up and down the weedy bottom of the marble basin, where little red crabs, water-spiders, sea-anemones, and odd shell-fish enjoyed themselves among the pebbles and coral branches lying here and there.

So busy was Blush that she *did* forget herself, for the first time in many days,—forgot her loss, her unhappiness, and began to smile again; for though the sprite was a curious creature, with long, green hair, and little fins upon her shoulders where the elf had wings,—though she wore no clothes, and her tiny hands were damp and cold,—she had such friendly ways with her, such loving eyes, and a voice so like the ripple of quiet waves upon the shore, that Blush grew very fond of her.

When the stars came out in the evening sky, and all the dwellers in the fountain crept into their watery beds, the sprite wrapped herself in a cloak of mist, and bade Blush come with her. Up they went, and with delight the elf breathed long breaths of the balmy upper air, and warmed herself in the golden heart of a rose, where the noonday heat still lingered.

"Now," said the sprite, "you shall see my work, and bear a share in it. Take a part of my dew-mantle about you, and fly to every flower in this long bed, brush away the dust of day, and bathe it in the drops that will continually gather on the edge of your cloak. Forget none, but refresh all, and, if any have received a hurt, touch it with this balm of moonlight, which is a sovereign cure for such wounds. I shall work on the upper terrace until dawn; but if you tire of this labor, you can leave it, only I can never befriend you any more, unless you are in earnest." And with that, the sprite floated away.

This was a hard task for Blush, because she knew that the care given to the plants made them grow fair and strong, and now it seemed as if she were giving her own loveliness away; besides, she was sure that sleepless nights, and days spent in the damp fountain, would not give her back her beauty. Long she stood with the dew-mantle in her hand, unable to decide, and at length stooped to lay it down, when from her bosom dropped the talisman, and lay shining on the grass. The face was so sorrowful, that, with a last sigh of selfish vanity, she folded herself in the chilly cloak, and saw, as she put it back into her bosom, that the mother's face was smiling on her now.

Then she fell to work, and washed every flower in the plot, though it must be owned that she scrubbed the naughty tulips till their cheeks glowed like fire, and they cried out. She could not forgive and love them yet, and as they did not know her in her misty cloak, she enjoyed that part of her work, and left such a big dew-drop in each cup, they thought there must have been a shower while they slept. Queen Minnie was more gently tended, for every leaf glistened, and the air was full of fragrance when the elf had done. Now that she had begun to care for others, she remembered the good counsel Mignonette had often given, and how scornfully she had received it; therefore she was anxious to atone for her unkindness, and did her careful work unseen in the stillness of the night.

Till dawn they worked, then back into the fountain for another quiet day, for the water-sprite could not bear the sun, and Blush would not leave her new-found friend. In this way a long time passed; Blush never looked into a mirror, tried heartily to forget that she had been so fair, endeavored to be self-denying, humble, and happy in the unseen work to which she gave her nights. Soon she found she could rejoice in the beauty of others without an envious feeling, and tended many a plant that once had been unkind to her so tenderly, that they wondered at her forgiving spirit, and longed to see her as she once had been. Night after night, when she came stealing to them, thinking them asleep, some one of them would be awake, and waiting for her with a drop of freshest honey, a breath of odor, or a loving kiss, to show their friendliness, and Blush would dance for joy, saying, as she went on with her dainty task:—

"Ah, this is better than to be a vain and selfish elf, unloved by any! I can be glad that I am ugly, if pity makes me friends like these. What more can I do for you, dear flowers? Let me bend this leaf, that the sun may not scorch you to-morrow; let me smooth away this fold in your petal, and be sure I will bring dew enough next time to bathe you from your tallest stamen to your lowest leaf."

While busied with these generous cares for others, Blush was unconscious that her beauty was returning, that the sprite, the waves, the winds, the plants, all lent their help to give her back the charms she had lost fourfold greater than before. Now the loveliness came from within, brightening her face until it seemed a little sun shining even in the darksome fountain. No one told her this, till the sprite could not keep the secret any longer, and bade Blush look into the mirrors of the crown imperial, where they had been busied late into the dawn. The elf believed she should behold the faded face she had last seen there, but smiled and looked bravely in, there to behold a sweeter face than any glass ever had reflected before. She knew it was her own, was glad to be again her winsome self, but now the vanity was so well cured, that, instead of looking proudly about her, she spread her hands before her face, and would not lift it up until the sprite placed her on the green tuft of leaves that crowned the flower, and set all the scarlet bells to ringing, that the other plants might wake and rejoice with Blush. Very soon the garden was alive with blooming faces and gay voices, as birds and blossoms joined in the song the happy fairy sang, while the sun climbed up the rosy sky, and on her bosom shone the talisman, undarkened by a single shadow.

> "O lesson well and wisely taught,
>     Stay with me to the last,
> That all my life may better be
>     For the trial that is past.
> O vanity, mislead no more!
>     Sleep, like passions, long!
> Wake, happy heart, and dance again
>     To the music of my song!
>
> "O summer days, flit fast away,
>     And bring the blithesome hour
> When we three wanderers shall meet
>     Safe in our household flower!
> O dear mamma, lament no more!
>     Smile on us as we come,
> Your grief has been our punishment,
>     Your love has led us home."

Mamma Rose sat alone longing for the merry voices that used to make the evening hour such a pleasant time. The Papa was teaching Tina to fly among the aspen-trees near by, and as the Mamma watched the only child now left her, tears dropped slowly down her cheeks, and she sighed: "When will they come? Ah, if they knew how I pine for them, they would not linger long away from me."

As the words left her lips there came a little rustle, and there before her, as if they had risen at her wish, stood Blush, Brier, and Moss, with a star shining on each forehead, while smiles and tears made rainbows on their happy faces. Gathered close to their mother's bosom, they were too full of joy for words, till the dear Papa came flying like the wind with Tina, whose locks were all blown about her face, and little garments sadly ruffled with his speed. But when she saw who waited for her, she fluttered from one to the other, eager to welcome them back, and show that she could fly as well as they. Then, lying in their mother's arms, they told all their wanderings, and the hope each cherished that the good Star's lessons had been so well learned that they could never be forgotten.

"But tell me, dearest children, what was the talisman Star gave to help and comfort you? I long to see the wondrous charm which has given me back my darlings so beautiful and good," said Mamma Rose, as she kissed the blooming faces clustering about her own.

Blush, Brier, and Moss drew closer still; and, folding their arms more tenderly about her, whispered, as they showed the magic drops glittering in their little bosoms: "See, dear mamma, here lies the talisman; for the strong, sweet spell that conquered passion, vanity, and indolence, and led us safely home, was our great love for you."

# What the Bells Saw and Said

"Bells ring others to church, but go not in themselves."

No one saw the spirits of the bells up there in the old steeple at midnight on Christmas Eve. Six quaint figures, each wrapped in a shadowy cloak and wearing a bell-shaped cap. All were gray-headed, for they were among the oldest bell-spirits of the city, and "the light of other days" shone in their thoughtful eyes. Silently they sat, looking down on the snow-covered roofs glittering in the moonlight, and the quiet streets deserted by all but the watchmen on their chilly rounds, and such poor souls as wandered shelterless in the winter night. Presently one of the spirits said, in a tone, which, low as it was, filled the belfry with reverberating echoes,—

"Well, brothers, are your reports ready of the year that now lies dying?"

All bowed their heads, and one of the oldest answered in a sonorous voice:—

"My report isn't all I could wish. You know I look down on the commercial part of our city and have fine opportunities for seeing what goes on there. It's my business to watch the business men, and upon my word I'm heartily ashamed of them sometimes. During the war they did nobly, giving their time and money, their sons and selves to the good cause, and I was proud of them. But now too many of them have fallen back into the old ways, and their motto seems to be, 'Every one for himself, and the devil take the hindmost.' Cheating, lying and stealing are hard words, and I don't mean to apply them to *all* who swarm about below there like ants on an ant-hill—*they* have other names for these things, but I'm old-fashioned and use plain words. There's a deal too much dishonesty in the world, and business seems to have become a game of hazard in which luck, not labor, wins the prize. When I was young, men were years making moderate fortunes, and were satisfied with them. They built them on sure foundations, knew how to enjoy them while they lived, and to leave a good name behind them when they died.

"Now it's anything for money; health, happiness, honor, life itself, are flung down on that great gaming-table, and they forget everything else in the excitement of success or the desperation of defeat. Nobody seems satis-

106

fied either, for those who win have little time or taste to enjoy their prosperity, and those who lose have little courage or patient to support them in adversity. They don't even fail as they used to. In my day when a merchant found himself embarrassed he didn't ruin others in order to save himself, but honestly confessed the truth, gave up everything, and began again. But now-a-days after all manner of dishonorable shifts there comes a grand crash; many suffer, but by some hocus-pocus the merchant saves enough to retire upon and live comfortably here or abroad. It's very evident that honor and honesty don't mean now what they used to mean in the days of old May, Higginson and Lawrence.

"They preach below here, and very well too sometimes, for I often slide down the rope to peep and listen during service. But, bless you! they don't seem to lay either sermon, psalm or prayer to heart, for while the minister is doing his best, the congregation, tired with the breathless hurry of the week, sleep peacefully, calculate their chances for the morrow, or wonder which of their neighbors will lose or win in the great game. Don't tell me! I've seen them do it, and if I dared I'd have startled every soul of them with a rousing peal. Ah, they don't dream whose eye is on them, they never guess what secrets the telegraph wires tell as the messages fly by, and little know what a report I give to the winds of heaven as I ring out above them morning, noon, and night." And the old spirit shook his head till the tassel on his cap jangled like a little bell.

"There are some, however, whom I love and honor," he said, in a benignant tone, "who honestly earn their bread, who deserve all the success that comes to them, and always keep a warm corner in their noble hearts for those less blest than they. These are the men who serve the city in times of peace, save it in times of war, deserve the highest honors in its gift, and leave behind them a record that keeps their memories green. For such an one we lately tolled a knell, my brothers; and as our united voices pealed over the city, in all grateful hearts, sweeter and more solemn than any chime, rung the words that made him so beloved,—

"'Treat our dead boys tenderly, and send them home to me.'"

He ceased, and all the spirits reverently uncovered their gray heads as a strain of music floated up from the sleeping city and died among the stars.

"Like yours, my report is not satisfactory in all respects," began the second spirit, who wore a very pointed cap and a finely ornamented cloak. But, though his dress was fresh and youthful, his face was old, and he had nodded several times during his brother's speech. "My greatest affliction during the past year has been the terrible extravagance which prevails. My post, as you know, is at the court end of the city, and I see all the fashionable vices and follies. It is a marvel to me how so many of these immortal creatures, with such opportunities for usefulness, self-improvement and genuine happiness can be content to go round and round in one narrow circle of unprofitable and unsatisfactory pursuits. I do my best to warn them; Sunday after Sunday I chime in their ears the beautiful old hymns that sweetly chide or cheer the hearts that truly listen and believe; Sunday after Sunday I look down on them as they pass in, hoping to see that my words have not fallen upon deaf ears; and Sunday after Sunday they listen to words that should teach them much, yet seem to go by them like the wind. They are told to love their neighbor, yet too many hate him because he possesses more of this world's goods or honours than they; they are told that a rich man cannot enter the kingdom of heaven, yet they go on laying up perishable wealth, and though often warned that moth and rust will corrupt, they fail to believe it till the worm that destroys enters and mars their own chapel of ease. Being a spirit, I see below external splendor and find much poverty of heart and soul under the velvet and the ermine which should cover rich and royal natures. Our city saints walk abroad in threadbare suits, and under quiet bonnets shine the eyes that make sunshine in the shady places. Often as I watch the glittering procession passing to and fro below me, I wonder if with all our progress, there is to-day as much real piety as in the times when our fathers, poorly clad, with weapon in one hand and Bible in the other, came weary distances to worship in the wilderness with fervent faith unquenched by danger, suffering and solitude.

"Yet in spite of my fault-finding I love my children, as I call them, for all are not butterflies. Many find wealth no temptation to forgetfulness of duty or hardness of heart. Many give freely of their abundance, pity the poor, comfort the afflicted, and make our city loved and honored in other lands as in our own. They have their cares, losses, and heartaches as well as the poor; it isn't all sunshine with them, and they learn, poor souls, that

> 'Into each life some rain must fall,
> Some days must be dark and dreary.'

"But I've hopes of them, and lately they have had a teacher so genial, so gifted, so well-beloved that all who listen to him must be better for the lessons of charity, good-will and cheerfulness which he brings home to them by the magic of tears and smiles. We know him, we love him, we always remember him as the year comes round, and the blithest song our brazen tongues utter is a Christmas carol to the Father of 'The Chimes!'"

As the spirit spoke his voice grew cheery, his old face shone, and in a burst of hearty enthusiasm he flung up his cap and cheered like a boy. So did the others, and as the fairy shout echoed through the belfry a troop of shadowy figures, with faces lovely or grotesque, tragical or gay, sailed by on the wings of the wintry wind and waved their hands to the spirits of the bells.

As the excitement subsided and the spirits reseated themselves, looking ten years younger for that burst, another spoke. A venerable brother in a dingy mantel, with a tuneful voice, and eyes that seemed to have grown sad with looking on much misery.

"He loves the poor, the man we've just hurrahed for, and he makes others love and remember them, bless him!" said the spirit. "I hope he'll touch the hearts of those who listen to him here and beguile them to open their hands to my unhappy children over yonder. If I could set some of the forlorn souls in my parish beside the happier creatures who weep over imaginary woes as they are painted by his eloquent lips, that brilliant scene would be better than any sermon. Day and night I look down on lives as full of sin, self-sacrifice and suffering as any in those famous books. Day and night I try to comfort the poor by my cheery voice, and to make their wants known by proclaiming them with all my might. But people seem to be so intent on business, pleasure or home duties that they have no time to hear and answer my appeal. There's a deal of charity in this good city, and when the people do wake up they work with a will; but I can't help thinking that if some of the money lavished on luxuries was spent on necessaries for the poor, there would be fewer tragedies like that which ended yesterday. It's a short story, easy to tell, though long and hard to live; listen to it.

"Down yonder in the garret of one of the squalid houses at the foot of my tower, a little girl has lived for a year, fighting silently and single-handed a good fight against poverty and sin. I saw her when she first came, a hopeful, cheerful, brave-hearted little soul, alone, yet not afraid. She used to sit all day sewing at her window, and her lamp burnt far into the night, for she was very poor, and all she earned would barely give her food and shelter. I watched her feed the doves, who seemed to be her only friends; she never forgot them, and daily gave them the few crumbs that fell from her meagre table. But there was no kind hand to feed and foster the little human dove, and so she starved.

"For a while she worked bravely, but the poor three dollars a week would not clothe and feed and warm her, though the things her busy fingers made sold for enough to keep her comfortably if she had received it. I saw the pretty color fade from her cheeks; her eyes grew hollow, her voice lost its cheery ring, her step its elasticity, and her face began to wear the haggard, anxious look that made its youth doubly pathetic. Her poor little gowns grew shabby, her shawl so thin she shivered when the pitiless wind smote her, and her feet were almost bare. Rain and snow beat on the patient little figure going to and fro, each morning with hope and courage faintly shining, each evening with the shadow of despair gathering darker round her. It was a hard time for all, desperately hard for her, and in her poverty, sin and pleasure tempted her. She resisted, but as another bitter winter came she feared that in her misery she might yield, for body and soul were weakened now by the long struggle. She knew not where to turn for help; there seemed to be no place for her at any safe and happy fireside; life's hard aspect daunted her, and she turned to death, saying confidingly, 'Take me while I'm innocent and not afraid to go.'

"I saw it all! I saw how she sold everything that would bring money and paid her little debts to the utmost penny; how she set her poor room in order for the last time; how she tenderly bade the doves goodby, and lay down on her bed to die. At nine o'clock last night as my bell rang over the city, I tried to tell what was going on in the garret where the light was dying out so fast. I cried to them with all my strength,—

"'Kind souls, below there! a fellow-creature is perishing for lack of charity! Oh, help her before it is too late! Mothers, with little daughters on your knees, stretch out your hands and take her in! Happy women, in the safe shelter of home, think of her desolation! Rich men, who grind the faces of the poor, remember that this soul will one day be required of you! Dear Lord, let not this little sparrow fall to the ground! Help, Christian men and women, in the name of Him whose birthday blessed the world!'

"Ah me! I rang, and clashed, and cried in vain. The passers-by only said, as they hurried home, laden with Christmas cheer: 'The old bell is merry to-night, as it should be at this blithe season, bless it!'

"As the clocks truck ten, the poor child lay down, saying, as she drank the last bitter draught life could give her, 'It's very cold, but soon I shall not feel it;' and with her quiet eyes fixed on the cross that glimmered in the moonlight above me, she lay waiting for the sleep that needs no lullaby.

"As the clock struck eleven, pain and poverty for her were over. It was bitter cold, but she no longer felt it. She lay serenely sleeping, with tired heart and hands, at rest forever. As the clocks struck twelve, the dear Lord remembered her, and with fatherly hand led her into the home where there is room for all. To-day I rung her knell, and though my heart was heavy, yet my soul was glad; for in spite of all her human woe and weakness, I am sure that little girl will keep a joyful Christmas up in heaven."

In the silence which the spirits for a moment kept, a breath of softer air than any from the snowy world below swept through the steeple and seemed to whisper, "Yes!"

"Avast there! fond as I am of salt water, I don't like this kind," cried the breezy voice of the fourth spirit, who had a tiny ship instead of a tassel on his cap, and who wiped his wet eyes with the sleeve of his rough blue cloak. "It won't take me long to spin my yarn; for things are pretty taut and ship-shape aboard our craft. Captain Taylor is an experienced sailor, and has brought many a ship safely into port in spite of wind and tide, and the devil's own whirlpools and hurricanes. If you want to see earnestness come aboard some Sunday when the Captain's on the quarter-deck, and take an observation. No danger of falling asleep there, no more than there is up aloft, 'when the stormy winds do blow.' Consciences get raked fore and aft, sins are blown clean out of the water, false colors are hauled down and true ones run up to the masthead, and many an immortal soul is warned to steer off in time from the pirates, rocks and quicksands of temptation. He's a regular revolving light, is the Captain,—a beacon always burning and saying plainly, 'Here are life-boats, ready to put off in all weathers and bring the shipwrecked into quiet waters.' He comes but seldom now, being laid up in the home dock, tranquilly waiting till his turn comes to go out with the tide and safely ride at anchor in the great harbor of the Lord. Our crew varies a good deal. Some of 'em have rather rough voyages, and come into port pretty well battered; land-sharks fall foul of a good many, and do a deal of damage; but most of 'em carry brave and tender hearts under the blue jackets, for their rough nurse, the sea, manages to keep something of the child alive in the grayest old tar that makes the world his picture-book. We try to supply 'em with life-preservers while at sea, and make 'em feel sure of a hearty welcome when ashore, and I believe the year '67 will sail away into eternity with a satisfactory cargo. Brother North-End made me pipe my eye; so I'll make him laugh to pay for it, by telling a clerical joke I heard the other day. Bell-ows didn't make it, though he might have done so, as he's a connection of ours, and knows how to use his tongue as well as any of us. Speaking of the bells of a certain town, a reverend gentleman affirmed that each bell uttered an appropriate remark so plainly, that the words were audible to all. The Baptist bell cried, briskly, 'Come up and be dipped! come up and be dipped!' The Episcopal bell slowly said, 'Apos-tol-ic suc-cess-ion! apos-tol-ic suc-cess-ion!' The Orthodox bell solemnly pronounced, 'Eternal damnation! eternal damnation!' and the Methodist shouted, invitingly, 'Room for all! room for all!'"

As the spirit imitated the various calls, as only a jovial bell-sprite could, the others gave him a chime of laughter, and vowed they would each adopt some tuneful summons, which should reach human ears and draw human feet more willingly to church.

"Faith, brother, you've kept your word and got the laugh out of us," cried a stout, sleek spirit, with a kindly face, and a row of little saints round his cap and a rosary at his side. "It's very well we are doing this year; the cathedral is full, the flock increasing, and the true faith holding its own entirely. Ye may shake your heads if you will and fear there'll be trouble, but I doubt it. We've warm hearts of our own, and the best of us don't forget that when we were starving, America—the saints bless the jewel!—sent us bread; when we were dying for lack of work, America opened her arms and took us in, and now helps us to build churches, homes and schools by giving us a share of the riches all men work for and win. It's a generous nation ye are, and a brave one, and we showed our gratitude by fighting for ye in the day of trouble and giving ye our Phil, and many another broth of a boy. The land is wide enough for us both, and while we work and fight and grow together, each may learn something from the other. I'm free to confess that your religion looks a bit cold and hard to me, even here in the good city where each man may ride his own hobby to death, and hoot at his neighbors as much as he will. You seem to keep your piety shut up all the week in your bare, white churches, and only let it out on Sundays, just a trifle musty with disuse. You set your rich, warm and soft to the fore, and leave the poor shivering at the door. You give your people bare walls to look upon, common-place music to listen to, dull sermons to put them asleep, and then wonder why they stay away, or take no interest when they come.

"We leave our doors open day and night; our lamps are always burning, and we may come into our Father's house at any hour. We let rich and poor kneel together, all being equal there. With us abroad you'll see prince and peasant side by side, school-boy and bishop, market-woman and noble lady, saint and sinner, praying to the Holy Mary, whose motherly arms are open to high and low. We make our churches inviting with immortal music, pictures by the world's great masters, and rites that are splendid symbols of the faith we hold. Call it mummery if ye like, but let me ask you why so many of your sheep stray into our fold? It's because they miss the warmth, the hearty, the maternal tenderness which all souls love and long for, and fail to find in your stern, Puritanical belief. By Saint Peter! I've seen many a lukewarm worshipper, who for years has nodded in your cushioned pews, wake and glow with something akin to genuine piety while kneeling on the stone pavement of one of our cathedrals, with Raphael's angels before his eyes, with strains of magnificent music in his

ears, and all about him, in shapes of power or beauty, the saints and mar-
tyrs who have saved the world, and whose presence inspires him to follow
their divine example. It's not complaining of ye I am, but just reminding ye
that men are but children after all, and need more tempting to virtue than
they do to vice, which last comes easy to 'em since the Fall. Do your best in
your own ways to get the poor souls into bliss, and good luck to ye. But
remember, there's room in the Holy Mother Church for all, and when your
own priests send ye to the divil, come straight to us and we'll take ye in."

"A truly Catholic welcome, bull and all," said the sixth spirit, who, in
spite of his old-fashioned garments, had a youthful face, earnest, fearless
eyes, and an energetic voice that woke the echoes with its vigorous tones.
"I've a hopeful report, brothers, for the reforms of the day are wheeling
into rank and marching on. The war isn't over nor rebeldom conquered yet,
but the Old Guard has been 'up and at 'em' through the year. There has
been some hard fighting, rivers of ink have flowed, and the Washington
dawdlers have signalized themselves by a 'masterly inactivity.' The political campaign has been an anxious one; some of the leaders have deserted;
some been mustered out; some have fallen gallantly, and as yet have received no monuments. But at the Grand Review the Cross of the Legion of
Honor will surely shine on many a brave breast that won no decoration but
its virtue here; for the world's fanatics make heaven's heroes, poets say.

"The flock of Nightingales that flew South during the 'winter of our discontent' are all at home again, some here and some in Heaven. But the
music of their womanly heroism still lingers in the nation's memory, and
makes a tender minor-chord in the battle-hymn of freedom.

"The reform in literature isn't as vigorous as I could wish; but a sharp
attack of mental and moral dyspepsia will soon teach our people that
French confectionery and the bad pastry of Wood, Braddon, Yates & Co. is
not the best diet for the rising generation.

"Speaking of the rising generation reminds me of the schools. They are
doing well; they always are, and we are justly proud of them. There may be
a slight tendency toward placing too much value upon book-learning; too
little upon home culture. Our girls are acknowledged to be uncommonly
pretty, witty and wise, but some of us wish they had more health and less
excitement, more domestic accomplishments and fewer ologies and isms,
and were contented with simple pleasures and the old-fashioned virtues,
and not quite so fond of the fast, frivolous life that makes them old so soon.
I am fond of our girls and boys. I love to ring for their christenings and
marriages, to toll proudly for the brave lads in blue, and tenderly for the

innocent creatures whose seats are empty under my old roof. I want to see them anxious to make Young America a model of virtue, strength and beauty, and I believe they will in time.

"There have been some important revivals in religion; for the world won't stand still, and we must keep pace or be left behind to fossilize. A free nation must have a religion broad enough to embrace all mankind, deep enough to fathom and fill the human soul, high enough to reach the source of all love and wisdom, and pure enough to satisfy the wisest and the best. Alarm bells have been rung, anathemas pronounced, and Christians, forgetful of their creed, have abused one another heartily. But the truth always triumphs in the end, and whoever sincerely believes, works and waits for it, by whatever name he calls it, will surely find his own faith blessed to him in proportion to his charity for the faith of others.

"But look!—the first red streaks of dawn are in the East. Our vigil is over, and we must fly home to welcome in the holidays. Before we part, join with me, brothers, in resolving that through the coming year we will with all our hearts and tongues,—

> 'Ring out the old, ring in the new,
> Ring out the false, ring in the true;
> Ring in the valiant man and free,
> Ring in the Christ that is to be.'"

Then hand in hand the spirits of the bells floated away, singing in the hush of dawn the sweet song the stars sung over Bethlehem,—"Peace on earth, good will to men."

# Shadow-Children

NED, POLLY, AND WILL sat on the steps one sunshiny morning, doing nothing, except wish they had something pleasant to do.

"Something new, something never heard of before,—wouldn't that be jolly?" said Ned, with a great yawn.

"It must be an amusing play, and one that we don't get tired of very soon," added Polly gravely.

"And something that didn't be wrong, else mamma wouldn't like it," said little Will, who was very good for a small boy.

As no one could suggest any thing to suit, they all sat silent a few minutes. Suddenly Ned said, rather crossly, "I wish my shadow wouldn't mock me. Every time I stretch or gape it does the same, and I don't like it."

"Poor thing, it can't help that: it has to do just what you do, and be your slave all day. I'm glad I ain't a shadow," said Polly.

"I try to run away from mine sometimes, but I can't ever. It will come after me; and in the night it scares me, if it gets big and black," said Will, looking behind him.

"Wouldn't it be fun to see shadows going about alone, and doing things like people?" asked Polly.

"I just wish they would. I'd like to see ours cut capers; that would be a jolly new game, wouldn't it?" said Ned.

No one had time to speak; for suddenly the three little shadows on the sunny wall behind them stood up straight, and began to bow.

"Mercy, me!" cried Polly, staring at them.

"By Jove, that's odd!" said Ned, looking queer.

"Are they alive?" asked Will, a little frightened.

"Don't be alarmed: they won't hurt you," said a soft voice. "To-day is midsummer-day, and whoever wishes a wish can have it till midnight. You want to see your shadows by themselves; and you can, if you promise to follow them as they have followed you so long. They will not get you into harm; so you may safely try it, if you like. Do you agree for the day to do as they do, and so have your wish?"

"Yes, we promise," answered the children.

"Tell no one till night, and be faithful shadows to the shadows."

The voice was silent, but with more funny little bows the shadows began to move off in different directions. The children each knew their own: for Ned's was the tallest, and had its hands in its pockets; Polly's had a frock on, and two bows where its hair was tied up; while Will's was a plump little shadow in a blouse, with a curly head and a pug nose. Each child went after its shadow, laughing, and enjoying the fun.

Ned's master went straight to the shed, took down a basket, and marched away to the garden, where it began to move its hands as if busily picking peas. Ned stopped laughing when he saw that, and looked rather ashamed; for he remembered that his mother had asked him to do that little job for her, and he had answered,—

"Oh, bother the old peas! I'm busy, and I can't."

"Who told you about this?" he asked, beginning to work.

The shadow shook its head, and pointed first to Ned's new jacket, then to a set of nice garden tools near by, and then seemed to blow a kiss from its shadowy fingers towards mamma, who was just passing the open gate.

"Oh! you mean that she does lots for me; so I ought to do what I can for her, and love her dearly," said Ned, getting a pleasanter face every minute.

The shadow nodded, and worked away as busily as the bees, tumbling heels over head in the great yellow squash blossoms, and getting as dusty as little millers. Somehow Ned rather liked the work, with such an odd comrade near by; for, though the shadow didn't really help a bit, it seemed to try, and set an excellent example. When the basket was full, the shadow took one handle, and Ned the other; and they carried it in.

"Thank you, dear. I was afraid we should have to give up our peas today: I'm so busy, I can't stop," said mamma, looking surprised and pleased.

Ned couldn't stop to talk; for the shadow ran away to the woodpile, and began to chop with all its might.

"Well, I suppose I must; but I never saw such a fellow for work as this shadow is. He isn't a bit like me, though he's been with me so long," said Ned, swinging the real hatchet in time with the shadowy one.

Polly's new mistress went to the dining-room, and fell to washing up the breakfast cups. Polly hated that work, and sulkily began to rattle the spoons and knock the things about. But the shadow wouldn't allow that; and Polly had to do just what it did, though she grumbled all the while.

"She don't splash a bit, or make any clatter; so I guess she's a tidy creature," said Polly. "How long she does rub each spoon and glass! We never shall get done. What a fuss she makes with the napkins, laying them all even in the drawer! and now she's at the salt-cellars, doing them just as mamma likes. I wish she'd live here, and do my work for me. Why, what's that?" And Polly stopped fretting to listen; for she seemed to hear the sound of singing,—so sweet, and yet so very faint she could catch no words, and only make out a cheerful little tune.

"Do you hear any one singing, mamma?" she asked.

"No: I wish I did." And mamma sighed; for baby was poorly, and piles of sewing lay waiting for her, and Biddy was turning things topsy-turvy in the kitchen for want of a word from the mistress, and Polly was looking sullen.

The little girl didn't say any more, but worked quietly and watched the shadow, feeling sure the faint song came from it. Presently she began to hum the tune she caught by snatches; and, before she knew it, she was singing away like a blackbird. Baby stopped crying, and mamma said, smiling,—

"Now I hear somebody singing, and it's the music I like best in the world."

That pleased Polly; but, a minute after, she stopped smiling, for the shadow went and took baby, or seemed to, and Polly really did. Now, baby was heavy, and cross with its teeth; and Polly didn't feel like tending it one bit. Mamma hurried away to the kitchen; and Polly walked up and down the room with poor baby hanging over her arm, crying dismally, with a pin in its back, a wet bib under its chin, and nothing cold and hard to bite with its hot, aching gums, where the little teeth were trying to come through.

"Do stop, you naughty, fretty baby. I'm tired of your screaming, and it's high time you went to sleep. Bless me! what's Miss Shadow doing with *her* baby?" said Polly.

Miss Shadow took out the big pin and laid it away, put on a dry bib, and gave *her* baby a nice ivory ring to bite; then began to dance up and down the room, till the shadowy baby clapped its hands and kicked delightedly. Polly laughed, and did the same, feeling sorry she had been so pettish. Presently both babies grew quiet, went to sleep, and were laid in the cradle.

"Now, I hope we shall rest a little," said Polly, stretching her arms.

But, no: down sat the shadow, and began to sew, making her needle fly like a real little seamstress.

"Oh, dear!" groaned Polly. "I promised to hem those handkerchiefs for Ned, and so I must; but I do think handkerchiefs are the most pokey things in the world to sew. I dare say you think you can sew faster than I can. Just wait a bit, and see what I can do, miss," she said to the shadow.

It took some time to find her thimble and needles and spools, for Polly wasn't a very neat little girl; but she got settled at last, and stitched away as if bent on beating her dumb friend.

Little Will's shadow went up to the nursery, and stopped before a basin of water. "Oh! ah! ain't this drefful?" cried Will, with a shiver; for he knew he'd got to have his face washed, because he wouldn't have it done properly when he got up, but ran away. Now, Will was a good child; but this one thing was his great trouble, and sometimes he couldn't bear it. Jane was so rough. She let soap get in his eyes, and water run down his neck, and she pinched his nose when she wiped him, and brushed his hair so hard that really it *was* dreadful; and even a bigger boy would have found it hard to bear. He shivered and sighed: but Jane came in; and, when he saw that the shadow stood still and took the scrubbing like a little hero, he tried to do the same, and succeeded so well that Jane actually patted his head and called him "a deary;" which was something new, for old Nurse Jane was always very busy and rather cross.

Feeling that nothing worse could possibly happen to him, Will ran after his shadow, as it flitted away into the barn, and began to feed the chickens.

"There, now! I forgetted all about my chickeys, and the shadow 'membered 'em; and I'm glad of it," said Will, scattering dabs of meal and water to the chirping, downy little creatures who pecked and fluttered at his feet. Little Shadow hunted for eggs, drove the turkeys out of the garden, and picked a basket of chips: then it went to play with Sammy, a neighbor's child; for, being a small shadow, it hadn't many jobs to do, and plenty of active play was good for it.

Sammy was a rough little boy and rather selfish: so, when they played ball, he wanted to throw all the time; and, when Will objected, he grew angry and struck him. The blow didn't hurt Will's cheek much, but it did his little feelings; and he lifted his hand to strike back, when he saw his shadow go and kiss Sammy's shadow. All his anger was gone in a minute, and he put his arm round Sammy's neck and kissed him. This kiss for a blow made him so ashamed that he began to cry, and couldn't be comforted till he had given Will his best marble and a ride on his pony.

About an hour before dinner, the three shadows and the children met in the garden, and had a grand game of play, after they had told each other what they had been doing since they parted. Now, the shadows didn't forget baby even then, but got out the wagon, and Miss Baby, all fresh from her nap, sat among her pillows like a queen, while Ned was horse, Polly footman, and Will driver; and in this way she travelled all round the garden and barn, up the lane and down to the brook, where she was much delighted with the water sparkling along and the fine splash of the stones they threw in.

When the dinner-bell rang, mamma saw four clean, rosy faces and four smooth heads at the table; for the shadow-children made themselves neat, without being told. Every one was merry and hungry and good-natured. Even poor baby forgot her teeth, and played a regular rub-a-dub with her spoon on her mug, and tried to tell about the fine things she saw on her drive. The children said nothing about the new play, and no one observed the queer actions of their shadows but themselves. They saw that there was no gobbling, or stretching over, or spilling of things, among the shadows; but that they waited to be helped, served others first, and ate tidily, which was a great improvement upon the usual state of things.

It was Saturday afternoon: the day was fine, and mamma told them they could go for a holiday frolic in the woods. "Don't go to the pond, and be home early," she said.

"Yes, mamma; we'll remember," they answered, as they scampered away to get ready.

"We shall go through the village, and Mary King will be looking out; so I shall wear my best hat. Mamma won't see me, if I slip down the back way; and I do so want Mary to know that my hat is prettier than hers," said Polly, up in her little room.

Now Polly was rather vain, and liked to prink; so she got out the new hat, and spent some time in smoothing her braids and putting on her blue ribbons. But when all was ready, and the boys getting impatient, she found her shadow, with a sun bonnet on, standing by the door, as if to prevent her going out.

"You tiresome thing! do you mean that I mustn't wear my hat, but that old bonnet?" asked Polly.

The shadow nodded and beckoned, and patted its head, as if it was all right.

"I wish I hadn't promised to do as you do; then I could do as I like, and not make a fright of myself," said Polly, rather sulkily, as she put away the hat, and tied on the old bonnet with a jerk.

Once out in the lovely sunshine, she soon forgot the little disappointment; and, as they didn't go through the village, but by a green lane, where she found some big blackberries, she was quite contented. Polly had a basket to hold fruit or flowers, Ned his jackknife, and Will a long stick on which he rode, fancying that this sort of horse would help his short legs along; so they picked, whittled, and trotted their way to the wood, finding all manner of interesting things on the road.

The wood was full of pleasant sights and sounds; for wild roses bloomed all along the path, ferns and scarlet berries filled the little dells, squirrels chattered, birds sang, and pines whispered musically overhead.

"I'm going to stop here and rest, and make a wreath of these pretty wild roses for baby: it's her birthday, and it will please mamma," said Polly, sitting down on a mound of moss, with a lapful of flowers.

"I'm going to cut a fishing-pole, and will be back in a minute." And Ned went crashing into the thickest part of the wood.

"I shall see where that rabbit went to, and maybe I'll find some berries," said Will, trotting down the path the wild rabbit had gone.

The sound of the boys' steps died away, and Polly was wondering how it would seem to live all alone in the wood, when a little girl came trudging by, with a great pail of berries on her arm. She was a poor child: her feet were bare, her gown was ragged, she wore an old shawl over her head, and walked as if lame. Polly sat behind the ferns, and the child did not see her till Polly called out. The sudden sound startled her; and she dropped her pail, spilling the berries all over the path. The little girl began to cry, and Polly to laugh, saying, in a scornful tone,—

"How silly to cry for a few berries!"

"I've been all day picking 'em," said the girl; "and I'm so tired and hungry; 'cause I didn't dare to go home till my pail was full,—mother scolds if I do,—and now they're all spoilt. Oh, dear! dear me!" And she cried so hard that great tears fell on the moss.

Polly was sorry now, and sat looking at her till she saw her shadow down on its knees, picking up the berries; then it seemed to fold its little handkerchief round the girl's bruised foot, and give her something from its pocket. Polly jumped up and imitated the kind shadow, even to giving the great piece of gingerbread she had brought for fear she should be hungry.

"Take this," she said gently. "I'm sorry I frightened you. Here are the berries all picked up, and none the worse for falling in the grass. If you'll take them to the white house on the hill, my mamma will buy them, and then your mother won't scold you."

"Oh, thank you, miss! It's ever so good. I'll take the berries to your mother, and bring her more whenever she likes," said the child gratefully, as she walked away munching the gingerbread, and smiling till there were little rainbows in her tears.

Meanwhile Ned had poked about in the bushes, looking for a good pole. Presently he saw a willow down by the pond, and thought that would give him a nice, smooth pole. He forgot his promise, and down he went to the pond; where he cut his stick, and was whittling the end, when he saw a boat by the shore. It was untied, and oars lay in it, as if waiting for some one to come and row out.

"I'll just take a little pull across, and get those cardinal-flowers for Polly," he said; and went to the boat.

He got in, and was about to push off, when he saw his shadow standing on the shore.

"Don't be a fool; get in, and come along," he said to it, remembering his promise now, but deciding to break it, and ask pardon afterwards.

But the shadow shook its head; pointed to the swift stream that ran between the banks, the rocks and mud on the opposite side, and the leaky boat itself.

"I ain't afraid: mamma won't mind, if I tell her I'm sorry; and it will be such fun to row alone. Be a good fellow, and let me go," said Ned, beckoning.

But the shadow would not stir, and Ned was obliged to mind. He did so very reluctantly, and scolded the shadow well as he went back to Polly; though all the time he felt he was doing right, and knew he should be glad afterwards.

Will trotted after the rabbit, but didn't find it; he found a bird's-nest instead with four little birds in it. He had an empty cage at home, and longed for something to put in it; for kittens didn't like it, and caterpillars and beetlebugs got away. He chose the biggest bird, and, holding him carefully, walked away to find Polly. The poor mother-bird chirped and fluttered in great distress; but Will kept on till his little shadow came before him, and tried to make him turn back.

"No, no, I want him," said Will. "I won't hurt him, and his mother has three left: she won't mind if I take one."

Here the mother-bird chirped so loud it was impossible to help seeing that she *did* care very much; and the shadow stamped its foot and waved its hand, as if ordering the young robber to carry back the baby-bird. Will stood still, and thought a minute; but his little heart was a very kind one, and he soon turned about, saying pleasantly,—

"Yes, it *is* naughty, and I won't do it. I'll ask mamma to get me a canary, and will let this birdie stay with his brothers."

The shadow patted him on the shoulder, and seemed to be delighted as Will put the bird in the nest and walked on, feeling much happier than if he had kept it. A bush of purple berries grew by the path, and Will stopped to pick some. He didn't know what they were, and mamma had often told him never to eat strange things. But they smelt so good, and looked so nice, he couldn't resist, and lifted one to his mouth, when little shadow motioned for him to stop.

"Oh, dear! you don't let me do anything I want to," sighed Will. "I shall ask Polly if I tarn't eat these; and, if she says I may, I shall, so now."

He ran off to ask Polly; but she said they were poisonous, and begged him to throw them away.

"Good little shadow, to keep me safe!" cried Will. "I like you; and I'll mind better next time, 'cause you are always right."

The shadow seemed to like this, and bobbed about so comically it made Will laugh till his eyes were full of tears. Ned came back, and they went on, having grand times in the wood. They found plenty of berries to fill the basket; they swung down on slender birches, and got rolls of white bark for canoes; they saw all sorts of wild-wood insects and birds; and frolicked till they were tired. As they crossed a field, a cow suddenly put down her head and ran at them, as if she was afraid they meant to hurt her calf. All turned, and ran as fast as they could toward the wall; but poor Will in his fright tumbled down, and lay screaming. Ned and Polly had reached the wall, and, looking back, saw that their shadows had not followed. Ned's stood before Will, brandishing his pole; and Polly's was flapping a shadowy sun-bonnet with all its might. As soon as they saw that, back they went,—Ned to threaten till he broke his pole, and Polly to flap till the strings came off. As if anxious to do its part, the bonnet flew up in the air, and coming down lit on the cross cow's head; which so astonished her that she ran away as hard as she could pelt.

"Wasn't that funny?" said Will, when they had tumbled over the wall, and lay laughing in the grass on the safe side.

"I'm glad I wore the old bonnet; for I suppose my best hat would have gone just the same," said Polly thankfully.

"The calf don't know its own mother with that thing on," laughed Ned.

"How brave and kind you were to come back and save me! I'd have been deaded if you hadn't," said Will, looking at his brother and sister with his little face full of grateful admiration.

They turned towards home after this flurry, feeling quite like heroes. When they came to the corner where two roads met, Ned proposed they should take the river-road; for, though the longest, it was much the pleasantest.

"We shan't be home at supper-time," said Polly. "You won't be able to do your jobs, Ned, nor I mine, and Will's chickens will have to go to bed hungry."

"Never mind: it's a holiday, so let's enjoy it, and no bother," answered Ned.

"We promised mamma we'd come home early," said Will.

They stood looking at the two roads,—one sandy, hot, and hilly; the other green and cool and level, along the river-side. They all chose the pleasant path, and walked on till Ned cried out, "Why, where are our shadows?"

They looked behind, before, and on either side; but nowhere could they see them.

"They were with us at the corner," said Will.

"Let's run back, and try to find them," said Polly.

"No, let 'em go: I'm tired of minding mine, and don't care if I never see it again," said Ned.

"Don't say so; for I remember hearing about a man who sold his shadow, and then got into lots of trouble because he had none. We promised to follow them, and we must," said Polly.

"I wish," began Ned in a pet; but Polly clapped her hand over his mouth, saying,—

"Pray, don't wish now; for it may come to pass as the man's wish in the fairy tale did, and the black pudding flew up and stuck tight to his wife's nose."

This made Ned laugh, and they all turned back to the corner. Looking up the hilly road, they saw the three shadows trudging along, as if bent on getting home in good time. Without saying a word, the children followed; and, when they got to the garden-gate, they all said at once,—

"Aren't you glad you came?"

Under the elm-tree stood a pretty tea-table, covered with bread and butter, custards, and berries, and in the middle a fine cake with sugar-roses on the top; and mamma and baby, all nicely dressed, were waiting to welcome them to the birth-day feast. Polly crowned the little queen, Ned gave her a willow whistle he had made, and Will some pretty, bright pebbles he had found; and Miss Baby was as happy as a bird, with her treasures.

A pleasant supper-time; then the small duties for each one; and then the go-to-bed frolic. The nursery was a big room, and in the evening a bright wood-fire always burned there for baby. Mamma sat before it softly, rubbing baby's little rosy limbs before she went to bed, singing and telling stories meanwhile to the three children who pranced about in their long nightgowns. This evening they had a gay time; for the shadows amused them by all sorts of antics, and kept them laughing till they were tired. As they sat resting on the big sofa, they heard a soft, sweet voice singing. It wasn't mamma; for she was only talking to baby, and this voice sang a real song. Presently they saw mamma's shadow on the wall, and found it was the shadow-mother singing to the shadow-children. They listened intently, and this is what they heard:—

> "Little shadows, little shadows,
>    Dancing on the chamber wall,
> While I sit beside the hearthstone
>    Where the red flames rise and fall.
> Caps and nightgowns, caps and nightgowns,
>    My three antic shadows wear;
> And no sound they make in playing,
>    For the six small feet are bare.
>
> 'Dancing gayly, dancing gayly,
>    To and fro all together,
> Like a family of daisies
>    Blown about in windy weather;
> Nimble fairies, nimble fairies,
>    Playing pranks in the warm glow,
> While I sing the nursery ditties
>    Childish phantoms love and know.
>
> "Now what happens, now what happens?
>    One small shadow's tumbled down:
> I can see it on the carpet,
>    Softly rubbing its hurt crown.
> No one whimpers, no one whimpers;
>    A brave-hearted sprite is this:
> See! the others offer comfort
>    In a silent, shadowy kiss.
>
> "Hush! they're creeping; hush! they're creeping,
>    Up about my rocking-chair:
> I can feel their loving fingers
>    Clasp my neck and touch my hair.
> Little shadows, little shadows,
>    Take me captive, hold me tight,
> As they climb and cling and whisper,
>    'Mother dear, good night! good night!'"

# What the Swallows Did

A MAN LAY ON A PILE of new-made hay, in a great barn, looking up at the swallows who darted and twittered above him. He envied the cheerful little creatures; for he wasn't a happy man, though he had many friends, much money, and the beautiful gift of writing songs that everybody loved to sing. He had lost his wife and little child, and would not be comforted; but lived alone, and went about with such a gloomy face that no one liked to speak to him. He took no notice of friends and neighbors; neither used his money for himself nor others; found no beauty in the world, no happiness anywhere; and wrote such sad songs it made one's heart ache to sing them.

As he lay alone on the sweet-smelling hay, with the afternoon sunshine streaming in, and the busy birds chirping overhead, he said sadly to himself,—

"Happy swallows, I wish I was one of you; for you have no pains nor sorrows, and your cares are very light. All summer you live gayly together; and, when winter comes, you fly away to the lovely South, unseparated still."

"Neighbors, do you hear what that lazy creature down there is saying?" cried a swallow, peeping over the edge of her nest, and addressing several others who sat on a beam near by.

"We hear, Mrs. Skim; and quite agree with you that he knows very little about us and our affairs," answered one of the swallows with a shrill chirp, like a scornful laugh. "We work harder than he does any day. Did he build his own house, I should like to know? Does he get his daily bread for himself? How many of his neighbors does he help? How much of the world does he see, and who is the happier for his being alive?"

"Cares indeed!" cried another: "I wish he'd undertake to feed and teach my brood. Much he knows about the anxieties of a parent." And the little mother bustled away to get supper for the young ones, whose bills were always gaping wide.

"Sorrows we have, too," softly said the fourth swallow. "He would not envy *me*, if he knew how my nest fell, and all my children were killed; how my dear husband was shot, and my old mother died of fatigue on our spring journey from the South."

"Dear Neighbor Dart, he *would* envy you, if he knew how patiently you bear your troubles; how tenderly you help us with our little ones; how cheerfully you serve your friends; how faithfully you love your lost mate; and how trustfully you wait to meet him again in a lovelier country than the South."

As Skim spoke, she leaned down from her nest to kiss her neighbor; and, as the little beaks met, the other birds gave a grateful and approving murmur, for Neighbor Dart was much beloved by all the inhabitants of Twittertown.

"I, for my part, don't envy *him*," said Gossip Wing, who was fond of speaking her mind. "Men and women call themselves superior beings; but, upon my word, I think they are vastly inferior to us. Now, look at that man, and see how he wastes his life. There never was any one with a better chance for doing good, and being happy; and yet he mopes and dawdles his time away most shamefully."

"Ah! he has had a great sorrow, and it is hard to be gay with a heavy heart, an empty home; so don't be too severe, Sister Wing." And the white tie of the little widow's cap was stirred by a long sigh as Mrs. Dart glanced up at the nook where her nest once stood.

"No, my dear, I won't; but really I do get out of patience when I see so much real misery which that man might help, if he'd only forget himself a little. It's my opinion he'd be much happier than he now is, wandering about with a dismal face and a sour temper."

"I quite agree with you; and I dare say he'd thank any one for telling him how he may find comfort. Poor soul! I wish he could understand me; for I sympathize with him, and would gladly help him if I could."

And, as she spoke, kind-hearted Widow Dart skimmed by him with a friendly chirp, which did comfort him; for, being a poet, he *could* understand them, and lay listening, well pleased while the little gossips chattered on together.

"I am so tied at home just now, that I know nothing of what is going on, except the bits of news Skim brings me; so I enjoy your chat immensely. I'm interested in your views on this subject, and beg you'll tell me what you'd have that man do to better himself," said Mrs. Skim, settling herself on her eggs with an attentive air.

"Well, my dear, I'll tell you; for I've seen a deal of the world, and any one is welcome to my experience," replied Mrs. Wing, in an important manner; for she was proud of her "views," and very fond of talking. "In my daily flights about the place, I see a great deal of poverty and trouble, and often wish I could lend a hand. Now, this man has plenty of money and time; and he might do more good than I can tell, if he'd only set about it. Because he is what they call a poet is no reason he should go moaning up and down, as if he had nothing to do but make songs. We sing, but we work also; and are wise enough to see the necessity of both, thank goodness!"

"Yes, indeed, we do," cried all the birds in a chorus; for several more had stopped to hear what was going on.

"Now, what I say is this," continued Mrs. Wing impressively. "If I were that man, I'd make myself useful at once. There is poor little Will getting more and more lame every day, because his mother can't send him where he can be cured. A trifle of that man's money would do it, and he ought to give it. Old Father Winter is half starved, alone there in his miserable hovel; and no one thinks of the good old man. Why don't that lazy creature take him home, and care for him, the little while he has to live? Pretty Nell is working day and night, to support her father, and is too proud to ask help, though her health and courage are going fast. The man might make her's the gayest heart alive, by a little help. There in a lonely garret lives a young man studying his life away, longing for books and a teacher. The man has a library full, and might keep the poor boy from despair by a little help and a friendly word. He mourns for his own lost baby: I advise him to adopt the orphan whom nobody will own, and who lies wailing all day untended on the poor-house floor. Yes: if he wants to forget sorrow and find peace, let him fill his empty heart and home with such as these, and life won't seem dark to him any more."

"Dear me! how well you express yourself, Mrs. Wing! it's quite a pleasure to hear you; and I heartily wish some persons could hear you, it would do 'em a deal of good," said Mrs. Skim; while her husband gave an approving nod as he dived off the beam, and vanished through the open doors.

"I know it would comfort that man to do these things; for I have tried the same cure in my small way, and found great satisfaction in it," began little Madam Dart, in her soft voice; but Mrs. Wing broke in, saying with a pious expression of countenance:—

"I flew into church one day, and sat on the organ enjoying the music; for every one was singing, and I joined in, though I didn't know the air. Opposite me were two great tablets with golden letters on them. I can read a little, thanks to my friend, the learned raven; and so I spelt out some of the words. One was, 'Love thy neighbor;' and as I sat there, looking down on the people, I wondered how they could see those words week after week, and yet pay so little heed to them. Goodness knows, *I* don't consider myself a perfect bird; far from it; for I know I am a poor, erring fowl; but I believe I may say I *do* love my neighbor, though I *am* 'an inferior creature.'" And Mrs. Wing bridled up, as if she resented the phrase immensely.

"Indeed you do, gossip," cried Dart and Skim; for Wing was an excellent bird, in spite of the good opinion she had of herself.

"Thank you: well, then, such being the known fact, I may give advice on the subject as one having authority; and, if it were possible, I'd give that man a bit of my mind."

"You have, madam, you have; and I shall not forget it. Thank you, neighbors, and good night," said the man, as he left the barn, with the first smile on his face which it had worn for many days.

"Mercy on us! I do believe the creature heard every thing we said," cried Mrs. Wing, nearly tumbling off the beam, in her surprise.

"He certainly did; so I'm glad I was guarded in my remarks," replied Mrs. Skim, laughing at her neighbor's dismay.

"Dear me! dear me! what did I say?" cried Mrs. Wing, in a great twitter.

"You spoke with more than your usual bluntness, and some of your expressions were rather strong, I must confess; but I don't think any harm will come of it. We are of too little consequence for our criticisms or opinions to annoy him," said Mrs. Dart consolingly.

"I don't know that, ma'am," returned Mrs. Wing, sharply; for she was much ruffled and out of temper. "A cat may look at a king; and a bird may teach a man, if the bird is the wisest. He may destroy my nest, and take my life; but I feel that I have done my duty, and shall meet affliction with a firmness which will be an example to that indolent, ungrateful man."

In spite of her boasted firmness, Mrs. Wing dropped her voice, and peeped over the beam, to be sure the man was gone before she called him names; and then flew away, to discover what he meant to do about it.

For several days, there was much excitement in Twittertown; for news of what had happened flew from nest to nest, and every bird was anxious to know what revenge the man would take for the impertinent remarks which had been made about him.

Mrs. Wing was in a dreadful state of mind, expecting an assault, and the destruction of her entire family. Every one blamed her. Her husband lectured; the young birds chirped, "Chatterbox, chatterbox," as she passed; and her best friends were a little cool. All this made her very meek for a time; and she scarcely opened her bill, except to eat.

A guard was set day and night, to see if any danger approached; and a row of swallows might be seen on the ridgepole at all hours. If any one entered the barn, dozens of little black heads peeped cautiously over the edges of the nests, and there was much flying to and fro with reports and rumors; for all the birds in the town soon knew that something had happened.

The day after the imprudent conversation, a chimney-swallow came to call on Mrs. Wing; and, the moment she was seated on the beam, she began:—

"My dear creature, I feel for you in your trying position,—indeed I do, and came over at once to warn you of your danger."

"Mercy on us! what is coming?" cried Mrs. Wing, covering her brood with trembling wings, and looking quite wild with alarm.

"Be calm, my friend, and bear with firmness the consequences of your folly," replied Mrs. Sooty-back, who didn't like Mrs. Wing, because she prided herself on her family, and rather looked down on chimney-swallows. "You know, ma'am, I live at the great house, and am in the way of seeing and hearing all that goes on there. No fire is lit in the study now; but my landlord still sits on the hearth, and I can overhear every word he says. Last evening, after my darlings were asleep, and my husband gone out, I went down and sat on the andiron, as I often do; for the fireplace is full of oak boughs, and I can peep out unseen. My landlord sat there, looking a trifle more cheerful than usual, and I heard him say, in a very decided tone,—

"'I'll catch them, one and all, and keep them here; that is better than pulling the place down, as I planned at first. Those swallows little know what they have done; but I'll show them I don't forget.'"

On hearing this a general wail arose, and Mrs. Wing fainted entirely away. Madam Sooty-back was quite satisfied with the effect she had produced, and departed, saying loftily,—

"I'm sorry for you, Mrs. Wing, and forgive your rude speech about my being related to chimney-sweeps. One can't expect good manners from persons brought up in mud houses, and entirely shut out from good society. If I hear any thing more, I'll let you know."

Away she flew; and poor Mrs. Wing would have had another fit, if they hadn't tickled her with a feather, and fanned her so violently that she was nearly blown off her nest by the breeze they raised.

"What shall we do?" she cried.

"Nothing, but wait. I dare say, Mrs. Sooty-back is mistaken; at any rate, we can't get away without leaving our children, for they can't fly yet. Let us wait, and see what happens. If the worst comes, we shall have done our duty, and will all die together."

As no one could suggest any thing better, Mrs. Dart's advice was taken, and they waited. On the afternoon of the same day, Dr. Banks, a sand-swallow, who lived in a subterranean village over by the great sand-bank, looked in to see Mrs. Wing, and cheered her by the following bit of news:—

"The man was down at the poor-house to-day, and took away little Nan, the orphan baby. I saw him carry her to Will's mother, and heard him ask her to take care of it for a time. He paid her well, and she seemed glad to do it; for Will needs help, and now he can have it. An excellent arrangement, I think. Bless me, ma'am! what's the matter? Your pulse is altogether too fast, and you look feverish."

No wonder the doctor looked surprised; for Mrs. Wing suddenly gave a skip, and flapped her wings, with a shrill chirp, exclaiming, as she looked about her triumphantly,—

"Now, who was right? Who has done good, not harm, by what you call 'gossip'? Who has been a martyr, and patiently borne all kinds of blame, injustice, and disrespect? Yes, indeed! the man saw the sense of my words; he took my advice; he will show his gratitude by some good turn yet; and, if half a dozen poor souls are helped, it will be my doing, and mine alone."

Here she had to stop for breath; and her neighbors all looked at one another, feeling undecided whether to own they were wrong, or to put Mrs. Wing down. Every one twittered and chirped, and made a great noise; but no one would give up, and all went to roost in a great state of uncertainty. But, the next day, it became evident that Mrs. Wing was right; for Major Bumble-bee came buzzing in to tell them that old Daddy Winter's hut was empty, and his white head had been seen in the sunny porch of the great house.

After this, the swallows gave in; and, as no harm came to them, they had a jubilee in honor of the occasion. Mrs. Wing was president, and received a vote of thanks for the good she had done, and the credit she had bestowed upon the town by her wisdom and courage. She was much elated by all this; but her fright had been of service, and she bore her honors more meekly than one would have supposed. To be sure, she cut Mrs. Sooty-back when they met; assumed an injured air, when some of her neighbors passed her; and said, "I told you so," a dozen times a day to her husband, who got so many curtain lectures that he took to sleeping on the highest rafter, pretending that the children's noise disturbed him.

All sorts of charming things happened after that, and such a fine summer never was known before; for not only did the birds rejoice, but people also. A good spirit seemed to haunt the town, leaving help and happiness wherever it passed. Some unseen hand scattered crumbs over the barn-floor, and left food at many doors. No dog or boy or gun marred the tranquillity of the birds, insects, and flowers who lived on the great estate. No want, care, or suffering, that love or money could prevent, befell the poor folk whose cottages stood near the old house. Sunshine and peace seemed to reign there; for its gloomy master was a changed man now, and the happiness he earned for himself, by giving it to others, flowed out in beautiful, blithe songs, and went singing away into the world, making him friends, and bringing him honor in high places as well as low.

He did not forget the wife and little child whom he had loved so well; but he mourned no longer, for cheerful daisies grew above their graves, and he knew that he should meet them in the lovely land where death can never come. So, while he waited for that happy time to come, he made his life a cheery song,—as every one may do, if they will; and went about dropping kind words and deeds as silently and sweetly as the sky drops sunshine and dew. Every one was his friend, but his favorites were the swallows. Every day he went to see them, carrying grain and crumbs, hearing their chat, sharing their joys and sorrows, and never tiring of their small friendship; for to them, he thought, he owed all the content now his.

When autumn leaves were red, and autumn winds blew cold, the inhabitants of Twittertown prepared for their journey to the South. They lingered longer than usual this year, feeling sorry to leave their friend. But the fields were bare, the frosts began to pinch, and the young ones longed to see the world; so they must go. The day they started, the whole flock flew to the great house, to say good-by. Some dived and darted round and round it, some hopped to and fro on the sere lawn, some perched on the chimney-tops, and some clung to the window ledges; all twittering a loving farewell.

Chirp, Dart, and Wing peeped everywhere, and everywhere found something to rejoice over. In a cosey room, by a bright fire, sat Daddy Winter and Nell's old father, telling stories of their youth, and basking in the comfortable warmth. In the study, surrounded by the books he loved, was the poor young man, happy as a king now, and learning many things which no book could teach him; for he had found a friend. Then, down below was Will's mother, working like a bee; for she was housekeeper, and enjoyed her tasks as much as any mother-bird enjoys filling the little mouths of her brood. Close by was pretty Nell, prettier than ever now; for her heavy care was gone, and she sung as she sewed, thinking of the old father, whom nothing could trouble any more.

But the pleasantest sight the three gossips saw was the man with Baby Nan on his arm and Will at his side, playing in the once dreary nursery.

How they laughed and danced! for Will was up from his bed at last, and hopped nimbly on his crutches, knowing that soon even they would be unneeded. Little Nan was as plump and rosy as a baby should be, and babbled like a brook, as the man went to and fro, cradling her in his strong arms, feeling as if his own little daughter had come back when he heard the baby voice call him father.

"Ah, how sweet it is!" cried Mrs. Dart, glad to see that he had found comfort for his grief.

"Yes, indeed: it does one's heart good to see such a happy family," added Mrs. Skim, who was a very motherly bird.

"I don't wish to boast; but I *will* say that I am satisfied with my summer's work, and go South feeling that I leave an enviable reputation behind me." And Mrs. Wing plumed herself with an air of immense importance, as she nodded and bridled from her perch on the window-sill.

The man saw the three, and hastened to feed them for the last time, knowing that they were about to go. Gratefully they ate, and chirped their thanks; and then, as they flew away, the little gossips heard their friend singing his good-by:—

> "Swallow, swallow, neighbor swallow,
>     Starting on your autumn flight,
> Pause a moment at my window,
>     Twitter softly your good-night;
> For the summer days are over,
>     All your duties are well done,
> And the happy homes you builded
>     Have grown empty, one by one.
> Swallow, swallow, neighbor swallow,
>     Are you ready for your flight?
> Are all the feather cloaks completed?
>     Are the little caps all right?
> Are the young wings strong and steady
>     For the journey through the sky?
> Come again in early spring-time;
>     And till then, good-by, good-by!"

# Little Gulliver

UP IN THE LIGHT-HOUSE TOWER lived Davy, with Old Dan the keeper. Most little boys would have found it very lonely; but Davy had three friends, and was as happy as the day was long. One of Davy's friends was the great lamp, which was lit at sunset, and burnt all night, to guide the ships into the harbor. To Dan it was only a lamp; but to the boy it seemed a living thing, and he loved and tended it faithfully. Every day he helped Dan clear the big wick, polish the brass-work, and wash the glass lantern which protected the flame. Every evening he went up to see it lighted, and always fell asleep, thinking, "No matter how dark or wild the night, my good Shine will save the ships that pass, and burn till morning."

Davy's second friend was Nep, the Newfoundland, who was washed ashore from a wreck, and had never left the island since. Nep was rough and big, but had such a loyal and loving heart that no one could look in his soft brown eyes and not trust him. He followed Davy's steps all day, slept at his feet all night, and more than once had saved his life when Davy fell among the rocks, or got caught by the rising tide.

But the dearest friend of all was a sea-gull. Davy found him, with a broken wing, and nursed him carefully till he was well; then let him go, though he was very fond of "Little Gulliver," as he called him in fun. But the bird never forgot the boy, and came daily to talk with him, telling all manner of wild stories about his wanderings by land and sea, and whiling away many an hour that otherwise would have been very lonely.

Old Dan was Davy's uncle,—a grim, gray man, who said little, did his work faithfully, and was both father and mother to Davy, who had no parents, and no friends beyond the island. That was his world; and he led a quiet life among his playfellows,—the winds and waves. He seldom went to the main land, three miles away; for he was happier at home. He watched the sea-anemones open below the water, looking like fairy-plants, brilliant and strange. He found curious and pretty shells, and sometimes more valuable treasures, washed up from some wreck. He saw little yellow crabs, ugly lobsters, and queer horse-shoes with their stiff tails. Sometimes a whale or a shark swam by, and often sleek black seals came up to bask on the warm rocks. He gathered lovely sea-weeds of all kinds, from tiny red cobwebs to great scalloped leaves of kelp, longer than himself. He heard the waves dash and roar unceasingly; the winds howl or sigh over the island; and the gulls scream shrilly as they dipped and dived, or sailed away to follow the ships that came and went from all parts of the world.

With Nep and Gulliver he roamed about his small kingdom, never tired of its wonders; or, if storms raged, he sat up in the tower, safe and dry, watching the tumult of sea and sky. Often in long winter nights he lay awake, listening to the wind and rain, that made the tower rock with their violence; but he never was afraid, for Nep nestled at his feet, Dan sat close by, and overhead the great lamp shone far out into the night, to cheer and guide all wanderers on the sea.

Close by the tower hung the fog-bell, which, being wound up, would ring all night, warningly. One day Dan found that something among the chains was broken; and, having vainly tried to mend it, he decided to go to the town, and get what was needed. He went once a week, usually, and left Davy behind; for in the daytime there was nothing to do, and the boy was not afraid to stay.

"A heavy fog is blowing up: we shall want the bell tonight, and I must be off at once. I shall be back before dark, of course; so take care of yourself, boy," said Dan.

Away went the little boat; and the fog shut down over it, as if a misty wall had parted Davy from his uncle. As it was dull weather, he sat and read for an hour or two; then fell asleep, and forgot everything till Nep's cold nose on his hand waked him up. It was nearly dark; and, hoping to find Dan had come, he ran down to the landing-place. But no boat was there, and the fog was thicker than ever.

Dan never had been gone so long before, and Davy was afraid something had happened to him. For a few minutes he was in great trouble; then he cheered up, and took courage.

"It is sunset by the clock; so I'll light the lamp, and, if Dan is lost in the fog, it will guide him home," said Davy.

Up he went, and soon the great star shone out above the black-topped light-house, glimmering through the fog, as if eager to be seen. Davy had his supper, but no Dan came. He waited hour after hour, and waited all in vain. The fog thickened, till the lamp was hardly seen; and no bell rung to warn the ships of the dangerous rocks. Poor Davy could not sleep, but all night long wandered from the tower to the door, watching, calling, and wondering; but Dan did not come.

At sunrise he put out the light, and, having trimmed it for the next night, ate a little breakfast, and roved about the island hoping to see some sign of Dan. The sun drew up the fog at last; and he could see the blue bay, the distant town, and a few fishing-boats going out to sea. But nowhere was the island-boat with gray Old Dan in it; and Davy's heart grew heavier and heavier, as the day passed, and still no one came. In the afternoon Gulliver appeared: to him Davy told his trouble, and the three friends took counsel together.

"There is no other boat; and I couldn't row so far, if there was: so I can't go to find Dan," said David sorrowfully.

"I'd gladly swim to town, if I could; but it's impossible to do it, with wind and tide against me. I've howled all day, hoping some one would hear me; but no one does, and I'm discouraged," said Nep, with an anxious expression.

"I can do something for you; and I will, with all my heart. I'll fly to town, if I dont see him in the bay, and try to learn what has become of Dan. Then I'll come and tell you, and we will see what is to be done next. Cheer up, Davy dear: I'll bring you tidings, if any can be had." With these cheerful words, away sailed Gulliver, leaving Nep and his master to watch and wait again.

The wind blew hard, and the broken wing was not quite well yet, else Gulliver would have been able to steer clear of a boat that came swiftly by. A sudden gust drove the gull so violently against the sail that he dropped breathless into the boat; and a little girl caught him, before he could recover himself.

"Oh, what a lovely bird! See his black cap, his white breast, dove-colored wings, red legs and bill, and soft bright eyes. I wanted a gull; and I'll keep this one, for I don't think he is much hurt."

Poor Gulliver struggled, pecked, and screamed; but little Dora held him fast, and shut him in a basket till they reached the shore. Then she put him in a lobster-pot,—a large wooden thing, something like a cage,—and left him on the lawn, where he could catch glimpses of the sea, and watch the light-house tower, as he sat alone in this dreadful prison. If Dora had known the truth, she would have let him go, and done her best to help him; but she could not understand his speech, as Davy did, for very few people have the power of talking with birds, beasts, insects, and plants. To her, his prayers and cries were only harsh screams; and, when he sat silent, with drooping head and ruffled feathers, she thought he was sleepy: but he was mourning for Davy, and wondering what his little friend would do.

For three long days and nights he was a prisoner, and suffered much. The house was full of happy people, but no one took pity upon him. Ladies and gentlemen talked learnedly about him; boys poked and pulled him; little girls admired him, and begged his wings for their hats, if he died. Cats prowled about his cage; dogs barked at him; hens cackled over him; and a shrill canary jeered at him from the pretty pagoda in which it hung, high above danger. In the evening there was music; and the poor bird's heart ached as the sweet sounds came to him, reminding him of the airier melodies he loved. Through the stillness of the night, he heard the waves break on the shore; the wind came singing up from the sea; the moon shone kindly on him, and he saw the water-fairies dancing on the sand. But for three days no one spoke a friendly word to him, and he pined away with a broken heart.

On the fourth night, when all was quiet, little Gulliver saw a black shadow steal across the lawn, and heard a soft voice say to him,—

"Poor bird, you'll die, if yer stays here; so I'se gwine to let yer go. Specs little missy'll scold dreffle; but Moppet'll take de scoldin fer yer. Hi, dere! you is peart nuff now, kase you's in a hurry to go; but jes wait till I gits de knots out of de string dat ties de door, and den away you flies."

"But, dear, kind Moppet, wont you be hurt for doing this? Why do you care so much for me? I can only thank you, and fly away."

As Gulliver spoke, he looked up at the little black face bent over him, and saw tears in the child's sad eyes; but she smiled at him, and shook her fuzzy head, as she whispered kindly,—

"I dont want no tanks, birdie: I loves to let you go, kase you's a slave, like I was once; and it's a dreffle hard ting. I knows. I got away, and I means you shall. I'se watched you, deary, all dese days; and I tried to come 'fore, but dey didn't give me no chance."

"Do you live here? I never see you playing with the other children," said the gull, as Moppet's nimble fingers picked away at the knots.

"Yes: I lives here, and helps de cook. You didn't see me, kase I never plays; de chilen don't like me."

"Why not?" asked Gulliver, wondering.

"I'se black," said Moppet, with a sob.

"But that's silly in them," cried the bird, who had never heard of such a thing. "Color makes no difference: the peeps are gray, the seals black, and the crabs yellow; but we don't care, and are all friends. It is very unkind to treat you so. Haven't you any friends to love you, dear?"

"Nobody in de world keres fer me. Dey sold me way from my mammy when I was a baby, and I'se knocked roun eber since. De oder chilen has folks to lub an kere fer em, but Moppet's got no friends;" and here the black eyes grew so dim with tears that the poor child couldn't see that the last knot was out.

Gulliver saw it, and, pushing up the door, flew from his prison with a glad cry; and, hopping into Moppet's hand, looked into the little dark face with such grateful confidence that it cleared at once, and the brightest smile it had worn for months broke over it as the bird nestled its soft head against her cheek, saying gently,—

"I'm your friend, dear; I love you, and I never shall forget what you have done for me to-night. How can I thank you before I go?"

For a minute, Moppet could only hug the bird, and cry; for these were the first kind words she had heard for a long time, and they went straight to her lonely little heart.

"O my deary! I'se paid by dem words, and I don't want no tanks. Jes lub me, and come sometimes to see me ef you can, it's so hard livin' in dis yere place. I don't tink I'll bar it long. I wish I was a bird to fly away, or a oyster safe in de mud, and free to do as I'se a mind."

"I wish you could go and live with Davy on the island; he is so kind, so happy, and as free as the wind. Can't you get away, Moppet?" whispered Gulliver, longing to help this poor, friendless little soul. He told her all his story: and they agreed that he should fly at once to the island, and see if Dan was there; if not, he was to come back, and Moppet would try to get some one to help find him. When this was done, Davy and Dan were to take Moppet, if they could, and make her happy on the island. Full of hope and joy, Gulliver said good-by, and spread his wings; but, alas for the poor bird! he was too weak to fly. For three days he had hardly eaten any thing, had found no salt water to bathe in, and had sat moping in the cage till his strength was all gone.

"What shall I do? what shall I do?" he cried, fluttering his feeble wings, and running to and fro in despair.

"Hush, birdie, I'll take kere ob you till you's fit to fly. I knows a nice, quiet little cove down yonder, where no one goes; and dere you kin stay till you's better. I'll come and feed you, and you kin paddle, and rest, and try your wings, safe and free, honey."

As Moppet spoke, she took Gulliver in her arms, and stole away in the dim light, over the hill, down to the lonely spot where nothing went but the winds and waves, the gulls, and little Moppet, when hard words and blows made heart and body ache. Here she left the bird, and, with a loving "Good-night," crept home to her bed in the garret, feeling as rich as a queen, and much happier; for she had done a kind thing, and made a friend.

Next day, a great storm came: the wind blew a hurricane, the rain poured, and the sea thundered on the coast. If he had been well, Gulliver wouldn't have minded at all: but, being sick and sad, he spent an anxious day, sitting in a cranny of the rock, thinking of Davy and Moppet. It was so rough, even in the cove, that he could neither swim nor fly, so feeble was he; and could find no food but such trifles as he could pick up among the rocks. At nightfall the storm raged fiercer than ever, and he gave up seeing Moppet; for he was sure she wouldn't come through the pelting rain just to feed him. So he put his head under his wing, and tried to sleep; but he was so wet and weak, so hungry and anxious, no sleep came.

"What has happened to Davy alone on the island all this while? He will fall ill with loneliness and trouble; the lamp won't be lighted, the ships will be wrecked, and many people will suffer. O Dan, Dan, if we could only find you, how happy we should be!"

As Gulliver spoke, a voice cried through the darkness,—

"Is you dere, honey?" and Moppet came climbing over the rocks, with a basket full of such bits as she could get. "Poor birdie, is you starvin'? Here, jes go at dis, and joy yerself. Dere's fish and tings I tink you'd like. How is you now, dear?"

"Better, Moppet; but, it's so stormy, I can't get to Davy; and I worry about him," began Gulliver, pecking away at his supper: but he stopped suddenly, for a faint sound came up from below, as if some one called, "Help, help!"

"Hi! what's dat?" said Moppet, listening.

"Davy, Davy!" called the voice.

"It's Dan. Hurrah, we've found him!" and Gulliver dived off the rock so recklessly that he went splash into the water. But that didn't matter to him; and he paddled away, like a little steamer with all the engines in full blast. Down by the seaside, between two stones, lay Dan, so bruised and hurt he couldn't move, and so faint with hunger and pain he could hardly speak. As soon as Gulliver called, Moppet scrambled down, and fed the poor man with her scraps, brought him rain-water from a crevice near by, and bound up his wounded head with her little apron. Then Dan told them how his boat had been run down by a ship in the fog; how he was hurt, and cast ashore in the lonely cove; how he had lain there half dead, for no one heard his shouts, and he couldn't move; how the storm brought him back to life, when he was almost gone, and the sound of Moppet's voice told him help was near.

How glad they all were then! Moppet danced for joy; Gulliver screamed and flapped his wings; and Dan smiled, in spite of pain, to think he should see Davy again. He couldn't understand Gulliver; but Moppet told him all the story, and, when he heard it, he was more troubled for the boy than for himself.

"What will he do? He may get killed or scared, or try to come ashore. Is the lamp alight?" he cried, trying to move, and falling back with a moan of pain.

Gulliver flew up to the highest rock, and looked out across the dark sea. Yes, there it was,—the steady star shining through the storm, and saying plainly, "All is well."

"Thank heaven! if the lamp is burning, Davy is alive. Now, how shall I get to him?" said Dan.

"Never you fret, massa: Moppet'll see to dat. You jes lay still till I comes. Dere's folks in de house as'll tend to you, ef I tells em who and where you is."

Off she ran, and soon came back with help. Dan was taken to the house, and carefully tended; Moppet wasn't scolded for being out so late; and, in the flurry, no one thought of the gull. Next morning, the cage was found blown over, and every one fancied the bird had flown away. Dora was already tired of him; so he was soon forgotten by all but Moppet.

In the morning it was clear; and Gulliver flew gladly to the tower where Davy still watched and waited, with a pale face and heavy heart, for the three days had been very hard to bear, and, but for Nep and Shine, he would have lost his courage entirely. Gulliver flew straight into his bosom, and, sitting there, told his adventures; while Davy laughed and cried, and Nep stood by, wagging his tail for joy, while his eyes were full of sympathy. The three had a very happy hour together, and then came a boat to carry Davy ashore, while another keeper took charge of the light till Dan was well.

Nobody ever knew the best part of the story but Moppet, Davy, and Gulliver. Other people didn't dream that the boy's pet gull had any thing to do with the finding of the man, or the good fortune that came to Moppet. While Dan lay sick, she tended him, like a loving little daughter; and, when he was well, he took her for his own. He did not mind the black skin: he only saw the loneliness of the child, the tender heart, the innocent, white soul; and he was as glad to be a friend to her as if she had been as blithe and pretty as Dora.

It was a happy day when Dan and Davy, Moppet, Gulliver, and Nep sailed away to the island; for that was still to be their home, with stout young Ben to help.

The sun was setting; and they floated through waves as rosy as the rosy sky. A fresh wind filled the sail, and ruffled Gulliver's white breast as he sat on the mast-head crooning a cheery song to himself. Dan held the tiller, and Davy lay at his feet, with Nep bolt upright beside him; but the happiest face of all was Moppet's. Kneeling at the bow, she leaned forward, with her lips apart, her fuzzy hair blown back, and her eyes fixed on the island which was to be her home. Like a little black figurehead of Hope, she leaned and looked, as the boat flew on bearing her away from the old life into the new.

As the sun sunk, out shone the lamp with sudden brightness, as if the island bade them welcome. Dan furled the sail; and, drifting with the tide, they floated in, till the waves broke softly on the shore, and left them safe at home.

# The Whale's Story

FREDDY SAT THINKING on the seat under the trees. It was a wide, white seat, about four feet long, sloping from the sides to the middle, something like a swing; and was not only comfortable but curious, for it was made of a whale's bone. Freddy often sat there, and thought about it; for he was very much interested in it, and nobody could tell him any thing of it, except that it had been there a long time.

"Poor old whale, I wonder how you got here, where you came from, and if you were a good and happy creature while you lived," said Freddy, patting the old bone with his little hand.

It gave a great creak; and a sudden gust of air stirred the trees, as if some monster groaned and sighed. Then Freddy heard a strange voice, very loud, yet cracked and queer, as if some one tried to talk with a broken jaw.

"Freddy ahoy!" called the big voice. "I'll tell you all about it; for you are the only person who ever pitied me, or cared to know anything about me."

"Why, can you talk?" asked Freddy, very much astonished and a little frightened.

"Of course I can, for this is a part of my jaw-bone. I should talk better if my whole mouth was here; but I'm afraid my voice would then be so loud you wouldn't be able to hear it. I don't think any one but you would understand me, any way. It isn't every one that can, you know; but you are a thoughtful little chap, with a lively fancy as well as a kind heart, so you shall hear my story."

"Thank you, I should like it very much, if you would please to speak a little lower, and not sigh; for your voice almost stuns me, and your breath nearly blows me away," said Freddy.

"I'll try: but it's hard to suit my tone to such a mite, or to help groaning when I think of my sad fate; though I deserve it, perhaps," said the bone, more gently.

"Were you a naughty whale?" asked Freddy.

"I was proud, very proud, and foolish; and so I suffered for it. I dare say you know a good deal about us. I see you reading often, and you seem a sensible child."

"No: I haven't read about you yet, and I only know that you are the biggest fish there is," answered Freddy.

The bone creaked and shook, as if it was laughing, and said in a tone that showed it hadn't got over its pride yet,—

"You're wrong there, my dear: we are not fishes at all, though stupid mortals have called us so for a long time. We can't live without air; we have warm, red blood; and we don't lay eggs,—so we are *not* fishes. We certainly *are* the biggest creatures in the sea and out of it. Why, bless you! some of us are nearly a hundred feet long; our tails alone are fifteen or twenty feet wide; the biggest of us weigh five hundred thousand pounds, and have in them the fat, bone, and muscle of a thousand cattle. The lower jaw of one of my family made an arch large enough for a man on horseback to ride under easily, and my cousins of the sperm-family usually yield eighty barrels of oil."

"Gracious me, what monsters you are!" cried Freddy, taking a long breath, while his eyes got bigger and bigger as he listened.

"Ah! you may well say so; we are a very wonderful and interesting family. All our branches are famous in one way or another. Fin-backs, sperms, and rights are the largest; then come the norwhals, the dolphins, and porpoises,—which last, I dare say, you've seen."

"Yes: but tell me about the big ones, please. Which were you?" cried Freddy.

"I was a Right whale, from Greenland. The Sperms live in warm places; but to us the torrid zone is like a sea of fire, and we don't pass it. Our cousins do; and go to the East Indies by way of the North Pole, which is more than your famous Parrys and Franklins could do."

"I don't know about that; but I'd like to hear what you eat, and how you live, and why you came here," said Freddy, who thought the whale rather inclined to boast.

"Well, we haven't got any teeth,—our branch of the family; and we live on creatures so small, that you could only see them with a microscope. Yes, you may stare; but it's true, my dear. The roofs of our mouths are made of whalebone, in broad pieces from six to eight feet long, arranged one against the other; so they make an immense sieve. The tongue, which makes about five barrels of oil, lies below, like a cushion of white satin. When we want to feed, we rush through the water, which is full of the little things we eat, and catch them in our sieve, spirting the water through two holes in our heads. Then we collect the food with our tongue, and swallow it; for, though we are so big, our throats are small. We roam about in the ocean, leaping and floating, feeding and spouting, flying from our enemies, or fighting bravely to defend our young ones."

"Have you got any enemies? I shouldn't think you could have, you are so large," said Freddy.

"But we have, and many too,—three who attack us in the water, and several more that men use against us. The killer, the sword-fish, and the thrasher trouble us at home. The killer fastens to us, and won't be shaken off till he has worried us to death; the swordfish stabs us with his sword; and the thrasher whips us to death with his own slender, but strong and heavy, body. Then, men harpoon us, shoot or entrap us; and make us into oil and candles and seats, and stiffening for gowns and umbrellas," said the bone, in a tone of scorn.

Freddy laughed at the idea, and asked, "How about candles? I know about oil and seats and umbrellas; but I thought candles were made of wax."

"I can't say much on that point: I only know that, when a sperm whale is killed, they make oil out of the fat part as they do of ours; but the Sperms have a sort of cistern in their heads, full of stuff like cream, and rose-colored. They cut a hole in the skull, and dip it out; and sometimes get sixteen or twenty barrels. This is made into what you call spermaceti candles. *We* don't have any such nonsense about us; but the Sperms always were a light-headed set."

Here the bone laughed, in a cracked sort of roar, which sent Freddy flying off the seat on to the grass, where he stayed, laughing also, though he didn't see any joke.

"I beg your pardon, child. It isn't often that I laugh; for I've a heavy heart somewhere, and have known trouble enough to make me as sad as the sea is sometimes."

"Tell me about your troubles; I pity you very much, and like to hear you talk," said Freddy, kindly.

"Unfortunately we are very easily killed, in spite of our size; and have various afflictions besides death. We grow blind; our jaws are deformed sometimes; our tails, with which we swim, get hurt; and we have dyspepsia."

Freddy shouted at that; for he knew what dyspepsia was, because at the sea-side there were many sickly people who were always groaning about that disease.

"It's no laughing matter, I assure you," said the whale's bone. "We suffer a great deal, and get thin and weak and miserable. I've sometimes thought that's the reason we are blue."

"Perhaps, as you have no teeth, you don't chew your food enough, and so have dyspepsia, like an old gentleman I know," said Freddy.

"That's not the reason; my cousins, the Sperms, have teeth, and dyspepsia also."

"Are they blue?"

"No, black and white. But I was going to tell you my troubles. My father was harpooned when I was very young, and I remember how bravely he died. The Rights usually run away when they see a whaler coming; not from cowardice,—oh, dear no!—but discretion. The Sperms stay and fight, and are killed off very fast; for they are a very headstrong family. We fight when we can't help it; and my father died like a hero. They chased him five hours before they stuck him; he tried to get away, and dragged three or four boats and sixteen hundred fathoms of line from eight in the morning till four at night. Then they got out another line, and he towed the ship itself for more than an hour. There were fifteen harpoons in him: he chewed up a boat, pitched several men overboard, and damaged the vessel, before they killed him. Ah! he was a father to be proud of."

Freddy sat respectfully silent for a few minutes, as the old bone seemed to feel a good deal on the subject. Presently he went on again:—

"The Sperms live in herds; but the Rights go in pairs, and are very fond of one another. My wife was a charming creature, and we were very happy, till one sad day, when she was playing with our child,—a sweet little whaleling only twelve feet long, and weighing but a ton,—my son was harpooned. His mamma, instead of flying, wrapped her fins round him, and dived as far as the line allowed. Then she came up, and dashed at the boats in great rage and anguish, entirely regardless of the danger she was in. The men struck my son, in order to get her, and they soon succeeded; but even then, in spite of her suffering, she did not try to escape, but clung to little Spouter till both were killed. Alas! alas!"

Here the poor bone creaked so dismally, Freddy feared it would tumble to pieces, and bring the story to an end too soon.

"Don't think of those sorrowful things," he said; "tell me how you came to be here. Were you harpooned?"

"Not I; for I've been very careful all my life to keep out of the way of danger: I'm not like one of my relations, who attacked a ship, gave it such a dreadful blow that he made a great hole, the water rushed in, and the vessel was a wreck. But he paid dearly for that prank, for a few months afterward another ship harpooned him very easily, finding two spears still in him, and a wound in his head. I forgot to mention, that the Sperms have fine ivory teeth, and make ambergris,—a sort of stuff that smells very nice, and costs a great deal. I give you these little facts about my family, as you seem interested, and it's always well to improve the minds of young people."

"You are very kind; but will you be good enough to tell about yourself?" said Freddy again; for the bone seemed to avoid that part of the story, as if he didn't want to tell it.

"Well, if I must, I must; but I'm sorry to confess what a fool I've been. You know what coral is, don't you?"

"No," said Freddy, wondering why it asked.

"Then I must tell you, I suppose. There is a bit in the house there,—that rough, white, stony stuff on the table in the parlor. It's full of little holes, you know. Well, those holes are the front doors of hundreds of little polypes, or coral worms, who build the great branches of coral, and live there. They are of various shapes and colors,—some like stars; some fine as a thread, and blue or yellow; others like snails and tiny lobsters. Some people say the real coral-makers are shaped like little oblong bags of jelly, closed at one end, the other open, with six or eight little feelers, like a star, all round it. The other creatures are boarders or visitors: these are the real workers, and, when they sit in their cells and put out their feelers, they make all manner of lovely colors under the water,—crimson, green, orange, and violet. But, if they are taken up or touched, the coral people go in doors, and the beautiful hues disappear. They say there are many coral reefs and islands built by these industrious people, in the South Seas; but I can't go there to see, and I am contented with those I find in the northern latitudes. I knew such a community of coral builders, and used to watch them long ago, when they began to work. It was a charming spot, down under the sea; for all manner of lovely plants grew there; splendid fishes sailed to and fro; wonderful shells lay about; crimson and yellow prawns, long, gliding green worms, and purple sea-urchins, were there. When I asked the polypes what they were doing, and they answered, 'Building an island,' I laughed at them; for the idea that these tiny, soft atoms could make any thing was ridiculous. 'You may roar; but you'll see that we are right, if you live long enough,' said they. 'Our family have built thousands of islands and long reefs, that the sea can't get over, strong as it is.' That amused me immensely; but I wouldn't believe it, and laughed more than ever."

"It does seem very strange," said Freddy, looking at the branch of coral which he had brought out to examine.

"Doesn't it? and isn't it hard to believe? I used to go, now and then, to see how the little fellows got on, and always found them hard at it. For a long while there was only a little plant without leaves, growing slowly taller and taller; for they always built upward toward the light. By and by, the small shrub was a tree: flying fish roosted in its branches; sea-cows lay under its shadow; and thousands of jolly little polypes lived and worked in its white chambers. I was glad to see them getting on so well; but still I didn't believe in the island story, and used to joke them about their ambition. They were very good-natured, and only answered me, 'Wait a little longer, Friend Right.' I had my own affairs to attend to; so, for years at a time, I forgot the coral-workers, and spent most of my life up Greenland way, for warm climates don't agree with my constitution. When I came back, after a long absence, I was astonished to see the tree grown into a large umbrella-shaped thing, rising above the water. Sea-weed had washed up and clung there; sea-birds had made nests there; land-birds and the winds had carried seeds there, which had sprung up; trunks of trees had been cast there by the sea; lizards, insects, and little animals came with the trees, and were the first inhabitants; and, behold! it *was* an island."

"What did you say then," asked Freddy.

"I was angry, and didn't want to own that I was wrong; so I insisted that it wasn't a real island, without people on it. 'Wait a little longer,' answered the polypes; and went on, building broader and broader foundations. I flounced away in a rage, and didn't go back for a great while. I hoped something would happen to the coral builders and their island; but I was so curious that I couldn't keep away, and, on going back there, I found a settlement of fishermen, and the beginning of a thriving town. Now I should have been in a towering passion at this, if in my travels I hadn't discovered a race of little creatures as much smaller than polypes as a mouse is smaller than an elephant. I heard two learned men talking about diatoms, as they sailed to Labrador; and I listened. They said these people lived in both salt and fresh water, and were found in all parts of the world. They were a glassy shell, holding a soft, golden-yellow substance, and that they were so countless that banks were made of them, and that a town here in these United States were founded on them. They were the food of many little sea-animals, who, in turn, fed us big creatures, and were very interesting and wonderful. I saved up this story; and, when the polypes asked if they hadn't done what they intended, I told them I didn't think it so very remarkable, for the tiny diatoms made cities, and were far more astonishing animals than they. I thought that would silence them; but they just turned round, and informed me that my diatoms were plants, not animals,—so my story was all humbug. Then I *was* mad; and couldn't get over the fact that these little rascals had done what we, the kinds of the sea, couldn't do. I wasn't content with being the biggest creature there: I wanted to be the most skilful also. I didn't remember that every thing has its own place and use, and should be happy in doing the work for which it was made. I fretted over the matter a long while, and at last decided to make an island myself."

"How could you?" asked Freddy.

"I had my plans; and thought them very wise ones. I was so bent on outdoing the polypes that I didn't much care what happened; and so I went to work in my clumsy way. I couldn't pile up stones, or build millions of cells; so I just made an island of myself. I swam up into the harbor yonder one night; covered my back with sea weed; and lay still on the top of the water. In the morning the gulls came to see what it was, and pecked away at the weeds, telling me very soon that they knew what I was after, and that I couldn't gull them. All the people on shore turned out to see the wonder also; for a fisherman had carried the tidings, and every one was wild to behold the new island. After staring and chattering a long while, boats came off to examine the mystery. Loads of scientific gentlemen worked away at me with microscopes, hammers, acids, and all sorts of tests, to decide what I was; and kept up such a fire of long words that I was 'most dead. They couldn't make up their minds; and meanwhile news of the strange thing spread, and every sort of person came to see me. The gulls kept telling them the joke; but they didn't understand, and I got on capitally. Every night I dined and fed and frolicked till dawn; then put on my sea-weeds, and lay still to be stared at. I wanted some one to come and live on me; then I should be equal to the island of the polypes. But no one came, and I was beginning to be tired of fooling people, when I was fooled myself. An old sailor came to visit me: he had been a whaler, and he soon guessed the secret. But he said nothing till he was safely out of danger; then he got all ready, and one day, as I lay placidly in the sun, a horrible harpoon came flying through the air, and sunk deep into my back. I forgot every thing but the pain, and dived for my life. Alas! the tide was low; the harbor-bar couldn't be passed; and I found hundreds of boats chasing me, till I was driven ashore down there on the flats. Big and strong as we are, once out of water, and we are perfectly helpless. I was soon despatched; and my bones left to whiten on the sand. This was long ago; and, one by one, all my relics have been carried off or washed away. My jawbone has been used as a seat here, till it's worn out; but I couldn't crumble away till I'd told some one my story. Remember, child, pride goeth before a fall."

Then, with a great creak, the bone tumbled to pieces; and found a peaceful grave in the long green grass.

# A Strange Island

ONE DAY I LAY ROCKING in my boat, reading a very famous book, which all children know and love; and the name of which I'll tell you by and by. So busily was I reading, that I never minded the tide; and presently discovered that I was floating out to sea, with neither sail nor oar. At first I was very much frightened; for there was no one in sight on land or sea, and I didn't know where I might drift to. But the water was calm, the sky clear, and the wind blew balmily; so I waited for what should happen.

Presently I saw a speck on the sea, and eagerly watched it; for it drew rapidly near, and seemed to be going my way. When it came closer, I was much amazed; for, of all the queer boats I ever saw, this was the queerest. It was a great wooden bowl, very cracked and old; and in it sat three gray-headed little gentlemen with spectacles, all reading busily, and letting the boat go where it pleased. Now, right in their way was a rock; and I called out, "Sir, sir, take care."

But my call came too late: crash went the bowl, out came the bottom, and down plumped all the little gentlemen into the sea. I tried not to laugh, as the books, wigs, and spectacles flew about; and, urging my boat nearer, I managed to fish them up, dripping and sneezing, and looking like drowned kittens. When the flurry was over, and they had got their breath, I asked who they were, and where they were going.

"We are from Gotham, ma'am," said the fattest one, wiping a very wet face on a very wet handkerchief.

"We were going to that island yonder. We have often tried, but never got there: it's always so, and I begin to think the thing can't be done."

I looked where he pointed; and, sure enough, there was an island where I had never seen one before. I rubbed my eyes, and looked again. Yes: there is was,—a little island, with trees and people on it; for I saw smoke coming out of the chimney of a queerly-shaped house on the shore.

"What is the name of it?" I asked.

The little old gentleman put his finger on his lips, and said, with a mysterious nod,—

"I couldn't tell you, ma'am. It's a secret; but, if you manage to land there, you will soon know."

The other old men nodded at the same time; and then all went to reading again, with the water still dropping off the ends of their noses. This made me very curious; and, as the tide drifted us nearer and nearer, I looked well about me, and saw several things that filled me with a strong desire to land on the island. The odd house, I found, was built like a high-heeled shoe; and at every window I saw children's heads. Some were eating broth; some were crying; and some had nightcaps on. I caught sight of a distracted old lady flying about, with a ladle in one hand, and a rod in the other; but the house was so full of children (even up to the skylight,—out of which they popped their heads, and nodded at me) that I couldn't see much of the mamma of this large family; one seldom can, you know.

I had hardly got over my surprise at this queer sight, when I saw a cow fly up through the air, over the new moon that hung there, and come down and disappear in the woods. I really didn't know what to make of this, but had no time to ask the old men what it meant; for a cat, playing a fiddle, was seen on the shore. A little dog stood by, listening and laughing; while a dish and a spoon ran away over the beach with all their might. If the boat had not floated up to the land, I think I should have swam there,—I was so anxious to see what was going on; for there was a great racket on the island, and such a remarkable collection of creatures, it was impossible to help staring.

As soon as we landed, three other gentlemen came to welcome the ones I had saved, and seemed very glad to see them. They appeared to have just landed from a tub in which was a drum, rub-a-dub-dubbing all by itself. One of the new men had a white frock on, and carried a large knife; the second had dough on his hands, flour on his coat, and a hot-looking face; the third was very greasy, had a bundle of candles under his arm, and a ball of wicking half out of his pocket. The six shook hands, and walked away together, talking about a fair; and left me to take care of myself.

I walked on through a pleasant meadow, where a pretty little girl was looking sadly up at a row of sheep's tails hung on a tree. I also saw a little boy in blue, asleep by a hay-cock; and another boy taking aim at a cock-sparrow, who clapped his wings and flew away. Presently I saw two more little girls: one sat by a fire warming her toes; and, when I asked what her name was, she said pleasantly,—

"Polly Flinders, ma'am."

The other one sat on a tuft of grass, eating something that looked very nice; but, all of a sudden, she dropped her bowl, and ran away, looking very much frightened.

"What's the matter with her?" I asked of a gay young frog who came tripping along with his hat under his arm.

"Miss Muffet is a fashionable lady, and afraid of spiders, madam; also of frogs." And he puffed himself angrily up, till his eyes quite goggled in his head.

"And, pray, who are you, sir?" I asked, staring at his white vest, green coat, and fine cravat.

"Excuse me, if I don't give my name, ma'am. My false friend, the rat, got me into a sad scrape once; and Rowley insists upon it that a duck destroyed me, which is all gammon, ma'am,—all gammon."

With that, the frog skipped away; and I turned into a narrow lane, which seemed to lead toward some music. I had not gone far, when I heard the rumbling of a wheelbarrow, and saw a little man wheeling a little woman along. The little man looked very hot and tired; but the little woman looked very nice, in a smart bonnet and shawl, and kept looking at a new gold ring on her finger, as she rode along under her little umbrella. I was wondering who they were, when down went the wheelbarrow; and the little lady screamed so dismally that I ran away, lest I should get into trouble,—being a stranger.

Turning a corner, I came upon a very charming scene, and slipped into a quiet nook to see what was going on. It was evidently a wedding; and I was just in time to see it, for the procession was passing at that moment. First came a splendid cock-a-doodle, all in black and gold, like a herald, blowing his trumpet, and marching with a very dignified step. Then came a rook, in black, like a minister, with spectacles and white cravat. A lark and bullfinch followed,—friends, I supposed; and then the bride and bridegroom. Miss Wren was evidently a Quakeress; for she wore a sober dress, and a little white veil, through which her bright eyes shone. The bridegroom was a military man, in his scarlet uniform,—a plump, bold-looking bird, very happy and proud just then. A goldfinch gave away the bride, and a linnet was bridemaid. The ceremony was very fine; and, as soon as it was over, the blackbird, thrush, and nightingale burst out in a lovely song.

A splendid dinner followed, at which was nearly every bird that flies; so you may imagine the music there was. They had currant-pie in abundance; and cherry-wine, which excited a cuckoo so much, that he became quite rude, and so far forgot himself as to pull the bride about. This made the groom so angry that he begged his friend, the sparrow, to bring his bow and arrow, and punish the ruffian. But, alas! Sparrow had also taken a drop too much: he aimed wrong, and, with a dreadful cry, Mr. Robin sank dying into the arms of his wife, little Jane.

It was too much for me; and, taking advantage of the confusion that followed, I left the tragical scene as fast as possible.

A little farther on, I was shocked to see a goose dragging an old man down some steps that led to a little house.

"Dear me! what's the matter here?" I cried.

"He won't say his prayers," screamed the goose.

"But perhaps he was never taught," said I.

"It's never too late to learn: he's had his chance; he won't be pious and good, so away with him. Don't interfere, whatever you do: hold your tongue, and go about your business," scolded the goose, who certainly had a dreadful temper.

I dared say no more; and, when the poor old man had been driven away by this foul proceeding, I went up the steps and peeped in; for I heard some one crying, and thought the cross bird, perhaps, had hurt some one else. A little old woman stood there, wringing her hands in great distress; while a small dog was barking at her with all his might.

"Bless me! the fashions have got even here," thought I; for the old woman was dressed in the latest style,—or, rather, she had overdone it sadly; for her gown was nearly up to her knees, and she was nearly as ridiculous an object as some of the young ladies I had seen at home. She had a respectable bonnet on, however, instead of a straw saucer; and her hair was neatly put under a cap,—not made into a knob on the top of her head.

"My dear soul, what's the trouble?" said I, quite touched by her tears.

"Lud a mercy, ma'am! I've been to market with my butter and eggs,— for the price of both is so high, one can soon get rich now-a-days,—and, being tired, I stopped to rest a bit, but fell asleep by the road. Somebody—I think it's a rogue of a peddler who sold me wooden nutmegs, and a clock that wouldn't go, and some pans that came to bits the first time I used them—somebody cut my new gown and petticoat off all round, in the shameful way you see. I thought I never should get home; for I was such a fright, I actually didn't know myself. But, thinks I, my doggy will know me; and then I shall be sure I'm I, and not some bold-faced creature in short skirts. But, oh, ma'am! doggy *don't* know me; and I ain't myself, and I don't know what to do."

"He's a foolish little beast; so don't mind him, but have a cup of tea, and go to bed. You can make your gown decent to-morrow; and, if I see the tricksy pedler, I'll give him a scolding."

This seemed to comfort the old woman; though doggy still barked.

"My next neighbor has a dog who never behaves in this way," she said, as she put her teapot on the coals. "He's a remarkable beast; and you'd better stop to see him as you pass, ma'am. He's always up to some funny prank or other."

I said I would; and, as I went by the next house, I took a look in at the window. The closet was empty, I observed; but the dog sat smoking a pipe, looking as grave as a judge.

"Where is your mistress?" asked I.

"Gone for some tripe," answered the dog, politely taking the pipe out of his mouth, and adding, "I hope the smoke doesn't annoy you."

"I don't approve of smoking," said I.

"Sorry to hear it," said the dog, coolly.

I was going to lecture him on this bad habit; but I saw his mistress coming with a dish in her hand, and, fearing she might think me rude to peep in at her windows, I walked on, wondering what we were coming to when even four-legged puppies smoked.

At the door of the next little house, I saw a market-wagon loaded with vegetables, and a smart young pig just driving it away. I had heard of this interesting family, and took a look as I passed by. A second tidy pig sat blowing the fire; and a third was eating roast-beef, as if he had just come in from his work. The fourth, I was grieved to see, looked very sulky; for it was evident he had been naughty, and so lost his dinner. The little pig was at the door, crying to get in; and it was sweet to see how kindly the others let him in, wiped his tears, tied on his bib, and brought him his bread and milk. I was very glad to see these young orphans doing so well, and I knew my friends at home would enjoy hearing from them.

A loud scream made me jump; and the sudden splash of water made me run along, without stopping to pick up a boy and girl who came tumbling down the hill, with an empty pail, bumping their heads as they rolled. Smelling something nice, and feeling hungry, I stepped into a large room near by,—a sort of eating-house, I fancy; for various parties seemed to be enjoying themselves in their different ways. A small boy sat near the door, eating a large pie; and he gave me a fine plum which he had just pulled out. At one table was a fat gentleman cutting another pie, which had a dark crust, through which appeared the heads of a flock of birds, all singing gayly.

"There's no end to the improvements in cooking, and no accounting for tastes," I added, looking at a handsomely-dressed lady, who sat near, eating bread and honey.

As I passed this party, I saw behind the lady's chair a maid, with a clothes-pin in her hand, and no nose. She sobbingly told me a bird had nipped it off; and I gave her a bit of court-plaster, which I fortunately had in my pocket.

Another couple were dividing their meat in a queer way; for one took all the fat, and the other all the lean. The next people were odder still; for the man looked rather guilty, and seemed to be hiding a three-peck measure under his chair, while he waited for his wife to bring on some cold barley-pudding, which, to my surprise, she was frying herself. I also saw a queer moon-struck-looking man inquiring the way to Norridge; and another man making wry faces over some plum-pudding, with which he had burnt his mouth, because his friend came down too soon.

I ordered pease-porride hot, and they brought it cold; but I didn't wait for any thing else, being in a hurry to see all there was to be seen on this strange island. Feeling refreshed, I strolled on, passing a jolly old gentleman smoking and drinking, while three fiddlers played before him. As I turned into a road that led toward a hill, a little boy, riding a dapple-gray pony, and an old lady on a white horse, with bells ringing somewhere, trotted by me, followed by a little girl, who wished to know where she could buy a penny bun. I told her the best were at Newmarch's, in Bedford Street, and she ran on, much pleased; but I'm afraid she never found that best of bake-shops. I was going quietly along, when the sound of another horse coming made me look round; and there I saw a dreadful sight,—a wild horse, tearing over the ground, with fiery eyes and streaming tail. On his back sat a crazy man, beating him with a broom; a crazy woman was behind him, with her bonnet on wrong side before, holding one crazy child in her lap, while another stood on the horse; a third was hanging on by one foot, and all were howling at the top of their voices as they rushed by. I scrambled over the wall to get out of the way, and there I saw more curious sights. Two blind men were sitting on the grass, trying to see two lame men who were hobbling along as hard as they could; and, near by, a bull was fighting a bee in the most violent manner. This rather alarmed me; and I scrambled back into the road again, just as a very fine lady jumped over a barberry-bush near by, and a gentleman went flying after, with a ring in one hand and a stick in the other.

"What very odd people they have here!" I thought. Close by was a tidy little house under the hill, and in it a tidy little woman who sold things to eat. Being rather hungry, in spite of my porridge, I bought a baked apple and a cranberry-pie; for she said they were good, and I found she told the truth. As I sat eating my pie, some dogs began to bark; and by came a troop of beggars, some in rags, and some in old velvet gowns. A drunken grenadier was with them, who wanted a pot of beer; but as he had no money, the old woman sent him about his business.

On my way up the hill, I saw a little boy crying over a dead pig, and his sister, who seemed to be dead also. I asked his name, and he sobbed out,

"Johnny Pringle, ma'am;" and went on crying so hard I could do nothing to comfort him. While I stood talking to him, a sudden gust of wind blew up the road, and down came the bough of a tree; and, to my surprise, a cradle with a baby in it also. The baby screamed dreadfully, and I didn't know how to quiet it; so I ran back to the old woman, and left it with her, asking if that was the way babies were taken care of there.

"Bless you, my dear! its ma is making patty-cakes; and put it up there to be out of the way of Tom Tinker's dog. I'll soon hush it up," said the old woman; and, trotting it on her knee, she began to sing,—

> "Hey, my kitten, my kitten,
> Hey! my kitten, my deary."

Feeling that the child was in good hands, I hurried away; for I saw something was going on upon the hilltop. When I got to the hill-top, I was shocked to find some people tossing an old woman in a blanket. I begged them to stop; but one of the men, who, I found, was a Welchman, by the name of Taffy, told me the old lady liked it.

"But why does she like it?" I asked in great surprise.

"Tom, the piper's son, will tell you: it's my turn to toss now," said the man.

"Why, you see, ma'am," said Tom, "she is one of those dreadfully nice old women, who are always fussing and scrubbing, and worrying people to death, with everlastingly cleaning house. Now and then we get so tired out with her that we propose to her to clean the sky itself. She likes that; and, as this is the only way we can get her up, we toss till she sticks somewhere, and then leave her to sweep cobwebs till she is ready to come back and behave herself."

"Well, that is the oddest thing I ever heard. I know just an old lady, and when I go home I'll try your plan. It seems to me that you have a great many queer old ladies on this island," I said to another man, whom they called Peter, and who stood eating pumpkin all the time.

"Well, we do have rather a nice collection; but you haven't seen the best of all. We expect her every minute; and Margery Daw is to let us know the minute she lights on the island," replied Peter, with his mouth full.

"Lights?" said I, "you speak as if she flew."

"She rides on a bird. Hurrah! the old sweeper has lit. Now the cobwebs will fly. Don't hurry back," shouted the man; and a faint, far-off voice answered, "I shall be back again by and by."

The people folded up the blanket, looking much relieved; and I was examining a very odd house which was built by an ancient king called Boggen, when Margery Daw, a dirty little girl, came up the hill, screaming, at the top of her voice,—

"She's come! she's come!"

Every one looked up; and I saw a large white bird slowly flying over the island. On its back sat the nicest old woman that ever was seen: all the others were nothing compared to her. She had a pointed hat on over her cap, a red cloak, high-heeled shoes, and a crutch in her hand. She smiled and nodded as the bird approached; and every one ran and nodded, and screamed, "Welcome! welcome, mother!"

As soon as she touched the ground, she was so surrounded that I could only see the top of her hat; for hundreds and hundreds of little children suddenly appeared, like a great flock of birds,—rosy, happy, pretty children; but all looked unreal, and among them I saw some who looked like little people I had known long ago.

"Who are they?" I asked of a bonny lass, who was sitting on a cushion, eating strawberries and cream.

"They are the phantoms of all the little people who ever read and loved our mother's songs," said the maid.

"What did she write?" I asked, feeling very queer, and as if I was going to remember something.

"Songs that are immortal; and you have them in your hand," replied the bonny maid, smiling at my stupidity.

I looked; and there, on the cover of the book I had been reading so busily when the tide carried me away, I saw the words, "Mother Goose's Melodies." I was so delighted that I had seen her I gave a shout, and tried to get near enough to hug and kiss the dear old soul, as the swarm of children were doing; but my cry woke me, and I was *so* sorry to find it all a dream!

# Fancy's Friend

IT WAS A WAGON, shaped like a great square basket, on low wheels, and drawn by a stout donkey. There was one seat, on which Miss Fairbairn the governess sat; and all round her, leaning over the edge of the basket, were children, with little wooden shovels and baskets in their hands, going down to play on the beach. Away they went, over the common, through the stony lane, out upon the wide, smooth sands. All the children but one immediately fell to digging holes, and making ponds, castles, or forts. They did this every day, and were never tired of it; but little Fancy made new games for herself, and seldom dug in the sand. She had a garden of sea-weed, which the waves watered every day: she had a palace of pretty shells, where she kept all sorts of little water-creatures as fairy tenants; she had friends and playmates among the gulls and peeps, and learned curious things by watching crabs, horseshoes, and jellyfishes; and every day she looked for a mermaid.

It was of no use to tell her that there were no mermaids: Fancy firmly believed in them, and was sure she would see one some day. The other children called the seals mermaids; and were contented with the queer, shiny creatures who played in the water, lay on the rocks, and peeped at them with soft, bright eyes as they sailed by. Fancy was not satisfied with seals,—they were not pretty and graceful enough for her,—and she waited and watched for a real mermaid. On this day she took a breezy run with the beach-birds along the shore; she planted a pretty red weed in her garden; and let out the water-beetles and snails who had passed the night in her palace. Then she went to a rock that stood near the quiet nook where she played alone, and sat there looking for a mermaid as the tide came in; for it brought her many curious things, and it might perhaps bring a mermaid.

As she looked across the waves that came tumbling one over the other, she saw something that was neither boat nor buoy nor seal. It was a queer-looking thing, with a wild head, a long waving tail, and something like arms that seemed to paddle it along. The waves tumbled it about, so Fancy could not see very well: but, the longer she looked, the surer she was that this curious thing was a mermaid; and she waited eagerly for it to reach the shore. Nearer and nearer it came, till a great wave threw it upon the sand;

and Fancy saw that it was only a long piece of kelp, torn up by the roots. She was very much disappointed; but, all of a sudden, her face cleared up, she clapped her hands, and began to dance round the kelp, saying,—

"I'll make a mermaid myself, since none will come to me."

Away she ran, higher up the beach, and, after thinking a minute, began her work. Choosing a smooth, hard place, she drew with a stick the outline of her mermaid; then she made the hair of the brown marsh-grass growing near by, arranging it in long locks on either side the face, which was made of her prettiest pink and white shells,—for she pulled down her palace to get them. The eyes were two gray pebbles; the neck and arms of larger, white shells; and the dress of sea-weed,—red, green, purple, and yellow; very splendid, for Fancy emptied her garden to dress her mermaid.

"People say that mermaids always have tails; and I might make one out of this great leaf of kelp. But it isn't pretty, and I don't like it; for I want mine to be beautiful: so I won't have any tail," said Fancy, and put two slender white shells for feet, at the lower edge of the fringed skirt. She laid a wreath of little star-fish across the brown hair, a belt of small orange-crabs round the waist, buttoned the dress with violet snail-shells, and hung a tiny white pebble, like a pearl, in either ear.

"Now she must have a glass and a comb in her hand, as the song says, and then she will be done," said Fancy, looking about her, well pleased.

Presently she found the skeleton of a little fish, and his backbone made an excellent comb; while a transparent jelly-fish served for a glass, with a frame of cockle-shells round it. Placing these in the hands of her mermaid, and some red coral bracelets on her wrists, Fancy pronounced her done; and danced about her, singing,—

> "My pretty little mermaid,
>     Oh! come, and play with me:
> I'll love you, I'll welcome you;
>     And happy we shall be."

Now, while she had been working, the tide had crept higher and higher; and, as she sung, one wave ran up and wet her feet.

"Oh, what a pity I didn't put her farther up!" cried Fancy; "the tide will wash her all away; and I meant to keep her fresh, and show her to Aunt Fiction. My poor mermaid!—I shall lose her; but perhaps she will be happier in the sea: so I'll let her go."

Mounting her rock, Fancy waited to see her work destroyed. But the sea seemed to pity her; and wave after wave came up, without doing any harm.

At last one broke quite over the mermaid, and Fancy thought that would be the end of her. But, no; instead of scattering shells, stones, and weeds, the wave lifted the whole figure, without displacing any thing, and gently bore it back into the sea.

"Good by! good by!" cried Fancy, as the little figure floated away; then, as it disappeared, she put her hands before her face,—for she loved her mermaid, and had given all her treasures to adorn her; and now to lose her so soon seemed hard,—and Fancy's eyes were full of tears. Another great wave came rolling in; but she did not look up to see it break, and, a minute after, she heard steps tripping toward her over the sand. Still she did not stir; for, just then, none of her playmates could take the place of her new friend, and she didn't want to see them.

"Fancy! Fancy!" called a breezy voice, sweeter than any she had ever heard. But she did not raise her head, nor care to know who called. The steps came quite close; and the touch of a cold, wet hand fell on her own. Then she looked up, and saw a strange little girl standing by her, who smiled, showing teeth like little pearls, and said, in the breezy voice,—

"You wanted me to play with you, so I came."

"Who are you?" asked Fancy, wondering where she had seen the child before.

"I'm your mermaid," said the child.

"But the water carried her away," cried Fancy.

"The waves only carried me out for the sea to give me life, and then brought me back to you," answered the new comer.

"But are you really a mermaid?" asked Fancy, beginning to smile and believe.

"I am really the one you made: look, and see if I'm not;" and the little creature turned slowly round, that Fancy might be sure it was her own work.

She certainly was very like the figure that once lay on the sand,—only she was not now made of stones and shells. There was the long brown hair blowing about her face, with a wreath of starry shells in it. Her eyes were gray, her cheeks and lips rosy, her neck and arms white; and from under her striped dress peeped little bare feet. She had pearls in her ears, coral bracelets, a golden belt, and a glass and comb in her hands.

"Yes," said Fancy, drawing near, "you *are* my little mermaid; but how does it happen that you come to me at last?"

"Dear friend," answered the water-child, "you believed in me, watched and waited long for me, shaped the image of the thing you wanted out of your dearest treasures, and promised to love and welcome me. I could not help coming; and the sea, that is as fond of you as you are of it, helped me to grant your wish."

"Oh, I'm glad, I'm glad! Dear little mermaid, what is your name?" cried Fancy, kissing the cool cheek of her new friend, and putting her arms about her neck.

"Call me by my German cousin's pretty name,—Lorelei," answered the mermaid, kissing back as warmly as she could.

"Will you come home and live with me, dear Lorelei?" asked Fancy, still holding her fast.

"If you will promise to tell no one who and what I am, I will stay with you as long as you love and believe in me. As soon as you betray me, or lose your faith and fondness, I shall vanish, never to come back again," answered Lorelei.

"I promise; but won't people wonder who you are? and, if they ask me, what shall I say?" said Fancy.

"Tell them you found me on the shore; and leave the rest to me. But you must not expect other people to like and believe in me as you do. They will say hard things of me; will blame you for loving me; and try to part us. Can you bear this, and keep your promise faithfully?"

"I think I can. But why won't they like you?" said Fancy, looking troubled.

"Because they are not like you, dear," answered the mermaid, with salt tears in her soft eyes. "They have not your power of seeing beauty in all things, of enjoying invisible delights, and living in a world of your own. Your Aunt Fiction will like me; but your Uncle Fact won't. He will want to know all about me; will think I'm a little vagabond; and want me to be sent away somewhere, to be made like other children. I shall keep out of his way as much as I can; for I'm afraid of him."

"I'll take care of you, Lorelei dear; and no one shall trouble you. I hear Miss Fairbairn calling; so I must go. Give me your hand, and don't be afraid."

Hand in hand the two went toward the other children, who stopped digging, and stared at the new child. Miss Fairbairn, who was very wise and good, but rather prim, stared too, and said, with surprise,—

"Why, my dear, where did you find that queer child?"

"Down on the beach. Isn't she pretty?" answered Fancy, feeling very proud of her new friend.

"She hasn't got any shoes on; so she's a beggar, and we mustn't play with her," said one boy, who had been taught that to be poor was a very dreadful thing.

"What pretty earrings and bracelets she's got!" said a little girl, who thought a great deal of her dress.

"She don't look as if she knew much," said another child, who kept studying so hard that she never had time to dig and run, and make dirt-pies, till she fell ill, and had to be sent to the sea-side.

"What's your name? and who are your parents?" asked Miss Fairbairn.

"I've got no parents; and my name is Lorelei," answered the mermaiden.

"You mean Luly; mind your pronunciation, child," said Miss Fairbairn, who corrected every one she met in something or other. "Where do you live?"

"I haven't got any home now," said Lorelei, smiling at the lady's tone.

"Yes, you have: my home is yours; and you are going to stay with me always," cried Fancy heartily. "She is my little sister, Miss Fairbairn: I found her; and I'm going to keep her, and make her happy."

"Your uncle won't like it, my dear." And Miss Fairbairn shook her head gravely.

"Aunt will; and Uncle won't mind, if I learn my lessons well, and remember the multiplication table all right. He was going to give me some money, so I might learn to keep accounts; but I'll tell him to keep the money, and let me have Lorelei instead."

"Oh, how silly!" cried the boy who didn't like bare feet.

"No, she isn't; for, if she's kind to the girl, maybe she'll get some of her pretty things," said the vain little girl.

"Keeping accounts is a very useful and important thing. I keep mine; and mamma says I have great arth-met-i-cal talent," added the pale child, who studied too much.

"Come, children; it's time for dinner. Fancy, you can take the girl to the house; and your uncle will do what he thinks best about letting you keep her," said Miss Fairbairn, piling them into the basket-wagon.

Fancy kept Lorelei close beside her; and as soon as they reached the great hotel, where they all were staying with mothers and fathers, uncles or aunts, she took her to kind Aunt Fiction, who was interested at once in the friendless child so mysteriously found. She was satisfied with the little she could discover, and promised to keep her,—for a time, at least.

"We can imagine all kinds of romantic things about her; and, by and by, some interesting story may be found out concerning her. I can make her useful in many ways; and she shall stay."

As Aunt Fiction laid her hand on the mermaid's head, as if claiming her for her own, Uncle Fact came stalking in, with his note-book in his hand,

and his spectacles on his nose. Now, though they were married, these two persons were very unlike. Aunt Fiction was a graceful, picturesque woman; who told stories charmingly, wrote poetry and novels, was very much beloved by young folks, and was the friend of some of the most famous people in the world. Uncle Fact was a grim, grave, decided man; whom it was impossible to bend or change. He was very useful to every one; knew an immense deal; and was always taking notes of things he saw and heard, to be put in a great encyclopædia he was making. He didn't like romance, loved the truth, and wanted to get to the bottom of every thing. He was always trying to make little Fancy more sober, well-behaved, and learned; for she was a freakish, dreamy, yet very lovable and charming child. Aunt Fiction petted her to her heart's content, and might have done her harm, if Uncle Fact had not had a hand in her education; for the lessons of both were necessary to her, as to all of us.

"Well, well, well! who is this?" he said briskly, as he turned his keen eyes and powerful glasses on the newcomer.

Aunt Fiction told him all the children had said; but he answered impatiently,—

"Tut, tut! my dear: I want the facts of the case. You are apt to exaggerate; and Fancy is not to be relied on. If the child isn't a fool, she must know more about herself than she pretends. Now, answer truly, Luly, where did you come from?"

But the little mermaid only shook her head, and answered as before, "Fancy found me on the beach, and wants me to stay with her. I'll do her no harm: please, let me stay."

"She has evidently been washed ashore from some wreck, and has forgotten all about herself. Her wonderful beauty, her accent, and these ornaments show that she is some foreign child," said Aunt Fiction, pointing to the earrings.

"Nonsense! my dear: those are white pebbles, not pearls; and, if you examine them, you will find that those bracelets are the ones you gave Fancy as a reward for so well remembering the facts I gave her about coral," said the uncle, who had turned Lorelei round and round, pinched her cheek, felt her hair, and examined her frock through the glasses which nothing escaped.

"She may stay, and be my little playmate, mayn't she? I'll take care of her; and we shall be very happy together," cried Fancy eagerly.

"One can't be sure of that till one has tried. You say you will take care of her: have you got any money to pay her board, and buy her clothes?" asked her uncle.

"No; but I thought you'd help me," answered Fancy wistfully.

"Never say you'll do a thing till you are sure you can," said Uncle Fact, as he took notes of the affair, thinking they might be useful by and by. "I've no objection to your keeping the girl, if, after making inquiries about her, she proves to be a clever child. She can stay awhile; and, when we go back to town, I'll put her in one of our charity schools, where she can be taught to earn her living. Can you read, Luly?"

"No," said the mermaid, opening her eyes.

"Can you write and cipher?"

"What is that?" asked Lorelei innocently.

"Dear me! what ignorance!" cried Uncle Fact.

"Can you sew, or tend babies?" asked Aunt Fiction gently.

"I can do nothing but play and sing, and comb my hair."

"I see! I see!—some hand-organ man's girl. Well, I'm glad you keep your hair smooth,—that's more than Fancy does," said Uncle Fact.

"Let us hear you sing," whispered his little niece; and, in a voice as musical as the sound of ripples breaking on the shore, Lorelei sung a little song that made Fancy dance with delight, charmed Aunt Fiction, and softened Uncle Fact's hard face in spite of himself.

"Very well, very well, indeed: you have a good voice. I'll see that you have proper teaching; and, by and by, you can get your living by giving singing-lessons," he said, turning over the leaves of his book, to look for the name of a skilful teacher; for he had lists of every useful person, place, and thing under the sun.

Lorelei laughed at the idea; and Fancy thought singing for gold, not love, a hard way to get one's living.

Inquiries were made; but nothing more was discovered, and neither of the children would speak: so the strange child lived with Fancy, and made her very happy. The other children didn't care much about her; for with them she was shy and cold, because she knew, if the truth was told, they would not believe in her. Fancy had always played a good deal by herself, because she never found a mate to suit her; now she had one, and they enjoyed each other very much. Lorelei taught her many things besides new games; and Aunt Fiction was charmed with the pretty stories Fancy repeated to her, while Uncle Fact was astonished at the knowledge of marine plants and animals which she gained without any books. Lorelei taught her to swim, like a fish; and the two played such wonderful pranks in the water that people used to come down to the beach when they bathed. In return, Fancy tried to teach her friend to read and write and sew; but Lorelei couldn't learn much, though she loved her little teacher dearly, and every evening sung her to sleep with beautiful lullabies.

There was a great deal of talk about the curious stranger; for her ways were odd, and no one knew what to make of her. She would eat nothing but fruit and shell-fish, and drink nothing but salt water. She didn't like tight clothes; but would have run about in a loose, green robe, with bare feet and flying hair, if Uncle Fact would have allowed it. Morning, noon, and night, she plunged into the sea,—no matter what the weather might be; and she would sleep on no bed but one stuffed with dried sea-weed. She made lovely chains of shells; found splendid bits of coral; and dived where no one else dared, to bring up wonderful plants and mosses. People offered money for these things; but she gave them all to Fancy and Aunt Fiction, of whom she was very fond. It was curious to see the sort of people who liked both Fancy and her friend,—poets, artists; delicate, thoughtful children; and a few old people, who had kept their hearts young in spite of care and time and trouble. Dashing young gentlemen, fine young ladies, worldly-minded and money-loving men and women, and artificial, unchildlike children, the two friends avoided carefully; and these persons either made fun of them, neglected them entirely, or seemed to be unconscious that they were alive. The others they knew at a glance; for their faces warmed and brightened when the children came, they listened to their songs and stories, joined in their plays, and found rest and refreshment in their sweet society.

"This will do for a time; as Fancy is getting strong, and not entirely wasting her days, thanks to me! But our holiday is nearly over; and, as soon as I get back to town, I'll take that child to the Ragged Refuge, and see what they can make of her," said Uncle Fact, who was never quite satisfied about Lorelei; because he could find out so little concerning her. He was walking over the beach as he said this, after a hard day's work on his encyclopædia. He sat down on a rock in a quiet place; and, instead of enjoying the lovely sunset, he fell to studying the course of the clouds, the state of the tide, and the temperature of the air, till the sound of voices made him peep over the rock. Fancy and her friend were playing there, and the old gentleman waited to see what they were about. Both were sitting with their little bare feet in the water; Lorelei was stringing pearls, and Fancy plaiting a crown of pretty green rushes.

"I wish I could go home, and get you a string of finer pearls than these," said Lorelei, "but it is too far away, and I cannot swim now as I used to do."

"I must look into this. The girl evidently knows all about herself, and can tell, if she chooses," muttered Uncle Fact, getting rather excited over this discovery.

"Never mind the pearls: I'd rather have you, dear," said Fancy lovingly. "Tell me a story while we work, or sing me a song; and I'll give you my crown."

"I'll sing you a little song that has got what your uncle calls a moral to it," said Lorelei, laughing mischievously. Then, in her breezy little voice, she sang the story of—

## THE ROCK
## AND THE BUBBLE

Oh! a bare, brown rock
    Stood up in the sea,
The waves at its feet
    Dancing merrily.

A little bubble
    Once came sailing by,
And thus to the rock
    Did it gayly cry,—

"Ho! clumsy brown stone,
    Quick, make way for me:
I'm the fairest thing
    That floats on the sea.

"See my rainbow-robe,
    See my crown of light,
My glittering form,
    So airy and bright.

"O'er the waters blue,
    I'm floating away,
To dance by the shore
    With the foam and spray.

"Now, make way, make way;
    For the waves are strong,
And their rippling feet
    Bear me fast along."

But the great rock stood
    Straight up in the sea:

It looked gravely down,
　　And said pleasantly,—

"Little friend, you must
　　Go some other way;
For I have not stirred
　　This many a long day.

"Great billows have dashed,
　　And angry winds blown;
But my sturdy form
　　Is not overthrown.

"Nothing can stir me
　　In the air or sea;
Then, how can I move,
　　Little friend, for thee?"

Then the waves all laughed,
　　In their voices sweet;
And the sea-birds looked,
　　From their rocky seat,

At the bubble gay,
　　Who angrily cried,
While its round cheek glowed
　　With a foolish pride,—

"You *shall* move for me;
　　And you shall not mock
At the words I say,
　　You ugly, rough rock.

"Be silent, wild birds!
　　Why stare you so?
Stop laughing, rude waves,
　　And help me to go!

"For I am the queen
　　Of the ocean here,
And this cruel stone
　　Cannot make me fear."

Dashing fiercely up,
　　With a scornful word,
Foolish Bubble broke;
　　But Rock never stirred.

Then said the sea-birds,
  Sitting in their nests,
To the little ones
  Leaning on their breasts,—

"Be not like Bubble,
  Headstrong, rude, and vain,
Seeking by violence
  Your object to gain;

"But be like the rock,
  Steadfast, true, and strong,
Yet cheerful and kind,
  And firm against wrong.

"Heed, little birdlings,
  And wiser you'll be
For the lesson learned
  To-day by the sea."

"Well, to be sure, the song *has* got a moral, if that silly Fancy only sees it," said Uncle Fact, popping up his bald head again as the song ended.

"I thank you: that's a good little song for me. But, Lorelei, are you sorry you came to be my friend?" cried Fancy; for, as she bent to lay the crown on the other's head, she saw that she was looking wistfully down into the water that kissed her feet.

"Not yet: while you love me, I am happy, and never regret that I ceased to be a mermaid for your sake," answered Lorelei, laying her soft cheek against her friend's.

"How happy I was the day my play-mermaid changed to a real one!" said Fancy. "I often want to tell people all about that wonderful thing, and let them know who you really are: then they'd love you as I do, instead of calling you a little vagabond."

"Few would believe our story; and those that did would wonder at me,—not love me as you do. They would put me in a cage, and make a show of me; and I should be so miserable I should die. So don't tell who I am, will you?" said Lorelei earnestly.

"Never," cried Fancy, clinging to her.

"But, my deary, what will you do when uncle sends you away from me, as he means to do as soon as we go home? I can see you sometimes; but we cannot be always together, and there is no ocean for you to enjoy in the city."

"I shall bear it, if I can, for your sake; if I cannot, I shall come back here, and wait until you come again next year."

"No, no! I will not be parted from you; and, if uncle takes you away, I'll come here, and be a mermaid with you," cried Fancy.

The little friends threw their arms about each other, and were so full of their own feelings that they never saw Uncle Fact's tall shadow flit across them, as he stole away over the soft sand. Poor old gentleman! he was in a sad state of mind, and didn't know what to do; for in all his long life he had never been so puzzled before.

"A mermaid indeed!" he muttered. "I always thought that child was a fool, and now I'm sure of it. She thinks she is a mermaid, and has made Fancy believe it. I've told my wife a dozen times that she let Fancy read too many fairy tales and wonder-books. Her head is full of nonsense, and she is just ready to believe any ridiculous story that is told her. Now, what on earth shall I do? If I put Luly in an asylum, Fancy will break her heart, and very likely they will both run away. If I leave them together, Luly will soon make Fancy as crazy as she is herself, and I shall be mortified by having a niece who insists that her playmate is a mermaid. Bless my soul! how absurd it all is!"

Aunt Fiction had gone to town to see her publishers about a novel she had written, and he didn't like to tell the queer story to any one else; so Uncle Fact thought it over, and decided to settle the matter at once. When the children came in, he sent Fancy to wait for him in the library, while he talked alone with Lorelei. He did his best; but he could do nothing with her,—she danced and laughed, and told the same tale as before, till the old gentleman confessed that he had heard their talk on the rocks: then she grew very sad, and owned that she *was* a mermaid. This made him angry, and he wouldn't believe it for an instant; but told her it was impossible, and she must say something else.

Lorelei could say nothing else, and wept bitterly when he would not listen; so he locked her up and went to Fancy, who felt as if something dreadful was going to happen when she saw his face. He told her all he knew, and insisted that Lorelei was foolish or naughty to persist in such a ridiculous story.

"But, uncle, I really did make a mermaid; and she really did come alive, for I saw the figure float away, and then Lorelei appeared," said Fancy, very earnestly.

"It's very likely you made a figure, and called it a mermaid: it would be just the sort of thing you'd do," said her uncle. "But it is impossible that any coming alive took place, and I wont hear any such nonsense. You didn't see this girl come out of the water; for she says you never looked up, till she touched you. She was a real child, who came over the beach from somewhere; and you fancied she looked like your figure, and believed the silly tale she told you. It is my belief that she is a sly, bad child; and the sooner she is sent away the better for you."

Uncle Fact was so angry, and talked so loud, that Fancy felt frightened and bewildered; and began to think he might be right about the mermaid part, though she hated to give up the little romance.

"If I agree that she *is* a real child, won't you let her stay, uncle?" she said, forgetting that, if she lost her faith, her friend was lost also.

"Ah! then you have begun to come to your senses, have you? and are ready to own that you don't believe in mermaids and such rubbish?" cried Uncle Fact, stopping in his tramp up and down the room.

"Why, if you say there never were and never can be any, I suppose I *must* give up my fancy; but I'm sorry," sighed the child.

"That's my sensible girl! Now, think a minute, my dear, and you will also own that it is best to give up the child as well as the mermaid," said her uncle briskly.

"Oh! no: we love one another; and she is good, and I can't give her up," cried Fancy.

"Answer me a few questions; and I'll prove that she isn't good, that you don't love her, and that you *can* give her up," said Uncle Fact, and numbered off the questions on his fingers as he spoke.

"Didn't Luly want you to deceive us, and every one else, about who she was?"

"Yes, sir."

"Don't you like to be with her better than with your aunt or myself?"

"Yes, sir."

"Hadn't you rather hear her songs and stories than learn your lessons?"

"Yes, sir."

"Isn't it wrong to deceive people, to love strangers more than those who are a father and mother to you, and to like silly tales better than useful lessons?"

"Yes, sir."

"Very well. Then, don't you see, that, if Luly makes you do these wrong and ungrateful things, she is not a good child, nor a fit playmate for you?"

Fancy didn't answer; for she couldn't feel that it was so, though he made it seem so. When Uncle Fact talked in that way, she always got confused and gave up; for she didn't know how to argue. He was right in a certain way; but she felt as if she was right also in another way, though she could not prove it: so she hung her head, and let her tears drop on the carpet one by one.

Uncle Fact didn't mean to be unkind, but he did mean to have his own way; and, when he saw the little girl's sad face, he took her on his knee, and said, more mildly,—

"Do you remember the story about the German Lorelei, who sung so sweetly, and lured people to death in the Rhine?"

"Yes, uncle; and I like it," answered Fancy, looking up.

"Well, my dear, your Lorelei will lead you into trouble, if you follow her. Suppose she is what you think her,—a mermaid: it is her delight to draw people into the water, where, of course, they drown. If she is what I think her,—a sly, bad child, who sees that you are very simple, and who means to get taken care of without doing any thing useful,—she will spoil you in a worse way than if you followed her into the sea. I've got no little daughter of my own, and I want to keep you as safe and happy as if you were mine. I don't like this girl, and I want you to give her up for my sake. Will you, Fancy?"

While her uncle said these things, all the beauty seemed to fall away from her friend, all the sweetness from their love, and all her faith in the little dream which had made her so happy. Mermaids became treacherous, unlovely, unreal creatures; and Lorelei seemed like a naughty, selfish child, who deceived her, and made her do wrong things. Her uncle had been very kind to her all her life; and she loved him, was grateful, and wanted to show that she was, by pleasing him. But her heart clung to the friend she had made, trusted, and loved; and it seemed impossible to give up the shadow, even though the substance was gone. She put her hands before her face for a moment; then laid her arms about the old man's neck, and whispered, with a little sob,—

"I'll give her up; but you'll be kind to her, because I was fond of her once."

As the last word left Fancy's lips, a long, sad cry sounded through the room; Lorelei sprung in, gave her one kiss, and was seen to run swiftly toward the beach, wringing her hands. Fancy flew after; but, when she reached the shore, there was nothing to be seen but the scattered pebbles, shells, and weeds that made the mock mermaid, floating away on a receding wave.

"Do you believe now?" cried Fancy, weeping bitterly, as she pointed to the wreck of her friend, and turned reproachfully toward Uncle Fact, who had followed in great astonishment.

The old gentleman looked well about him; then shook his head, and answered decidedly,—

"No, my dear, I *don't*. It's an odd affair; but, I've no doubt, it will be cleared up in a natural way sometime or other."

But there he was mistaken; for this mystery never *was* cleared up. Other people soon forgot it, and Fancy never spoke of it; yet she made very few friends, and, though she learned to love and value Uncle Fact as well as Aunt Fiction, she could not forget her dearest playmate. Year after year she came back to the sea-side; and the first thing she always did was to visit the place where she used to play, and stretch her arms toward the sea, crying tenderly,—

"O my little friend! come back to me!"

But Lorelei never came again.

# Madam Cluck, and Her Family

THERE NEVER WAS A PROUDER mamma than Madam Cluck when she led forth her family of eight downy little chicks. Chanticleer, Strut, Snowball, Speckle, Peep, Peck, Downy, and Blot were their names; and no sooner were they out of the shell than they began to chirp and scratch as gayly as if the big world in which they suddenly found themselves was made for their especial benefit. It was a fine brood; but poor Madam Cluck had bad luck with her chicks, for they were her first, and she didn't know how to manage them. Old Aunt Cockletop told her that she didn't, and predicted that "those poor dears would come to bad ends."

Aunt Cockletop was right, as you will see, when I have told the sad history of this unfortunate family. The tragedy began with Chanty, who was the boldest little cockadoodle who ever tried to crow. Before he had a feather to his bit of a tail, Chanty began to fight, and soon was known as the most quarrelsome chick in the farm-yard. Having picked his brothers and sisters, he tried to do the same to his playmates, the ducklings, goslings, and young turkeys, and was so disagreeable that all the fowls hated him. One day, a pair of bantams arrived,—pretty little white birds, with red crests and nice yellow feet. Chanty thought he could beat Mr. Bantam easily, he was so small, and invited him to fight. Mr. B. declined. Then Chanty called him a coward, and gave Mrs. B. a peck, which so enraged her spouse that he flew at Chanty like a game-cock, and a dreadful fight followed, which ended in Chanty's utter defeat, for he died from his wounds.

Downy and Snowball soon followed; for the two sweet little things would swing on the burdock-leaves that grew over the brook. Sitting side by side, the plump sisters were placidly swaying up and down over the clear brown water rippling below, when—ah! sad to relate—the stem broke, and down went leaf, chickens and all, to a watery death.

"I'm the most unlucky hen ever hatched!" groaned poor Madam Cluck; and it did seem so, for the very next week, Speckle, the best and prettiest of the brood, went to walk with Aunt Cockletop, "grasshoppering" they called it, in the great field across the road. What a nice time Speckle did have, to be sure; for the grasshoppers were lively and fat, and aunt was in an unusually amiable mood.

"Never run away from any thing, but face danger and conquer it, like a brave chick," said the old biddy, as she went clucking through the grass, with her gray turban wagging in the wind. Speckle had hopped away from a toad with a startled chirp, which caused aunt to utter that remark. The words had hardly left her beak, when a shadow above made her look up, give one loud croak of alarm, and then scuttle away, as fast as legs and wings could carry her.

Little Speckle, remembering the advice, and unconscious of the danger, stood her ground as a great hawk came circling nearer and nearer, till, with a sudden dart, he pounced on the poor chicken, and bore it away chirping dismally, "Aunty told me not to run. Oh, dear! oh, dear! What shall I do?"

It was a dreadful blow to Mrs. Cluck; and Aunt Cockletop didn't show herself for a whole day after that story was known, for every fowl in the yard twitted her with the difference between her preaching and her practice.

Strut, the other son, was the vainest chick ever seen; and the great aim of his life was to crow louder than any other cock in the neighborhood. He was at it from morning till night, and every one was tired to death of hearing his shrill, small voice making funny attempts to produce hoarse little crows, as he sat on the wall and stretched his yellow neck, till his throat quite ached with the effort.

"Ah! if I could only fly to the highest beam in the barn, and give a splendid crow that every one could hear, I should be perfectly happy," said this silly little fowl, as he stared up at the loft where the old cock often sat.

So he tried every day to fly and crow, and at last managed to get up; then how he did strut and rustle his feathers, while his playmates sat below and watched him.

"You'll fall and get hurt," said his sister Blot.

"Hold your tongue, you ugly little thing, and don't talk to me. I'm going to crow, and can't be interrupted by any silly bit of a hen. Be quiet, down there, and hear if I can't do it as well as daddy."

The chicks stopped scratching and peeping, and sat in a row to hear Strut crow. Perching himself on the beam, he tried his best, but only a droll "cock-a-doodle-doo" came of it, and all the chicks laughed. That made Strut mad, and he resolved to crow, even if he killed himself doing it. He gave an angry cluck, flapped his wings, and tried again. Alas, alas, for poor Strut! he leaned so far forward in his frantic effort to get a big crow out, that he toppled over and fell bump on the hard barn-floor, killing himself instantly.

For some time after this, Mrs. Cluck kept her three remaining little ones close to her side, watching over them with maternal care, till they were heartily tired of her anxious cluckings. Peep and Peck were always together, being very fond of one another. Peep was a most inquisitive chicken, poking her head into every nook and corner, and never satisfied till she had seen all there was to see. Peck was a glutton, eating everything she could find, and often making herself ill by gobbling too fast, and forgetting to eat a little gravel to help digest her food.

"Don't go out of the barn, children. I'm going to lay an egg, and can't look after you just now," said their mother one day.

"Yes, ma'am," chirped the chickens; and then, as she went rustling into the hay-mow, they began to run about and enjoy themselves with all their might. Peep found a little hole into the meal-room, and slipped in, full of joy at the sight of the bags, boxes, and bins. "I'll eat all I want, and then I'll call Peck," she said; and having taken a taste of every thing, she was about to leave, when she heard the stable-man coming, and in her fright couldn't find the hole, so flew into the meal-bin and hid herself. Sam never saw her, but shut down the cover of the bin as he passed, and left poor Peep to die. No one knew what had become of her till some days later, when she was found dead in the meal, with her poor little claws sticking straight up, as if imploring help. Peck, meanwhile, got into mischief also; for, in her hunt for something good to eat, she strayed into the sheep-shed, and finding some salt, ate as much as she liked, not knowing that salt is bad for hens. Having taken all she wanted, she ran back to the barn, and was innocently catching gnats when her mamma came out of the hay-mow, with a loud "Cut-cut-cut-ca-dar-cut!"

"Where is Peep?" asked Mrs. Cluck.

"Don't know, ma. She"—there Peck stopped suddenly, rolled up her eyes, and began to stagger about as if she was tipsy.

"Mercy on us! What's the matter with the chick?" cried Mrs. Cluck, in great alarm.

"Fits, ma'am," answered Doctor Drake, who just then waddled by.

"Oh! what can I do?" screamed the distracted hen.

"Nothing, ma'am; it's fatal." And the doctor waddled on to visit Dame Partlet's son, who was ill of the pip.

"My child, my child! don't flap and stagger so! Let me hold you! Taste this mint-leaf! Have a drop of water! What shall I do?"

As poor Mrs. Cluck sighed and sobbed, her unhappy child went scuffling about on her back, gasping and rolling up her eyes in great anguish, for she had eaten too much of the fatal salt, and there was no help for her. When all was over, they buried the dead chicken under a currant-bush, covered the little grave with chickweed, and the bereaved parent wore a black string round her leg for a month.

Blot, "the last of that bright band," needed no mourning, for she was as black as a crow. This was the reason why her mother never had loved her as much as she did the others, who were all white, gray, or yellow. Poor little Blot had been much neglected by every one; but now her lonely mamma discovered how good and affectionate a chicken she was, for Blot was a great comfort to her, never running away or disobeying in any way, but always close to her side, ready to creep under her wing, or bring her a plump bug when the poor biddy's appetite failed her. They were very happy together till Thanksgiving drew near, when a dreadful pestilence seemed to sweep through the farm-yard; for turkeys, hens, ducks, and geese fell a prey to it, and were seen by their surviving relatives, feather-less, pale, and stiff, borne away to some unknown place whence no fowl returned. Blot was waked one night by a great cackling and fluttering in the hen-house, and peeping down from her perch, saw a great hand glide along the roost, clutch her beloved mother by the leg, and pull her off, screaming dolefully, "Good-by, good-by, my darling child!"

Aunt Cockletop pecked and croaked fiercely; but, tough as she was, the old biddy did not escape, and many another amiable hen and gallant cockadoodle fell a victim to that mysterious hand. In the morning few re-mained, and Blot felt that she was a forlorn orphan, a thought which caused her to sit with her head under her wing for several hours, brooding over her sad lot, and longing to join her family in some safe and happy land, where fowls live in peace. She had her wish very soon, for one day, when the first snowflakes began to flutter out of the cold, gray sky, Blot saw a little kitten mewing pitifully as it sat under the fence.

"What is the matter, dear?" asked kind Blot.

"I'm lost, and I can't find my way home," answered the kitten, shivering with cold. "I live at the red farm-house over the hill, only I don't know which road to take."

"I'll show you. Come at once, for night is coming on, and the snow will soon be too deep for us," said Blot.

So away they went, as fast as their small legs could carry them; but it was a long way, and dusk came on before the red farm-house appeared.

"Now I'm safe; thank you very much. Won't you come in, and stay all night? My mother will be glad to see you," said the kit, rubbing her soft white face against Blot's little black breast.

"It's against the rule to stay out all night, and I promised to be in early;

so, good-by, dear." And off trotted Blot along the snowy road, hoping to get home before the hen-house door was shut. Faster and faster fell the snow, darker and darker grew the night, and colder and colder became poor Blot's little feet as she waded through the drifts. The firelight was shining out into the gloom, as the half-frozen chicken came into the yard, to find all doors shut, and no shelter left for her but the bough of a leafless tree. Too stiff and weak to fly up, she crept as close as possible to the bright glow which shone across the door-step, and with a shiver put her little head under her wing, trying to forget hunger, weariness, and the bitter cold, and wait patiently for morning. But when morning came, little Blot lay frozen stiff under a coverlet of snow; and the tender-hearted children sighed as they dug a grave for the last of the unfortunate family of the Clucks.

# A Curious Call

I HAVE OFTEN WONDERED what the various statues standing about the city think of all day, and what criticisms they would make upon us and our doings, if they could speak. I frequently stop and stare at them, wondering if they don't feel lonely; if they wouldn't be glad of a nod as we go by; and I always long to offer my umbrella to shield their uncovered heads on a rainy day, especially to good Ben Franklin, when the snow lies white on his benevolent forehead. I was always fond of this old gentleman; and one of my favorite stories when a little girl, was that of his early life, and the time when he was so poor he walked about Philadelphia with a roll of bread under each arm, eating a third as he went. I never pass without giving him a respectful look, and wishing he could know how grateful I am for all he had done in the printing line; for, without types and presses, where would the books be?

Well, I never imagined that he understood why the tall woman in the big bonnet stared at him; but he did, and he liked it, and managed to let me know it in a very curious manner, as you shall hear.

As I look out, the first thing I see is the great gilt eagle on the City-Hall dome. There he sits, with open wings, all day long, looking down on the people, who must appear like ants scampering busily to and fro about an ant-hill. The sun shines on him splendidly in the morning; the gay flag waves and rustles in the wind above him sometimes; and the moonlight turns him to silver when she comes glittering up the sky. When it rains, he never shakes his feathers; snow beats on him without disturbing his stately repose; and he never puts his head under his wing at night, but keeps guard in darkness as in day, like a faithful sentinel. I like the big, lonely bird, call him my particular fowl, and often wish he'd turn his head and speak to me. One night he did actually do it, or seemed to; for I've never been able to decide whether I dreamed what I'm going to tell you, or whether it really happened.

It was a stormy night; and, as I drew down my curtain, I said to myself, after peering through the driving snow to catch a glimpse of my neighbor, "Poor Goldy! he'll have a rough time of it. I hope this northeaster won't blow him off his perch." Then I sat down by my fire, took my knitting, and began to meditate. I'm sure I didn't fall asleep; but I can't prove it, so we'll say no more about it. All at once there came a tap at my door, as I thought; and I said "Come in," just as Mr. Poe did when that unpleasant raven paid him a call. No one came, so I went to see who it was. Not a sign of a human soul in the long hall, only little Jessie, the poodle, asleep on her mat. Down I sat; but in a minute the tap came again; this time so loud that I knew it was at the window, and went to open it, thinking that one of my doves wanted to come in perhaps. Up went the sash, and in bounced something so big and so bright that it dazzled and scared me.

"Don't be frightened, ma'am; it's only me," said a hoarse voice. So I collected my wits, rubbed my eyes, and looked at my visitor. It was the gold eagle off the City Hall! I don't expect to be believed; but I wish you'd been here to see, for I give you my word, it was a sight to behold. How he ever got in at such a small window I can't tell; but there he was, strutting majestically up and down the room, his golden plumage rustling, and his keen eyes flashing as he walked. I really didn't know what to do. I couldn't imagine what he came for; I had my doubts about the propriety of offering him a chair; and he was so much bigger than I expected that I was afraid he might fly away with me, as the roc did with Sinbad; so I did nothing but sidle to the door, ready to whisk out, if my strange guest appeared to be peckishly inclined. My respectful silence seemed to suit him; for, after a turn or two, he paused, nodded gravely, and said affably, "Good-evening, ma'am. I stepped over to bring you old Ben's respects, and to see how you were getting on."

"I'm very much obliged, sir. May I inquire who Mr. Old-Ben is? I'm afraid I haven't the honor of his acquaintance."

"Yes, you have; it's Ben Franklin, of City-Hall yard. You know him; and he wished me to thank you for your interest in him."

"Dear me! how very odd! Will you sit down, sir?"

"Never sit! I'll perch here;" and the great fowl took his accustomed attitude just in front of the fire, looking so very splendid that I couldn't keep my eyes off of him.

"Ah! you often do that. Never mind; I rather like it," said the eagle, graciously, as he turned his brilliant eye upon me. I was rather abashed; but being very curious, I ventured to ask a few questions, as he seemed in a friendly mood.

"Being a woman, sir, I'm naturally of an inquiring turn; and I must confess that I have a strong desire to know how it happens that you take your walks abroad, when you are supposed to be permanently engaged at home?"

He shrugged his shoulders, and actually winked at me, as he replied,

"That's all people know of what goes on under, or rather over, their noses. Bless you, ma'am! I leave my roost every night, and enjoy myself in all sorts of larks. Excuse the expression; but, being ornithological, it is more proper for me than for some people who use it."

"What a gay old bird!" thought I, feeling quite at home after that. "Please tell me what you do, when the shades of evening prevail, and you go out for a frolic?"

"I am a gentleman; therefore I behave myself," returned the eagle, with a stately air. "I must confess, I smoke a great deal: but that's not my fault, it's the fault of the chimneys. They keep it up all day, and I have to take it; just as you poor ladies have to take cigar smoke, whether you like it or not. My amusements are of a wholesome kind. I usually begin by taking a long flight down the harbor, for a look at the lighthouses, the islands, the shipping, and the sea. My friends, the gulls, bring their reports to me; for they are the harbor-police, and I take notes of their doings. The school-ship is an object of interest to me, and I often perch on the mast-head, to see how the lads are getting on. Then I take a turn over the city, gossip with the weathercocks, pay my compliments to the bells, inspect the fire-alarm, and pick up information by listening at the telegraph wires. People often talk about 'a little bird' who spreads news; but they don't know how that figure of speech originated. It is the sparrows sitting on the wires, who receive the electric shock, and, being hollow-boned, the news go straight to their heads; they then fly about, chirping it on the housetops, and the air carries it everywhere. That's the way rumors rise and news spread."

"If you'll allow, I'll make a note of that interesting fact," said I, wondering if I might believe him. He appeared to fall into a reverie, while I jotted down the sparrow story, and it occurred to me that perhaps I ought to offer my distinguished guest some refreshment; but, when I modestly alluded to it, he said, with an aldermanic air, "No, thank you; I've just dined at the Parker House."

Now, I really could *not* swallow that; and so plainly betrayed my incredulity, that the eagle explained. "The savory smells which rise to my nostrils from that excellent hotel, with an occasional sniff from the Tremont, are quite sufficient to satisfy my appetite; for, having no stomach, I don't need much food, and I drink nothing but water."

"I wish others would follow your example in that latter habit," said I, respectfully, for I was beginning to see that there was something in my bird, though he *was* hollow. "Will you allow me to ask if the other statues in the city fly by night?"

"They promenade in the parks; and occasionally have social gatherings, when they discuss politics, education, medicine, or any of the subjects in which they are interested. Ah! we have grand times when you are all asleep. It quite repays me for being obliged to make an owl of myself."

"Do the statues come from the shops to these parties?" I asked, resolving to take a late walk the next moonlight night.

"Sometimes; but they get lazy and delicate, living in close, warm places. We laugh at cold and bad weather, and are so strong and hearty that I shouldn't be surprised if I saw Webster and Everett flying round the Common on the new-fashioned velocipedes, for they believed in exercise. Goethe and Schiller often step over from De Vries's window, to flirt with the goddesses, who come down from their niches on Horticultural Hall. Nice, robust young women are Pomona and Flora. If your niminy-piminy girls could see them run, they would stop tilting through the streets, and learn that the true Grecian Bend is the line of beauty always found in straight shoulders, well-opened chest, and an upright figure, firmly planted on active feet."

"In your rambles don't you find a great deal of misery?" said I, to change the subject, for he was evidently old-fashioned in his notions.

"Many sad sights!" And he shook his head with a sigh; then added, briskly, "But there is a deal of charity in our city, and it does its work beautifully. By the by, I heard of a very sweet charity the other day,—a church whose Sunday school is open to all the poor children who will come; and there, in pleasant rooms, with books, pictures, kindly teachers, and a fatherly minister to welcome them, the poor little creatures find refreshment for their hungry souls. I like that; it's a lovely illustration of the text, 'Suffer little children to come unto me;' and *I* call it practical Christianity."

He did like it, my benevolent old bird; for he rustled his great wings, as if he wanted to clap them, if there had only been room; and every feather shone as if a clearer light than that of my little fire had fallen on it as he spoke.

"You are a literary woman, hey?" he said suddenly, as if he'd got a new idea, and was going to pounce upon me with it.

"Ahem! I do a little in that line," I answered, with a modest cough.

"Then tell people about that place; write some stories for the children; go and help teach them; do something, and make others do what they can to increase the Sabbath sunshine that brightens one day in the week for the poor babies who live in shady places."

"I should be glad to do my best; and, if I'd known before"—I began.

"You might have known, if you'd looked about you. People are so wrapped up in their own affairs they don't do half they might. Now, then, hand me a bit of paper, and I'll give you the address, so you won't have any excuse for forgetting what I tell you."

"Mercy on us! what will he do next?" thought I, as he tweaked a feather out of his breast, gave the nib a peck, and then coolly wrote these words on the card I handed him: *"Church of the Disciples. Knock, and it shall be opened!"* There it was, in letters of gold; and, while I looked at it, feeling reproached that I hadn't known it sooner, my friend,—he didn't seem a stranger any more,—said in a business-like tone, as he put back his pen, "Now I must be off. Old Ben reads an article on the 'Abuses of the Press at the present day,' and I must be there to report."

"It must be very interesting. I suppose you don't allow mortals at your meetings?" said I, burning to go, in spite of the storm.

"No, ma'am. We meet on the Common; and, in the present state of the weather, I don't think flesh and blood would stand it. Bronze, marble, and wood, are sterner stuff, and can defy the elements."

"Good evening; pray, call again," I said, hospitably.

"I will; your eyrie suits me; but don't expect me to call in the daytime. I'm on duty then, and can't take my eye off my charge. The city needs a deal of watching, my dear. Bless me! it's striking eight. Your watch is seven minutes slow by the Old South. Good-night, good-night!"

And as I opened the window, the great bird soared away like a flash of light through the storm, leaving me so astonished at the whole performance that I haven't got over it yet.

# Fairy Pinafores

AFTER CINDERELLA WAS married and settled, her god-mother looked about for some other clever bit of work to do, for she was not only the best, but the busiest little old lady that ever lived. Now the city was in a sad state, for all it looked so fine and seemed so gay. The old king was very lazy and sat all day in his great easy-chair, taking naps and reading newspapers, while the old queen sat opposite in *her* easy-chair, taking naps and knitting gold-thread stockings for her son. The prince was a fine young man, but rather wild, and fonder of running after pretty young ladies with small feet than of attending to the kingdom.

The wise god-mother knew that Cinderella would teach him better things by and by, but the old lady could not wait for that. So, after talking the matter over with her ancient cat, Silverwhisker, she put on her red cloak, her pointed hat and high-heeled shoes, took her cane and trotted away to carry out her plan. She was so fond of making people happy that it kept her brisk and young in spite of her years; and, for all I know, she may be trotting up and down the world this very day, red cloak, pointed hat, high-heeled shoes, and all.

In her drives about the city, she had been much grieved to see so many beggar-children, ragged, hungry, sick, and cold, with no friends to care for them, no homes to shelter them, and no one to teach, help, or comfort them. When Cinderella's troubles were well over, the good god-mother resolved to attend to this matter, and set about it in the following manner:—

She went into the poor streets, and whenever she found a homeless child she bade it come with her; and so motherly was her face, so kind her voice, that not one feared or refused. Soon she had gathered a hundred little boys and girls,—a sad sight, for some were lame, some blind, some deformed, many black and many ugly, all hungry, ragged, and forlorn, but all dear children in her sight, for the little hearts were not spoilt, and her fairy power could work all miracles. When she had enough, she led them beyond the city gates into the beautiful country and no one saw them go, for she made them invisible to other eyes. Wondering, yet contented, they trooped along, delighted with all they saw. The strong helped the weak; those who could see described the lovely sights to the blind; the hungry found berries all along the road; the sick gladly breathed the fresh air, and to none did the way seem long, for green grass was underneath their feet, blue sky overhead, and summer sunshine everywhere.

As they came out from a pleasant wood, a great shouting arose, when the god-mother pointed to a lovely place and told them that was home. She had but to wish for any thing and it was hers; so she had wished for a Children's Home, and there it was. In a wide meadow stood a large, low house, with many blooming little gardens before it, and sunny fields behind it, full of pretty tame creatures, who came running as if to welcome and tell the children that their holiday had begun. In they went, and stood quite breathless with wonder and delight, all was so pleasant and so new. There were no stairs to tire little feet with climbing up, or to bump little heads with tumbling down, but four large rooms opening one into the other, with wide doors and sunny windows on every side.

In one stood a hundred clean white beds, with a hundred little, clean white caps and gowns ready for the night. Dark curtains made a comfortable twilight here, and through the room sounded a soft lullaby from an unseen instrument, so soothing that all the children gaped at once and began to nod like a field of poppies.

"Yes, yes, that will work well, I see; but it is not yet time for bed," said the god-mother, and, touching another spring, there instantly sounded a lively air, which would wake the soundest sleeper and make him skip gayly out of bed.

In the second room was a bath, so large that it looked like a shallow lake. A pretty marble child stood blowing bubbles in the middle, and pink and white shells, made of soap, lay along the brim. The pool was lined with soft sponges, and heaps of towels were scattered about, so that while the little folks splashed and romped they got finely washed and wiped before they knew it.

In the third room stood a long table, surrounded by low chairs, so no one could tip over. Two rows of bright silver porringers shone down the table; a fountain of milk played in the middle, and on a little railway, that ran round the table, went mimic cars loaded with bread, funny donkeys with panniers of berries on either side, and small men and women carrying trays of seed-cakes, gingerbread, and all the goodies that children may safely eat. Thus every one got quickly and quietly served, and meals would be merry-makings, not scenes of noise and confusion, as is often the case where many little mouths are to be filled.

The fourth room was larger than any of the others, being meant for both work and play. The walls were all pictures, which often changed, showing birds, beasts, and flowers, every country, and the history of the world; so one could study many things, you see. The floor was marked out for games of all kinds, and quantities of toys lay ready for the little hands that till now had owned so few. On one side long windows opened into the gardens, and on the other were recesses full of books to study and to read.

At first, the poor children could only look and sigh for happiness, finding it hard to believe that all this comfort could be meant for them. But the god-mother soon made them feel that this was home, for, gathering them tenderly about her, she said,—

"Dear little creatures, you have had no care, no love or happiness, all your short, sad lives; but now you are mine, and here you shall soon become the blithest, busiest children ever seen. Come, now, and splash in this fine pond; then we will have supper and play, and then to bed, for to-morrow will be a long holiday for all of us."

As she spoke, the children's rags vanished, and they sprang into the bath, eager to pick up the pretty shells and see the marble child, who, smiling, blew great bubbles that sailed away over their heads.

Great was the splashing and loud the laughter as the little people floated in the warm pool and romped among the towel-cocks, while the god-mother, in a quiet corner, bathed the sick and bound up the hurts of those whom cruel hands had wounded.

As fast as the children were washed, they were surprised to find themselves clothed all in a minute in pretty, comfortable suits, that pleased their eyes, and yet were not too fine for play. Soon a ring of happy faces shone round the table. The fountain poured its milky stream into every porringer, the mimic cars left their freight at each place, the donkeys trotted, and the little market-men and women tripped busily up and down, while the god-mother went tapping about, putting on bibs, helping the shy ones, and feeding the babies who could not feed themselves. When all were satisfied, the fountain ceased to play, the engine let off steam, the donkeys kicked up their heels to empty the panniers, the bibs folded themselves up, the porringers each turned a somerset and came down clean, and all was ready for breakfast.

Then the children played for an hour in the lovely play-room, often stopping to wonder if they wouldn't presently wake up and find it all a dream. Lest they should get quite wild with excitement, the god-mother soon led them to the great bedroom, and ordered on the caps and gowns, which was done before the children could wink. Then she taught them the little prayer all children love, and laid them in their cosey beds, with a good-night kiss for each. The lullaby-flute began to play, weary eyelids to close, and soon a hundred happy little souls lay fast asleep in the Children's Home.

For a long time the old lady let her family do nothing but enjoy themselves. Every morning they were led out into the meadow like a flock of lambs, there to frisk all day with their healthful playmates, sun and air, green grass, and exercise; for, being a wise woman, she left them to the magic of a better nurse than herself, and Nature, the dear god-mother of the world, did her work so well that soon no one would have known the rosy, happy troop for the forlorn little creatures who had come there.

Then the old lady was satisfied, and said to herself,—

"Now they may work a little, else they will learn to love idleness. What shall I give them to do that will employ their hands, make them happy, and be of use to others?"

Now, like many other excellent old ladies, the god-mother had a pet idea, and it was *pinafores*. In her day all children wore them, were simply dressed, healthy, gay, and good. At the present time foolish mothers dressed their little ones like dolls, and the poor things were half-smothered with finery. At home there was a constant curling and brushing, tying of sashes and fussing with frills, abroad there was no fun, for hats, top-heavy with feathers, burdened their heads, fine cloaks and coats were to be taken care of, smart boots, in which they couldn't run, were on their feet, and dainty little gloves prevented their ever making dear dirt-pies. Very cross and fretful were the poor little people made by all this, though they hardly knew what the matter was, and the foolish mammas wondered and sighed, sent for Dr. Camomile, and declared there were never seen such naughty children before.

"Put on pinafores, and let them romp at their ease, and you will mend all this," said the god-mother, who knew everybody.

But the fine ladies were shocked, and cried out: "My dear madam, it is impossible, for pinafores are entirely out of fashion," and there it ended.

But the old lady never gave up her idea, and when she had successfully tried it with her large family, she felt sure that much of the health and happiness of children lay in big, sensible pinafores and plenty of freedom.

"I'll show them the worth of my idea," she said as she sat thinking, with her eyes on the blue flax-fields shining in the sun. "These poor children shall help the rich ones, who never helped them, and we will astonish the city by the miracles we'll work."

With that she clapped her hands, and in a minute the room was filled with little looms and spinning-wheels, thimbles and needles, reels for winding thread, and all necessary tools for the manufacture of fairy pinafores. She could have wished for them already made, but she thought it better to teach the children some useful lessons, and keep them busy as well as happy.

Soon they were all at work, and no one was awkward or grew tired, for the wheels and looms were enchanted; so, though the boys and girls knew nothing of the matter when they began, they obeyed the old lady, who said,—

> "A good will
> Giveth skill,"

and presently were spinning and weaving, reeling and sewing, as if they had done nothing else all their lives.

Many days they worked, with long play spells between, and at last there lay a hundred wonderful pinafores before their eyes. Each was white as snow, smooth as satin, and all along the hem there shone a child-name curiously woven in gold or silver thread. But the charm of these "pinnies," as the children called them, was that they would never tear, get soiled, or wear out, but always remain as white and smooth and new as when first made, for they were woven of fairy flax. Another fine thing was that whoever wore one would grow gentle and good, for the friendly little weavers and spinners had put so much love and good-will into their work that it got into the pinafores and would never come out, but shone in the golden border, and acted like a charm on the childish hearts the aprons covered.

Very happy were the little people as they saw the pile grow higher and higher, for they knew what they were doing, and wondered who would wear each one.

"Now," said the god-mother, "which of my good children shall go to the city and sell our pinnies?"

"Send Babie, she is the best and has worked harder than all the rest," answered the children; and little Barbara quite blushed to be so praised.

"Yes, she shall go," said the god-mother, as she began to lay the aprons in a little old-fashioned basket.

As soon as the children saw it, they gathered about it like a swarm of bees, exclaiming,—

"See! see! it is Red Riding-Hood's little basket in which she carried the pot of butter. Dear grandma, where did you get it?"

"The excellent old lady whom the wolf ate up was a friend of mine, and after that sad affair I kept it to remember her by, my dears. It is an immortal basket, and all children love it, long to peep into it, and would give much to own it."

"What am I to do?" asked Babie, as the god-mother hung the basket on her arm.

"Go to the Royal Park, my dear, where all the young lords and ladies walk; stand by the great fountain, and when any children ask about the basket, tell them they may put in their hands and take what they find for a silver penny. They will gladly pay it, but each must kiss the penny and give it with a kind word, a friendly wish, before they take the pinnies. When all are sold, lay the silver pennies in the sunshine, and whatever happens, be sure that it is what I wish. Go, now, and tell no one where you come from nor why you sell your wares."

Then Babie put on her little red cloak, took the basket on her arm, and went away toward the city, while her playmates called after her,—

"Good luck! good-by! Come home soon and tell us all about it!"

When she came to the great gate, she began to fear she could not get in, for, though she had often peeped between the bars and longed to play with the pretty children, the guard had always driven her away, saying it was no place for her. Now, however, when she came up, the tall sentinel was so busy looking at her basket that he only stood smiling to himself, as if some pleasant recollection was coming back to him, and said slowly,—

"Upon my word, I think I must be asleep and dreaming, for there's little Red Riding-Hood come again. The wolf is round the corner, I dare say, Run in, my dear, run in before he comes; and I'll give the cowardly fellow the beating I've owed him ever since I was a boy."

Babie laughed, and slipped through the gate so quickly that the guard rubbed his eyes, looked about him, and said,—

"Yes, yes, I thought I was asleep. Very odd that I should dream of the old fairy-tale I haven't read this twenty years."

In a green nook near the great fountain, Babie placed herself, looking like a pretty picture with her smiling face, bright eyes, and curly hair blowing in the wind. Presently little Princess Bess came running by to hide from her maid, of whom she was sadly tired. When she saw Babie, she forgot every thing else, and cried out,—

"O the pretty basket! I must have it. Will you sell it, little girl?"

"No, my lady, for it isn't mine; but if you like to pay a silver penny, you may put in your hand and take what you find."

"Will it be the little pot of butter?" said the Princess, as she pulled out her purse.

"A much more useful and wonderful thing than that, my lady. Something that will never spoil nor wear out, but keep you always good and happy while you wear it," answered Babie.

"That's splendid! Take the penny, lift the lid, and let me see," cried Bess.

"First kiss it, with a kind word, a friendly wish, please, my lady; for these are fairy wares, and can be had in no other way," said Babie.

Princess Bess tossed her head at this, but she wanted the fairy gift, so she kissed the silver penny, said the word, and wished the wish; then in went her hand and out came the white pinafore, with a golden Bess shining all along the hem, and little crowns embroidered on the sleeves.

"O the pretty thing! Put it on, put it on before Primmins comes, else she won't let me wear it," cried the princess, throwing her hat and cloak on the grass, and hurrying on the pinafore.

She clapped her hands and danced about as if bewitched, for on each corner of the apron hung a tiny silver bell, which rang such a merry peal it made one dance and sing to hear it. Suddenly she stood quite still, while a soft look came into her face, as all the pride and wilfulness faded away. She touched the smooth, white pinafore, looked down at the golden name, listened to the fairy bells, and in that little pause seemed to become another child; for presently she put her arms round Babie's neck and kissed her, quite forgetting that one was a king's daughter and the other a beggar child.

"Dear little girl, thank you very much for my lovely pinny. Wait here till I call my playmates, that they too may buy your fairy wares."

Away she ran, and was soon back again with a troop of children so gayly dressed they looked like a flock of butterflies. The maids came with them, and all crowded about the wonderful basket, pushing and screaming, for these fine children had not fine manners. Babie was rather frightened, but Bess stood by her and rang her little bells, so that all stopped to listen. One by one each paid the penny, with the friendly word and wish, and then drew out the magic pinafore, which always showed the right name. The maids were so much interested when they learned that these aprons made their wearers good, that they gladly put them on; for, having gold and silver woven in them, the fine linen was not thought too plain for such noble little people to wear.

How they all changed as the pinnies went on! No more screaming, pushing, or fretting; only smiling faces, gentle voices, and the blithe ringing of the fairy bells: The poor maids almost cried for joy, they were so tired of running after naughty children; and every thing looked so gay that people stopped to peep at the pretty group in the Royal Park.

When the last apron was sold, Babie told them that something strange was going to happen, and they might see it if they liked. So they made a wide ring round a sunny spot where she had laid the hundred silver pennies. Presently from each coin sprang a little pair of wings; on one the kind word, on the other the friendly wish that had been uttered over them, and, lifted by their magic, the pennies rose into the air like a flock of birds, and flew away over the tree-tops, shining as they went.

All the children were so eager to see where they would alight that they ran after. No one stumbled, no one fell, though they followed through crowded streets and down among strange places where they had never been before. All the maids ran after the children, and the stately papas and mammas followed the maids, quite distracted by the strange behavior of their children and servants. A curious sight it was, and the city was amazed, but the pennies flew on till they came to a bleak and barren spot, where many poor children tried to play in the few pale rays of sunshine that crept between the tall roofs that stood so thickly crowded on every side. Here the pennies folded their wings and fell like a silver shower, to be welcomed by cries of joy and wonder by the ragged children.

The poor mothers and fathers left their work to go and see the sight, and were as much amazed to find a crowd of fine people as the fine people were to see them; for, though they had heard of each other, they had never met, and did not know how sad was the contrast between them.

No one knew what to do at first, it was all so strange and new. But the magic that had got into the pinafores began to work, and soon Princess Bess was seen emptying her little purse among the poor children. The other boys and girls began at once to do the same, then the fine ladies felt their hearts grow pitiful, and they looked kindly at the poor, sad-faced women as they spoke friendly words and promised help. At sight of this, the lords and gentlemen were ashamed to be outdone by their wives and children, and the heavy purses came out when the little ones failed, till all about the dreary place there was played a beautiful new game called "give away."

No one ever knew who did it, but, as the city clock struck noon, all the bells in all the steeples began to ring, and the tune they played was the same blithe one the little bells had chimed. Other wonders happened, for as the clear peal went sounding through the air the sun came glancing through all manners of chinks never seen before, and shone warm and bright upon the rich and poor standing together like one family. The third wonder was that when the fine folk came to put their purses back into their pockets, they were fuller than before, because for every bit of money given away there were two in its place, shining brighter than any gold, and marked with a little cross.

This was the beginning, but it would take a long time to tell all the good done by the fairy pinafores. Nobody guessed they were at the bottom of the changes which came about, but people thought some blessing had befallen the children, so blooming, good, and gay did they become. Busied with their own affairs, the older people would have forgotten the poor folk and the promises made them, if the children had not reminded them. Some little girl who wore a fairy pinny would climb into her mother's lap and say,—

"Mamma, I'm tired of my dolls; I want to make some clothes for the ragged children we saw the day I bought my pretty pinafore. Will you show me how?"

Then the mother would kiss the little face she loved so well, and give the child her wish, finding much happiness in seeing the comfortable suits go on, and receiving the thanks of less fortunate women; for motherly hearts are the same under rags and silk. The boys, though small fellows, were never tired of playing the new game with silver pennies, and made their fathers play with them, till many men who began it to please the little lads went on for the love of charity.

Princess Bess ordered the Park gates to stand open for the poor as well as the rich, and soon one could hardly tell the difference; for the poor children were comfortably clothed, and the foolish mammas, finding their little sons and daughters grew rosy strong, and happy in the plain pinafores, grew wiser, and left off fretting them with useless finery, finding that their own innocent gayety and beauty were their sweetest ornaments, and learning that the good old fashion of simplicity was the best for all.

Things were prospering in this way when news of the fairy pinafores reached the old king. He seldom troubled himself about matters, but when he read accounts of the kind things his people were doing, he was so much interested that he forgot his nap, and the queen counted her stitches all amiss while listening. Cinderella and the Prince heard of it also, and felt quite reproached that they had forgotten every one but themselves. It was talked of at court, and everybody wished pinafores for their children; but the unknown child with the famous basket had vanished no one knew whither.

At last, after searching through the city, a sentinel was found who remembered seeing Babie come in from the country. When the king heard this, he ordered his carriage, the old queen put by her work to go with him, and the Prince with Cinderella got into the famous pumpkin coach, for they too wished to see the wonderful child.

Away they drove, followed by their lords and ladies, through the wood, and there beyond they saw the Children's Home. Full of curiosity, yet fearing to alarm the dwellers in that quiet place, every one alighted and went softly toward the house.

Every thing was so still and pleasant, all were charmed, and felt as if a spell were falling on them. When the court gentlemen heard the song of the birds overhead, they felt ashamed of the foolish speeches they were making; when the fine ladies saw the flowers blooming in the little gardens, their gay dresses seemed less beautiful; the old king and queen felt quite young and lively all at once, and Cinderella and her Prince longed for another race, such as they had when the glass slipper was lost.

Presently they found a little lad reading in the sun, and of him the king asked many questions. The child, forgetting that the god-mother wished to remain unknown, told all she had done, and bade them look in at the window, and see if what he said was not true. Every one peeped, and there they saw the children sitting at the looms and wheels motionless; for the dear old lady had fallen fast asleep, and no one stirred lest they should wake her. Like a room full of breathing, smiling images they sat, and, as the heads came at the windows, all looked up and whispered, "Hush!" like a soft wind sighing through the place.

Cinderella, who dearly loved her god-mother, felt reproached that she had done so little while the good old lady had done so much, and, stepping in, she began to stitch away on one of the new set of pinafores which they were making. At that, the lively young Prince skipped in after her, and whisking a small boy out of his seat before a loom, began to weave with all his might; for, as the old lady said,—

"A good will
Giveth skill."

"I'll not be outdone by those children!" cried the king, and began briskly winding the thread which hung on blind Nanny's outstretched hands.

"Neither will I, my dear!" returned the queen, and whipping on her spectacles she cut out a pinafore on the spot.

After that, of course, every one else came rushing in, and soon all the wheels buzzed, looms jangled, needles flew, and scissors snipped, while the children stood by smiling at the sight of the fine folks working as if for their lives.

The noise woke the god-mother, who understood the matter at once, and was glad to see things in such good train. As she wished to say a word, she gave a smart tap with her staff, and every one stopped but the king, who was so busy winding his thread that he kept on till the skein was done, when he patted Nanny on the head, saying, in such a brisk tone his people hardly knew him for the lazy old king,—

"There, I feel better for that. We'll do another presently, my fine little girl." Then he nodded to the god-mother with twinkling eyes, for being a fairy he respected her very much. She nodded back at him, and said gravely,—

"Your majesty is very welcome, and I am glad you have waked up at last. Don't fall asleep again, but go and make homes for all your poor, so that when you do fall asleep for the last time you will leave your son as happy a kingdom as you have found here. And you, my dear Cinderella, remember this: let your children be children while they may, and be sure they all wear pinafores."

# The Moss People

"Rain, rain, go away,
come again another day,"

SANG little Marnie, as she stood at the window watching the drops patter on the pane, the elm-boughs toss in the wind, and the clover-blossoms lift up their rosy faces to be washed. But the rain did not go away, and, finding that mamma had fallen asleep over her book, Marnie said to herself,—

"I will go and play quietly with my fairy-land till mamma wakes up and cuts me some paper fairies to put in it."

Marnie's fairy-land was as pretty a plaything as any child could wish for, and, as every child can make one in the summer-time, let us tell what it was. The little girl firmly believed in elves, and was always wishing she could go to fairy-land. That rainy day, when she had longed for something to do, her mother said,—

"As you can't go to fairy-land, why don't you make one for yourself?"

Such a happy thought, and such a busy little girl as Marnie was, working away, forgetful of rain or loneliness! Mamma was so kind and helpful in suggesting ways and supplying means, that the new fairy-land really did seem to rise as if by enchantment.

A long, shallow box, filled with earth, which was covered with moss of all kinds, gathered by Marnie the day before; some green as grass, some soft as velvet, some full of red-brimmed cups, some feathery and tall, some pale and dry: marsh, rock, tree, and field had given their share, and out of this the little hands fashioned a dainty pleasure-ground for the elves. Ferns and spires of evergreen were the trees fencing in the garden, standing in groups or making shady avenues. Silver-white mushrooms with rosy lining stood here and there, like little tables, and mossy mounds or colored pebbles served for seats. Marnie's china bowl was sunk deep in the moss, filled with water, on which floated pea-pod boats with rose-leaf sails. Acorn-cups, with blue and white comfits for eggs, were fastened in the trees, and toy-birds brooded over their nests in the most natural manner. Dead butterflies, lady-bugs, and golden-green beetles from Marnie's museum, hung here and there, as if alive. On a small mound stood a pretty Swiss châlet, with some droll wooden men and women near it. One girl was churning, another rocking a mite of a baby, a man and his donkey were just going up the hill, and a family of wooden bears from Berne sat round a table eating dinner. A little marble hound with a golden chain about its neck guarded this child's paradise, and nothing was wanted to make it quite perfect but some of the winged paper dolls with prettily painted faces that mamma made so nicely.

"I must wait till she wakes up," said Marnie, with a patient sigh, as she drew her little chair before the table where the box stood, and, leaning her chin on her chubby hand, sat looking admiringly at her work.

The ruddy glow of the fire shone warmly over the green hills and dales of fairy-land, the soft patter of the rain sounded like tiny feet tripping to and fro, and all the motionless inhabitants of the garden seemed waiting for some spell to break their sleep. Marnie never knew how it happened, but, as she sat looking at the Swiss cottage, she suddenly heard a rustling inside, and saw something pass before the open windows. She thought the chrysalis she had put in there had come to life, and waited, hoping to see a pretty butterfly pop its head out. But what a start she gave when suddenly the little door opened and a wee man came marching out. Yes, actually a living tiny man, dressed like a hunter, in green from top to toe, with a silver horn slung over his shoulder and a bow in his hand.

Marnie held her breath lest she should blow him away, and peeped with all her eyes from behind the hemlock-boughs, wondering what would happen next. Up the steps ran the little man to the balcony that always hangs outside a Swiss châlet, and lifting his horn to his lips blew a blast so soft and clear it sounded like the faint, far-off carol of a bird. Three times the fairy bugle sounded, and at the third blast, swarming up from the moss below, dropping from the ferns above, floating on the ripples of the mimic lake, and turning somersaults over the mushrooms, came hundreds of lovely little creatures, all gay, all graceful, all in green. How they danced to and fro, airy as motes in a sunbeam! how they sung and shouted as they peeped everywhere! and how their tiny faces shone as they rejoiced over the pleasant land they had found! For the same peal that brought the moss people from their beds woke up every inanimate thing in fairy-land.

The toy-birds began to sing, the butterflies and lady-bugs fluttered gayly about, the white hound broke his chain and frisked away, the wooden maid began to churn, the mother set the cradle rocking, while the mite of a baby kicked up its wooden legs, and the man whipped the donkey, which gave such a natural bray Marnie couldn't help laughing, it was so droll. Smoke rose from the Swiss cottage, as if fairy feasts were being cooked within; and the merry moss people, charmed with the pretty house, crowded it so full that every window showed half-a-dozen bright faces, the balcony quite creaked with the weight of them, and green caps came bobbing out at the chimney-top.

Dear me, what fun they did have! Marnie never saw such capital games before; and the best of it was, every one joined in them,—moss men and women, wee moss children, even moss grandfathers and mothers, as gray as the lichens from which they came. Delightful little folk they were, so lovely in face, so quaint in dress, so blithe and brisk in spirit, so wonderful and bewitching altogether that Marnie longed to call her mother, but did not, lest a word should frighten them away.

Presently she caught the sound of delicate noises, and, listening intently, she discovered that they were talking of her.

"Ha! ha! isn't this a fine pleasure-ground for us this rainy day!" cried one merry moss boy, as he paused to settle his pointed cap, after turning somersaults till he looked like a leaf blown about by the wind.

"Hush, Prance," whispered a pretty little moss girl, with a wreath of coral in her hair, "you will wake the child if you shout so loud, and then she will no longer see and hear us, which would be a pity; for we amuse her, as one may guess by the smile on her face."

Now that surprised Marnie very much, for she was sure she was wide awake, and would have said so, if she had not remembered that it was not polite to contradict.

"What shall we do to thank this child for making us a pretty garden?" said Prance, skipping because he couldn't keep still.

"Let us put her baby-house in order," answered little Trip, who was a tidy body.

"So we will, and play in it afterward," cried all the moss children, whisking away to the corner of the nursery where Marnie's toys were tumbling about. Such busy, helpful little people as they were! and such wonders as they worked with their fairy fingers! Marnie forgot to be ashamed of the disorderly baby-house in her delight at the change they soon wrought.

The boys mended broken chairs and tables, pots and pans, trundled the small furniture to its proper place, and attended to the wooden cows and horses in the topsy-turvy barn. The little maids swept and dusted, put the doll's clothes in order, ran about the kitchen, washing cups and dishes, or rubbed up the mirrors in the drawing-room, which was a very fine apartment. Yes, indeed! for the curtains were of red damask, the sofa had real pillows, a tiny piano tinkled its six notes, and the centre-table held a vase of elegant wax-flowers, not to mention that there was a grate, gilt clock, two fine candlesticks, and portraits of all the dolls painted by mamma.

"There!" said Prance, when not a speck of dust remained: "now things look as they should, and I hope Miss Marnie will take the hint and keep her house tidy. Now what shall we play?"

"I've been thinking this would be a nice chance to try living like real people, as we have often wanted to. Let some be servants, some fine ladies and gentlemen, and all do as much like these persons in the house as we can."

As Trip spoke, all the moss children clapped their hands, and skipped about, crying,—

"We will! we will!"

The dear little sprites had no idea that servants were not as nice parts to play as master and mistress; so one was Byelow the nurse, and put on a cap and shawl, and took some very young moss folk into the doll's nursery to play be the fine people's children. Another was cook, and clattered the pans about in the kitchen with a big apron on, and her little dress pinned up. A third was Dimity the maid, very smart indeed, and full of airs. A stoutish moss boy was coachman, and began to rub down the painted horses, and furbish up the little carriages in the stable; while another with plump legs put powder on his head and played footman.

Prance and Trip took the hardest parts of all, for they said they would be master and mistress. There was no trouble about clothes, for some fashion-books lay on the table, and these queer little things only had to choose what costume they would have, when, lo and behold! there it was all made and on. Marnie didn't think them half so pretty in the fashionable finery as in their own simple green suits, and she laughed heartily at the funny mistakes they made in getting their furbelows and feathers properly arranged. Poor Prance quite gasped in his little broadcloth suit as he put on a tiny beaver, smoothed his gloves, and shouldered a doll's umbrella, saying so like Marnie's papa that she quite started,—

"Mrs. Prance, I wish to dine at three: don't be behind hand."

"Yes, dear," meekly answered Trip, who had whisked into an elegant morning-dress and cap, and nodded from the window as Mr. Prance went by to his office.

"What will you have for dinner, ma'am?" asked Skillet the cook, popping her head into the parlor where madam was playing read a novel on the sofa.

"Mercy on us! I'm sure I don't know;" and little Mrs. Prance ran down to see what there was in the pantry.

Mr. Prance was evidently not a good provider; for all she could find was a pea which came out of one of the boats, some jelly, sugar, milk, and cake which Marnie had been playing with, and a whole dinner in wood, painted brilliantly and stuck on to the dishes.

"It's a rainy day, and no one is likely to come to dinner, so we will have a pease pudding with jelly, and warm up these dishes, for every thing is very high,—we must economize," said Mrs. Prance, shaking her head, just as mamma often did when she visited the kitchen.

"Very well, ma'am," returned Skillet, retiring into the closet to eat cake and jelly, and drink the milk as soon as her mistress left the room.

"It's time to dress, I suppose, for some one may call. Get out my blue silk and lace head-dress, Dimity," said Mrs. Prance, going up to her chamber, too busy about her toilet to mind the baby, who was crying in the nursery.

"Lace me tightly. I'm growing stout, I do believe, and my figure will be ruined if I allow it," said madam; and Dimity squeezed her into such a tight dress that Trip got a pain in her side directly. "I can bear it a little while, but I don't see how ladies can do it all the time,—it's dreadful!" she sighed, as Dimity piled her pretty hair in a fuzzy bunch on the top of her head, and hung jewels in her little ears, after putting costly bits of lace here and there, and poking her tiny feet into high-heeled boots that made her totter when she tried to walk. These and her train nearly tripped her up, for, if Dimity had not caught her, Mrs. Prance would have tumbled downstairs.

Hardly was she safe in the parlor when the bell rang, and Buttons showed in several very fashionable ladies, who sat down and began to talk about dress, servants, gentlemen, and the opera, so exactly like some of mamma's callers that Marnie wondered where the sly little moss people could have been hidden to know how to imitate them so well. As soon as one lady left, all the rest said sharp things about her; and when they got out, after saying good-by most tenderly, they all abused Mrs. Prance, who said to herself when alone,—

"Tiresome, ill-natured creatures, I can't bear any of them; but I must return their calls as soon as my new bonnet comes from Paris."

By the time the last gossip was gone, it was past two, and Mrs. Prance was dying for her dinner, being quite exhausted. Imagine her dismay when her husband arrived with two gentlemen to dine. She clasped her hands and flew into the kitchen, where she found Skillet fuming over the little stove, and scolding because it wasn't a range like the one she used in her last place. Every thing was in confusion, and the prospect of dinner a gloomy one.

"We must have soup," cried distracted Mrs. Prance.

"No meat to make it of, ma'am," said Skillet, crossly.

"Boil two or three of these caraway-seeds in a pot of hot water, pepper it well, and add the leg of that fly to give it a relish, then call it by some French name, and it will be all right," returned Mrs. Prance, who was suddenly inspired by this bright thought. "Dissolve some of the jelly for wine, and send up those nuts and raisins for dessert. Do your best, Skillet, and don't keep us waiting."

"I'd like to give you a week's warning, ma'am, the place don't suit me," said the red-faced cook, with her arms akimbo.

"Don't be impertinent, Skillet! You can go tomorrow, if you wish, but till then behave yourself," and Mrs. Prance retired with dignity.

Dressing her tired countenance in smiles, she went to welcome her un-desired guests, and thank them for "this unexpected pleasure." Mr. William Wisp and Mr. Robin Goodfellow were two very elegant little gentlemen, with ruffled shirt-fronts, eye-glasses, and curled-up mustaches, quite splendid to behold. They chatted with their host and hostess in the most affable manner, affecting not to see that Mr. Prance's face grew more and more stern every minute, and that poor Mrs. Prance cast despairing glances at the clock, which plainly said "half-past three."

It really was becoming awkward, when Buttons announced, "Dinner, ma'am," and the cloud lifted suddenly from the faces of all. Skillet had done her best, fearing she wouldn't get her wages if she didn't; and the first course did very well.

Greasy warm water, flavored with pepper, was so like a French soup no one knew the difference, and everybody took a few sips and pretended to like it; but to airy creatures, fed on sun and dew, it wasn't nice, of course. There was no fish, for the tin ones melted in the frying-pan; and there was no time to get any more. The wooden leg of mutton got burnt in the oven, and the painted vegetables were not very satisfactory, though they looked quite fine. Mr. Prance frowned as he chipped away at the meat, and Mrs. Prance wanted to sob behind her napkin as he gave her a black look, saying sternly,—

"Mrs. P., your cook is unbearable. I desire that you will dismiss her at once."

"I have, my dear," meekly answered his wife; and then good-natured Mr. Wisp struck in with a droll anecdote, while every one pecked at the painted feast, and was glad when the pudding came.

Here was another blow; for instead of leaving the pea in its skin, and sending it up a nice, round little pudding, Skillet had taken the skin off as if it was the cloth it was boiled in, and nothing remained but a mealy ruin.

Mrs. Prance groaned, and then coughed to hide the sound of woe, and served out her dish with the calmness of despair. The jelly didn't go round, the cook had eaten so much on the sly; and when the wine came, Mr. Prance looked disgusted, it was so weak. However, the nuts and raisins were all right; and after one sip of currant-water, in answer to the gentlemen when they drank her health, unhappy Mrs. Prance left the table, wishing that she never had been born.

Trip was a clever little sprite, and entered into the spirit of her part so heartily that she really dropped a tear or two as she sat alone in her fine drawing-room. Presently the gentlemen came to say good-by, for they were going to try Prance's horses. Tired Mrs. Prance wished her husband would ask her to join them,—a drive would be so refreshing; but he only nodded grimly, and went away without a word. Mrs. Prance immediately took to her bed, for she was to have a party in the evening, and feared she never would live through it if she didn't rest.

But very little repose did the poor lady get that afternoon, for the children acted as if possessed. Flibberty-Gibbet fell off his rocking-horse and broke the bridge of his nose. Midget set her little dress a-fire, and frightened every one out of their wits. Poppet ran out of the back gate, and was lost for a whole hour; while Weewee, the baby, had a fit, owing to Mrs. Byelow's giving him a pickle when he cried for it. If poor, dear Mrs. Prance was hustled off her bed once that afternoon, she was a dozen times, and at last gave it up entirely, whipped the children all round, scolded every servant in the house, had a good cry and a strong cup of tea, and felt better.

The gentlemen, meantime, had each lighted a tiny cigarette, made from one stolen from papa's box, and had driven off in great style. Mr. Prance had the tin gig, with Silver-gray for a horse; Mr. Wisp took the straw chaise and yellow Bill harnessed with red; Mr. Goodfellow chose the smart dog-cart with the creaking wheels, and black Jerry, who had lost his tail, but was a fine beast nevertheless. With their hats on one side, and puffing their cigars, the little gentlemen drove gayly round the squares in the carpet, till Prance proposed a race from one end of a long seam to the other.

Away they went, with much cracking of whips, and crying out "Hi, yar!" looking like three distracted bugs skimming along at a great rate. Prance would have certainly won, if, just as he passed Mr. Wisp, the wheel of the gig had not ran against a big knot in the seam, which upset Mr. Prance right in the way of Mr. Wisp, whose straw chaise turned over them all like an extinguisher, leaving nothing to be seen but yellow Bill's legs sticking straight up in the air.

Mr. Goodfellow passed the wreck, but soon returned in alarm to pull the wounded from the ruins. Prance was only shaken, but poor Mr. Wisp was so much bruised he could not rise, and when they looked about for a carriage in which to get him home, not one of the three could be had, for two were smashed, and Jerry had galloped off with the dog-cart, never pausing till he had reached the barn. With much difficulty they lifted the groaning Wisp on to a visiting-card, which fortunately lay on the floor, and bore him away to the residence of Mr. Prance.

The house had just subsided after the baby's fit, when this arrival set it all in confusion again. Wisp was put into the best bed, where, after a drop of arnica had been applied to his bruises, and a doll's smelling-bottle of hot water to his feet, he groaned himself to sleep.

Leaving his friend Robin to take care of him, Mr. and Mrs. Prance snatched a hasty cup of tea, and hurried to dress for their party.

Mr. Prance, I regret to say, was in a bad humor, for his dinner distressed him, his broken carriages annoyed him, and he didn't feel at all like seeing company. He pulled the bell down ringing for hot water, told the footman he was a "blockhead" because his boots were not blacked to his mind, and asked his wife "why the dickens the buttons were always off his shirts?"

Mrs. Prance was likewise out of sorts, and nothing went well. The new pink lace dress was not becoming. Dimity didn't dress her hair well, and she looked so pale and nervous that she was quite discouraged.

When master and mistress met at last in the lighted drawing-room, two crosser little faces were seldom seen. Trip threw herself into an arm-chair with a sigh, and put on her gloves in silence. Prance, who was a waggish moss boy, marched solemnly up and down the room with his hands in his pockets, and an air of offended dignity, that made Marnie shake with laughter.

"Mrs. Prance, you gave us a very bad dinner to-day, and I was much mortified. If you can't manage better, madam, I shall give up housekeeping."

"I sincerely wish you would, my dear, for what with servants, and children, and company, I am nearly worn out," and Mrs. Prance sobbed behind her lace handkerchief.

"I thought when I married you that you were able to look after things properly," said Mr. Prance, still marching up and down with a frown on his face.

"I never was taught to do any thing but look pretty," sighed Mrs. Prance.

"Don't be a goose, my dear."

"You used to call me an angel."

Here the bell rang. Mr. Prance took his hands out of his pockets, Mrs. Prance dried her tears, and both looked quite gay and beaming when the guests appeared.

Such dashing little beaux and belles as did arrive, dressed in the most astonishing style,—the ladies with bits of bouquets and fans, satin slippers, and trailing skirts. The gentlemen had stiff collars, gay ties, wee boots and gloves, and twirled their eye-glasses as if they had been going to parties all their lives. Every one simpered and chatted, laughed and flirted, looked at each other's clothes, and whispered gossip round the room. Then a band of moss people, led by the green huntsman's horn, struck up the blithest dancing tune ever heard, and the little company began to spin round in couples like a party of teetotums. It was not the airy, graceful gambols Marnie had admired in her fairy-land, but it was the fashionable step, and therefore must be elegant. There seemed to be a good deal of romping, and the gentlemen twisted the ladies about till they looked quite flushed.

They kept up the dancing as hard as they could till supper-time, when every one ate as if exhausted. Where the supper came from, Marnie didn't know; but there it was,—ice, salad, cake, coffee, oysters, and wine, all complete, and the company made themselves uncomfortable eating all sorts of stuff at that late hour. After supper, several of the young ladies sang, opening their mouths very wide, and screaming small screams without any music in them, while the little piano tottered under the banging it received. Then Misses Moth, Cobweb, and Peaseblossom gave an air from the famous opera of *Oberon,* and every one said, "How sweet!" as they patted their gloves together and tried to look as if they knew all about it.

After a good deal of noise, there was dancing again, and Marnie observed that the company got more and more excited. Some of the gentlemen were very silly, but the ladies did not seem to mind it. Poor Mr. and Mrs. Prance were so tired they could hardly keep their eyes open, and when at last their guests began to go they could scarcely hide their joy.

"Such a charming party!" "Had a most delightful time!" said the people, bidding them good-night; and then added as soon as the door was shut: "Wasn't it a miserable affair?" "Those Prances are very ordinary people, and I shall not go again,"—quite in the regular way.

I'm sorry to say that Mr. Prance was one of those who had taken too much wine; and when Mrs. Prance fell into a chair exhausted, he sat down upon the fender and began to sing,—

"Where the bee sucks, there suck I,"

in a sleepy voice, nodding like an owl.

This was very trying to Mrs. Prance's feelings: she lost her temper, and scolded him as well as she knew how. Marnie was quite frightened to hear the lecture she gave her naughty husband, who sat smiling and blinking till his little coat-tails took fire. The instant a bright blaze shot up behind him as he skipped off the fender, Mrs. Prance stopped scolding, and ran to put the fire out like a devoted little wife. But, oh! sad to tell, her dress caught, and in a minute two blazes flew about the room like a pair of lively Will-o'-the-wisps. Every one screamed and ran, men and maids, Mr. Goodfellow and his patient, the children tumbled out of bed, and came scampering downstairs, and Weewee roared in his cradle as loud as if he tried to call "Fire! Fire!"

Marnie was so frightened at the idea of those cunning, tricksy imps being burnt up, that she screamed also with all her might, and in a minute every sign of the moss people vanished. She rubbed her eyes, but all was quiet,—nothing stirred in fairy-land; the doll's house was topsy-turvy as before, and all she saw were hundreds of motes dancing in the sunshine that now shone brightly on her face. Marnie was so sorry to lose her new playmates, that she would have cried about it if mamma had not waked up just then and asked what was the matter. When Marnie had told her all about it, she laughed at the funny dream, and then looked sober, as she said, with a kiss,—

"If these sly rogues are going to come and imitate us to amuse our little children, we must be careful what we do that we may set them a good example."

"You and papa are not so bad as Mr. and Mrs. Prance, though you do some of the things they did. But the droll little moss boys and girls set *me* a good example in one way, and I'm going to show them that I don't forget it," said Marnie, beginning to put her playthings in order.

"So am I," added mamma, laughing again as she put away her novel and took up her sewing, thinking to herself that she really would attend more to the comfort of home, and not care so much for fashionable society.

So you see some good was done after all by the merry little phantoms of a dream, for Marnie and mamma did not forget the moss people.

# What Fanny Heard

SHE WAS LYING ON THE RUG, in the twilight, all alone, seeing pictures in the fire, and talking to herself.

It hadn't been a happy day, and Fanny felt a little sad, though she wouldn't own that the reason was because she had been idle, disobedient, and wilful.

"Nobody cares for me or takes any pains to make me happy," grumbled Fanny. "Since mamma died, and papa went to England, I've been just as miserable as I could be. Cousin Mary is so sober and strict and fussy, I don't have a bit of fun, but study, sew, walk, go to bed and get up, like the hateful little story-book girls, who never do wrong or get tired of going on as regularly as a clock. Oh, dear! if I had some friends and playmates, this big, quiet house wouldn't seem so dismal."

Fanny laid her face on her arm and tried to cry, but not having any thing to cry for, she couldn't squeeze out a single tear. Suddenly she heard a chime of delicate bells ringing sweetly in the room, and filling the air with perfume.

"Bless me, what's that?" and Fanny popped up her head to see. But every thing was still and in its place, and when she spoke the bells ceased.

So she lay down again, and presently heard a sweet little voice say sorrowfully,—

"What an ungrateful child Fanny is to say she has no friends, when the house is full of them, if she would only learn to see them! Her good cousin took her home, and tries to be a mother to her, though she is feeble and fond of quiet. It was very kind of her to have a noisy, spoilt child always about; for, though it worries her, she never complains, but tries to make Fanny a gentle, helpful, happy child."

The blue hyacinth standing in the window said this, and the lovely pink one answered warmly,—

"Yes, indeed! and I often wonder that Fanny doesn't see this, and try to return some of the patient care by affectionate little acts, and grateful words, and cheerful looks. Why, she might make this house perfectly charming, if she chose: it was too lonely and still before, but now a bright-faced, gentle little girl, with her merry ways, would delight us all.

"I bloom my best to please her, and send out my perfume to attract her, for I love her much, and want her to feel that I am her friend. But she takes no notice of me, she doesn't care for my love, she is blind to my beauty, and gives no answer to my sweet invitation, though she longs for playmates all the time."

With a soft sigh the flowers shook their delicate heads, and said no more. But before Fanny could speak, Goldy, the canary, gave a little skip on his perch, and cried out, in a shrill chirp,—

"I quite agree with you, ladies: that child doesn't know how to enjoy her blessings, or recognize her friends when she sees them. Here I sit day after day, telling her in all sorts of ways how glad I am she is come; how fond I am of her, and how much I want to talk with her. I get quite excited sometimes, and sing till my throat aches, trying to make her understand all this; but she won't, and all I get for my pains is a pettish, 'Do stop screaming, you noisy bird,' and a cloth over the cage to keep me quiet. It's very hard;" and Goldy shook a little tear out of his round black eye. "I love the sun, and air, and blithe company so dearly, and she won't let me have any of them.

"She promised to take care of me, but she doesn't, and I go hungry, thirsty, and untidy, while she mopes and wishes she had something pleasant to do.

"To-day, now, I've had neither seed nor water; no sniff of fresh air, no fly about the room, not a bit of apple, not a kind word or look, but have sat in the dark, with the cover over my cage, because I tried to tell how glad I was to see the sun, in spite of my hunger and thirst, loneliness and homesickness. Ah, well! some day she may be kinder to me, and then I'll show her what a loving friend I can be."

And with a last peck at the husks that lay in the cage, a last sad look about his gloomy house, Goldy put his head under his wing and tried to forget his troubles in sleep.

Fanny was going to start up and feed and pet him, with remorseful tenderness, when a new voice sounded behind her, and she waited to listen.

It was the piano, and every thing it said went to a sort of tune, because it couldn't help being musical at all times.

"When first she came to stay, little Fanny used to play and sing like any lark, between the daylight and the dark, and our mistress loved it well. But now, I grieve to tell, she scarcely sings a note; no more the sweet songs float like spirits through the gloom, making gay the quiet room.

"I cannot tell how much her little fingers' touch ever thrills me with delight; how my keys, black and white, love to dance as she plays; how my pedal quick obeys, and bass and treble blend, to please our little friend.

"But now she sits apart, with discord in her heart, forgetting I am here with power to soothe and cheer; that she'd better sing than sigh, better laugh than cry, for hearts get out of tune, and should be mended soon.

"Little Fanny, sing again, like a bird in spite of rain. Fill the house with music gay, make a concert of each day; and when others play on you, answer sweetly, as I do."

"Why, it's talking poetry, I do believe!" cried Fanny, as the last words went echoing through the room and died away.

"How any one can be lonely with us for friends is hard to understand," said another voice from the bookcase. "Here we are, lots of us, rows of us, regiments of us; every sort of story book; here's fairy tales new and old; here's Robinson Crusoe and dear old Mother Goose, Mrs. Barbauld and Miss Edgeworth; here's German picture books and French fables, English games and American notions, of every kind. Come and read us, come and read us, and never say again you have no friends, and nothing to do."

There was such a noise that no one heard Fanny laugh out, for each book was shouting its own title and making such a stir it sounded like a wind blowing dry leaves about.

"I don't wish to intrude myself, for I'm not literary, nor musical, nor botanical; but I am domestic, and have an eye for all useful things," said a needle, in a sharp tone, as it sat bolt upright in Fanny's topsy-turvy basket, on the table.

"I am woman's friend, and with my help she does a deal of good, whiles away many long hours, and finds a good deal of quiet happiness in my society. Little girls don't care much for me until they have doll children to sew for; even then some of them neglect and abuse me, and don't learn to use me nicely. I know a young lady who hasn't a rag to her back; and yet her mamma takes no pains to clothe her, though a charming blue dress, and white apron, and nice little underclothes lie all ready cut out and basted.

"I pity that poor doll so much that I'd gladly sew for her alone, if I could. I'm afraid I should be thought rude, if I suggested to the mamma to sew instead of fretting, so I wouldn't say a word on any account; but I see more than people would believe, and judge accordingly."

After which pointed remarks, the needle actually winked at the thimble, and then sat stiffer than ever in the unfinished blue gown.

Fanny was so ashamed that she turned her face toward the fire, just in time to see a brilliant spark-spirit standing in a cave of glowing coals. Waving its tiny hand, the spirit said,—

"Years ago a little girl lived here, who made this the happiest home ever seen, by her gentle ways, her loving heart, her cheerful voice, and willing hands.

"Every one loved her, and she was always happy, for duty was pleasant. The world was bright, and she was never out of tune.

"She tended flowers in the window yonder, and grew as beautiful as they; she touched the old piano, and filled the house with music; she fed her little bird, and was as cheerful as he; she read and studied those books, growing wise and good and gay on the food they gave her; she sewed busily, clothing naked children as well as dolls, and many blessed her. She often lay where you lie now, not discontented and sad, but with a happy heart, a busy fancy, and the love of many friends to keep her always blithe.

"We loved her well, and we love you for her dear sake. If you would see her image, look up and try to imitate her."

Rather startled at the serious manner of the sprite, Fanny lifted her eyes, and there hung the picture of her mother, when a little girl. She had often seen it before, but it never had seemed so beautiful and dear as now, when, looking at it with full eyes, little Fanny said softly to herself,—

"O dear mamma, I will be like you, if I can: I'll find friends where you found them; I'll make home happy as you did I'll try to be loved for your sake, and grow a useful, cheerful, good woman, like you."

# A Marine Merry-Making

"ARE YOU GOING TO Mrs. Turtle's this evening?" asked a gay young Periwinkle of his friend Cockle, as they met on the sands.

"Well, I don't know: what is to be done, and who will be there?" replied Cockle, rather languidly, for it had been a very gay season, and he was decidedly "used up."

"There will be no dancing, for the alderman doesn't approve of it; but there is to be singing, tableaux, and a supper of course. It's the last night of the season; and, as they are having a farewell hop up at the hotel, we thought we would get up some sort of fun among ourselves. Lovely Lily Crab will be there; the Lobsters, Barnacles, Horseshoes, and Sea-snails, besides the Mosquitoes, Fireflies, and Water-beetles. I hear there are also to be strangers of distinction, a Flying-fish, a Water-shrew, and Mother Carey's Chickens."

"Hum, ha, well; maybe I'll look in for an hour. I rather fancy Lily Crab; and the alderman gives capital suppers. I'm going to enjoy a weed; so ta-ta, till this evening."

Young Cockle didn't mean a cigar, but a nap under the sea-weed. Periwinkle took a weed also; and both were so much refreshed that they were among the first at the party.

The Turtles were a very aristocratic family, for they were both ancient and honorable. Their coat-of-arms was a globe resting on a turtle's back; and so many of their ancestors had been aldermen, it was vain to try to count them. Even their diseases were aristocratic, for they always died of apoplexy or gout. Some people said it was because they were such high livers; but the turtles insisted that it was hereditary, and couldn't be helped. They were very slow, and rather heavy, but intensely dignified and well-bred. They lived elegantly, gave fine parties, and had one son, who was considered a very eligible young Turtle. It was thought that he would marry the beautiful Lily Crab, the belle of the bay; but she flirted sadly with Oceanicus Lobster, and no one could tell which she would take.

The Turtles had chosen a fine, smooth place on the beach, with a pretty pool near by, for such of the guests as could not remain long out of water. A flat rock at one end was set apart as a stage for the tableaux; and at the other end the supper was spread. The alderman waddled importantly about before the company arrived, looking very portly and imposing; while his wife, in black velvet and gold ornaments, sat tranquilly by, and took a little rest before the labors of the evening began. Columbus, the son, was elegantly got up in a new suit of black, with a white tie, and a flower in his button-hole. The moon served for a chandelier; and a party of fireflies had promised to act as footlights when they were needed. The tide was coming in; and, instead of carriages, wave after wave rolled up and left its load at the Turtles' door.

The Barnacles and Mussels came first, for they seldom left home, and always got back again at an early hour. Miss Mosquito arrived, full of scandal and gossip, and kept up a perpetual hum in some one's ear, though everybody disliked, and tried to get rid of her. She was a vixenish spinster, thin, satirical, sharp-tongued, and so bad-tempered that people said her name, which was Xantippe, suited her excellently. A modest little Watershrew, in Quaker drab, came with the Beetles, who took their places near the pool, being unused to crowds. The Lobsters, always a peculiar family, came straggling in, one by one, in their usual awkward way, and were soon followed by the Periwinkles and Cockles. A party of Petrels came marching in with the Flying-fish, who looked, and doubtless felt, entirely out of his element. The bustle caused by the arrival of the distinguished strangers had just subsided, when Columbus Turtle and Oceanicus Lobster were seen to rush toward the door; young Cockle put his glass in his eye, and Periwinkle sighed. There was a stir among the ladies, and Miss Mosquito spitefully remarked to her Cousin Firefly, "Dear me! what a fuss they do make about those vulgar people!"

"Commodore Crab, Mrs. Crab, and Miss Crab!" announced the servant, and in they came. The commodore had taken part in many sea-fights, and was famous for never letting go when once he had grappled with a foe. But he was rather shy in company, and so was madame; and often, when any one approached to speak to them, they both precipitately retreated backward, so retiring were the dispositions of this excellent couple. The commodore wore his orange uniform, and limped, having lost a leg in battle. Mrs. C. was elegantly attired in green, with red ornaments. But Miss Crab,—how shall I paint that lovely creature? She was in snowy white from head to foot, a perfect blonde, and carried in her hand an exquisite bouquet of rosy seaweed, the sight of which caused young Turtle to glare at young Lobster, for both had sent bouquets, and Lily had chosen his rival's. Now her parents wished the young lady to accept Columbus, for he was rich; but she loved him not, for she had given her heart to Oceanicus, who was poor. Still, having been fashionably brought up, she felt it was her duty to secure a fine establishment; and so she tried to like dull Columbus, while she flirted with sprightly Oceanicus. Matters had reached a crisis, and it was very evident that something would be decided that very night, for both gentlemen haunted the fair Lily's steps, and scowled at one another tragically.

"I always thought there would be mischief there, for that girl's behavior is scandalous. There was a case very much like this at the hotel last year, and it ended in an elopement and a suicide," buzzed Miss Mosquito in the ear of Madame Turtle, who drew herself up, as she replied, in her most dignified tone, glancing at her son,—

"I have no fears in that quarter: such affairs are conducted with propriety in our first families. Excuse me: I have a word for Mrs. Crab."

"If that is a sample of the manners of 'our first families,' I'm glad I don't belong to 'em," scolded Miss Mosquito to herself. "Ah, if I had my way, I'd soon spoil your beauty, miss," she muttered, looking at Lily Crab. And so she would; for this spiteful creature used to delight in stinging the pretty girls up at the hotel, especially their poor dear noses, till they weren't fit to be seen.

The Snails came late, as they always did; and one of them, on being introduced to the Shrew-mouse, began to complain of her servants, as fashionable ladies are apt to do when they get together.

"There never was such a perfect slave to a house as I am to mine," she said. "We see a great deal of company, and things must be in order; but they never are, though we keep ten servants. How do you manage, ma'am? You look quite plump and serene; and here am I worn to the bone, with my worries and cares."

"I come from the brook over the hill, and we country people live much more simply than you city folks. I keep no servants at all, but do every thing myself, and bring up my eight children without help," answered the Shrew-mouse, settling the folds of her white shawl with a tranquil air.

"Dear me! how remarkable! But, you see, an active life doesn't suit me. You have always been used to that sort of thing, I dare say, and so get on very well. *I* was brought up differently." And, with a cool stare, the handsome violet Snail moved slowly away, while the Shrew-mouse and the Beetles laughed among themselves.

"Pray, how came a person who does her own work to get into our set?" asked Madam Snail of a testy old Horse-shoe whom she much respected.

"Because she is a very charming person, and I advised Turtle to invite her," replied the Horse-shoe, in a tone as sharp as his tail.

"Dear me! what are we coming to?" sighed the Snail, who, being very conservative, disliked progress of all kinds.

"My dear sir, I assure you, it's a splendid investment,—perfectly safe, and very desirable," said old Lobster to the alderman, whom he held by the button-hole in a corner.

"Are you the president of the bank?" asked old Turtle, with a sly twinkle of the eye.

"No, sir, not even a director; but I take an interest in it, and, if I had your means, I'd invest there, for the safest bank I know is that of my friends Oyster, Mussel, and Company," replied Lobster, who was as deep an old party as ever swam.

"I'll think of it, and make inquiries, and, if it's all satisfactory, I'll take your advice, for I value your opinion, and have confidence in your judgment," said Turtle, who considered Lobster an unprincipled speculator.

"Praise from you, sir, may well make me proud. You will certainly be reelected, and remain an alderman to the day of your death, if the influence and vote of A. Lobster can keep you in place," answered the other, who looked upon Turtle as a thick-headed, easy-going old gentleman, whom it would not be difficult to defraud of his money in some strictly business-like way.

"It's all right: he'll nibble, and we shall float in spite of fate," whispered Lobster to his friend Hercules Mussel, in a tone of exultation, for the fact was the bank of Oyster, Mussel, and Company was in a very desperate state, though few suspected it.

Meantime Miss Lily was driving her lovers to despair, by being extremely amiable to both. She sat on a sea-green sofa, fanning herself with a tiny coral fan, while the two gentlemen stood before her, trying to annoy each other and amuse her.

"Sad affair, that of Bessie Barnacle and young Cockle, wasn't it?" said Columbus, in his slow way, thinking it would please Lily to pity or condemn her former rival.

"What was it? I've been shut up for a week with a sad cold, and have heard nothing," replied the young lady, fixing her large eyes on Columbus in a way that confused him dreadfully in his story.

"Why, you know, she was all but engaged to Phillip Periwinkle, cousin to Tom who is here tonight; but just as the thing was considered settled, Charley Cockle cut in, and they eloped. Her family insist that she was torn away; but I doubt it."

"So do I. Any girl of sense would prefer a fine fellow like Charley, with-

out a cent, to a noodle worth half a million, like Phil Periwinkle," said
Oceanicus, in a tone that made the blood of Columbus boil.

"It was a most improper and ungentlemanly thing to do, and no one but
a low-born puppy would have done it," he answered grimly.

"Well, I should say Phil was the puppy, to take a beating so quietly. I
consider it a spirited thing on Charley's part, and I fancy Miss Lily agrees
with me," returned Oceanicus, with an insinuating smile and bow.

"You oughtn't to ask me such naughty questions," simpered Lily behind her fan. "It was dreadfully improper, and all that sort of thing, I know;
but then it was so romantic, and I adore romance,—don't you, Mr. Turtle?"

"Decidedly not that style of it. In good families such things are not allowed; but it is no more than I should expect of a Cockle," remarked Columbus, with scorn.

"Now, really, my dear fellow, you ought not to be so severe, when your
Cousin Theresa did the same thing, you know."

As Oceanicus said this, he looked straight at young Turtle in the most
impertinent manner. But for once Columbus was his match, for he said
coolly, "Old Barnacle vows he will have Cockle imprisoned, if he can find a
fit place for such a young rascal, and I advised him to try a lobster-pot."

Now that was a direct insult, for Oceanicus had been caught in one not
long ago, on his way home from a frolic, and would have been boiled if his
friends had not gone to the rescue. It was considered a sad disgrace to die
by boiling, or to be caught in any way; so the Lobster family hushed it up as
carefully as the Turtles did Theresa's runaway match. Oceanicus gave Columbus a look which he long remembered, but said nothing to him; and
turning to Miss Crab, as if they were alone, he murmured regretfully, "My
dear Lily, it must be dreadfully dull for you with no dancing. Won't you let
me bring you something to eat? I see they have begun supper at last."

"I was about to take Miss Crab down myself," said young Turtle,
haughtily.

"Now don't quarrel and be absurd about me. I am going to stay here,
and you may each bring me something. I could fancy a shrimp, and a glass
of briny," said Miss Lily, hoping to soothe the angry gentlemen.

Both rushed away; but Oceanicus, who was always brisk, got back first,
and whispered, as he handed the glass, "Remember after the tableaux."

"Oh, dear, no! I couldn't think of it!" cried Miss Lily, with a little scream.
"Now you may hold my things, while I eat. Be careful not to break that, for
I value it very much," she added, as she handed Turtle the fan he had given
her. "How sweet they are! I do *so* love flowers," she went on taking a long

sniff at her bouquet before she gave it to Lobster to hold. Then, taking off her gloves, she coquettishly sipped her wine; and, holding the shrimp in one delicate claw, she daintily picked off its legs, putting them bit by bit into her mouth, till nothing but the tail remained, which Turtle kept as a love-token.

"My dear creature, how miserably you are looking: I'm afraid this gay season has been too much for you. People at your time of life should be careful of themselves," said Miss Mosquito to Fanny Firefly, who was a universal favorite, being a bright, merry little lady.

"I'm very well, thank you, dear, and none the worse for my gayeties. If you can stand a dissipated season, I guess I can, for you are older than me, you know," returned Miss Fanny, sweetly, as she walked away with Tom Periwinkle, who shunned "Miss Skeet," as he called her, as if she had been a walking pest,—a flying one she certainly was.

"Poor girl! I'm sorry she is losing her good looks so fast, and getting so sharp and sour. She used to be rather pretty and amiable, but she is quite spoilt, and having neither money nor accomplishments she will soon be quite forgotten," said Xantippe, with a sigh that said plainly, "If she was like me, now, she'd be every thing that was good and charming."

"How are the Horse-shoes getting on, Miss Mosquito?" asked Mrs. Turtle.

"I don't see much of them, they are not in my set, you know. People who rose from mud, and still have relations living there, are not the sort of persons with whom I care to associate," replied Xantippe, with a scornful perk of her long nose.

Now both the Turtles and Lobsters had connections in Mudville, and so of course were offended by that speech. Old Mrs. Lobster turned as red as if she had been boiled; but Mrs. Turtle never forgot herself, and changed the subject by saying politely, "We are going to have supper early on account of the tableaux: as you are going to act, won't you step down with me and have some refreshment before the rush begins?"

"Thank you, I'm going to supper at the hotel by and by. I'm rather delicate, you know, and I find the things I get there agree with me better than common suppers. I see Mrs. Barnacle is expecting me to come and amuse her, so I must fly. Pray take care and not excite yourself, my dear lady, for you know apoplexy is sadly fatal to your family. You, Mrs. Lobster, are happy in being free from that aristocratic complaint." And with these farewell stings, Miss Mosquito buzzed away, leaving the two old ladies to exclaim angrily, as they settled their cap-ribbons, "Xantippe gets quite unbearable. She is regularly blood-thirsty, and stabs right and left with her cruel tongue. Let us go and have a comfortable dish of tea, my dear; I'm sure we need it."

It was very amusing to see the company at supper; the alderman trying to think of his guests before himself; the young ladies delicately picking at their food, and pretending to have no appetite after taking a hearty tea at home; the young men eating every thing they could lay their hands on, and drinking more than was good for them. The old ladies were rather neglected, but made the best of it, and slipped a few trifles into their pockets for the dears at home; while their stout husbands stuffed till they were speechless.

After supper, there was singing; and the Petrels came out splendidly, for they were a glee club, and sung all sorts of sea-songs in fine style, particularly "A Life on the Ocean Wave," and "Rocked in the Cradle of the Deep." Miss Mosquito, in a shrill small voice, sang Tennyson's "Blow, Bugle, blow;" and Mrs. Shrew-mouse gave a lullaby very sweetly. Old Lobster, who was a gay fellow still, warbled "I know a bank," which made Old Turtle laugh till they thought he would certainly go off in a fit; and, to Lily's delight, young Lobster's serenade entirely eclipsed young Turtle's *barcarolle*. After this, the Flying-Fish performed some wonderful feats in the pool; and the Beetles were allowed as a special favor to show the young people the new Grasshopper-step which was all the rage.

Then came the tableaux. A row of fireflies made capital foot-lights; a thick cobweb was the curtain, and two spiders were engaged to work it. Monsieur Hyla, a tree-frog, piped sweetly between the pictures, and every thing went smoothly. The first was a scene from "The Tempest." A venerable Horse-shoe was Prospero, and his stiff tail was very effective as the magic wand. Lily Crab was Miranda, and looked lovely as she gazed admiringly at Oceanicus, who played Ferdinand. A Hedgehog did Caliban; a Firefly was Ariel; and the picture was a great success everybody said but Columbus Turtle.

The alderman himself consented to appear in the next as the Ancient Mariner telling his story to the wedding guest. His face was wanting in expression, and he was rather stout for the haunted man; but as several members of his family had led seafaring lives, and died at fabulously great ages, he felt it was an appropriate part for him. Young Lobster was the detained guest, and was really fine in the longing look he gave at the bridal train just passing by. Columbus was the bridegroom, and Lily the bride, and very sweet she looked under her veil; while Turtle was absolutely brilliant with momentary excitement.

The "Three Fishers" followed, and was the gem of the whole, for one of the Petrels chanted the words as the scenes were shown. First, the fishers were seen "sailing out into the west" on the pool in large shells. A Jelly-fish, young Cockle, and Tom Periwinkle were the fishers, and the ladies applauded violently, as they rowed gallantly away. Then the three wives appeared up in the light-house tower, which was made by collecting fire-flies on the top of the rock, while the Shrew-mouse, Miss Beetle, and Miss Snail, as the wives, looked anxiously out for the boats "that would never come back to the land." The gentlemen quite brought down the house at this, but the ladies thought it "just a trifle flat." The last scene was really thrilling, for the "three corpses lay out on the shining sands," and "the women were weeping and wringing their hands" most tragically. Young Jelly-fish was very ghostly, and the anguish of Mrs. Shrew-mouse so capitally acted it was evident she had known sorrow. "The Lily Maid of Astolat" followed, for that and the "Fishers" are always favorites at the seaside. Of course Lily Crab was the maid, laid on a bed of splendid sea-weeds in the great rosy-lipped shell which was the boat. In the prow sat a toad, as the faithful old dwarf who steered her down to Camelot, and his ugliness made her beauty more dazzling. On the shore of the pool stood the handsomest Petrel, as King Arthur; another was Lancelot; and a pretty Miss Periwinkle was Guinevere. A good many of the company had not read "Idyls of the King," and hadn't the least idea what it all meant; but they took care to look as if they did, and patted their hands with an approving, "Very sweet," "Quite exquisite;" "Really, it does the young people a vast deal of credit;" "Altogether *commy la faut,*" as old Mrs. Lobster said, trying to be elegant, though she was a very ordinary woman, who could do nothing but make salads, for her father kept a restaurant years ago.

The last one was the "Corsair's Bride." Columbus was the stern papa, and Lily the lovely daughter, both in the Greek costume, and it is easy for one to imagine how becoming it must have been.

This was an acted tableau; for, as Haidee lay listlessly on her divan, thinking of the gallant being who had sung under her window one moon-light night, the same gallant being magnificently got up as a corsair burst into the room, followed by his band. Oceanicus looked as dark, fierce, and melodramatic as half-a-dozen Byrons, and quite electrified the audience by knocking down the stately papa, exclaiming, "Tyrant, I defy thee! Ha! ha! she is mine!" and rushing from the stage with Lily on his arm.

This thrilling display of tragic power produced round after round of tu-multuous applause, and cries of "Lob! Lob!" from all parts of the house. The curtain rose, but no one appeared except Columbus, still on the ground, having been half-stunned and wholly bewildered by the attack, that not having been planned beforehand. He lay staring blankly, and looking so forlorn that the wags who had pulled up the curtain dropped it, and raised him instead. Everybody laughed at him, and praised Oceanicus. The Lobsters quite glowed with pride; the young ladies declared it was "perfectly thrilling;" and the young gentlemen vowed that "Lob outdid himself, by Jove!"

By the time the excitement subsided, people began to wonder why the "stars" didn't appear to receive their honors. But nowhere could they be found, and Mrs. Crab began to look anxious. Some one suggested that they might be strolling on the beach to cool and compose themselves. A careful search was made, but no trace of them was discovered, till an old Jelly-fish who was lying on the sand informed them that a young couple had sailed away not long before, and that he heard them say there would be just time to stop at the Rev. Dr. Cod's before they caught the outward-bound steamer.

When this dreadful intelligence was carried back to the party, Mrs. Crab fainted dead away, and the Commodore stamped about, using very strong language. Miss Mosquito triumphantly exclaimed, "I told you so;" and every one was much excited.

The party broke up at once, and as the last wave left the door Mrs. Turtle said with a long sigh, "For my part, I'm glad the season's over, that we are done with fashion and frivolity, and can go back to our simple, sensible ways, and live like respectable creatures."

# The Autobiography of an Omnibus

I was born in Springfield,–excuse me if I don't mention how many years ago, for my memory is a little treacherous on some points, and it does not matter in the least. I was a gay young 'bus, with a long, red body, yellow wheels, and a picture of Washington on each side. Beautiful portraits, I assure you, with powdered hair, massive nose, and a cataract of shirt-frill inundating his buff vest. His coat and eyes were wonderfully blue, and he stared at the world in general with superb dignity, no matter how much mud might temporarily obscure his noble countenance.

Yes, I was an omnibus to be proud of; for my yellow wheels rumbled sonorously as they rolled; my cushions were soft, my springs elastic, and my varnish shone with a brilliancy which caused the human eye to wink as it regarded me.

Joe Quimby first mounted my lofty perch, four fine gray horses drew me from obscurity, and Bill Buffum hung gayly on behind as conductor; for in my early days there were no straps to jerk, and passengers did not plunge in and out in the undignified way they do now.

How well I remember my first trip, one bright spring day! I was to run between Roxbury and Boston, and we set out in great style, and an admiring crowd to see us off. That was the beginning of a long and varied career,—a useful one too, I hope; for never did an omnibus desire to do its duty more sincerely than I did. My heart yearned over every one whom I saw plodding along in the dust; my door opened hospitably to rich and poor, and no hand beckoned to me in vain. Can every one say as much?

For years I trundled to and fro punctually at my appointed hours, and many curious things I saw—many interesting people I carried. Of course, I had my favorites, and though I did my duty faithfully to all, there were certain persons whom I loved to carry, whom I watched for and received into my capacious bosom with delight.

Several portly old gentlemen rode down to their business every day for years, and I felt myself honored by such eminently respectable passengers. Nice, motherly women, with little baskets, daily went to market; for in earlier days housewives attended to these matters and were notable managers. Gay young fellows would come swarming up beside Joe, and crack jokes all the way into town, amusing me immensely.

But my especial pets were the young girls,—for we had girls then,— blithe, bonny creatures, with health on their cheeks, modesty in their bright eyes, and the indescribable charm of real maidenliness about them. So simply dressed, so quiet in manner, so unconscious of display, and so full of innocent gayety, that the crustiest passenger could not help softening as they came in. Bless their dear hearts! what would they say if they could see the little fashion-plates school-girls are now? The seven-story hats with jet daggers, steel arrows, and gilt horse-shoes on the sides, peacocks' tails in front, and quantities of impossible flowers tumbling off behind. The jewelry, the frills and bows, the frizzled hair and high-heeled boots, and, worst of all, the pale faces, tired eyes, and ungirlish manners.

Well, well, I must not scold the poor dears, for they are only what the times make them,—fast and loud, frivolous and feeble. All are not spoilt, thank heaven; for now and then, a fresh, modest face goes by, and then one sees how lovely girlhood may be.

I saw many little romances, and some small tragedies, in my early days, and learned to take such interest in human beings, that I have never been able to become a mere machine.

When one of my worthy old gentlemen dropped away, and I saw him no more, I mourned for him like a friend. When one of my housewifely women came in with a black bonnet on, and no little lad or lass clinging to her hand, I creaked my sympathy for her loss, and tried not to jolt the poor mother whose heart was so heavy. When one of my pretty girls entered, blushing and smiling, with a lover close behind, I was as pleased and proud as if she had been my own, and every black button that studded my red cushion twinkled with satisfaction.

I had many warm friends among the boys who were allowed to "hang on behind," for I never gave a dangerous lurch when they were there, and never pinched their fingers in the door. No, I gave a jolly rumble when the steps were full; and I kept the father of his country beaming so benignly at them that they learned to love his old face, to watch for it, and to cheer it as we went by.

I was a patriotic 'bus; so you may imagine my feelings when, after years of faithful service on that route, I was taken off and sent to the paint-shop, where a simpering damsel, with lilies in her hair, replaced G. Washington's honored countenance. I was re-christened "The Naiad Queen," which disgusted me extremely, and kept to carry picnic parties to a certain lake.

Earlier in my life I should have enjoyed the fun; but I was now a middleaged 'bus, and felt as if I wanted more serious work to do. However, I resigned myself and soon found that the change did me good; for in the city I was in danger of getting grimy with mud, battered with banging over stones, and used up with the late hours, noise and excitement of town life.

Now I found great refreshment in carrying loads of gay young people into the country for a day of sunshine, green grass, and healthful pleasure. What jolly parties they were, to be sure! Such laughing and singing, feasting and frolicking; such baskets of flowers and fresh boughs as they carried home; and, better still, such blooming cheeks, happy eyes, and hearts bubbling over with the innocent gayety of youth! They soon seemed as fond of me as I was of them, for they welcomed me with shouts when I came, played games and had banquets inside of me when sun or rain made shelter pleasant, trimmed me up with wreaths as we went home in triumph, and gave three rousing cheers for the old 'bus when we parted. That was a happy time, and it furnished many a pleasant memory for duller days.

After several seasons of picnicking, I was taken to an asylum for the deaf, dumb, and blind, and daily took a dozen or so out for an airing. You can easily imagine this was a great contrast to my last place; for now, instead of rollicking parties of boys and girls, I took a sad load of affliction; and it grieved me much to know that while some of the poor little creatures could see nothing of the beauty round them, the others could hear none of the sweet summer sounds, and had no power to express their happiness in blithe laughter or the gay chatter one so loves to hear.

But it did me good; for, seeing them so patient with their great troubles, I was ashamed to grumble about my small ones. I was now getting to be an elderly 'bus, with twinges of rheumatism in my axletrees, many cracks like wrinkles on my once smooth paint, and an asthmatic creak to the hinges of the door that used to swing so smartly to and fro. Yes, I was evidently getting old, for I began to think over my past, to recall the many passengers I had carried, the crusty or jolly coachmen I had known, the various horses who had tugged me over stony streets or dusty roads, and the narrow escapes I had had in the course of my career.

Presently I found plenty of time for such reminiscences, for I was put away in an old stable and left there undisturbed a long, long time. At first, I enjoyed the rest and quiet; but I was of a social turn, and soon longed for the stirring life I had left. I had no friends but a few gray hens, who roosted on my pole, laid eggs in the musty straw on my floor, and came hopping gravely down my steps with important "cut, cut, ka da cuts!" when their duty was done. I respected these worthy fowls, and had many a gossip with them; but their views were very limited, and I soon tired of their domestic chat.

Chanticleer was coachman now, as in the days of Partlet and the nuts;

but he never drove out, only flew up to my roof when he crowed, and sat there, in his black and yellow suit, like a diligence-driver sounding his horn. Interesting broods of chickens were hatched inside, and took their first look at life from my dingy windows. I felt a grandfatherly fondness for the downy things, and liked to have them chirping and scratching about me, taking small flights from my steps, and giving funny little crows in imitation of their splendid papa.

Sundry cats called often, for rats and mice haunted the stable, and these gray-coated huntsmen had many an exciting chase among my moth-eaten cushions, over the lofts, and round the grain-bags.

"Here I shall end my days," I thought, and resigned myself to obscurity. But I was mistaken; for just as I was falling out of one long doze into another, a terrible commotion among the cats, hens, and mice woke me up, and I found myself trundling off to the paint-shop again.

I emerged from that fragrant place in a new scarlet coat, trimmed with black and ornamented with a startling picture of a salmon-colored Mazeppa, airily dressed in chains and a blue sheet, hanging by one foot to the back of a coal-black steed with red nostrils and a tempestuous tail, who was wildly careering over a range of pea-green mountains on four impossible legs. It was much admired; but I preferred George Washington, like the loyal 'bus that I am.

I found I was to live in the suburbs and carry people to and from the station of a new railway, which, with the town, seemed to have sprung up like mushrooms. Well, I bumped passengers about the half-finished streets; but I did not like it, for every thing had changed much during my retirement. Everybody seemed in a tearing hurry now,—the men to be rich, the women to be fine; the boys and girls couldn't wait to grow up, but flirted before they were in their teens; and the very babies scrambled out of their cradles as if each was bent on toddling farther and faster than its neighbor. My old head quite spun round at the whirl every thing was in, and my old wheels knew no rest, for the new coachman drove like Jehu.

It is my private opinion that I should soon have fallen to pieces if a grand smash had not settled the matter for me. A gay young fellow undertook to drive, one dark night, and upset his load in a ditch, fortunately breaking no bones but mine. So I was sent to a carriage factory for repairs; but, apparently, my injuries were past cure, for I was left on a bit of waste land behind the factory, to go to ruin at leisure.

"This is the end of all things," I said, with a sigh, as year after year went by and I stood there alone, covered with wintry snow or blistered by summer sunshine. But how mistaken I was! for just when all seemed most sad and solitary, the happiest experience of my life came to me, and all the world was brightened for me by the coming of my dearest friends.

One chilly spring night, when rain was falling, and the wind sighed dismally over the flats, I was waked from a nap by voices and the rustling of straw inside my still strong body.

"Some tramp," I thought, with a yawn, for I had often taken lodgers for a night, rent free. But the sounds I now heard were the voices of children, and I listened with interest to the little creatures chirping and nestling in there like the chickens I told you of.

"It's as nice as a house, Hans, and so warm I'll soon be dry," said one of the homeless birds who had taken shelter in my bosom.

"It's nicer than a house, Gretchen, because we can push it about if we like. I wish we could stay here always; I'm so tired of the streets," sighed another young voice.

"And I'm so hungry; I do wish mother would come," cried a very tired baby voice, with a sob.

"Hush, go to sleep, my Lina! I'll wake you if mother brings us bread, and if not you will feel no disappointment, dear."

Then the elder sister seemed to wrap the little one close, and out of my bosom came a soft lullaby, as one child gave the other all she had,—love and care.

"In the shed yonder I saw a piece of carpet; I shall go and bring it to cover us, then you will not shiver so, dear Gretchen," said the boy; and out into the rainy darkness he went, whistling to keep his spirits up and hide his hunger.

Soon he came hurrying back with the rude coverlet, and another voice was heard, saying, in the tone that only mothers use,—

"Here is supper, dear children. Eat all; I have no wish for any more. People were very good to me, and there is enough for every one."

Then, with cries of joy, the hungry birds were fed, the motherly wings folded over them, and all seemed to sleep in the poor nest they had found.

All night the rain pattered on my old roof, but not a drop went through; all night the chilly wind crept round my windows, and breathed in at every broken pane, but the old carpet kept the sleepers warm, and weariness was a sure lullaby. How pleased and proud I felt that I could still be useful, and how eagerly I waited for day to see yet more of my new tenants! I knew they would go soon and leave me to my loneliness, so I longed to see and hear all I could.

The first words the mother said, as she sat upon the step in the warm April sun, pleased me immensely, for they were of me.

"Yes, Hans, it will be well to stay here a day at least, if we may, for Lina is worn out and poor Gretchen so tired she can go no more. You shall guard them while they sleep, and I will go again for food, and may get work. It is better out here in the sun than in some poor place in the city, and I like it well, this friendly old carriage that sheltered us when most we needed it."

So the poor woman trudged away, like a true mother-bird, to find food for the ever-hungry brood, and Hans, a stout lad of twelve, set about doing his part manfully.

When he heard the workmen stirring in the great factory, he took courage, and, going in, told his sad tale of the little tired sisters sleeping in the old omnibus, the mother seeking work, the father lately dead, and he (the young lad) left to guard and help the family. He asked for nothing but leave to use the bit of carpet, and for any little job whereby he might earn a penny.

The good fellows had fatherly hearts under their rough jackets, and lent a helping hand with the readiness the poor so often show in lightening one another's burdens. Each did what he could; and when the mother came back, she found the children fed and warmed, cheered by kind words and the promise of help.

Ah! it was a happy day for me when the Schmidts came wandering by and found my door ajar! A yet happier one for them, since the workmen and their master befriended the poor souls so well that in a week the house-less family had a home, and work whereby to earn their bread.

They had taken a fancy to me, and I was their home; for they were a hardy set and loved the sun and air. Clever Hans and his mother made me as neat and cosy as possible, stowing away their few possessions as if on shipboard. The shed was given to mother Schmidt for a wash-house, and a gypsy fire built on the ground, with an old kettle slung over it, in which to boil the clothes she washed for such of the men as had no wives. Hans and Gretchen soon found work selling chips and shavings from the factory, and bringing home the broken food they begged by the way. Baby Lina was a universal pet, and many a sixpence found its way into her little hand from the pockets of the kindly men, who took it out in kisses, or the pretty songs she sang them.

All that summer my family prospered, and I was a happy old 'bus. A proud one, too; for the dear people loved me well, and, in return for the shelter I gave them, they beautified me by all the humble means in their power. Some one gave Gretchen a few scarlet beans, and these she planted among the dandelions and green grass that had grown about my wheels. The gay runners climbed fast, and when they reached the roof, Hans made a trellis of old barrel hoops, over which they spread their broad leaves and bright flowers till Lina had a green little bower up aloft, where she sat, as happy as a queen, with the poor toys which her baby fancy changed to playthings of the loveliest sort.

Mother Schmidt washed and ironed busily all day in her shed, cooked the soup over her gypsy fire, and when the daily work was done sat in the shadow of the old omnibus with her children round her, a grateful and contented woman. If any one asked her what she would do when our bitter winter came, the smile on her placid face grew graver, but did not vanish, as she laid her worn hands together and answered, with simple faith,—

"The good Gott who gave us this home and raised up these friends will not forget us, for He has such as we in His especial charge."

She was right; for the master of the great factory was a kind man, and something in the honest, hard-working family interested him so much that he could not let them suffer, but took such friendly thought for them that he wrought one of the pleasant miracles which keep a rich man's memory green in grateful hearts, though the world may never know of it.

When autumn came and the pretty bower began to fade, the old omnibus to be cold at night, and the shed too gusty even for the hardy German laundress, a great surprise was planned and gayly carried out. On the master's birthday the men had a holiday, and bade the Schmidts be ready to take part in the festival, for all the factory people were to have a dinner in one of the long rooms.

A jovial time they had; and when the last bone had been polished off, the last health drunk, and three rousing cheers for the master given with a will, the great joke took place. First the Schmidts were told to go and see what had been left for them in the 'bus, and off they ran, little dreaming what was to come. *I* knew all about it, and was in a great twitter, for I bore a grand part in it.

The dear unsuspecting family piled in, and were so busy having raptures over certain bundles of warm clothes found there that they did not mind what went on without. A dozen of the stoutest men quietly harnessed themselves to the rope fastened to my pole, and at a signal trotted away with me at a great pace, while the rest, with their wives and children, came laughing and shouting after.

Imagine the amazement of the good Schmidts at this sudden start, their emotions during that triumphal progress, and their unspeakable surprise and joy when their carriage stopped at the door of a tidy little house in a lane not far away, and they were handed out to find the master waiting to welcome them home.

Dear heart, how beautiful it all was! I cannot describe it, but I would not have missed it for the world, because it was one of the scenes that do everybody so much good and leave such a pleasant memory behind.

That was my last trip, for the joyful agitation of that day was too much for me, and no sooner was I safely landed in the field behind the little house than one of my old wheels fell all to pieces, and I should have tumbled over, like a decrepit old creature, if the men had not propped me up. But I did not care; my travelling days were past, and I was quite content to stand there under the apple-trees, watching my family safe and busy in their new home.

I was not forgotten, I assure you; for Germans have much sentiment, and they still loved the old omnibus that sheltered them when most forlorn. Even when Hans was a worker in the factory he found time to mend me up and keep me tidy; pretty Gretchen, in spite of much help given to the hard-working mother, never forgot to plant some common flower to beautify and cheer her old friend; and little Lina, bless her heart! made me her baby-house. She played there day after day, a tiny matron, with her dolls, her kitten and her bits of furniture, as happy a child as ever sang "Bye-low" to a dirty-faced rag-darling. She is my greatest comfort and delight; and the proudest moment of my life was when Hans painted her little name on my door and gave me to her for her own.

Here my story ends; for nothing now remains to me but to crumble slowly to ruin and go where the good 'busses go; very slowly, I am sure, for my little mistress takes great care of me, and I shall never suffer from rough usage any more. I am quite happy and contented as I stand here under the trees that scatter their white petals on my rusty roof each spring; and well I may be, for after my busy life I am at rest; the sun shines kindly on me, the grass grows greenly round me, good friends cherish me in my old age, and a little child nestles in my heart, keeping it tender to the last.

# Rosa's Tale

"Now, I believe every one has had a Christmas present and a good time. Nobody has been forgotten, not even the cat," said Mrs. Ward to her daughter, as she looked at Pobbylinda, purring on the rug, with a new ribbon round her neck and the remains of a chicken bone between her paws.

It was very late, for the Christmas-tree was stripped, the little folks abed, the baskets and bundles left at poor neighbors' doors, and everything ready for the happy day which would begin as the clock struck twelve. They were resting after their labors, while the yule log burned down; but the mother's words reminded Belinda of one good friend who had received no gift that night.

"We've forgotten Rosa! Her mistress is away, but she *shall* have a present nevertheless. Late as it is, she will like some apples and cake and a Merry Christmas from the family."

Belinda jumped up as she spoke, and, having collected such remnants of the feast as a horse would relish, she put on her hood, lighted a lantern, and trotted off to the barn.

As she opened the door of the loose box in which Rosa was kept, she saw her eyes shining in the dark as she lifted her head with a startled air. Then, recognizing a friend, she rose and came rustling through the straw to greet her late visitor. She was evidently much pleased with the attention, and rubbed her nose against Miss Belinda gratefully, but seemed rather dainty, and poked over the contents of the basket, as if a little suspicious, though apples were her favorite treat.

Knowing that she would enjoy the little feast more if she had company while she ate it, for Rosa was a very social beast, Miss Belinda hung up the lantern, and, sitting down on an inverted bucket, watched her as she munched contentedly.

"Now really," said Miss Belinda, when telling her story afterwards, "I am not sure whether I took a nap and dreamed what follows, or whether it actually happened, for strange things do occur at Christmas time, as every one knows.

"As I sat there the town clock struck twelve, and the sound reminded me of the legend which affirms that all dumb animals are endowed with speech for one hour after midnight on Christmas eve, in memory of the animals about the manger when the blessed Child was born.

"'I wish the pretty fancy was a fact, and our Rosa could speak, if only for an hour, because I am sure she has an interesting history, and I long to know it.'

"I said this aloud, and to my utter amazement the bay mare stopped eating, fixed her intelligent eyes upon my face, and answered in a language I understood perfectly well,—

"'You shall know it, for whether the legend is true or not I feel as if I could confide in you and tell you all I feel. I was lying awake listening to the fun in the house, thinking of my dear mistress over the sea and feeling very sad, for I heard you say I was to be sold. That nearly broke my heart, for no one has ever been so kind to me as Miss Merry, and nowhere shall I be taken care of, nursed, and loved as I have been since she bought me. I know I am getting old, and stiff in the knees, and my forefoot is lame, and sometimes I'm cross when my shoulder aches; but I do try to be a patient, grateful beast. I've got fat with good living, my work is not hard, I dearly love to carry those who have done so much for me, and I'll tug for them till I die in harness, if they will only keep me.'

"I was so astonished at this address that I tumbled off the pail, and sat among the straw staring up at Rosa, as dumb as if I had lost the power she had gained. She seemed to enjoy my surprise, and added to it by letting me hear a genuine *horse laugh,* hearty, shrill, and clear, as she shook her pretty head, and went on talking rapidly in the language which I now perceived to be a mixture of English and the peculiar dialect of the horse-country Gulliver visited.

"'Thank you for remembering me to-night, and in return for the goodies you bring I'll tell my story as fast as I can, for I have often longed to recount the trials and triumphs of my life. Miss Merry came last Christmas eve to bring me sugar, and I wanted to speak, but it was too early and I could not say a word, though my heart was full.'

"Rosa paused an instant, and her fine eyes dimmed as if with tender tears at the recollection of the happy year which had followed the day she was brought from the drudgery of a livery-stable to be a lady's pet. I stroked her neck as she stooped to sniff affectionately at my hood, and said eagerly,—

"'Tell away, dear, I'm full of interest, and understand every word you say.'

"Thus encouraged, Rosa threw up her head, and began with an air of pride which plainly proved, what we had always suspected, that she belonged to a good family.

"'My father was a famous racer, and I am very like him; the same color, spirit, and grace, and but for the cruelty of man I might have been as renowned as he. I was a very happy colt, petted by my master, tamed by love, and never struck a blow while he lived. I gained one race for him, and promised so well that when he died I brought a great price. I mourned for him, but was glad to be sent to my new owner's racing-stable and made much of, for people predicted that I should be another Goldsmith Maid or Flora Temple. Ah, how ambitious and proud I was in those days! Vain of my good blood, my speed, and my beauty; for indeed I *was* handsome then, though you may find it hard to believe now.' And Rosa sighed regretfully as she stole a look at me, and took the attitude which showed to advantage the fine lines about her head and neck.

"'I do not find it hard, for we have always said you had splendid points about you. Miss Merry saw them, though you were a skeleton, when she bought you; so did the skilful Cornish blacksmith when he shod you. And it is easy to see that you belong to a good family by the way you hold your head without a check-rein and carry your tail like a plume,' I said, with a look of admiration which comforted her as much as if she had been a *passée* belle.

"'I must hurry over this part of my story, because, though brilliant, it was very brief, and ended in a way which made it the bitterest portion of my life,' continued Rosa. 'I won several races, and great fame was predicted for me. You may guess how high my reputation was when I tell you that before my last fatal trial thousands were bet on me, and my rival trembled in his shoes. I was full of spirit, eager to show my speed and sure of success. Alas, how little I knew of the wickedness of human nature then, how dearly I bought the knowledge, and how it has changed my whole life! You do not know much about such matters, of course, and I won't digress to tell you all the tricks of the trade; only beware of jockeys and never bet.

"'I was kept carefully out of every one's way for weeks, and only taken out for exercise by my trainer. Poor Bill! I was fond of him, and he was so good to me that I never have forgotten him, though he broke his neck years ago. A few nights before the great race, as I was getting a good sleep, carefully tucked away in my roomy stall, some one stole in and gave me a warm mash. It was dark, I was half awake, and I ate it like a fool, though I knew by instinct that it was not Bill who fed it to me. I was a confiding creature then, and as all sorts of queer things had been done to prepare me I thought it was all right. But it was not, and that deceit has caused me to be suspicious about my food ever since, for the mash was dosed in some way; it made me very ill, and my enemies nearly triumphed, thanks to this cowardly trick.

"'Bill worked over me day and night, that I might be fit to run. I did my best to seem well and gay, but there was not time for me to regain my lost strength and spirit, and pride alone kept me up. "I'll win for my master if I die in doing it," I said to myself, and when the hour came pranced to my place trying to look as well as ever, though my heart was very heavy and I trembled with excitement. "Courage, my lass, and we'll beat in spite of their black tricks," whispered Bill, as he sprung to his place.

"'I lost the first heat, but won the second, and the sound of the cheering gave me strength to walk away without staggering, though my legs shook under me. What a splendid minute that was when, encouraged and re-freshed by my faithful Bill, I came on the track again! I knew my enemies began to fear, for I had borne myself so bravely they fancied I was quite well, and now, excited by that first success, I was mad with impatience to be off and cover myself with glory.'

"Rosa looked as if the 'splendid minute' had come again, for she arched her neck, opened wide her red nostrils, and pawed the straw with one little foot, while her eyes shone with sudden fire, and her ears were pricked up as if to catch again the shouts she heard that day.

"'I wish I had been there to see you!' I exclaimed, quite carried away by her ardor.

"'I wish you had, for I won, I won! The big black horse did his best, but I had vowed to win or die, and I kept my word, for I beat him by a head, and then dropped as if dead. I might as well have died then, people thought, for the poison, the exertion, and the fall ruined me for a racer. My master cared no more for me, and would have had me shot if Bill had not saved my life. I was pronounced good for nothing, and he bought me cheap. I was lame and useless for a long time, but his patient care did wonders, and just as I was able to be of use to him he was killed.

"'A gentleman in want of a saddle-horse purchased me because my easy gait and quiet temper suited him; for I was meek enough now, and my size fitted me to carry his delicate daughter.

"'For more than a year I served little Miss Alice, rejoicing to see how rosy her pale cheeks became, how upright her feeble figure grew, thanks to the hours spent with me; for my canter rocked her as gently as if she were in a cradle, and fresh air was the medicine she needed. She often said she owed her life to me, and I liked to think so, for she made *my* life a very easy one.

"'But somehow my good times never lasted long, and when Miss Alice went West I was sold. I had been so well treated that I *looked* as handsome and gay as ever, though my shoulder never was strong again, and I often had despondent moods, longing for the excitement of the race-course with the instinct of my kind; so I was glad when, attracted by my spirit and beauty, a young army officer bought me and I went to the war. Ah! you never guessed that, did you? Yes, I did my part gallantly and saved my master's life more than once. You have observed how martial music delights me, but you don't know that it is because it reminds me of the proudest hour of my life. I've told you about the saddest; let me relate this also, and give me a pat for the brave action which won my master his promotion, though I got no praise for my part of the achievement.

"'In one of the hottest battles my captain was ordered to lead his men to a most perilous exploit. They hesitated, so did he; for it must cost many lives, and, brave as they were, they paused an instant. But *I* settled the point, for I was wild with the sound of drums, the smell of powder, the excitement of the hour, and, finding myself sharply reined in, I rebelled, took the bit between my teeth, and dashed straight away into the midst of the fight, spite of all my rider could do. The men thought their captain led them on, and with a cheer they followed, carrying all before them.

"'What happened just after that I never could remember, except that I got a wound here in my neck and a cut on my flank; the scar is there still, and I'm proud of it, though buyers always consider it a blemish. But when the battle was won my master was promoted on the field, and I carried him up to the general as he sat among his officers under the torn flags.

"'Both of us were weary and wounded, both were full of pride at what we had done; but *he* got all the praise and the honor, *I* only a careless word and a better supper than usual.

"'I thought no one knew what I had done, and resented the ingratitude of your race; for it was the horse, not the man, who led that forlorn hope, and I did think I should have a rosette at least, when others got stars and bars for far less dangerous deeds. Never mind, my master knew the truth, and thanked me for my help by keeping me always with him till the sad day when he was shot in a skirmish, and lay for hours with none to watch and mourn over him but his faithful horse.

"'Then I knew how much he loved and thanked me, for his hand stroked me while it had the strength, his eye turned to me till it grew too dim for seeing, and when help came, among the last words he whispered to a comrade were these, "Be kind to Rosa and send her safely home; she has earned her rest."

"'I *had* earned it, but I did not get it, for when I was sent home the old mother's heart was broken at the loss of her son, and she did not live long to cherish me. Then my hard times began, for my next owner was a fast young man, who ill used me in many ways, till the spirit of my father rose within me, and I gave my brutal master a grand run-away and smash-up.

"'To tame me down, I was sold for a car horse; and that almost killed me, for it was dreadful drudgery to tug, day after day, over the hard pavement with heavy loads behind me, uncongenial companions beside me, and no affection to cheer my life.

"'I have often longed to ask why Mr. Bergh does not try to prevent such crowds from piling into those cars; and now I beg you to do what you can to stop such an unmerciful abuse.

"'In snow-storms it was awful, and more than one of my mates dropped dead with overwork and discouragement. I used to wish I could do the same, for my poor feet, badly shod, became so lame I could hardly walk at times, and the constant strain on the up grades brought back the old trouble in my shoulder worse than ever.

"'Why they did not kill me I don't know, for I was a miserable creature then; but there must be something attractive about me, I fancy, for people always seem to think me worth saving. What can it be, ma'am?'

"'Now, Rosa, don't be affected; you know you are a very engaging little animal, and if you live to be forty will still have certain pretty ways about you, that win the hearts of women, if not of men. *They* see your weak points, and take a money view of the case; but *we* sympathize with your afflictions, are amused with your coquettish airs, and like your affectionate nature. Now hurry up and finish, for I find it a trifle cold out here.'

"I laughed as I spoke, for Rosa eyed me with a sidelong glance and gently waved the docked tail, which was her delight; for the sly thing liked to be flattered and was as fond of compliments as a girl.

"'Many thanks. I will come now to the most interesting portion of my narrative. As I was saying, instead of knocking me on the head I was packed off to New Hampshire, and had a fine rest among the green hills, with a dozen or so of weary friends. It was during this holiday that I acquired the love of nature which Miss Merry detected and liked in me, when she found me ready to study sunsets with her, to admire new landscapes, and enjoy bright summer weather.

"'In the autumn a livery-stable keeper brought me, and through the winter fed me up till I was quite presentable in the spring. It was a small town, but through the summer many city people visited there, so I was kept on the trot while the season lasted, because ladies could drive me. You, Miss Belinda, were one of the ladies, and I never shall forget, though I have long ago forgiven it, how you laughed at my queer gait the day you hired me.

"'My tender feet and stiff knees made me tread very gingerly, and amble along with short mincing steps, which contrasted oddly, I know, with my proudly waving tail and high-carried head. You liked me nevertheless, because I didn't rattle you down the steep hills, was not afraid of locomotives, and stood patiently while you gathered flowers and enjoyed the lovely prospects.

"'I have always felt a regard for you since you did not whip me, and admired my eyes, which, I may say without vanity, have always been considered unusually fine. But no one ever won my whole heart like Miss Merry, and I never shall forget the happy day when she came to the stable to order a saddle-horse. Her cheery voice made me prick up my ears, and when she said, after looking at several showy beasts, "No, they don't suit me. This one now has the right air; can I ride her?" my heart danced within me and I looked round with a whinny of delight. She understood my welcome, and came right up to me, patted me, peered into my face, rubbed my nose, and looked at my feet with an air of interest and sympathy, that made me feel as if I'd like to carry her round the world.

"'Ah, what rides we had after that! What happy hours trotting gayly through the green woods, galloping over the breezy hills, or pacing slowly along quiet lanes, where I often lunched luxuriously on clover-tops, while Miss Merry took a sketch of some picturesque bit with me in the foreground.

"'I liked that, and we had long chats at such times, for she seemed to understand me perfectly. She was never frightened when I danced for pleasure on the soft turf, never chid me when I snatched a bite from the young trees as we passed through sylvan ways, never thought it a trouble to let me wet my tired feet in babbling brooks, or to dismount and take out the stones that plagued me.

"'Then how well she rode! So firm yet light a seat, so steady a hand, so agile a foot to spring on and off, and such infectious spirits, that no matter how despondent or cross I might be, in five minutes I felt gay and young again when dear Miss Merry was on my back.'

"Here Rosa gave a frisk that sent the straw flying, and made me shrink into a corner, while she pranced about the box with a neigh which waked the big brown colt next door, and set poor Buttercup to lowing for her calf, the loss of which she had forgotten for a little while in sleep.

"'Ah, Miss Merry never ran away from me! She knew my heels were to be trusted, and she let me caper as I would, glad to see me lively. Never mind, Miss Belinda, come out and I'll be sober, as befits my years,' laughed Rosa, composing herself, and adding, so like a woman that I could not help smiling in the dark,—

"'When I say "years" I beg you to understand that I am *not* as old as that base man declared, but just in the prime of life for a horse. Hard usage has made me seem old before my time, and I am good for years of service yet.'

"'Few people have been through as much as you have, Rosa, and you certainly *have* earned the right to rest,' I said consolingly, for her little whims and vanities amused me much.

"'You know what happened next,' she continued; 'but I must seize this opportunity to express my thanks for all the kindness I've received since Miss Merry bought me, in spite of the ridicule and dissuasion of all her friends.

"'I know I didn't look like a good bargain, for I *was* very thin and lame and shabby; but she saw and loved the willing spirit in me, pitied my hard lot, and felt that it would be a good deed to buy me even if she never got much work out of me.

"'I shall always remember that, and whatever happens to me hereafter, I never shall be as proud again as I was the day she put my new saddle and bridle on, and I was led out, sleek, plump, and handsome, with blue rosettes at my ears, my tail cut in the English style, and on my back Miss Merry in her London hat and habit, all ready to head a cavalcade of eighteen horsemen and horsewomen. *We* were the most perfect pair of all, and when the troop caracoled down the wide street six abreast, *my* head was the highest, *my* rider the straightest, and *our* two hearts the friendliest in all the goodly company.

"'Nor is it pride and love alone that binds me to her, it is gratitude as well, for did not she often bathe my feet herself, rub me down, water me, blanket me, and daily come to see me when I was here alone for weeks in the winter time? Didn't she study horses' feet and shoes, that I might be cured if possible? Didn't she write to the famous friend of my race for advice, and drive me seven miles to get a good smith to shoe me well? Have not my poor contracted feet grown much better, thanks to the weeks of rest without shoes which she gave me? Am I not fat and handsome, and, barring the stiff knees, a very presentable horse? If I am, it is all owing to her; and for that reason I want to live and die in her service.

"'*She* doesn't want to sell me, and only bade you do it because you didn't want the care of me while she is gone. Dear Miss Belinda, please keep me! I'll eat as little as I can. I won't ask for a new blanket, though your old army one is very thin and shabby. I'll trot for you all winter, and try not to show it if I am lame. I'll do anything a horse can, no matter how humble, to earn my living, only don't, pray don't send me away among strangers who have neither interest nor pity for me!'

"Rosa had spoken rapidly, feeling that her plea must be made now or never, for before another Christmas she might be far away and speech of no use to win her wish. I was much touched, though she was only a horse; for she was looking earnestly at me as she spoke, and made the last words very eloquent by preparing to bend her stiff knees and lie down at my feet. I stopped her, and answered, with an arm about her neck and her soft nose in my hand,—

"'You shall *not* be sold, Rosa! you shall go and board at Mr. Town's great stable, where you will have pleasant society among the eighty horses who usually pass the winter there. Your shoes shall be taken off, and you shall rest till March at least. The best care will be taken of you, dear, and I will come and see you; and in the spring you shall return to us, even if Miss Merry is not here to welcome you.'

"'Thanks, many, many thanks! But I wish I could do something to earn my board. I hate to be idle, though rest *is* delicious. Is there nothing I can do to repay you, Miss Belinda? Please answer quickly, for I know the hour is almost over,' cried Rosa, stamping with anxiety; for, like all her sex, she wanted the last word.

"'Yes, you can,' I cried, as a sudden idea popped into my head. 'I'll write down what you have told me, and send the little story to a certain paper I know of, and the money I get for it will pay your board. So rest in peace, my dear; you *will* have earned your living, and may feel that your debt is paid.'

"Before she could reply the clock struck one, and a long sigh of satisfaction was all the response in her power. But we understood each other now, and, cutting a lock from her mane for Miss Merry, I gave Rosa a farewell caress and went away, wondering if I had made it all up, or if she had really broken a year's silence and freed her mind.

"However that may be, here is the tale, and the sequel to it is, that the bay mare has really gone to board at a first-class stable," concluded Miss Belinda. "I call occasionally and leave my card in the shape of an apple, finding Madam Rosa living like an independent lady, with her large box and private yard on the sunny side of the barn, a kind ostler to wait upon her, and much genteel society from the city when she is inclined for company.

"What more could any reasonable horse desire?"

# What Becomes of the Pins

MISS ELLEN WAS MAKING a new pincushion, and a very pretty one it promised to be, for she had much taste, and spent half her time embroidering chair-covers, crocheting tidies, and all sorts of dainty trifles. Her room was full of them; and she often declared that she did wish some one would invent a new sort of fancy-work, since she had tried all the old kinds till she was tired of them. Painting china, carving wood, button-holing butterflies and daisies onto Turkish towelling, and making peacock-feather trimming, amused her for a time; but as she was not very successful she soon gave up trying these branches, and wondered if she would not take a little plain sewing for a change.

The old cushion stood on her table beside the new one; which was ready for its trimming of lace and ribbon. A row of delicate new pins also lay waiting to adorn the red satin mound, and in the old blue one still remained several pins that had evidently seen hard service.

Miss Ellen was putting a dozen needles into her book, having just picked them out of the old cushion, and, as she quilted them through the flannel leaves, she said half aloud,—

"It is very evident where the needles go, but I really do wish I knew what becomes of the pins."

"I can tell you," answered a small, sharp voice, as a long brass pin tried to straighten itself up in the middle of a faded blue cornflower, evidently prepared to address the meeting.

Miss Ellen stared much surprised, for she had used this big pin a good deal lately, but never heard it speak before. As she looked at it she saw for the first time that its head had a tiny face, with silvery hair, two merry eyes, and a wee mouth out of which came the metallic little voice that pierced her ear, small as it was.

"Dear me!" she said; then added politely, "if you can tell I should be very happy to hear, for it has long been a great mystery, and no one could explain it."

The old pin tried to sit erect, and the merry eye twinkled as it went on like a garrulous creature, glad to talk after long silence:—

"Men make many wonderful discoveries, my dear, but they have never found that out, and never will, because we belong to women, and only a

233

feminine ear can hear us, a feminine mind understand our mission, or sympathize with our trials, experiences, and triumphs. For we have all these as well as human beings, and there really is not much difference between us when we come to look into the matter."

This was such a curious statement that Miss Ellen forgot her work to listen intently, and all the needles fixed their eyes on the audacious pin. Not a whit abashed it thus continued:—

"I am called 'Granny' among my friends, because I have had a long and eventful life. I am hearty and well, however, in spite of this crick in my back, and hope to serve you a good while yet, for you seem to appreciate me, stout and ordinary as I look.

"Yes, my dear, pins and people *are* alike, and that rusty darning-needle need not stare so rudely, for I shall prove what I say. We are divided into classes by birth and constitution, and each can do much in its own sphere. I am a shawl pin, and it would be foolish in me to aspire to the duties of those dainty lace pins made to fasten a collar. I am contented with my lot, however, and, being of a strong make and enterprising spirit, have had many adventures, some perils, and great satisfactions since I left the factory long ago. I well remember how eagerly I looked about me when the paper in which I lived, with some hundreds of relations, was hung up in a shop window, to display our glittering ranks and tempt people to buy. At last a purchaser came, a dashing young lady who bought us with several other fancy articles, and carried us away in a smart little bag, humming and talking to herself, in what I thought a very curious way.

"When we were taken out I was all in a flutter to see where I was and what would happen next. There were so many of us, I could hardly hope to go first, for I was in the third row, and most people take us in order. But Cora was a hasty, careless soul, and pulled us out at random, so I soon found myself stuck up in a big untidy cushion, with every sort of pin you can imagine. Such a gay and giddy set I never saw, and really, my dear, their ways and conversation were quite startling to an ignorant young thing like me. Pearl, coral, diamond, jet, gold, and silver heads, were all around me as well as vulgar brass knobs, jaunty black pins, good for nothing as they snap at the least strain, and my own relations, looking eminently neat and respectable among this theatrical rabble. For I will not disguise from you, Miss Ellen, that my first mistress was an actress, and my life a very gay one at the beginning. Merry, kind, and careless was the pretty Cora, and I am bound to confess I enjoyed myself immensely, for I was taken by chance with half a dozen friends to pin up the folds of her velvet train and mantle, in a fairy spectacle where she played the queen. It was very splendid, and, snugly settled among the soft folds, I saw it all, and probably felt that I too had my part; humble as it was, it was faithfully performed, and I never once deserted my post for six weeks.

"Among the elves who went flitting about with silvery wings and spangled robes was one dear child who was the good genius of the queen, and was always fluttering near her, so I could not help seeing and loving the dear creature. She danced and sung, came out of flowers, swung down from trees, popped up from the lower regions, and finally, when all the queen's troubles are over, flew away on a golden cloud, smiling through a blaze of red light, and dropping roses as she vanished.

"When the play ended, I used to see her in an old dress, a thin shawl, and shabby hat, go limping home with a tired-looking woman who dressed the girls.

"I thought a good deal about 'Little Viola,' as they called her,—though her real name was Sally, I believe,—and one dreadful night I played a heroic part, and thrill now when I remember it."

"Go on, please, I long to know," said Miss Ellen, dropping the needle-book into her lap, and leaning forward to listen better.

"One evening the theatre took fire," continued the old pin impressively. "I don't know how, but all of a sudden there was a great uproar, smoke, flames, water pouring, people running frantically about, and such a wild panic I lost my small wits for a time. When I recovered them, I found Cora was leaning from a high window, with something wrapped closely in the velvet mantle that I pinned upon the left shoulder just under a paste buckle that only sparkled while *I* did all the work.

"A little golden head lay close by me, and a white face looked up from the crimson folds, but the sweet eyes were shut, the lips were drawn with pain, a horrible odor of burnt clothes came up to me, and the small hand that clutched Cora's neck was all blistered with the cruel fire which would have devoured the child if my brave mistress had not rescued her at the risk of her own life. *She* could have escaped at first, but she heard Sally cry to her through the blinding smoke, and went to find and rescue her. I dimly recalled that, and pressed closer to the white shoulder, full of pride and affection for the kind soul whom I had often thought too gay and giddy to care for anything but pleasure.

"Now she was calling to the people in the street to put up a ladder, and, as she leaned and called, I could see the crowds far down, the smoke and flame bursting out below, and hear the hiss of water as it fell upon the blazing walls. It was a most exciting moment, as we hung there, watching the gallant men fix the long ladder, and one come climbing up till we could see his brave face, and hear him shout cheerily,—

"'Swing from the window-sill, I'll catch you.'

"But Cora answered, as she showed the little yellow head that shone in the red glare,—

"'No, save the child first!'

"'Drop her then, and be quick: it's hot work here,' and the man held up his arms with a laugh, as the flames licked out below as if to eat away the frail support he stood on.

"All in one breathless moment, Cora had torn off the mantle, wrapped the children in it, bound her girdle about it, and finding the gaudy band would not tie, caught out the first pin that came to hand, and fastened it. *I* was that pin; and I felt that the child's life almost depended upon me, for as the precious bundle dropped into the man's hands he caught it by the cloak, and, putting it on his shoulder, went swiftly down. The belt strained, the velvet tore, I felt myself bending with the weight, and expected every minute to see the child slip, and fall on the stones below. But I held fast, I drove my point deeply in, I twisted myself round so that even the bend should be a help, and I called to the man, 'Hold tight, I'm trying my best, but what can one pin do!'

"Of course he did not hear me, but I really believe my desperate efforts were of some use; for, we got safely down, and were hurried away to the hospital where other poor souls had already gone.

"The good nurse who undid that scorched, drenched, and pitiful bundle, stuck me in her shawl, and resting there, I saw the poor child laid in a little bed, her burns skilfully cared for, and her scattered senses restored by tender words and motherly kisses. How glad I was to hear that she would live, and still more rejoiced to learn next day that Cora was near by, badly burned but not in danger, and anxious to see the child she had saved.

"Nurse Benson took the little thing in her arms to visit my poor mistress, and I went too. But alas! I never should have known the gay and blooming girl of the day before. Her face and hands were terribly burnt, and she would never again be able to play the lovely queen on any stage, for her fresh beauty was forever lost.

"Hard days for all of us; I took my share of trouble with the rest, though I only suffered from the strain to my back. Nurse Benson straightened me out and kept me in use, so I saw much of pain and patience in that great house, because the little gray shawl which I fastened covered a tender heart, and on that motherly bosom many aching heads found rest, many weary creatures breathed their last, and more than one unhappy soul learned to submit.

"Among these last was poor Cora, for it was very hard to give up beauty, health, and the life she loved, so soon. Yet I do not think she ever regretted the sacrifice when she saw the grateful child well and safe, for little Sally was her best comforter, and through the long weeks she lay there half blind and suffering, the daily visit of the little one cheered her more than anything else. The poor mother was lost in the great fire, and Cora adopted the orphan as her own, and surely she had a right to what she had so dearly bought.

"They went away together at last, one quite well and strong again, the other a sad wreck, but a better woman for the trial, I think, and she carried comfort with her. Poor little Sally led her, a faithful guide, a tender nurse, a devoted daughter to her all her life."

Here the pin paused, out of breath, and Miss Ellen shook a bright drop off the lace that lay in her lap, as she said in a tone of real interest,—

"What happened next? How long did you stay in the hospital?"

"I stayed a year, for Nurse used me one day to pin up a print at the foot of a poor man's bed, and he took such comfort in it they let it hang till he died. A lovely picture of a person who held out his arms to all the suffering and oppressed, and they gathered about him to be comforted and saved. The forlorn soul had led a wicked life, and now lay dying a long and painful death, but something in that divine face taught him to hope for pardon, and when no eye but mine saw him in the lonely nights he wept, and prayed, and struggled to repent. I think he was forgiven, for when at last he lay dead a smile was on his lips that never had been there before. Then the print was taken down, and I was used to pin up a bundle of red flannel by one of the women, and for months I lay in a dark chest, meditating on the lessons I had already learned.

"Suddenly I was taken out, and when a queer round pin-ball of the flannel had been made by a nice old lady, I was stuck in it with a party of fat needles, and a few of my own race, all with stout bodies and big heads.

"'The dear boy is clumsy with his fingers, and needs strong things to use,' said the old lady, as she held the tomato cushion in both hands and kissed it before she put it into a soldier's 'comfort bag.'

"'Now I shall have a lively time!' I thought, and looked gaily about me, for I liked adventures, and felt that I was sure of them now.

"I cannot begin to tell you all I went through with that boy, for he was brave as a lion and got many hard knocks. We marched, and camped, and fought, and suffered, but we *never* ran away, and when at last a Minie ball came smashing through the red cushion (which Dick often carried in his pocket as a sort of charm to keep him safe, for men seldom use pins), I nearly lost my head, for the stuffing flew out, and we were all knocked about in a dreadful way. The cushion and the old wallet together saved Dick's life, however, for the ball did not reach his brave heart, and the last I saw of him as I fell out of the hasty hand that felt for a wound was a soft look in the brave bright eyes, as he said to himself with a smile,—

"'Dear old mother hasn't lost her boy yet, thank God!'

"A colored lad picked me up, as I lay shining on the grass, and pins being scarce in those parts, gave me to his mammy, who kept me to fasten her turban. Quite a new scene I found, for in the old cabin were a dozen children and their mothers making ready to go North. The men were all away fighting or serving the army, so mammy led the little troop, and they marched off one day following the gay turban like a banner, for she had a valiant soul, and was bound to find safety and freedom for her children at all risks.

"In my many wanderings to and fro, I never made so strange a journey as that one, but I enjoyed it, full of danger, weariness and privation as it was; and every morning when mammy put on the red and yellow hand-kerchief I was proud to sit aloft on that good gray head, and lead the forlorn little army toward a land of liberty.

"We got there at last, and she fell to work over a washtub to earn the bread for the hungry mouths. I had stood by her through all those weary weeks, and did not want to leave her now, but went off pinning a paper round some clean clothes on a Saturday morning.

"'Now I wonder what will come next!' I thought, as Thomas Jefferson, or 'Jeff,' as they called him, went whistling away with the parcel through the streets.

"Crossing the park, he spied a lovely butterfly which had strayed in from the country; caught and pinned it on his hat to please little Dinah when he got home. The pretty creature soon writhed its delicate life away, but its beauty attracted the eye of a pale girl hurrying along with a roll of work under her arm.

"'Will you sell me that?' she asked, and Jeff gladly consented, wondering what she would do with it. So did I, but when we got to her room I soon saw, for she pinned the impaled butterfly against a bit of blue paper, and painted it so well that its golden wings seemed to quiver as they did in life. A very poor place it was, but full of lovely things, and I grew artistic with just looking about me at the pictures on the walls, the flowers blooming on plates and panels, birds and insects kept for copies, and gay bits of stuff used as back-grounds.

"But more beautiful than anything she made was the girl's quiet, busy life alone in the big city; for, she was hoping to be an artist, and worked day and night to compass her desire. So poor, but so happy, I used to wonder why no one helped her and kept her from such hard, yet patient, waiting. But no one did, and I could watch her toiling away as I held the butterfly against the wall, feeling as if it was a symbol of herself, beating her delicate wings in that close place till her heart was broken, by the cruel fate that held her there when she should have been out in the free sunshine. But she found a good customer for her pretty work, in a rich lady who had nothing to do but amuse herself, and spent much time and money in fancy-work.

"I know all about it; for, one day an order came from the great store where her designs were often bought, and she was very happy painting some purple pansies upon velvet, and she copied her yellow butterfly to float above them.

"The poor insect was very dry, and crumbled at a touch, so my task there was done, and as my mistress rolled up the packet, she took me to fasten it securely, singing as she did so, for every penny was precious.

"We all went together to the rich lady, and she embroidered the flowers on a screen very like that one yonder. I thought she would throw me away, I was so battered now, but she took a fancy to use me in various ways about her canvas work, and I lived with her all winter. A kind lady, my dear, but I often wished I could suggest to her better ways of spending her life than everlasting fancy-work. She never seemed to see the wants of those about her, never lent an ear to the poor, or found delight in giving of her abundance to those who had little to brighten their lives; but sighed because she had nothing to do when the world was full of work, and she blessed with so many good gifts to use and to enjoy. I hope she will see her mistake some day, and not waste all her life on trifles, else she will regret it sadly by and by."

Here the pin paused with a keen glance at Miss Ellen, who had suddenly begun to sew with a bright color in her cheeks, for the purple pansies were on the screen that stood before her fire-place, and she recognized the portrait of herself in that last description. But she did not fancy being lectured by a pin, so she asked with a smile as she plaited up her lace,—

"That is all very interesting, but you have not yet told me what becomes of the pins, Granny."

"Pins, like people, shape their own lives, in a great measure, my dear, and go to their reward when they are used up. The good ones sink into the earth and turn to silver, to come forth again in a new and precious form. The bad ones crumble away to nothing in cracks and dust heaps, with no hope of salvation, unless some human hand lifts them up and gives them a chance to try again. Some are lazy, and slip out of sight to escape service, some are too sharp, and prick and scratch wherever they are. Others are poor, weak things, who bend up and lose their heads as soon as they are used. Some obtrude themselves on all occasions, and some are never to be found in times of need. All have the choice to wear out or to rust out. I chose the former, and have had a useful, happy life so far. I'm not as straight as I once was, but I'm bright still, my point is sharp, my head firm, and age has not weakened me much, I hope, but made me wiser, better, and more contented to do my duty wherever I am, than when I left my native paper long ago."

Before Miss Ellen could express her respect for the worthy old pin, a dismal groan was heard from the blue cushion, and a small voice croaked aloud,—

"Alas, alas, I chose to rust out, and here I am, a miserable, worthless thing, whom no one can use or care for. Lift the ruffle, and behold a sad contrast to the faithful, honest, happy Granny, who has told us such a varied tale."

"Bless me, what possesses everything to-day!" exclaimed Miss Ellen, looking under the frill of the old cushion to see who was speaking now. There to be sure she found a pin hidden away, and so rusty that she could hardly pull it out. But it came creaking forth at the third tug, and when it was set up beside Granny, she cried out in her cheery way,—

"Try Dr. Emery, he can cure most cases of rust, and it is never too late to mend, neighbor."

"Too late for me!" sighed the new comer. "The rust of idleness has eaten into my vitals while I lay in my silken bed, and my chance is gone forever. I was bright, and strong, and sharp once, but I feared work and worry, and I hid, growing duller, dimmer, and more useless every day. I am good for nothing, throw me away, and let the black pins mourn for a wasted life."

"No," said Miss Ellen, "you are not useless, for you two shall sit together in my new cushion, a warning to me, as well as to the other pins, to choose the right way in time, and wear out with doing our duty, rather than rust out as so many do. Thank you, Granny, for your little lecture, I will not forget it, but go at once and find that poor girl, and help her all I can. Rest here, you good old soul, and teach these little things to follow your example."

As she spoke, Miss Ellen set the two pins in the middle of the red satin cushion, stuck the smaller pins round them, and hastened to put on her shawl lest something should prevent her from going.

"Take me with you; I'm not tired, I love to work! use me, dear mistress, and let me help in the good work!" cried Granny, with a lively skip that sent her out upon the bureau.

So Miss Ellen pinned the shawl with the old pin instead of the fine brooch she had in her hand, and they went gaily away together, leaving the rusty one to bemoan itself, and all the little ones to privately resolve that they would not hide away from care and labor, but take their share bravely and have a good record to show when they went, at last where the good pins go.

# The Dolls' Journey from Minnesota to Maine

Mr. Plum lived in St. Paul, Minnesota, U.S.A. There were six little Plums, all girls, varying in ages from fourteen to seven, and named Kate, Lucy, Susy, Lizzy, Marjory and Maggie. There was no mamma, but Mrs. Gibbs, the housekeeper, was a kind old soul, and papa did everything he could to make the small daughters good and happy.

One stormy Saturday afternoon the children were all together in the school-room, and papa busy at his desk in the library, with the door open because he liked to hear the pleasant voices and catch glimpses of the droll plays that went on there.

Kate lay on the sofa reading "The Daisy Chain" for the fourth time. Susy, Lucy and Lizzie were having a select tea party in their own recess, the entrance to which was barricaded with chairs to keep out the "babies," as they called the little ones, who were much offended at being excluded and sat up in the cushioned window-seat pensively watching the rain.

"If it had only waited till to-morrow we should have had time for our journey; now we can't go till next Saturday. Flora is so disappointed she would cry if I had not taught her to behave," said Maggie with a sigh, as she surveyed the doll on her knee in its new summer suit.

"So is Dora. Just see how sweet she looks with her hat and cape on and her travelling-bag all ready. Couldn't we play travel in the house? It is such a pity to wait when the children are in such a hurry to go," answered Marjory, settling the tiny bag that held Dora's night-cap and gown as well as the morsels of cake that were to serve for her lunch.

"No," said Maggie decidedly, "we can't do it, because there is no room for carriages, and boats, and railroads, and hotels, and accidents. It is a long journey from Minnesota to Maine, and we couldn't get it all into one room I'm sure."

"I don't think papa would mind our coming into the library, if we didn't ring the car bells very loud or scream much when the accidents happen," said Marjory, who hated to give up the plan they had been cherishing all the week.

"What is it, little ones? Come and tell me what is the matter," called Mr.

242

Plum, hearing his name and the magic word "railroad," for he was the president of one and had his hands full just then.

Down jumped the little girls and ran to perch on either arm of his chair, pouring out their small tribulations as freely as if he had been the most sympathizing of mothers.

"We planned to take a long, long journey round the garden with our dolls to-day, and play go to Maine and see Aunt Maria. You know she asked us, and we looked out the way on the map and got all ready, and now it rains and we are dreadfully disappointed," said Maggie, while Marjory sighed as she looked at the red D. worked on the inch square travelling-bag.

"As you can't go, why not send the dolls to make aunty a visit, and she will send them back when they get homesick," proposed Mr. Plum, smiling, as if a sudden idea had popped into his head.

"Really?" cried Maggie.

"How could we?" asked Marjory.

"They could go and come by mail, and tell you all about their adventures when they got back," said papa.

Both children were speechless for a moment, then as the full splendor of this proposition dawned upon them they clapped their hands, crying eagerly:

"We will! we will! Let's do it at once."

"What? where? who?" asked Susy, Lucy, and Lizzie, forgetting their tea party to run and see what was going on.

They were told, and in their turn exclaimed so loudly that Kate came to join in the fun.

After a great deal of talking and laughing, the dolls were prepared for the long journey. They were common wooden-headed dollies, a hand long, with stuffed bodies and stout legs ornamented with very small feet in red and blue boots. Dora was a blonde and Flora a brunette, otherwise they were just alike and nearly new. Usually when people go travelling they put on their hats and cloaks, but these pilgrims, by papa's advice, left all encumbrances behind them, for they were to travel in a peculiar way, and blue gingham dresses were chosen for the expedition.

"It is possible that they may never come back. Accidents will happen you know. Are you prepared for that?" asked Mr. Plum, pausing with the brown paper spread out before him.

"I am," answered Maggie firmly, as she laid Flora on the table, her black eyes staring as if rather alarmed at this sudden start.

Marjory hesitated a moment, clasping Dora to her bosom with a face full of maternal anxiety. But Susy, Lucy and Lizzy cried: "Let her go, do let her go, and if she is lost papa will give you a new doll."

"Good-by, my darling dear. Have a splendid time, and be sure you come back to me," whispered Marjory, with a tender farewell kiss as she gave up her child.

All stood watching silently while papa tied the dolls back to back with the ribbon Kate pulled from her neck, then folded them carefully in strong brown paper, leaving their heads out that they might see the world as they went along. Being carefully fastened up with several turns of cord, Mr. Plum directed the precious parcel to "Miss Maria Plum, Portland, Maine. With care." Then it was weighed, stamped, and pronounced ready for the post.

"I shall write and tell aunty they are coming, because she will want to be prepared for such distinguished visitors," said papa, taking up his pen with a glance at the six excited little faces round him.

Silence reigned while the letter was written, and as he sealed it up Mr. Plum said solemnly, with his hand on the parcel:

"For the last time, shall they go?"

"Yes!" answered the Spartan mothers with one voice, while the other sisters danced round them, and Kate patted the curly heads approvingly.

"Going, going, gone!" answered papa as he whisked on his coat and hat, and slammed the door behind him.

The children clustered at the window to see him set out on this momentous errand, and he often looked back waving his umbrella at them, till he vanished round the corner, with a reassuring pat on the pocket out of which dear Do and Flo popped their heads for a last look at their sweet home.

"Now let us take out poor old Lucinda and Rose Augusta to play with. I know their feelings were hurt at our leaving them for the new dolls," said Maggie, rummaging in the baby-house, whither Margery soon followed her to reinstate the old darlings in the place of the departed new ones.

"Safely off," reported Mr. Plum, when he came into tea, "and we may expect to hear from them in a week or two. Parcels go more slowly than letters, and this is Aunty's busy season, so wait patiently and see what will happen."

"We will," said the little girls; and they did, but week after week went by and nothing was heard of the wanderers.

We, however, can follow them and learn much that their anxious mothers never knew.

As soon as Flora and Dora recovered from the bewilderment occasioned by the confusion of the post office, they found themselves in one of the many leathern mail bags rumbling Eastward. As it was perfectly dark they could not see their companions, so listened to the whispering and rustling that went on about them. The newspapers all talked politics, and some of them used such bad language that the dolls would have covered their ears, if their hands had not been tied down. The letters were better behaved and more interesting, for they told one another the news they carried, because nothing is private in America, and even gummed envelopes cannot keep gossip from leaking out.

"It is very interesting, but I should enjoy it more if I was not grinding my nose against the rough side of this leather bag," whispered Dora, who lay under most just then.

"So should I, if a heavy book was not pinching my toes. I've tried to kick it away, but it won't stir, and keeps droning on about reports and tariffs and such dull things," answered Flora, with a groan.

"Do you like travelling?" asked Dora, presently, when the letters and papers fell asleep, lulled by the motion of the cars.

"Not yet, but I shall when I can look about me. This bundle near by says the mails are often sorted in the cars, and in that way we shall see something of the world, I hope," answered Flora, cheering up, for, like her mama, she was of an enquiring turn.

The dolls took a nap of some hours, and were roused by a general tumbling out on a long shelf, where many other parcels lay, and lively men sent letters and papers flying here and there as if a whirl-wind was blowing. A long box lay beside the dolls who stood nearly erect leaning against a pile of papers. Several holes were cut in the lid, and out of one of them was thrust a little black nose, as if trying to get air.

"Dear me! what can be in it?" said Flora, who was nearest.

"I'm a poor little alligator, going to a boy in Chicago, if you please, and I want my mother," sobbed a voice from the box, and there was a rap on the lid as of an agitated tail.

"Mercy on us! I hope we shall not have to travel with the monster," whispered Dora, trying to see over her shoulder.

"I'm not afraid. He can't be very dreadful, for the box is not any longer than we are. Natural history is very useful; I've heard mamma say so, and I shall talk with him while we rest here," answered Flo, nodding toward the eye which now took the place of the nose.

So the little alligator told her something of his home on the banks of a great river, where he was just learning to play happily with his brothers and sisters, when he was caught and sent away to pine in captivity.

The dolls comforted him as well as they could, and a pair of baby's shoes travelling in an envelope sympathized with him, while a shabby bundle directed to "Michael Dolan, at Mrs. Judy Quin's, next door to Mr. Pat Murphy, Boston, North street," told them to "Whisht and slape quite till they came forninst the place."

"Such low people!" whispered Do to Flo, and both stood primly silent till they were tumbled into another mail bag, and went rattling on again with a new set of companions.

"I hope that poor baby will go safely and the boy be good to him," said Flora, for the little alligator went with the live stock in some other way.

"Thank goodness he didn't go with us! I shall dream about that black nose and winking eye, I'm sure. The dangers of travelling are great, but we are safe and comfortable now, I think," and Dora settled down in a cozy corner of the bag, wondering when they should reach Chicago.

"I like adventures and hope we shall have some," answered Flora, briskly, little dreaming how soon her wish was to be granted.

A few hours later there came a bump, a crash, a cry, and then all the mail bags rolled one over the other with the car down an embankment into a river.

"Now we are dead!" shrieked the poor dolls, clinging together as they heard the splash of water, the shouting of men, the splintering of wood, and the hiss of steam.

"Don't be frightened, ladies, mail bags are always looked after," said a large envelope with an official seal and the name of a Senator on it.

"Any bones broken, dear madam?" asked a jaunty pink letter, with a scent of musk about it, evidently a love-letter.

"I think one foot is hurt, and my clothes are dripping," sighed Dora, faintly.

"Water won't hurt calico," called out a magazine full of fashion plates, adding dolefully, as its gay colors began to run, "I shall be in a nice mess if I ever get out of this. People will wear odd fashions if they follow me this time."

"Hope they will telegraph news of this accident in time for the evening papers," said a dingy sheet called the "Barahoo Thunderbolt," as it lay atop of the heap in its yellow wrapper.

"Be calm, my friends, and wait with fortitude for death or deliverance, as I do." With which philosophic remark "The St. Louis Cosmos" folded the pages which for the first time since the paper was started, were not dry.

Here the water rose over the topmost letter and a moist silence prevailed till a sudden jerk fished up the bag, and before the dolls could recover their wits they were spread out on the floor of a mail car to dry, while several busy men sorted and saved such papers and letters as still held together.

"Now we shall see something," said Flora, feeling the warm air blow over her as they spun along, for a slight accident like this did not delay the energetic Westerners a moment longer than absolutely necessary.

"I can't see you, dear, but I hope you look better than I do, for the yellow of my hair has washed into my eyes and the red of my cheeks is quite gone, I'm sure," answered Dora, as her wet dress flopped in the breeze and the broken foot sticking up showed her that her blue boots were ruined.

"I don't care a bit how I look. It's great fun now we are safe. Pop up your head and see the wide prairie flying past. I do hope that poor baby got away and swam home to his mother. The upset into the river was quite to his taste, I fancy," said Flora, who was much excited by her adventure and eager for more.

Presently one of the men set the dolls up in the corner of a window to dry, and there they stood viewing the fine landscape with one eye while the other watched the scene of devastation within. Everything was in great confusion after the accident, so it is not strange that the dolls were not missed when they slowly slid lower and lower till a sudden lurch of the car sent them out of the window to roll into a green field where cows were feeding and children picking strawberries.

"This is the end of us! Here we shall lie and mould forgotten by everybody," said Dora, who always took a tragical view of things.

"Not a bit of it! I see cows eating toward us and they may give us a lift. I've heard of their tossing people up, though I don't know just how it's done. If they don't, we are in the path and some of those children are sure to find us," answered Flora cheerfully, though she stood on her head with a bunch of burrs pricking her nose.

She was right. A bright-eyed little German girl presently came trotting along the path with a great basket full of berries on her head arranged in pretty pottles ready for the market. Seeing the red cow sniffing at a brown paper parcel she drove her away, picked it up and peeped in at the open end.

The sight of two dolls in such a place made her feel as if fairies had dropped them there for her. She could not read the direction and hurried home to show her treasure to her brothers and sisters of whom there were eight.

"What will become of us now!" exclaimed Dora, as eager hands slipped them out of the wrapper and smoothed their damp skirts in a room that seemed swarming with boys and girls of all sizes.

"Don't worry, we shall get on nicely, I'm sure, and learn German of these young persons. It is a great relief to be able to stretch one's limbs and stand up, isn't it?" answered Flora, undismayed by anything that had happened as yet.

"Yes, dear, I love you but I *am* tired of being tied to you all day. I hope we shall live through this noise and get a little rest, but I give up the idea of ever seeing Portland," answered Dora, staring with all her blue eyes at the display of musical instruments about the room and longing to stop her ears, for several of the children were playing on the violin, flute, horn or harp. They were street musicians, and even the baby seemed to be getting ready to take part in the concert, for he sat on the floor beside an immense bass horn taller than himself, with his rosy lips at the mouth piece and his cheeks puffed out in vain attempts to make a "boom! boom!" as brother Fritz did.

Flora was delighted, and gave skips on her red boots in time to the lively tooting of the boys, while the girls gazed at the lovely dolls and jabbered away with their yellow braids quivering with excitement.

The wrapper was laid aside till a neighbor who read English came in to translate it. Meantime they enjoyed the new toys immensely, and even despondent Dora was cheered up by the admiration she received; while they in their turn were deeply interested in the pretty dolls' furniture some of the children made.

Beds, tables and chairs covered the long bench, and round it sat the neat-handed little maidens gluing, tacking and trimming, while they sang and chatted at their work as busy and happy as a hive of bees.

All day the boys went about the streets playing, and in the evening trooped off to the beer gardens to play again, for they lived in Chicago, and the dolls got so far on their way to Aunt Maria, as they soon discovered.

For nearly two months they lived happily with Minna, Gretchen and Nanerl, then they set out on their travels again, and this was the way it happened. A little girl came to order a set of furniture for her new baby-house, and seeing two shabby dolls reposing in a fine bed she asked about them. Her mamma spoke German so Minna told how they were found, and showed the old wrapper, saying that they always meant to send the dolls on their way but grew so fond of them they kept putting it off.

"I am going as far as New York very soon and will take them along if you like, for I think little Miss Maria Plum must have been expecting her dolls all this time. Shall I?" asked the mamma, as she read the address and saw the dash under "With care," as if the dollies were of great importance to some one.

"Ja, ja," answered Minna, glad to oblige a lady who bought two whole sets of their best furniture and paid for it at once.

So again the dolls were put in their brown paper cover and sent away with farewell kisses.

"This now is genteel and just suits me," said Dora, as they drove along with little Clara to the handsome house where she was staying.

"I have a feeling that she is a spoilt child, and we shall not be as happy with her as with the dear Poppleheimers. We shall see," answered Flora, wisely, for Clara had soon tossed the dolls into a corner and was fretting because mamma would not buy her the big horn to blow on.

The party started for New York in a day or two, and to the delight of Flo and Do they were left out of the trunks for Clara to play with on the way, her own waxen Blanche Marie Annabel being too delicate to be used.

"Oh my patience, this is worse than tumbling about in a mail-bag," groaned Dora, after hours of great suffering, for Clara treated the poor dolls as if they had no feeling.

She amused herself with knocking their heads together, shutting them in the window with their poor legs hanging out, swinging them by one arm, and drawing lines with a pencil all over their faces till they looked as if tattooed by savages. Even brave Flora was worn out and longed for rest, finding her only comfort in saying, "I told you so," when Clara banged them about, or dropped them on the dusty floor to be trampled on by passing feet.

There they were left, and would have been swept away if a little dog had not found them as the passengers were leaving the car and carried them after his master, trotting soberly along with the bundle in his mouth, for fortunately Clara had put them into the paper before she left them, so they were still together in the trials of the journey.

"Hullo, Jip, what have you got?" asked the young man as the little dog jumped up on the carriage seat and laid his load on his master's knee, panting and wagging his tail as if he had done something to be praised for.

"Dolls, I declare! What can a bachelor do with the poor things? Wonder who Maria Plum is? Midge will like a look at them before we send them along;" and into the young man's pocket they went, trembling with fear of the dog, but very grateful for being rescued from destruction.

Jip kept his eye on them, and gave an occasional poke with his cold nose to be sure they were there as they drove through the bustling streets of New York to a great house with an inscription over the door.

"I do hope Midge will be a nicer girl than Flora. Children ought to be taught to be kind to dumb dolls as well as dumb animals," said Dora, as the young man ran up the steps and hurried along a wide hall.

"I almost wish we were at home with our own kind little mothers," began Flo, for even her spirits were depressed by bad treatment, but just then a door opened and she cried out in amazement," "Bless my heart, this man has more children than even Mr. Poppleheimer!"

She might well think so, for all down both sides of the long room stood little white beds with a small pale face on every pillow. All the eyes that were open brightened when Jip and his master came in, and several thin hands were outstretched to meet them.

"I've been good, Doctor, let me pat him first," cried one childish voice.

"Did you bring me a flower, please?" asked another feeble one.

"I know he's got something nice for us, I see a bundle in his pocket," and a little fellow who sat up among his pillows gave a joyful cough as he could not shout.

"Two dollies for Midge to play with. Jip found them, but I think the little girl they are going to will lend them for a few days. We shall not need them longer I'm afraid," added the young man to a rosy faced nurse who came along with a bottle in her hand.

"Dear no, the poor child is very low to-day. But she will love to look at the babies if she isn't strong enough to hold 'em," said the woman, leading the way to a corner where the palest of all the pale faces lay smiling on the pillow, and the thinnest of the thin hands were feebly put up to greet the Doctor.

"So nice!" she whispered when the dolls were laid beside her, while Jip proudly beat his tail on the floor to let her know that she owed the welcome gift to him.

For an hour Flo and Do lay on the arm of poor Midge who never moved except to touch them now and then with a tender little finger, or to kiss them softly, saying, "Dear babies, it is very nice not to be all alone. Are you comfy, darlings?" till she fell asleep still smiling.

"Sister, do you think this can be the Heaven we hear people talk about? It is so still and white, and may be these children are angels," whispered Dora, looking at the sweet face turned toward her with the long lashes lying on the colorless cheek, and the arms outstretched like wings.

"No, dear, it is a hospital, I heard that man say so, and those are sick children come to be cured. It is a sweet place, I think, and this child much nicer than that horrid Clara," answered Flo, who was quicker to hear, see and understand what went on than Dora.

"I love to lie here safe and warm, but there doesn't seem to be much breath to rock me," said Do, who lay nearest the little bosom that very slowly rose and fell with the feeble flutter of the heart below.

"Hush, we may disturb her," and lively Flo controlled her curiosity, contenting herself with looking at the other children and listening to their quiet voices, for pain seemed to have hushed them all.

For a week the dolls lay in Midge's bed, and though their breasts were full of saw-dust and their heads were only wood, the sweet patience of the little creature seemed to waken something like a heart in them, and set them thinking, for dolls don't live in vain, I am firmly persuaded.

All day she tended them till the small hands could no longer hold them, and through the weary nights she tried to murmur bits of lullabies lest the dollies would not be able to sleep because of the crying or the moans some of the poor babies could not repress. She often sent one or the other to cheer up some little neighbor, and in this way Do and Flo became small sisters of charity, welcomed eagerly, reluctantly returned, and loved by all, although they never uttered a word and their dingy faces could not express the emotion that stirred their saw-dust bosoms.

When Saturday night came they were laid in their usual place on Midge's arm. She was too weak to kiss them now, and nurse laid their battered cheeks against the lips that whispered faintly, "Be sure you send 'em to the little girl, and tell her—tell her—all about it." Then she turned her cheek to the pillow with a little sigh and lay so still the dolls thought she had gone to sleep.

She had, but the sweet eyes did not open in the morning, and there was no breath in the little breast to rock the dolls any more.

"I knew she was an angel, and now she has flown away," said Dora softly, as they watched the white image carried out in the weeping nurse's arms, with the early sunshine turning all the pretty hair to gold.

"I think that is what they call dying, sister. It is a much lovelier way to end than as we do in the dust bin or rag-bag. I wonder if there is a little Heaven anywhere for good dolls?" answered Flora, with what looked like a tear on her cheek; but it was only a drop from the violets sent by the kind Doctor last night.

"I hope so, for I think the souls of little children might miss us if they loved us as dear Midge did," whispered Dora, trying to kiss the blue flower in her hand, for the child had shared her last gift with these friends.

"Why didn't you let her take them along, poor motherless baby?" asked the doctor when he saw the dolls lying as she had left them.

"I promised her they should go to the girl they were sent to, and please, I'd like to keep my word to the little darling," answered Nurse with a sob.

"You shall," said the Doctor, and put them in his breast pocket with the faded violets, for everybody loved the pauper child sent to die in a hospital, because Christian charity makes every man and woman father and mother to these little ones.

All day the dolls went about in the busy Doctor's pocket, and I think the violets did them good, for the soft perfume clung to them long afterward like the memory of a lovely life, as short and sweet as that of the flowers.

In the evening they were folded up in a fresh paper and re-directed carefully. The Doctor wrote a little note telling why he had kept them, and was just about to put on some stamps when a friend came in who was going to Boston in the morning.

"Anything to take along, Fred?" asked the newcomer.

"This parcel, if you will. I have a feeling that I'd rather not have it knock about in a mail-bag," and the Doctor told him why.

It was pleasant to see how carefully the traveller put away the parcel after that, and to hear him say that he was going through Boston to the mountains for his holiday, and would deliver it in Portland to Miss Plum herself.

"Now there is some chance of our getting there," said Flora, as they set off next day in a new Russia leather bag.

On the way they overheard a long chat between some New York and Boston ladies which impressed them very much. Flora liked to hear the fashionable gossip about clothes and people and art and theatres, but Dora preferred the learned conversation of the young Boston ladies, who seemed to know a little of everything, or think they did.

"I hope Mamma will give me an entirely new wardrobe when I get home; and we will have dolls' weddings and balls, and a play, and be as fine and fashionable as those ladies down there," said Flora, after listening a while.

"You have got your head full of dressy ideas and high life, sister. I don't care for such things, but mean to cultivate my mind as fast as I can. That girl says she is in college, and named over more studies than I can count. I do wish we were to stop and see a little of the refined society of Boston," answered Dora, primly.

"Pooh!" said Flo, "don't you try to be intellectual, for you are only a wooden-headed doll. I mean to be a real Westerner, and just enjoy myself as I please, without caring what other folks do or think, Boston is no better than the rest of the world, I guess."

Groans from every article in the bag greeted this disrespectful speech, and an avalanche of Boston papers fell upon the audacious doll. But Flo was undaunted, and shouted from underneath the pile: "I don't care! Minnesota forever!" till her breath gave out.

Dora was so mortified that she never said a word till they were let out in a room at the Parker House. Here she admired everything, and read all the evening in a volume of Emerson's Poems from the bag, for Mr. Mt. Vernon Beacon was a Boston man, and never went anywhere without a wise book or two in his pocket.

Flo turned up her nose at all she saw, and devoted herself to a long chat with the smart bag which came from New York and was full of gossip.

The next afternoon they really got to Portland, and as soon as Mr. Beacon had made his toilet he set out to find little Miss Plum. When the parlor door opened to admit her he was much embarrassed, for, advancing with a paternal smile and the dolls extended to the expected child, he found himself face to face with a pretty young lady, who looked as if she thought him a little mad.

A few words explained the errand, however, and when she read the note Aunt Maria's bright eyes were full of tears as she said, hugging the dilapidated dolls:

"I'll write the story of their travels, and send the dear old things back to the children as soon as possible."

And so she did with Mr. Beacon's help, for he decided to try the air of Portland, and spent his vacation there. The dolls were re-painted and redressed till they were more beautiful than ever, and their clothes fine enough to suit even Flo.

They were a good while doing this, and when all was ready, Aunt Maria took it into her head to run out to St. Paul and surprise the children. By a singular coincidence Mr. Beacon had railroad business in that direction, so they set off together, with two splendid dolls done up in a gay box.

All that was ever known about that journey was that these travellers stopped at the hospital in New York, and went on better friends than before after hearing from the good Doctor all the pathetic story of little Midge.

The young Plums had long ago given up the hope of ever seeing Do and Flo again, for they started in June and it was early in September when Aunt Maria appeared before them without the least warning, accompanied by a pleasant gentleman from Boston.

Six kisses had hardly resounded from Aunty's blooming cheeks when a most attractive box was produced from the Russia leather bag, and the wandering dolls restored to the arms of their enraptured mammas.

A small volume neatly written and adorned with a few pictures of the most exciting incidents of the trip also appeared.

"Every one writes or prints a book in Boston, you know, so we did both," said Aunt Maria, laughing, as she handed over the remarkable history which she had composed and Mr. Beacon illustrated.

It was read with intense interest, and was as true as most stories are nowadays.

"Nothing more delightful can happen now!" exclaimed the children, as they laid by the precious work and enthroned the travelled dolls in the place of honor on the roof of the baby-house.

But something much more delightful did happen, for at Thanksgiving time there was a wedding at the Plums'. Not a doll's wedding, as Flo had planned, but a real one, for the gentleman from Boston actually married Aunt Maria.

There were six bridesmaids, all in blue, and Flora and Dora, in the loveliest of new pink gowns, were set aloft among the roses on the wedding-cake, their proper place as everyone said, for there never would have been any marriage at all but for this Doll's Journey From Minnesota to Maine.

# A Christmas Dream, and How It Came True

"I'M SO TIRED OF CHRISTMAS I wish there never would be another one!" exclaimed a discontented-looking little girl, as she sat idly watching her mother arrange a pile of gifts two days before they were to be given.

"Why, Effie, what a dreadful thing to say! You are as bad as old Scrooge; and I'm afraid something will happen to you, as it did to him, if you don't care for dear Christmas," answered mamma, almost dropping the silver horn she was filling with delicious candies.

"Who was Scrooge? What happened to him?" asked Effie, with a glimmer of interest in her listless face, as she picked out the sourest lemon-drop she could find; for nothing sweet suited her just then.

"He was one of Dickens's best people, and you can read the charming story some day. He hated Christmas until a strange dream showed him how dear and beautiful it was, and made a better man of him."

"I shall read it; for I like dreams, and have a great many curious ones myself. But they don't keep me from being tired of Christmas," said Effie, poking discontentedly among the sweeties for something worth eating.

"Why are you tired of what should be the happiest time of all the year?" asked mamma, anxiously.

"Perhaps I shouldn't be if I had something new. But it is always the same, and there isn't any more surprise about it. I always find heaps of goodies in my stocking. Don't like some of them, and soon get tired of those I do like. We always have a great dinner, and I eat too much, and feel ill next day. Then there is a Christmas tree somewhere, with a doll on top, or a stupid old Santa Claus, and children dancing and screaming over bon-bons and toys that break, and shiny things that are of no use. Really, mamma, I've had so many Christmases all alike that I don't think I *can* bear another one." And Effie laid herself flat on the sofa, as if the mere idea was too much for her.

Her mother laughed at her despair, but was sorry to see her little girl so discontented, when she had everything to make her happy, and had known but ten Christmas days.

"Suppose we don't give you *any* presents at all,—how would that suit you?" asked mama, anxious to please her spoiled child.

"I should like one large and splendid one, and one dear little one, to remember some very nice person by," said Effie, who was a fanciful little body, full of odd whims and notions, which her friends loved to gratify, regardless of time, trouble, or money; for she was the last of three little girls, and very dear to all the family.

"Well, my darling, I will see what I can do to please you, and not say a word until all is ready. If I could only get a new idea to start with!" And mamma went on tying up her pretty bundles with a thoughtful face, while Effie strolled to the window to watch the rain that kept her in-doors and made her dismal.

"Seems to me poor children have better times than rich ones. I can't go out, and there is a girl about my age splashing along, without any maid to fuss about rubbers and cloaks and umbrellas and colds. I wish I was a beggar-girl."

"Would you like to be hungry, cold, and ragged, to beg all day, and sleep on an ash-heap at night?" asked mamma, wondering what would come next.

"Cinderella did, and had a nice time in the end. This girl out here has a basket of scraps on her arm, and a big old shawl all round her, and doesn't seem to care a bit, though the water runs out of the toes of her boots. She goes paddling along, laughing at the rain, and eating a cold potato as if it tasted nicer than the chicken and ice-cream I had for dinner. Yes, I do think poor children are happier than rich ones."

"So do I, sometimes. At the Orphan Asylum to-day I saw two dozen merry little souls who have no parents, no home, and no hope of Christmas beyond a stick of candy or a cake. I wish you had been there to see how happy they were, playing with the old toys some richer children had sent them."

"You may give them all mine; I'm so tired of them I never want to see them again," said Effie, turning from the window to the pretty baby-house full of everything a child's heart could desire.

"I will, and let you begin again with something you will not tire of, if I can only find it." And mamma knit her brows trying to discover some grand surprise for this child who didn't care for Christmas.

Nothing more was said then; and wandering off to the library, Effie found "A Christmas Carol," and curling herself up in the sofa corner, read it all before tea. Some of it she did not understand; but she laughed and cried over many parts of the charming story, and felt better without knowing why.

All the evening she thought of poor Tiny Tim, Mrs. Cratchit with the pudding, and the stout old gentleman who danced so gayly that "his legs twinkled in the air." Presently bedtime arrived.

"Come, now, and toast your feet," said Effie's nurse, "while I do your pretty hair and tell stories."

"I'll have a fairy tale to-night, a very interesting one," commanded Effie, as she put on her blue silk wrapper and little fur-lined slippers to sit before the fire and have her long curls brushed.

So Nursey told her best tales; and when at last the child lay down under her lace curtains, her head was full of a curious jumble of Christmas elves, poor children, snow-storms, sugar-plums, and surprises. So it is no wonder that she dreamed all night; and this was the dream, which she never quite forgot.

She found herself sitting on a stone, in the middle of a great field, all alone. The snow was falling fast, a bitter wind whistled by, and night was coming on. She felt hungry, cold, and tired, and did not know where to go nor what to do.

"I wanted to be a beggar-girl, and now I am one; but I don't like it, and wish somebody would come and take care of me. I don't know who I am, and I think I must be lost," thought Effie, with the curious interest one takes in one's self in dreams.

But the more she thought about it, the more bewildered she felt. Faster fell the snow, colder blew the wind, darker grew the night; and poor Effie made up her mind that she was quite forgotten and left to freeze alone. The tears were chilled on her cheeks, her feet felt like icicles, and her heart died within her, so hungry, frightened, and forlorn was she. Laying her head on her knees, she gave herself up for lost, and sat there with the great flakes turning her to a little white mound, when suddenly the sound of music reached her, and starting up, she looked and listened with all her eyes and ears.

Far away a dim light shone, and a voice was heard singing. She tried to run toward the welcome glimmer, but could not stir, and stood like a small statue of expectation while the light grew nearer, and the sweet words of the song grew clearer.

> From our happy home
> Through the world we roam
> One week in all the year,
> Making winter spring

With the joy we bring,
For Christmas-tide is here.

Now the eastern star
Shines from afar
To light the poorest home;
Hearts warmer grow,
Gifts freely flow,
For Christmas-tide has come.

Now gay trees rise
Before young eyes,
Abloom with tempting cheer;
Blithe voices sing,
And blithe bells ring,
For Christmas-tide is here.

Oh, happy chime,
Oh, blessed time,
That draws us all so near!
"Welcome, dear day,"
All creatures say,
For Christmas-tide is here.

A child's voice sang, a child's hand carried the little candle; and in the circle of soft light it shed, Effie saw a pretty child coming to her through the night and snow. A rosy, smiling creature, wrapped in white fur, with a wreath of green and scarlet holly on its shining hair, the magic candle in one hand, and the other outstretched as if to shower gifts and warmly press all other hands.

Effie forgot to speak as this bright vision came nearer, leaving no trace of footsteps in the snow, only lighting the way with its little candle, and filling the air with the music of its song.

"Dear child, you are lost, and I have come to find you," said the stranger, taking Effie's cold hands in his, with a smile like sunshine, while every holly berry glowed like a little fire.

"Do you know me?" asked Effie, feeling no fear, but a great gladness, at his coming.

"I know all children, and go to find them; for this is my holiday, and I gather them from all parts of the world to be merry with me once a year."

"Are you an angel?" asked Effie, looking for the wings.

"No; I am a Christmas spirit, and live with my mates in a pleasant place, getting ready for our holiday, when we are let out to roam about the world, helping make this a happy time for all who will let us in. Will you come and see how we work?"

"I will go anywhere with you. Don't leave me again," cried Effie, gladly.

"First I will make you comfortable. That is what we love to do. You are cold, and you shall be warm; hungry, and I will feed you; sorrowful, and I will make you gay."

With a wave of his candle all three miracles were wrought,—for the snow-flakes turned to a white fur cloak and hood on Effie's head and shoulders; a bowl of hot soup came sailing to her lips, and vanished when she had eagerly drunk the last drop; and suddenly the dismal field changed to a new world so full of wonders that all her troubles were forgotten in a minute.

Bells were ringing so merrily that it was hard to keep from dancing. Green garlands hung on the walls, and every tree was a Christmas tree full of toys, and blazing with candles that never went out.

In one place many little spirits sewed like mad on warm clothes, turning off work faster than any sewing-machine ever invented, and great piles were made ready to be sent to poor people. Other busy creatures packed money into purses, and wrote checks which they sent flying away on the wind,—a lovely kind of snow-storm to fall into a world below full of poverty.

Older and graver spirits were looking over piles of little books, in which the records of the past year were kept, telling how different people had spent it, and what sort of gifts they deserved. Some got peace, some disappointment, some remorse and sorrow, some great joy and hope. The rich had generous thoughts sent them; the poor, gratitude and contentment. Children had more love and duty to parents; and parents renewed patience, wisdom, and satisfaction for and in their children. No one was forgotten.

"Please tell me what splendid place this is?" asked Effie, as soon as she could collect her wits after the first look at all these astonishing things.

"This is the Christmas world; and here we work all the year round, never tired of getting ready for the happy day. See, these are the saints just setting off; for some have far to go, and the children must not be disappointed."

As he spoke the spirit pointed to four gates, out of which four great sleighs were just driving, laden with toys, while a jolly old Santa Claus sat in the middle of each, drawing on his mittens and tucking up his wraps for a long cold drive.

"Why, I thought there was only one Santa Claus, and even he was a humbug," cried Effie, astonished at the sight.

"Never give up your faith in the sweet old stories, even after you come to see that they are only the pleasant shadow of a lovely truth."

Just then the sleighs went off with a great jingling of bells and pattering of reindeer hoofs, while all the spirits gave a cheer that was heard in the lower world, where people said, "Hear the stars sing."

"I never will say there isn't any Santa Claus again. Now, show me more."

"You will like to see this place, I think, and may learn something here perhaps."

The spirit smiled as he led the way to a little door, through which Effie peeped into a world of dolls. Baby-houses were in full blast, with dolls of all sorts going on like live people. Waxen ladies sat in their parlors elegantly dressed; black dolls cooked in the kitchens; nurses walked out with the bits of dollies; and the streets were full of tin soldiers marching, wooden horses prancing, express wagons rumbling, and little men hurrying to and fro. Shops were there, and tiny people buying legs of mutton, pounds of tea, mites of clothes, and everything dolls use or wear or want.

But presently she saw that in some ways the dolls improved upon the manners and customs of human beings, and she watched eagerly to learn why they did these things. A fine Paris doll driving in her carriage took up a black worsted Dinah who was hobbling along with a basket of clean clothes, and carried her to her journey's end, as if it were the proper thing to do. Another interesting china lady took off her comfortable red cloak and put it round a poor wooden creature done up in a paper shift, and so badly painted that its face would have sent some babies into fits.

"Seems to me I once knew a rich girl who didn't give her things to poor girls. I wish I could remember who she was, and tell her to be as kind as that china doll," said Effie, much touched at the sweet way the pretty creature wrapped up the poor fright, and then ran off in her little gray gown to buy a shiny fowl stuck on a wooden platter for her invalid mother's dinner.

"We recall these things to people's minds by dreams. I think the girl you speak of won't forget this one." And the spirit smiled, as if he enjoyed some joke which she did not see.

A little bell rang as she looked, and away scampered the children into the red-and-green school-house with the roof that lifted up, so one could see how nicely they sat at their desks with mites of books, or drew on the inch-square blackboards with crumbs of chalk.

"They know their lessons very well, and are as still as mice. We make a great racket at our school, and get bad marks every day. I shall tell the girls they had better mind what they do, or their dolls will be better scholars than they are," said Effie, much impressed, as she peeped in and saw no rod in the hand of the little mistress, who looked up and shook her head at the intruder, as if begging her to go away before the order of the school was disturbed.

Effie retired at once, but could not resist one look in at the window of a fine mansion, where the family were at dinner, the children behaved so well at table, and never grumbled a bit when their mamma said they could not have any more fruit.

"Now, show me something else," she said, as they came again to the low door that led out of Doll-land.

"You have seen how we prepare for Christmas; let me show you where we love best to send our good and happy gifts," answered the spirit, giving her his hand again.

"I know. I've seen ever so many," began Effie, thinking of her own Christmases.

"No, you have never seen what I will show you. Come away, and remember what you see to-night."

Like a flash that bright world vanished, and Effie found herself in a part of the city she had never seen before. It was far away from the gayer places, where every store was brilliant with lights and full of pretty things, and every house wore a festival air, while people hurried to and fro with merry greetings. It was down among the dingy streets where the poor lived, and where there was no making ready for Christmas.

Hungry women looked in at the shabby shops, longing to buy meat and bread, but empty pockets forbade. Tipsy men drank up their wages in the bar-rooms; and in many cold dark chambers little children huddled under the thin blankets, trying to forget their misery in sleep.

No nice dinners filled the air with savory smells, no gay trees dropped toys and bonbons into eager hands, no little stockings hung in rows beside the chimney-piece ready to be filled, no happy sounds of music, gay voices, and dancing feet were heard; and there were no signs of Christmas anywhere.

"Don't they have any in this place?" asked Effie, shivering, as she held fast the spirit's hand, following where he led her.

"We come to bring it. Let me show you our best workers." And the spirit pointed to some sweet-faced men and women who came stealing into the poor houses, working such beautiful miracles that Effie could only stand and watch.

Some slipped money into the empty pockets, and sent the happy mothers to buy all the comforts they needed; others led the drunken men out of temptation, and took them home to find safer pleasures there. Fires were kindled on cold hearths, tables spread as if by magic, and warm clothes wrapped round shivering limbs. Flowers suddenly bloomed in the chambers of the sick; old people found themselves remembered; sad hearts were consoled by a tender word, and wicked ones softened by the story of Him who forgave all sin.

But the sweetest work was for the children; and Effie held her breath to watch these human fairies hang up and fill the little stockings without which a child's Christmas is not perfect, putting in things that once she would have thought very humble presents, but which now seemed beautiful and precious because these poor babies had nothing.

"That is so beautiful! I wish I could make merry Christmases as these good people do, and be loved and thanked as they are," said Effie, softly, as she watched the busy men and women do their work and steal away without thinking of any reward but their own satisfaction.

"You can if you will. I have shown you the way. Try it, and see how happy your own holiday will be hereafter."

As he spoke, the spirit seemed to put his arms about her, and vanished with a kiss.

"Oh, stay and show me more!" cried Effie, trying to hold him fast.

"Darling, wake up, and tell me why you are smiling in your sleep," said a voice in her ear; and opening her eyes, there was mamma bending over her, and morning sunshine streaming into the room.

"Are they all gone? Did you hear the bells? Wasn't it splendid?" she asked, rubbing her eyes, and looking about her for the pretty child who was so real and sweet.

"You have been dreaming at a great rate,—talking in your sleep, laughing, and clapping your hands as if you were cheering some one. Tell me what was so splendid," said mamma, smoothing the tumbled hair and lifting up the sleepy head.

Then, while she was being dressed, Effie told her dream, and Nursey thought it very wonderful; but mamma smiled to see how curiously things the child had thought, read, heard, and seen through the day were mixed up in her sleep.

"The spirit said I could work lovely miracles if I tried; but I don't know how to begin, for I have no magic candle to make feasts appear, and light up groves of Christmas trees, as he did," said Effie, sorrowfully.

"Yes, you have. We will do it! we will do it!" And clapping her hands, mamma suddenly began to dance all over the room as if she had lost her wits.

"How? how? You must tell me, mamma," cried Effie, dancing after her, and ready to believe anything possible when she remembered the adventures of the past night.

"I've got it! I've got it!—the new idea. A splendid one, if I can only carry it out!" And mamma waltzed the little girl round till her curls flew wildly in the air, while Nursey laughed as if she would die.

"Tell me! tell me!" shrieked Effie.

"No, no; it is a surprise,—a grand surprise for Christmas day!" sung mamma, evidently charmed with her happy thought. "Now, come to breakfast; for we must work like bees if we want to play spirits to-morrow. You and Nursey will go out shopping, and get heaps of things, while I arrange matters behind the scenes."

They were running downstairs as mamma spoke, and Effie called out breathlessly,—

"It won't be a surprise; for I know you are going to ask some poor children here, and have a tree or something. It won't be like my dream; for they had ever so many trees, and more children than we can find anywhere."

"There will be no tree, no party, no dinner, in this house at all, and no presents for you. Won't that be a surprise?" And mamma laughed at Effie's bewildered face.

"Do it. I shall like it, I think; and I won't ask any questions, so it will all burst upon me when the time comes," she said; and she ate her breakfast thoughtfully, for this really would be a new sort of Christmas.

All that morning Effie trotted after Nursey in and out of shops, buying dozens of barking dogs, woolly lambs, and squeaking birds; tiny tea-sets, gay picture-books, mittens and hoods, dolls and candy. Parcel after parcel was sent home; but when Effie returned she saw no trace of them, though she peeped everywhere. Nursey chuckled, but wouldn't give a hint, and went out again in the afternoon with a long list of more things to buy; while Effie wandered forlornly about the house, missing the usual merry stir that went before the Christmas dinner and the evening fun.

As for mamma, she was quite invisible all day, and came in at night so tired that she could only lie on the sofa to rest, smiling as if some very pleasant thought made her happy in spite of weariness.

"Is the surprise going on all right?" asked Effie, anxiously; for it seemed an immense time to wait till another evening came.

"Beautifully! better than I expected; for several of my good friends are helping, or I couldn't have done it as I wish. I know you will like it, dear, and long remember this new way of making Christmas merry."

Mamma gave her a very tender kiss, and Effie went to bed.

The next day was a very strange one; for when she woke there was no stocking to examine, no pile of gifts under her napkin, no one said "Merry Christmas!" to her, and the dinner was just as usual to her. Mamma vanished again, and Nursey kept wiping her eyes and saying: "The dear things! It's the prettiest idea I ever heard of. No one but your blessed ma could have done it."

"Do stop, Nursey, or I shall go crazy because I don't know the secret!" cried Effie, more than once; and she kept her eye on the clock, for at seven in the evening the surprise was to come off.

The longed-for hour arrived at last, and the child was too excited to ask questions when Nurse put on her cloak and hood, led her to the carriage, and they drove away, leaving their house the one dark and silent one in the row.

"I feel like the girls in the fairy tales who are led off to strange places and see fine things," said Effie, in a whisper, as they jingled through the gay streets.

"Ah, my deary, it *is* like a fairy tale, I do assure you, and you *will* see finer things than most children will to-night. Steady, now, and do just as I tell you, and don't say one word whatever you see," answered Nursey, quite quivering with excitement as she patted a large box in her lap, and nodded and laughed with twinkling eyes.

They drove into a dark yard, and Effie was led through a back door to a little room, where Nurse coolly proceeded to take off not only her cloak and hood, but her dress and shoes also. Effie stared and bit her lips, but kept still until out of the box came a little white fur coat and boots, a wreath of holly leaves and berries, and a candle with a frill of gold paper round it. A long "Oh!" escaped her then; and when she was dressed and saw herself in the glass, she started back, exclaiming, "Why, Nursey, I look like the spirit in my dream!"

"So you do; and that's the part you are to play, my pretty! Now whist, while I blind your eyes and put you in your place."

"Shall I be afraid?" whispered Effie, full of wonder; for as they went out she heard the sound of many voices, the tramp of many feet, and, in spite of the bandage, was sure a great light shone upon her when she stopped.

"You needn't be; I shall stand close by, and your ma will be there."

After the handkerchief was tied about her eyes, Nurse led Effie up some steps, and placed her on a high platform, where something like leaves touched her head, and the soft snap of lamps seemed to fill the air.

Music began as soon as Nurse clapped her hands, the voices outside sounded nearer, and the tramp was evidently coming up the stairs.

"Now, my precious, look and see how you and your dear ma have made a merry Christmas for them that needed it!"

Off went the bandage; and for a minute Effie really did think she was asleep again, for she actually stood in "a grove of Christmas trees," all gay and shining as in her vision. Twelve on a side, in two rows down the room, stood the little pines, each on its low table; and behind Effie a taller one rose to the roof, hung with wreaths of popcorn, apples, oranges, horns of candy, and cakes of all sorts, from sugary hearts to gingerbread Jumbos. On the smaller trees she saw many of her own discarded toys and those Nursey bought, as well as heaps that seemed to have rained down straight from that delightful Christmas country where she felt as if she was again.

"How splendid! Who is it for? What is that noise? Where is mamma?" cried Effie, pale with pleasure and surprise, as she stood looking down the brilliant little street from her high place.

Before Nurse could answer, the doors at the lower end flew open, and in marched twenty-four little blue-gowned orphan girls, singing sweetly, until amazement changed the song to cries of joy and wonder as the shining spectacle appeared. While they stood staring with round eyes at the wilderness of pretty things about them, mamma stepped up beside Effie, and holding her hand fast to give her courage, told the story of the dream in a few simple words, ending in this way:—

"So my little girl wanted to be a Christmas spirit too, and make this a happy day for those who had not as many pleasures and comforts as she has. She likes surprises, and we planned this for you all. She shall play the good fairy, and give each of you something from this tree, after which every one will find her own name on a small tree, and can go to enjoy it in her own way. March by, my dears, and let us fill your hands."

Nobody told them to do it, but all the hands were clapped heartily before a single child stirred; then one by one they came to look up wonderingly at the pretty giver of the feast as she leaned down to offer them great yellow oranges, red apples, bunches of grapes, bonbons, and cakes, till all were gone, and a double row of smiling faces turned toward her as the children filed back to their places in the orderly way they had been taught.

Then each was led to her own tree by the good ladies who had helped mamma with all their hearts; and the happy hubbub that arose would have satisfied even Santa Claus himself,—shrieks of joy, dances of delight, laughter and tears (for some tender little things could not bear so much pleasure at once, and sobbed with mouths full of candy and hands full of toys). How they ran to show one another the new treasures! how they peeped and tasted, pulled and pinched, until the air was full of queer noises, the floor covered with papers, and the little trees left bare of all but candles!

"I don't think heaven can be any gooder than this," sighed one small girl, as she looked about her in a blissful maze, holding her full apron with one hand, while she luxuriously carried sugar-plums to her mouth with the other.

"Is that a truly angel up there?" asked another, fascinated by the little white figure with the wreath on its shining hair, who in some mysterious way had been the cause of all this merry-making.

"I wish I dared to go and kiss her for this splendid party," said a lame child, leaning on her crutch, as she stood near the steps, wondering how it seemed to sit in a mother's lap, as Effie was doing, while she watched the happy scene before her.

Effie heard her, and remembering Tiny Tim, ran down and put her arms about the pale child, kissing the wistful face, as she said sweetly, "You may; but mamma deserves the thanks. She did it all; I only dreamed about it."

Lame Katy felt as if "a truly angel" was embracing her, and could only stammer out her thanks, while the other children ran to see the pretty spirit, and touch her soft dress, until she stood in a crowd of blue gowns laughing as they held up their gifts for her to see and admire.

Mamma leaned down and whispered one word to the older girls; and suddenly they all took hands to dance round Effie, singing as they skipped.

It was a pretty sight, and the ladies found it hard to break up the happy revel; but it was late for small people, and too much fun is a mistake. So the girls fell into line, and marched before Effie and mamma again, to say good-night with such grateful little faces that the eyes of those who looked grew dim with tears. Mamma kissed every one; and many a hungry childish heart felt as if the touch of those tender lips was their best gift. Effie shook so many small hands that her own tingled; and when Katy came she pressed a small doll into Effie's hand, whispering, "You didn't have a single present, and we had lots. Do keep that; it's the prettiest thing I got."

"I will," answered Effie, and held it fast until the last smiling face was gone, the surprise all over, and she safe in her own bed, too tired and happy for anything but sleep.

"Mamma, it *was* a beautiful surprise, and I thank you so much! I don't see how you did it; but I like it best of all the Christmases I ever had, and mean to make one every year. I had my splendid big present, and here is the dear little one to keep for love of poor Katy; so even that part of my wish came true."

And Effie fell asleep with a happy smile on her lips, her one humble gift still in her hand, and a new love for Christmas in her heart that never changed through a long life spent in doing good.

# The Candy Country

"I SHALL TAKE MAMMA'S red sun-umbrella, it is so warm, and none of the children at school will have one like it," said Lily, one day, as she went through the hall.

"The wind is very high; I'm afraid you'll be blown away if you carry that big thing," called Nurse from the window, as the red umbrella went bobbing down the garden walk with a small girl under it.

"I wish it would; I always wanted to go up in a balloon," answered Lily, as she struggled out of the gate.

She got on very well till she came to the bridge and stopped to look over the railing at the water running by so fast, and the turtles sunning themselves on the rocks. Lily was fond of throwing stones at them; it was so funny to watch them tumble, heels over head, splash into the water. Now, when she saw three big fellows close by, she stooped for a stone, and just at that minute a gale of wind nearly took the umbrella out of her hand. She clutched it fast; and away she went like a thistle-down, right up in the air, over river and hill, houses and trees, faster and faster, till her head spun round, her breath was all gone, and she had to let go. The dear red umbrella flew away like a leaf; and Lily fell down, down, till she went crash into a tree which grew in such a curious place that she forgot her fright as she sat looking about her, wondering what part of the world it could be.

The tree looked as if made of glass or colored sugar; for she could see through the red cherries, the green leaves, and the brown branches. An agreeable smell met her nose; and she said at once, as any child would, "I smell candy!" She picked a cherry and ate it. Oh, how good it was!—all sugar and no stone. The next discovery was such a delightful one that she nearly fell off her perch; for by touching her tongue here and there, she found that the whole tree was made of candy. Think what fun to sit and break off twigs of barley sugar, candied cherries, and leaves that tasted like peppermint and sassafras!

Lily rocked and ate till she finished the top of the little tree; then she climbed down and strolled along, making more surprising and agreeable discoveries as she went.

What looked like snow under her feet was white sugar; the rocks were lumps of chocolate, the flowers of all colors and tastes; and every sort of fruit grew on these delightful trees. Little white houses soon appeared; and here lived the dainty candy-people, all made of the best sugar, and painted to look like real people. Dear little men and women, looking as if they had stepped off of wedding cakes and bonbons, went about in their gay sugar clothes, laughing and talking in the sweetest voices. Bits of babies rocked in open-work cradles, and sugar boys and girls played with sugar toys in the most natural way. Carriages rolled along the jujube streets, drawn by the red and yellow barley horses we all love so well; cows fed in the green fields, and sugar birds sang in the trees.

Lily listened, and in a moment she understood what the song said,—

> "Sweet! Sweet!
> Come, come and eat,
> Dear little girls
> With yellow curls;
> For here you'll find
> Sweets to your mind.
> On every tree
> Sugar-plums you'll see;
> In every dell
> Grows the caramel.
> Over every wall
> Gum-drops fall;
> Molasses flows
> Where our river goes.
> Under your feet
> Lies sugar sweet;
> Over your head
> Grow almonds red.
> Our lily and rose
> Are not for the nose;
> Our flowers we pluck
> To eat or suck.
> And, oh! what bliss
> When two friends kiss,
> For they honey sip
> From lip to lip!
> And all you meet,
> In house or street,
> At work or play,
> Sweethearts are they.
> So, little dear,

Pray feel no fear;
Go where you will;
Eat, eat your fill.
Here is a feast
From west to east;
And you can say,
Ere you go away,
'At last I stand
In dear Candy-land,
And no more can stuff;
For once I've enough.'
Sweet! Sweet!
Tweet! Tweet!
Tweedle-dee!
Tweedle-dee!"

"That is the most interesting song I ever heard," said Lily, clapping her sticky hands and dancing along toward a fine palace of white cream candy, with pillars of striped peppermint stick, and a roof of frosting that made it look like the Milan Cathedral.

"I'll live here, and eat candy all day long, with no tiresome school or patchwork to spoil my fun," said Lily.

So she ran up the chocolate steps into the pretty rooms, where all the chairs and tables were of different colored candies, and the beds of spun sugar. A fountain of lemonade supplied drink; and floors of ice-cream that never melted kept people and things from sticking together, as they would have done had it been warm.

For a long while Lily was quite happy, going about tasting so many different kinds of sweeties, talking to the little people, who were very amiable, and finding out curious things about them and their country.

The babies were made of plain sugar, but the grown people had different flavors. The young ladies were flavored with violet, rose, and orange; the gentlemen were apt to have cordials of some sort inside of them, as she found when she ate one now and then slyly, and got her tongue bitten by the hot, strong taste as a punishment. The old people tasted of peppermint, clove, and such comfortable things, good for pain; but the old maids had lemon, hoarhound, flag-root, and all sorts of sour, bitter things in them, and did not get eaten much. Lily soon learned to know the characters of her new friends by a single taste, and some she never touched but once. The dear babies melted in her mouth, and the delicately flavored young ladies she was very fond of. Dr. Ginger was called to her more than once when so

"The Candy Country." From *St. Nicholas* 13 (Nov. 1885): 1.
Courtesy of Rare Book Collection, University of North Carolina at Charlotte.

much candy made her teeth ache, and she found him a very hot-tempered little man; but he stopped the pain, so she was glad to see him.

A lime-drop boy and a little pink checker-berry girl were her favorite playmates; and they had fine times making mud-pies by scraping the chocolate rocks and mixing this dust with honey from the wells near by. These they could eat; and Lily thought this much better than throwing away the pies, as she had to do at home. They had candy-pulls very often, and made swings of long loops of molasses candy, and bird's-nests with almond eggs, out of which came birds who sang sweetly. They played football with big bull's-eyes, sailed in sugar boats on lakes of syrup, fished in rivers of molasses, and rode the barley horses all over the country.

Lily discovered that it never rained, but snowed white sugar. There was no sun, as it would have been too hot; but a large yellow lozenge made a nice moon, and red and white comfits were the stars.

The people all lived on sugar, and never quarrelled. No one was ill; and if any got broken, as sometimes happened with such brittle creatures, they just stuck the parts together and were all right again. The way they grew old was to get thinner and thinner till there was danger of their vanishing. Then the friends of the old person put him in a neat coffin, and carried him to the great golden urn which stood in their largest temple, always full of a certain fine syrup; and here he was dipped and dipped till he was stout and strong again, and went home to enjoy himself for a long time as good as new.

This was very interesting to Lily, and she went to many funerals. But the weddings were better still; for the lovely white brides were so sweet Lily longed to eat them. The feasts were delicious; and everybody went in their best clothes, and danced at the ball till they got so warm half-a-dozen would stick together and have to be taken to the ice-cream room to cool off. Then the little pair would drive away in a fine carriage with white horses to a new palace in some other part of the country, and Lily would have another pleasant place to visit.

But by and by, when she had seen everything, and eaten so much sweet stuff that at last she longed for plain bread and butter, she began to get cross, as children always do when they live on candy; and the little people wished she would go away, for they were afraid of her. No wonder, when she would catch up a dear sugar baby and eat him, or break some respectable old grandmamma all into bits because she reproved her for naughty ways. Lily calmly sat down on the biggest church, crushing it flat, and even tried to poke the moon out of the sky in a pet one day. The king ordered her to go home; but she said, "I won't!" and bit his head off, crown and all.

Such a wail went up at this awful deed that she ran away out of the city, fearing some one would put poison in her candy, since she had no other food.

"I suppose I shall get somewhere if I keep walking; and I can't starve, though I hate the sight of this horrid stuff," she said to herself, as she hurried over the mountains of Gibraltar Rock that divided the city of Saccharissa from the great desert of brown sugar that lay beyond.

Lily marched bravely on for a long time, and saw at last a great smoke in the sky, smelt a spicy smell, and felt a hot wind blowing toward her.

"I wonder if there are sugar savages here, roasting and eating some poor traveller like me," she said, thinking of Robinson Crusoe and other wanderers in strange lands.

She crept carefully along till she saw a settlement of little huts very like mushrooms, for they were made of cookies set on lumps of the brown sugar; and queer people, looking as if made of gingerbread, were working very busily round several stoves which seemed to bake at a great rate.

"I'll creep nearer and see what sort of people they are before I show myself," said Lily, going into a grove of spice-trees, and sitting down on a stone which proved to be the plummy sort of cake we used to call Brighton Rock.

Presently one of the tallest men came striding toward the trees with a pan, evidently after spice; and before she could run, he saw Lily.

"Hollo, what do you want?" he asked, starring at her with his black currant eyes, while he briskly picked the bark off a cinnamon-tree.

"I'm travelling, and would like to know what place this is, if you please," answered Lily, very politely, being a little frightened.

"Cake-land. Where do you come from?" asked the gingerbread man, in a crisp tone of voice.

"I was blown into the Candy country, and have been there a long time; but I got tired of it, and ran away to find something better."

"Sensible child!" and the man smiled till Lily thought his cheeks would crumble. "You'll get on better here with us Brownies than with the lazy Bonbons, who never work and are all for show. They won't own us, though we are all related through our grandparents Sugar and Molasses. We are busy folks; so they turn up their noses and don't speak when we meet at parties. Poor creatures, silly and sweet and unsubstantial! I pity 'em."

"Could I make you a visit? I'd like to see how you live, and what you do. I'm sure it must be interesting," said Lily, picking herself up after a tumble, having eaten nearly all the stone, she was so hungry.

"I know you will. Come on! I can talk while I work." And the funny gingerbread man trotted off toward his kitchen, full of pans, rolling-pins, and molasses jugs.

"Sit down. I shall be at leisure as soon as this batch is baked. There are still some wise people down below who like gingerbread, and I have my hands full," he said, dashing about, stirring, rolling out, and slapping the brown dough into pans, which he whisked into the oven and out again so fast that Lily knew there must be magic about it somewhere.

Every now and then he threw her a delicious cooky warm from the oven. She liked the queer fellow, and presently began to talk, being very curious about this country.

"What is your name, sir?"

"Ginger Snap."

Lily thought it a good one; for he was very quick, and she fancied he could be short and sharp if he liked.

"Where does all this cake go to?" she asked, after watching the other kitchens full of workers, who were all of different kinds of cake, and each set of cooks made its own sort.

"I'll show you by and by," answered Snap, beginning to pile up the heaps of gingerbread on a little car that ran along a track leading to some unknown storeroom, Lily thought.

"Don't you get tired of doing this all the time?"

"Yes; but I want to be promoted, and I never shall be till I've done my best, and won the prize here."

"Oh, tell me about it! What is the prize, and how are you promoted? Is this a cooking-school?"

"Yes; the prize for best gingerbread is a cake of condensed yeast. That puts a soul into me, and I begin to rise till I am able to go over the hills yonder into the blessed land of bread, and be one of the happy creatures who are always wholesome, always needed, and without which the world below would be in a bad way."

"Bless me! that is the queerest thing I've heard yet. But I don't wonder you want to go; I'm tired of sweets myself, and long for a good piece of bread, though I used to want cake and candy at home."

"Ah, my dear, you'll learn a good deal here; and you are lucky not to have got into the clutches of Giant Dyspepsia, who always gets people if they eat too much of such rubbish and scorn wholesome bread. I leave my ginger behind when I go, and get white and round and beautiful, as you will see. The Gingerbread family have never been as foolish as some of the other cakes. Wedding is the worst; such extravagance in the way of wine and spice and fruit I never saw, and such a mess to eat when it's done! I don't wonder people get sick; serves 'em right." And Snap flung down a pan with such a bang that it made Lily jump.

"Sponge cake isn't bad, is it? Mamma lets me eat it, but I like frosted pound better," she said, looking over to the next kitchen, where piles of that sort of cake were being iced.

"Poor stuff. No substance. Ladies' fingers will do for babies, but pound has too much butter ever to be healthy. Let it alone, and eat cookies or seed-cakes, my dear. Now, come along; I'm ready." And Snap trundled away his car-load at a great pace.

Lily ran behind to pick up whatever fell, and looked about her as she went, for this was certainly a very queer country. Lakes of eggs all beaten up, and hot springs of saleratus foamed here and there ready for use. The earth was brown sugar or ground spice; and the only fruits were raisins, dried currants, citron, and lemon peel. It was a very busy place; for every one cooked all the time, and never failed and never seemed tired, though they got so hot that they only wore sheets of paper for clothes. There were piles of it to put over the cake, so that it shouldn't burn; and they made cook's white caps and aprons of it, and looked very nice. A large clock made of a flat pancake, with cloves to mark the hours and two toothpicks for hands, showed them how long to bake things; and in one place an ice wall was built round a lake of butter, which they cut in lumps as they wanted it.

"Here we are. Now, stand away while I pitch 'em down," said Snap, stopping at last before a hole in the ground where a dumb-waiter hung ready, with a name over it.

There were many holes all round, and many waiters, each with its name; and Lily was amazed when she read "Weber," "Copeland," "Dooling," and others, which she knew very well.

Over Snap's place was the name "Newmarch;" and Lily said, "Why, that's where mamma gets her hard gingerbread, and Weber's is where we go for ice-cream. Do *you* make cake for them?"

"Yes, but no one knows it. It's one of the secrets of the trade. We cook for all the confectioners, and people think the good things come out of the cellars under their saloons. Good joke, isn't it?" And Snap laughed till a crack came in his neck and made him cough.

Lily was so surprised she sat down on a warm queen's cake that happened to be near, and watched Snap send down load after load of gingerbread to be eaten by children, who would have liked it much better if they had only known where it came from, as she did.

As she sat, the clatter of many spoons, the smell of many dinners, and the sound of many voices calling, "One vanilla, two strawberries, and a Charlotte Russe," "Three stews, cup coffee, dry toast," "Roast chicken and apple without," came up the next hole, which was marked "Copeland."

"Dear me! it seems as if I was there," said Lily, longing to hop down, but afraid of the bump at the other end.

"I'm done. Come along, I'll ride you back," called Snap, tossing the last cooky after the dumb-waiter as it went slowly out of sight with its spicy load.

"I wish you'd teach me to cook. It looks great fun, and mamma wants me to learn; only our cook hates to have me mess round, and is so cross that I don't like to try at home," said Lily, as she went trundling back.

"Better wait till you get to Bread-land, and learn to make that. It's a great art, and worth knowing. Don't waste your time on cake, though plain gingerbread isn't bad to have in the house. I'll teach you that in a jiffy, if the clock doesn't strike my hour too soon," answered Snap, helping her down.

"What hour?"

"Why, of my freedom. I never know when I've done my task till I'm called by the chimes and go to get my soul," said Snap, turning his currant eyes anxiously to the clock.

"I hope you *will* have time." And Lily fell to work with all her might, after Snap had put on her a paper apron and a cap like his.

It was not hard; for when she was going to make a mistake a spark flew out of the fire and burnt her in time to remind her to look at the receipt, which was a sheet of gingerbread in a frame of pie-crust hung up before her, with the directions written while it was soft and baked in. The third sheet she made came out of the oven spicy, light, and brown; and, Snap, giving it one poke, said, "That's all right. Now you know. Here's your reward."

He handed her a receipt-book made of thin sheets of sugar-gingerbread held together by a gelatine binding, with her name stamped on the back, and each leaf crimped with a cake-cutter in the most elegant manner.

Lily was charmed with it, but had no time to read all it contained; for just then the clock began to strike, and a chime of bells to ring,—

> "Gingerbread,
> Go to the head.
> Your task is done;
> A soul is won.

Take it and go
Where muffins grow,
Where sweet loaves rise
To the very skies,
And biscuits fair
Perfume the air.
Away, away!
Make no delay;
In the sea of flour
Plunge this hour.
Safe in your breast
Let the yeast-cake rest,
Till you rise in joy,
A white bread boy!"

"Ha, ha! I'm free! I'm free!" cried Snap, catching up the silver-covered square that seemed to fall from heaven; and running to a great white sea of flour, he went in head first, holding the yeast-cake clasped to his breast as if his life depended on it.

Lily watched breathlessly, while a curious working and bubbling went on, as if Snap was tumbling about down there like a small earthquake. The other cake-folk stood round the shore with her; for it was a great event, and all were glad that the dear fellow was promoted so soon. Suddenly a cry was heard, and up rose a beautiful white figure on the farther side of the sea. It moved its hand, as if saying "Good-by," and ran over the hills so fast they had only time to see how plump and fair he was, with a little knob on the top of his head like a crown.

"He's gone to the happy land, and we shall miss him; but we'll follow his example and soon find him again," said a gentle Sponge cake, with a sigh, as all went back to their work; while Lily hurried after Snap, eager to see the new country, which was the best of all.

A delicious odor of fresh bread blew up from the valley as she stood on the hill-top and looked down on the peaceful scene below. Fields of yellow grain waved in the breeze; hop-vines grew from tree to tree; and many windmills whirled their white sails as they ground the different grains into fresh, sweet meal, for the loaves of bread that built the houses like bricks and paved the streets, or in many shapes formed the people, furniture, and animals. A river of milk flowed through the peaceful land, and fountains of yeast rose and fell with a pleasant foam and fizz. The ground was a mixture of many meals, and the paths were golden Indian, which gave a very gay look to the scene. Buckwheat flowers bloomed on their rosy stems, and tall corn-stalks rustled their leaves in the warm air that came from the ovens hidden in the hillsides; for bread needs a slow fire, and an obliging volcano did the baking here.

"What a lovely place!" cried Lily, feeling the charm of the homelike landscape, in spite of the funny plump people moving about.

Two of these figures came running to meet her as she slowly walked down the yellow path from the hill. One was a golden boy, with a beaming face; the other a little girl in a shiny brown cloak, who looked as if she would taste very nice. They each put a warm hand into Lily's, and the boy said,—

"We are glad to see you. Muffin told us you were coming."

"Thank you. Who is Muffin?" asked Lily, feeling as if she had seen both these little people before, and liked them.

"He was Ginger Snap once, but he's a Muffin now. We begin in that way, and work up to the perfect loaf by degrees. My name is Johnny Cake, and she's Sally Lunn. You know us; so come on and have a race."

Lily burst out laughing at the idea of playing with these old friends of hers; and all three ran away as fast as they could tear, down the hill, over a bridge, into the middle of the village, where they stopped, panting, and sat down on some very soft rolls to rest.

"What do you all do *here?*" asked Lily, when she got her breath again.

"We farm, we study, we bake, we brew, and are as merry as grigs all day long. It's school-time now, and we must go; will you come?" said Sally, jumping up as if she liked it.

"Our schools are not like yours; we only study two things,—grain and yeast. I think you'll like it. We have yeast to-day, and the experiments are very jolly," added Johnny, trotting off to a tall brown tower of rye and Indian bread, where the school was kept.

Lily never liked to go to school, but she was ashamed to own it; so she went along with Sally, and was so amused with all she saw that she was glad she came. The brown loaf was hollow, and had no roof; and when she asked why they used a ruin, Sally told her to wait and see why they chose strong walls and plenty of room overhead. All round was a circle of very small biscuits like cushions, and on these the Bread-children sat. A square loaf in the middle was the teacher's desk, and on it lay an ear of wheat, with several bottles of yeast well corked up. The teacher was a pleasant, plump lady from Vienna, very wise, and so famous for her good bread that she was a Professor of Grainology.

When all were seated, she began with the wheat ear, and told them all about it in such an interesting way that Lily felt as if she had never known anything about the bread she ate before. The experiments with the yeast were quite exciting,—for Fraulein Pretzel showed them how it would work till it blew the cork out, and go fizzing up to the sky if it was kept too long; how it would turn sour or flat, and spoil the bread if care was not taken to use it just at the right moment; and how too much would cause the loaf to rise till there was no substance to it.

The children were very bright; for they were fed on the best kinds of oatmeal and Graham bread, with very little white bread or hot cakes to spoil their young stomachs. Hearty, happy boys and girls they were, and their yeasty souls were very lively in them; for they danced and sung, and seemed as bright and gay as if acidity, heaviness, and mould were quite unknown.

Lily was very happy with them, and when school was done went home with Sally and ate the best bread and milk for dinner that she ever tasted. In the afternoon Johnny took her to the cornfield, and showed her how they kept the growing ears free from mildew and worms. Then she went to the bakehouse; and here she found her old friend Muffin hard at work making Parker House rolls, for he was such a good cook he was set to work at once on the lighter kinds of bread.

"Well, isn't this better than Candy-land or Saccharissa?" he asked, as he rolled and folded his bits of dough with a dab of butter tucked inside.

"Ever so much!" cried Lily. "I feel better already, and mean to learn all I can. Mamma will be so pleased if I can make good bread when I go home. She is rather old-fashioned, and likes me to be a nice housekeeper. I didn't think bread interesting then, but I do now; and Johnny's mother is going to teach me to make Indian cakes to-morrow."

"Glad to hear it. Learn all you can, and tell other people how to make healthy bodies and happy souls by eating good plain food. Not like this, though these rolls are better than cake. I have to work my way up to the perfect loaf, you know; and then, oh, then, I'm a happy thing."

"What happens then? Do you go on to some other wonderful place?" asked Lily, as Muffin paused with a smile on his face.

"Yes; I am eaten by some wise, good human being, and become a part of him or her. That is immortality and heaven; for I may nourish a poet and help him sing, or feed a good woman who makes the world better for being in it, or be crumbed into the golden porringer of a baby prince who is to rule a kingdom. Isn't that a noble way to live, and an end worth working for?" asked Muffin, in a tone that made Lily feel as if some sort of fine yeast had got into her, and was setting her brain to work with new thoughts.

"Yes, it is. I suppose all common things are made for that purpose, if we only knew it; and people should be glad to do anything to help the world along, even making good bread in a kitchen," answered Lily, in a sober way that showed that her little mind was already digesting the new food it had got.

She stayed in Bread-land a long time, and enjoyed and learned a great deal that she never forgot. But at last, when she had made the perfect loaf, she wanted to go home, that her mother might see and taste it.

"I've put a good deal of myself into it, and I'd love to think I had given her strength or pleasure by my work," she said, as she and Sally stood looking at the handsome loaf.

"You can go whenever you like; just take the bread in your hands and wish three times, and you'll be wherever you say. I'm sorry to have you go, but I don't wonder you want to see your mother. Don't forget what you have learned, and you will always be glad you came to us," said Sally, kissing her good-by.

"Where is Muffin? I can't go without seeing him, my dear old friend," answered Lily, looking round for him.

"He is here," said Sally, touching the loaf. "He was ready to go, and chose to pass into your bread rather than any other; for he said he loved you and would be glad to help feed so good a little girl."

"How kind of him! I must be careful to grow wise and excellent, else he will be disappointed and have died in vain," said Lily, touched by his devotion.

Then, bidding them all farewell, she hugged her loaf close, wished three times to be in her own home, and like a flash she was there.

Whether her friends believed the wonderful tale of her adventures I cannot tell; but I know that she was a nice little housekeeper from that day, and made such good bread that other girls came to learn of her. She also grew from a sickly, fretful child into a fine, strong woman, because she ate very little cake and candy, except at Christmas time, when the oldest and the wisest love to make a short visit to Candy-land.

# The Skipping Shoes

ONCE THERE WAS a little girl, named Kitty, who never wanted to do what people asked her. She said "I won't" and "I can't," and did not run at once pleasantly, as obliging children do.

One day her mother gave her a pair of new shoes; and after a fuss about putting them on, Kitty said, as she lay kicking on the floor,—

"I wish these were seven-leagued boots, like Jack the Giant Killer's; then it would be easy to run errands all the time. Now, I hate to keep trotting, and I don't like new shoes, and I won't stir a step."

Just as she said that, the shoes gave a skip, and set her on her feet so suddenly that it scared all the naughtiness out of her. She stood looking at these curious shoes; and the bright buttons on them seemed to wink at her like eyes, while the heels tapped on the floor a sort of tune. Before she dared to stir, her mother called from the next room,—

"Kitty, run and tell the cook to make a pie for dinner; I forgot it."

"I don't want to," began Kitty, with a whine as usual.

But the words were hardly out of her mouth when the shoes gave one jump, and took her downstairs, through the hall, and landed her at the kitchen door. Her breath was nearly gone; but she gave the message, and turned round, trying to see if the shoes would let her walk at all. They went nicely till she wanted to turn into the china-closet where the cake was. She was forbidden to touch it, but loved to take a bit when she could. Now she found that her feet were fixed fast to the floor, and could not be moved till her father said, as he passed the window close by,—

"You will have time to go to the post-office before school and get my letters."

"I can't," began Kitty; but she found she could, for away went the shoes, out of the house at one bound, and trotted down the street so fast that the maid who ran after her with her hat could not catch her.

"I can't stop!" cried Kitty; and she did not till the shoes took her straight into the office.

"What's the hurry to-day?" asked the man, as he saw her without any hat, all rosy and breathless, and her face puckered up as if she did not know whether to laugh or to cry.

"I won't tell any one about these dreadful shoes, and I'll take them off as soon as I get home. I hope they will go back slowly, or people will think I'm crazy," said Kitty to herself, as she took the letters and went away.

The shoes walked nicely along till she came to the bridge; and there she wanted to stop and watch some boys in a boat, forgetting school and her father's letters. But the shoes wouldn't stop, though she tried to make them, and held on to the railing as hard as she could. Her feet went on; and when she sat down they still dragged her along so steadily that she had to go, and she got up feeling that there was something very strange about these shoes. The minute she gave up, all went smoothly, and she got home in good time.

"I won't wear these horrid things another minute," said Kitty, sitting on the doorstep and trying to unbutton the shoes.

But not a button could she stir, though she got red and angry struggling to do it.

"Time for school; run away, little girl," called mamma from upstairs, as the clock struck nine.

"I won't!" said Kitty, crossly.

But she did; for those magic shoes danced her off, and landed her at her desk in five minutes.

"Well, I'm not late; that's one comfort," she thought, wishing she had come pleasantly, and not been whisked away without any luncheon.

Her legs were so tired with the long skips that she was glad to sit still; and that pleased the teacher, for generally she was fussing about all lesson time. But at recess she got into trouble again; for one of the children knocked down the house of corn-cobs she had built, and made her angry.

"Now, I'll kick yours down, and see how you like it, Dolly."

Up went her foot, but it didn't come down; it stayed in the air, and there she stood looking as if she were going to dance. The children laughed to see her, and she could do nothing till she said to Dolly in a great hurry,—

"Never mind; if you didn't mean to, I'll forgive you."

Then the foot went down, and Kitty felt so glad about it that she tried to be pleasant, fearing some new caper of those dreadful shoes. She began to see how they worked, and thought she would try if she had any power over them. So, when one of the children wanted his ball, which had bounced over the hedge, she said kindly,—

"Perhaps I can get it for you, Willy."

And over she jumped as lightly as if she too were an india-rubber ball.

"How could you do it?" cried the boys, much surprised; for not one of them dared try such a high leap.

Kitty laughed, and began to dance, feeling pleased and proud to find there was a good side to the shoes after all. Such twirlings and skippings as she made, such pretty steps and airy little bounds it was pretty to see; for it seemed as if her feet were bewitched, and went of themselves. The little girls were charmed, and tried to imitate her; but no one could, and they stood in a circle watching her dance till the bell rang, then all rushed in to tell about it.

Kitty said it was her new shoes, and never told how queerly they acted, hoping to have good times now. But she was mistaken.

On the way home she wanted to stop and see her friend Bell's new doll; but at the gate her feet stuck fast, and she had to give up her wishes and go straight on, as mamma had told her always to do.

"Run and pick a nice little dish of strawberries for dinner," said her sister, as she went in.

"I'm too ti—" There was no time to finish, for the shoes landed her in the middle of the strawberry bed at one jump.

"I might as well be a grasshopper if I'm to skip round like this," she said, forgetting to feel tired out there in the pleasant garden, with the robins picking berries close by, and a cool wind lifting the leaves to show where the reddest and ripest ones hid.

The little dish was soon filled, and she wanted to stay and eat a few, warm and sweet from the vines; but the bell rang, and away she went, over the wood-pile, across the piazza, and into the dining-room before the berry in her mouth was half eaten.

"How this child does rush about to-day!" said her mother. "It is so delightful to have such a quick little errand-girl that I shall get her to carry some bundles to my poor people this afternoon.

"Oh, dear me! I do hate to lug those old clothes and bottles and baskets of cold victuals round. Must I do it?" sighed Kitty, dismally, while the shoes tapped on the floor under the table, as if to remind her that she must, whether she liked it or not.

"It would be right and kind, and would please me very much. But you may do as you choose about it. I am very tired, and some one must go; for the little Bryan baby is sick and needs what I send," said mamma, looking disappointed.

Kitty sat very still and sober for some time, and no one spoke to her. She was making up her mind whether she would go pleasantly or be whisked about like a grasshopper against her will. When dinner was over, she said in a cheerful voice,—

"I'll go, mamma; and when all the errands are done, may I come back through Fairyland, as we call the little grove where the tall ferns grow?"

"Yes, dear; when you oblige me, I am happy to please you."

"I'm glad I decided to be good; now I shall have a lovely time," said Kitty to herself, as she trotted away with a basket in one hand, a bundle in the other, and some money in her pocket for a poor old woman who needed help.

The shoes went quietly along, and seemed to know just where to stop. The sick baby's mother thanked her for the soft little nightgowns; the lame girl smiled when she saw the books; the hungry children gathered round the basket of food, like young birds eager to be fed; and the old woman gave her a beautiful pink shell that her sailor son brought home from sea.

When all the errands were done Kitty skipped away to Fairyland, feeling very happy, as people always do when they have done kind things. It was a lovely place; for the ferns made green arches tall enough for little girls to sit under, and the ground was covered with pretty green moss and wood-flowers. Birds flew about in the pines, squirrels chattered in the oaks, butterflies floated here and there, and from the pond near by came the croak of frogs sunning their green backs on the mossy stones.

"I wonder if the shoes will let me stop and rest; it is so cool here, and I'm so tired," said Kitty, as she came to a cosey nook at the foot of a tree.

The words were hardly out of her mouth when her feet folded under her, and there she sat on a cushion of moss, like the queen of the wood on her throne. Something lighted with a bump close by her; and looking down she saw a large black cricket with a stiff tail, staring at her curiously.

"Bless my heart! I thought you were some relation of my cousin Grasshopper's. You came down the hill with long leaps just like him; so I stopped to say, How d'ye do," said the cricket, in its creaky voice.

"I'm not a grasshopper; but I have on fairy shoes to-day, and so do many things that I never did before," answered Kitty, much surprised to be able to understand what the cricket said.

"It is midsummer day, and fairies can play whatever pranks they like. If you didn't have those shoes on, you couldn't understand what I say. Hark, and hear those squirrels talk, and the birds, and the ants down here. Make the most of this chance; for at sunset your shoes will stop skipping, and the fun all be over."

While the cricket talked Kitty did hear all sorts of little voices, singing, laughing, chatting in the gayest way, and understood every word they said. The squirrels called to one another as they raced about,—

> "Here's a nut, there's a nut;
> Hide it quick away,

In a hole, under leaves,
  To eat some winter day.
Acorns sweet are plenty,
  We will have them all:
Skip and scamper lively
  Till the last ones fall."

The birds were singing softly,—

"Rock a bye, babies,
  Your cradle hangs high;
Soft down your pillow,
  Your curtain the sky.
Father will feed you,
  While mother will sing,
And shelter our darlings
  With her warm wing."

And the ants were saying to one another as they hurried in and out of
their little houses,—

"Work, neighbor, work!
  Do not stop to play;
Wander far and wide,
  Gather all you may.
We are never like
  Idle butterflies,
But like the busy bees,
  Industrious and wise."

"Ants always were dreadfully good, but butterflies are ever so much
prettier," said Kitty, listening to the little voices with wonder and pleasure.

"Hollo! hollo!
Come down below,—
It's lovely and cool
Out here in the pool;
On a lily-pad float
For a nice green boat.
Here we sit and sing
In a pleasant ring;
Or leap-frog play,

In the jolliest way.
Our games have begun,
Come join in the fun."

"Dear me! what could I do over there in the mud with the queer green frogs?" laughed Kitty, as this song was croaked at her.

"No, no, come and fly
Through the sunny sky,
Or honey sip
From the rose's lip,
Or dance in the air,
Like spirits fair.
Come away, come away;
'T is our holiday."

A cloud of lovely yellow butterflies flew up from a wild-rose bush, and went dancing away higher and higher, till they vanished in the light beyond the wood.

"That is better than leap-frog. I wish my skipping shoes would let me fly up somewhere, instead of carrying me on errands and where I ought to go all the time," said Kitty, watching the pretty things glitter as they flew.

Just at that minute a clock struck, and away went the shoes over the pool, the hill, the road, till they pranced in at the gate as the tea-bell rang. Kitty amused the family by telling what she had done and seen; but no one believed the Fairyland part, and her father said, laughing,—

"Go on, my dear, making up little stories, and by and by you may be as famous as Hans Christian Andersen, whose books you like so well."

"The sun will soon set, and they my fun will be over; so I must skip while I can," thought Kitty, and went waltzing round the lawn so prettily that all the family came to see her.

"She dances so well that she shall go to dancing-school," said her mother, pleased with the pretty antics of her little girl.

Kitty was delighted to hear that; for she had longed to go, and went on skipping as hard as she could, that she might learn some of the graceful steps the shoes took before the day was done.

"Come, dear, stop now, and run up to your bath and bed. It has been a long hot day, and you are tired; so get to sleep early, for Nursey wants to go out," said her mother, as the sun went down behind the hills with a last bright glimmer, like the wink of a great sleepy eye.

"Oh, please, a few minutes more," began Kitty, but was off like a flash; for the shoes trotted her upstairs so fast that she ran against old Nursey, and down she went, splashing the water all over the floor, and scolding in such a funny way that it made Kitty laugh so that she could hardly pick her up again.

By the time she was ready to undress the sun was quite gone, and the shoes she took off were common ones again, for midsummer day was over. But Kitty never forgot the little lessons she had learned: she tried to run willingly when spoken to; she remembered the pretty steps and danced like a fairy; and best of all, she always loved the innocent and interesting little creatures in the woods and fields, and whenever she was told she might go to play with them, she hurried away almost as quickly as if she still wore the skipping shoes.

# Cockyloo

IN THE BARNYARD a gray hen sat on her nest, feeling very happy because it was time for her eggs to hatch, and she hoped to have a fine brood of chickens. Presently crack, crack, went the shells; "Peep, peep!" cried the chicks; "Cluck, cluck!" called the hen; and out came ten downy little things one after the other, all ready to run and eat and scratch,—for chickens are not like babies, and don't have to be tended at all.

There were eight little hens and two little cockerels, one black and one as white as snow, with yellow legs, bright eyes, and a tiny red comb on his head. This was Cockyloo, the good chick; but the black one was named Peck, and was a quarrelsome bad fowl, as we shall see.

Mrs. Partlet, the mamma, was very proud of her fine family; for the eight little daughters were all white and very pretty. She led them out into the farmyard, clucking and scratching busily; for all were hungry, and ran chirping round her to pick up the worms and seeds she found for them. Cocky soon began to help take care of his sisters; and when a nice corn or a fat bug was found, he would step back and let little Downy or Snowball have it. But Peck would run and push them away, and gobble up the food greedily. He chased them away from the pan where the meal was, and picked the down off their necks if they tried to get their share. His mother scolded him when the little ones ran to hide under her wings; but he didn't care, and was very naughty. Cocky began to crow when he was very young, and had such a fine voice that people liked to hear his loud, clear "Cock-a-doodle-doo!" early in the morning; for he woke before the sun was up, and began his song. Peck used to grumble at being roused at dawn, for he was lazy; but the hens bustled up, and were glad to get out of the hen-house.

The father cock had been killed by a dog; so they made Cocky king of the farmyard, and Peck was very jealous of him.

"I came out of the shell first, and I am the oldest; so I ought to be king," he said.

"But we don't like you, because you are selfish, cross, and lazy. We want Cocky; he is so lively, kind, and brave. He will make a splendid bird, and *he* must be our king," answered the hens; and Peck had to mind, or they would have pulled every feather out of his little tail.

He resolved to do some harm to his good brother, and plagued him all he could. One day, when Cocky was swinging with three of his sisters on a bush that hung over the brook, Peck asked a stupid donkey feeding near to come and put his heavy foot on the bush. He did it, and crack went the branch, splash went the poor chicks into the water, and all were drowned but Cocky, who flew across and was saved. Poor little Hop, Chirp, and Downy went floating down the brook like balls of white foam, and were never seen again. All the hens mourned for them, and put a black feather in their heads to show how sorry they were. Mamma Partlet was heart-broken to lose three darlings at once; but Cocky comforted her, and never told how it happened, because he was ashamed to have people know what a bad bird Peck was.

A butterfly saw it all, and he told Granny Cockletop about it; and the hens were so angry that they turned Peck out of the barnyard, and he had to go and live in the woods alone. He said he didn't care; but he did, and was very unhappy, and used to go and peep into the pleasant field where the fowls scratched and talked together. He dared not show himself, for they would have driven him out. But kind Cocky saw him, and would run with some nice bit and creep through the fence into the wood, saying,—

"Poor brother, I'm sorry for you, and I'll come and play with you, and tell you the news."

Now in this wood lived a fox, and he had been planning to eat Peck as soon as he was fat; for he missed the good corn and meal he used to have, and grew very thin living on grasshoppers and berries. While he waited the sly fellow made friends with Peck, though the bird knew that foxes ate hens.

"I'm not afraid, and I don't believe old Granny Cockletop's tales. I can take care of myself, I guess," he said, and went on playing with the fox, who got him to tell all about the hen-house,—how the door was fastened, and where the plump chickens roosted, and what time they went to bed,— so that he could creep in and steal a good supper by and by. Silly Peck never guessed what harm he was doing, and only laughed when Cocky said,—

"You will be sorry if you play with the fox. He is a bad fellow; so be careful and sleep on a high branch, and keep out of his way, as I do."

Cocky was fat and large, and the fox longed to eat him, but never could, because he wisely ran home whenever he saw the rogue hiding in the wood. This made Peck angry, for he wanted his brother to stay and play; and so one day, when Cocky ran off in the midst of a nice game, Peck said to the fox,—

"See here, if you want to catch that fellow, I'll tell you how to do it. He has promised to bring me some food to-night, when all the rest are at roost. He will hide and not get shut up; then, when those cross old biddies are asleep, he will cluck softly, and I am to go in and eat all I want out of the pan. You hide on the top of the hen-house; and while he talks to me, you can pounce on him. Then I shall be the only cock here, and they will have to make me king."

"All right," said the fox, much pleased with the plan, and very glad that Peck had a chance to get fatter.

So when it was night, Peck crept through the broken paling and waited till he heard the signal. Now, good Cocky had saved up nice bits from his own dinner, and put them in a paper hidden under a bush. He spread them all out in the barnyard and called; and Peck came in a great hurry to eat them, never stopping to say, "Thank you."

Cocky stood by talking pleasantly till a little shower came up.

"Peck, dear, put this nice thick paper over you; then you will be dry, and can go on eating. I'll step under that burdock leaf and wait till you are done," said Cocky; and Peck was too busy gobbling up the food to remember anything else.

Now the fox had just crept up on the hen-house roof; and when he peeped down, there was just light enough to see a white thing bobbing about.

"Ah, ha! that's Cockyloo; now for a good supper!" And with a jump he seized Peck by the head before he could explain the mistake.

One squawk, and the naughty bird was dead; but though the paper fell off, and the fox saw what he had done, it was too late, and he began to eat Peck up, while Cocky flew into a tree and crowed so loud that the farmer ran with his gun and shot the fox before he could squeeze through the hole in the fence with the fowl in his mouth.

After that the hens felt safe, for there were no more foxes; and when they heard about Peck they did not mourn at all, but liked Cocky better than ever, and lived happily together, with nothing to trouble them.

King Cockyloo grew to be a splendid bird,—pure white, with a tall red comb on his head, long spurs on his yellow legs, many fine feathers in his tail, and eyes that shone like diamonds. His crow was so loud that it could be heard all over the neighborhood, and people used to say, "Hark! hear Farmer Hunt's cock crow. Isn't it a sweet sound to wake us in the dawn?" All the other cocks used to answer him, and there was a fine matinée concert every day.

He was a good brother, and led his five little sisters all about the field, feeding, guarding, and amusing them; for mamma was lame now, and could not stir far from the yard. It was a pretty sight to see Cocky run home with a worm in his bill or a nice berry, and give it to his mother, who was very proud of her handsome son. Even old Granny Cockletop, who scolded about everything, liked him; and often said, as the hens sat scuffling in the dust,—

"A fine bird, my dears, a very fine bird, and I know he will do something remarkable before he dies."

She was right for once; and this is what he did.

One day the farmer had to go away and stay all night, leaving the old lady alone with two boys. They were not afraid; for they had a gun, and quite longed for a chance to fire it. Now it happened that the farmer had a good deal of money in the house, and some bad men knew it; so they waited for him to go away that they might steal it. Cocky was picking about in the field when he heard voices behind the wall, and peeping through a hole saw two shabby men hiding there.

"At twelve, to-night, when all are asleep, we will creep in at the kitchen window and steal the money. You shall watch on the outside and whistle if any one comes along while I'm looking for the box where the farmer keeps it," said one man.

"You needn't be afraid; there is no dog, and no one to wake the family, so we are quite safe," said the other man; and then they both went to sleep till night came.

Cocky was much troubled, and didn't know what to do. He could not tell the old lady about it; for he could only cackle and crow, and she would not understand that language. So he went about all day looking very sober, and would not chase grasshoppers, play hide-and-seek under the big burdock leaves, or hunt the cricket with his sisters. At sunset he did not go into the hen-house with the rest, but flew up to the shed roof over the kitchen, and sat there in the cold ready to scare the robbers with a loud crow, as he could do nothing else.

At midnight the men came creeping along; one stopped outside, and the other went in. Presently he handed a basket of silver out, and went back for the money. Just as he came creeping along with the box, Cocky gave a loud, long crow, that frightened the robbers and woke the boys. The man with the basket ran away in such a hurry that he tumbled into a well; the other was going to get out of the window, when Cocky flew down and picked at his eyes and flapped his wings in his face, so that he turned to run some other way, and met the boys, who fired at him and shot him in the legs. The old lady popped her head out of the upper window and rang the dinner-bell, and called "Fire! fire!" so loud that it roused the neighbors, who came running to see what the trouble could be.

They fished one man out of the well and picked up the wounded one, and carried them both off to prison.

"Who caught them?" asked the people.

"We did," cried the boys, very proud of what they had done; "but we shouldn't have waked if our good Cocky had not crowed, and scared the rascals. He deserves half the praise, for this is the second time he has caught a thief."

So Cocky was brought in, and petted, and called a fine fellow; and his family were so proud of him they clucked about it for weeks afterward.

When the robbers were tried, it was found that they were the men who had robbed the bank, and taken a great deal of money; so every one was glad to have them shut up for twenty years. It made a great stir, and people would go to see Cocky and tell how he helped catch the men; and he was so brave and handsome, they said at last,—

"We want a new weather-cock on our court-house, and instead of an arrow let us have a cock; and he shall look like this fine fellow."

"Yes, yes," cried the young folks, much pleased; for they thought Cocky ought to be remembered in some way.

So a picture was taken, and Cocky stood very still, with his bright eye on the man; then one like it was made of brass, and put high up on the court-house, where all could see the splendid bird shining like gold, and twirling about to tell which way the wind was. The children were never tired of admiring him; and all the hens and chickens went in a procession one moonlight night to see it,—yes, even Mamma Partlet and Granny Cockletop, though one was lame and the other very old, so full of pride were they in the great honor done King Cockyloo.

This was not the end of his good deeds; and the last was the best of all, though it cost him his life. He ruled for some years, and kept his kingdom in good order; for no one would kill him, when many of the other fowls were taken for Thanksgiving and Christmas dinners. But he did die at last; and even then he was good and brave, as you shall hear.

One of the boys wanted to smoke a pipe, and went behind the hen-house, so nobody should see him do such a silly thing. He thought he heard his father coming, and hid the pipe under the house. Some straw and dry leaves lay about, and took fire, setting the place in a blaze; for the boy ran away when he saw the mischief he had done, and the fire got to burning nicely before the cries of the poor hens called people to help. The door was locked, and could not be opened, because the key was in the pocket of the naughty boy; so the farmer got an axe and chopped down the wall, letting the poor biddies fly out, squawking and smoking.

"Where is Cocky?" cried the other boy, as he counted the hens and missed the king of the farmyard.

"Burnt up, I'm afraid," said the farmer, who was throwing water on the flames.

Alas! yes, he was; for when the fire was out they found good old Cocky sitting on a nest, with his wide wings spread over some little chicks whose mother had left them. They were too small to run away, and sat chirping sadly till Cocky covered and kept them safe, though the smoke choked *him* to death.

Every one was very sorry; and the children gave the good bird a fine funeral, and buried him in the middle of the field, with a green mound over him, and a white stone, on which was written,—

> Here lies the bravest cock that ever crew:
> We mourn for him with sorrow true.
> Now nevermore at dawn his music shall we hear,
> Waking the world like trumpet shrill and clear.
> The hens all hang their heads, the chickens sadly peep;
> The boys look sober, and the girls all weep.
> Good-by, dear Cocky: sleep and rest,
> With grass and daisies on your faithful breast;
> And when you wake, brave bird, so good and true,
> Clap your white wings and crow, "Cock-a-doodle-doo."

# Rosy's Journey

ROSY WAS A NICE LITTLE GIRL who lived with her mother in a small house in the woods. They were very poor, for the father had gone away to dig gold, and did not come back; so they had to work hard to get food to eat and clothes to wear. The mother spun yarn when she was able, for she was often sick, and Rosy did all she could to help. She milked the red cow and fed the hens; dug the garden, and went to town to sell the yarn and the eggs.

She was very good and sweet, and every one loved her; but the neighbors were all poor, and could do little to help the child. So, when at last the mother died, the cow and hens and house had to be sold to pay the doctor and the debts. Then Rosy was left all alone, with no mother, no home, and no money to buy clothes and dinners with.

"What will you do?" said the people, who were very sorry for her.

"I will go and find my father," answered Rosy, bravely.

"But he is far away, and you don't know just where he is, up among the mountains. Stay with us and spin on your little wheel, and we will buy the yarn, and take care of you, dear little girl," said the kind people.

"No, I must go; for mother told me to, and my father will be glad to have me. I'm not afraid, for every one is good to me," said Rosy, gratefully.

Then the people gave her a warm red cloak, and a basket with a little loaf and bottle of milk in it, and some pennies to buy more to eat when the bread was gone. They all kissed her, and wished her good luck; and she trotted away through the wood to find her father.

For some days she got on very well; for the wood-cutters were kind, and let her sleep in their huts, and gave her things to eat. But by and by she came to lonely places, where there were no houses; and then she was afraid, and used to climb up in the trees to sleep, and had to eat berries and leaves, like the Children in the Wood.

She made a fire at night, so wild beasts would not come near her; and if she met other travellers, she was so young and innocent no one had the heart to hurt her. She was kind to everything she met; so all little creatures were friends to her, as we shall see.

One day, as she was resting by a river, she saw a tiny fish on the bank, nearly dead for want of water.

"Poor thing! go and be happy again," she said, softly taking him up, and dropping him into the nice cool river.

"Thank you, dear child; I'll not forget, but will help you some day," said the fish, when he had taken a good drink, and felt better.

"Why, how can a tiny fish help such a great girl as I am?" laughed Rosy.

"Wait and see," answered the fish, as he swam away with a flap of his little tail.

Rosy went on her way, and forgot all about it. But she never forgot to be kind; and soon after, as she was looking in the grass for strawberries, she found a field-mouse with a broken leg.

"Help me to my nest, or my babies will starve," cried the poor thing.

"Yes, I will; and bring these berries so that you can keep still till your leg is better, and have something to eat."

Rosy took the mouse carefully in her little hand, and tied up the broken leg with a leaf of spearmint and a blade of grass. Then she carried her to the nest under the roots of an old tree, where four baby mice were squeaking sadly for their mother. She made a bed of thistle-down for the sick mouse, and put close within reach all the berries and seeds she could find, and brought an acorn-cup of water from the spring, so they could be comfortable.

"Good little Rosy, I shall pay you for all this kindness some day," said the mouse, when she was done.

"I'm afraid you are not big enough to do much," answered Rosy, as she ran off to go on her journey.

"Wait and see," called the mouse; and all the little ones squeaked, as if they said the same.

Some time after, as Rosy lay up in a tree, waiting for the sun to rise, she heard a great buzzing close by, and saw a fly caught in a cobweb that went from one twig to another. The big spider was trying to spin him all up, and the poor fly was struggling to get away before his legs and wings were helpless.

Rosy put up her finger and pulled down the web, and the spider ran away at once to hide under the leaves. But the happy fly sat on Rosy's hand, cleaning his wings, and buzzing so loud for joy that it sounded like a little trumpet.

"You've saved my life, and I'll save yours, if I can," said the fly, twinkling his bright eye at Rosy.

"You silly thing, you can't help me," answered Rosy, climbing down, while the fly buzzed away, saying, like the mouse and fish,—

"Wait and see; wait and see."

Rosy trudged on and on, till at last she came to the sea. The mountains were on the other side; but how should she get over the wide water? No ships were there, and she had no money to hire one if there had been any; so she sat on the shore, very tired and sad, and cried a few big tears as salt as the sea.

"Hullo!" called a bubbly sort of voice close by; and the fish popped up his head.

Rosy ran to see what he wanted.

"I've come to help you over the water," said the fish.

"How can you, when I want a ship, and some one to show me the way?" answered Rosy.

"I shall just call my friend the whale, and he will take you over better than a ship, because he won't get wrecked. Don't mind if he spouts and flounces about a good deal, he is only playing; so you needn't be frightened."

Down dived the little fish, and Rosy waited to see what would happen; for she didn't believe such a tiny thing could really bring a whale to help her.

Presently what looked like a small island came floating through the sea; and turning round, so that its tail touched the shore, the whale said, in a roaring voice that made her jump,—

"Come aboard, little girl, and hold on tight. I'll carry you wherever you like."

It was rather a slippery bridge, and Rosy was rather scared at this big, strange boat; but she got safely over, and held on fast; then, with a roll and a plunge, off went the whale, spouting two fountains, while his tail steered him like the rudder of a ship.

Rosy liked it, and looked down into the deep sea, where all sorts of queer and lovely things were to be seen. Great fishes came and looked at her; dolphins played near to amuse her; the pretty nautilus sailed by in its transparent boat; and porpoises made her laugh with their rough play. Mermaids brought her pearls and red coral to wear, sea-apples to eat, and at night sung her to sleep with their sweet lullabies.

So she had a very pleasant voyage, and ran on shore with many thanks to the good whale, who gave a splendid spout, and swam away.

Then Rosy travelled along till she came to a desert. Hundreds of miles of hot sand, with no trees or brooks or houses.

"I never can go that way," she said; "I should starve, and soon be worn out walking in that hot sand. What *shall* I do?"

> "Quee, quee!
> Wait and see:
> You were good to me;
> So here I come,
> From my little home,
> To help you willingly,"

said a friendly voice; and there was the mouse, looking at her with its bright eyes full of gratitude.

"Why, you dear little thing, I'm very glad to see you; but I'm sure you can't help me across this desert," said Rosy, stroking its soft back.

"That's easy enough," answered the mouse, rubbing its paws briskly. "I'll just call my friend the lion; he lives here, and he'll take you across with pleasure."

"Oh, I'm afraid he'd rather eat me. How dare you call that fierce beast?" cried Rosy, much surprised.

"I gnawed him out of a net once, and he promised to help me. He is a noble animal, and he will keep his word."

Then the mouse sang, in its shrill little voice,—

> "O lion, grand,
> Come over the sand,
> And help me now, I pray!
> Here's a little lass,
> Who wants to pass;
> Please carry her on her way."

In a moment a loud roar was heard, and a splendid yellow lion, with fiery eyes and a long mane, came bounding over the sand to meet them.

"What can I do for you, tiny friend?" he said, looking at the mouse, who was not a bit frightened, though Rosy hid behind a rock, expecting every moment to be eaten.

Mousie told him, and the good lion said pleasantly,—

"I'll take the child along. Come on, my dear; sit on my back and hold fast to my mane, for I'm a swift horse, and you might fall off."

Then he crouched down like a great cat, and Rosy climbed up, for he was so kind she could not fear him; and away they went, racing over the sand till her hair whistled in the wind. As soon as she got her breath, she thought it great fun to go flying along, while other lions and tigers rolled

"Rosy's Journey." From *Lulu's Library, Vol. 1:
A Christmas Dream*, 1886.

their fierce eyes at her, but dared not touch her; for this lion was king of all, and she was quite safe. They met a train of camels with loads on their backs; and the people travelling with them wondered what queer thing was riding that fine lion. It looked like a very large monkey in a red cloak, but went so fast they never saw that it was a little girl.

"How glad I am that I was kind to the mouse; for if the good little creature had not helped me, I never could have crossed this desert," said Rosy, as the lion walked awhile to rest himself.

"And if the mouse had not gnawed me out of the net I never should have come at her call. You see, little people can conquer big ones, and make them gentle and friendly by kindness," answered the lion.

Then away they went again, faster than ever, till they came to the green country. Rosy thanked the good beast, and he ran back; for if any one saw him, they would try to catch him.

"Now I have only to climb up these mountains and find father," thought Rosy, as she saw the great hills before her, with many steep roads winding up to the top; and far, far away rose the smoke from the huts where the men lived and dug for gold. She started off bravely, but took the wrong road, and after climbing a long while found the path ended in rocks over which she could not go. She was very tired and hungry; for her food was gone, and there were no houses in this wild place. Night was coming on, and it was so cold she was afraid she would freeze before morning, but dared not go on lest she should fall down some steep hole and be killed. Much discouraged, she lay down on the moss and cried a little; then she tried to sleep, but something kept buzzing in her ear, and looking carefully she saw a fly prancing about on the moss, as if anxious to make her listen to his song,—

> "Rosy, my dear,
> Don't cry,—I'm here
> To help you all I can.
> I'm only a fly,
> But you'll see that I
> Will keep my word like a man."

Rosy couldn't help laughing to hear the brisk little fellow talk as if he could do great things; but she was very glad to see him and hear his cheerful song, so she held out her finger, and while he sat there told him all her troubles.

"Bless your heart! my friend the eagle will carry you right up the mountains and leave you at your father's door," cried the fly; and he was off with a flirt of his gauzy wings, for he meant what he said.

Rosy was ready for her new horse, and not at all afraid after the whale and the lion; so when a great eagle swooped down and alighted near her, she just looked at his sharp claws, big eyes, and crooked beak as coolly as if he had been a cock-robin.

He liked her courage, and said kindly in his rough voice,—

"Hop up, little girl, and sit among my feathers. Hold me fast round the neck, or you may grow dizzy and get a fall."

Rosy nestled down among the thick gray feathers, and put both arms round his neck; and whiz they went, up, up, up, higher and higher, till the trees looked like grass, they were so far below. At first it was very cold, and Rosy cuddled deeper into her feather bed; then, as they came nearer to the sun, it grew warm, and she peeped out to see the huts standing in a green spot on the top of the mountain.

"Here we are. You'll find all the men are down in the mine at this time. They won't come up till morning; so you will have to wait for your father. Good-by; good luck, my dear." And the eagle soared away, higher still, to his nest among the clouds.

It was night now, but fires were burning in all the houses; so Rosy went from hut to hut trying to find her father's, that she might rest while she waited: at last in one the picture of a pretty little girl hung on the wall, and under it was written, "My Rosy." Then she knew that this was the right place; and she ate some supper, put on more wood, and went to bed, for she wanted to be fresh when her father came in the morning.

While she slept a storm came on,—thunder rolled and lightning flashed, the wind blew a gale, and rain poured,—but Rosy never waked till dawn, when she heard men shouting outside,—

"Run, run! The river is rising! We shall all be drowned!"

Rosy ran out to see what was the matter, though the wind nearly blew her away; she found that so much rain had made the river overflow till it began to wash the banks away.

"What shall I do? what shall I do?" cried Rosy, watching the men rush about like ants, getting their bags of gold ready to carry off before the water swept them away, if it became a flood.

As if in answer to her cry, Rosy heard a voice say close by,—

"Splash, dash!
Rumble and crash!

> Here come the beavers gay;
>> See what they do,
>> Rosy, for you,
> Because you helped *me* one day."

And there in the water was the little fish swimming about, while an army of beavers began to pile up earth and stones in a high bank to keep the river back. How they worked, digging and heaping with teeth and claws, and beating the earth hard with their queer tails like shovels!

Rosy and the men watched them work, glad to be safe, while the storm cleared up; and by the time the dam was made, all danger was over. Rosy looked into the faces of the rough men, hoping her father was there, and was just going to ask about him, when a great shouting rose again, and all began to run to the pit hole; saying,—

"The sand has fallen in! The poor fellows will be smothered! How can we get them out? how can we get them out?

Rosy ran too, feeling as if her heart would break; for her father was down in the mine, and would die soon if air did not come to him. The men dug as hard as they could; but it was a long job, and they feared they would not be in time.

Suddenly hundreds of moles came scampering along, and began to burrow down through the earth, making many holes for air to go in; for they know how to build galleries through the ground better than men can. Every one was so surprised they stopped to look on; for the dirt flew like rain as the busy little fellows scratched and bored as if making an underground railway.

"What does it mean?" said the men. "They work faster than we can, and better; but who sent them? Is this strange little girl a fairy?"

Before Rosy could speak, all heard a shrill, small voice singing,—

> "They come at my call;
>> And though they are small,
> They'll dig the passage clear:
>> I never forget;
>> We'll save them yet,
> For love of Rosy dear."

Then all saw a little gray mouse sitting on a stone, waving her tail about, and pointing with her tiny paw to show the moles where to dig.

The men laughed; and Rosy was telling them who she was, when a cry came from the pit, and they saw that the way was clear so they could pull the buried men up. In a minute they got ropes, and soon had ten poor fellows safe on the ground; pale and dirty, but all alive, and all shouting as if they were crazy,—

"Tom's got it! Tom's got it! Hooray for Tom!"

"What is it?" cried the others; and then they saw Tom come up with the biggest lump of gold ever found in the mountains.

Every one was glad of Tom's luck; for he was a good man, and had worked a long time, and been sick, and couldn't go back to his wife and child. When he saw Rosy, he dropped the lump, and caught her up, saying,—

"My little girl! she's better than a million pounds of gold."

Then Rosy was very happy, and went back to the hut, and had a lovely time telling her father all about her troubles and her travels. He cried when he heard that the poor mother was dead before she could have any of the good things the gold would buy them.

"We will go away and be happy together in the pleasantest home I can find, and never part any more, my darling," said the father, kissing Rosy as she sat on his knee with her arms round his neck.

She was just going to say something very sweet to comfort him, when a fly lit on her arm and buzzed very loud,—

> "Don't drive me away,
> But hear what I say:
> Bad men want the gold;
> They will steal it to-night,
> And you must take flight;
> So be quiet and busy and bold."

"I was afraid some one would take my lump away. I'll pack up at once, and we will creep off while the men are busy at work; though I'm afraid we can't go fast enough to be safe, if they miss us and come after," said Tom, bundling his gold into a bag and looking very sober; for some of the miners were wild fellows, and might kill him for the sake of that great lump.

But the fly sang again,—

> "Slip away with me,
> And you will see
> What a wise little thing am I;

> For the road I show
> No man can know,
> Since it's up in the pathless sky."

Then they followed Buzz to a quiet nook in the wood; and there were the eagle and his mate waiting to fly away with them so fast and so far that no one could follow. Rosy and the bag of gold were put on the mother eagle; Tom sat astride the king bird; and away they flew to a great city, where the little girl and her father lived happily together all their lives.

# The Fairy Box

I wish I had a magic bracelet like Rosamond's, that would prick me when I was going to do wrong," said little May, as she put down the story she had been reading.

There was no one else in the room, but she heard a sweet voice sing these words close to her ear:—

> "Now hark, little May,
>     If you want to do right,
> Under your pillow
>     Just look every night.
> If you have been good
>     All through the day,
> A gift you will find,
>     Useful or gay;
> But if you have been
>     Cross, selfish, or wild,
> A bad thing will come
>     For the naughty child.
> So try, little dear,
>     And soon you will see
> How easy and sweet
>     To grow good it will be."

May was very much surprised at this, and looked everywhere to see who spoke, but could find no one.

"I guess I dreamed it; but my eyes are wide open, and I can't make up poetry, asleep or awake."

As she said that, some one laughed; and the same voice sang again,—

> "Ha, ha! you can't see,
>     Although I am here;
> But listen to what
>     I say in your ear.

Tell no one of this,
　　Because, if you do,
My fun will be spoilt,
　　And so will yours too.
But if you are good,
　　And patient, and gay,
A real fairy will come
　　To see little May."

"Oh, how splendid that will be! I'll try hard, and be as good as an angel if I can only get one peep at a live fairy. I always said there were such people, and now I shall know how they look," cried the little girl, so pleased that she danced all about the room, clapping her hands.

Something bright darted out of the window from among the flowers that stood there, and no more songs were heard; so May knew that the elf had gone.

"I've got a fine secret all to myself, and I'll keep it carefully. I wonder what present will come to-night," she said, thinking this a very interesting play.

She was very good all day, and made no fuss about going to bed, though usually she fretted, and wanted to play, and called for water, and plagued poor Nursey in many ways. She got safely into her little nest, and then was in such a hurry to see what was under her pillow that she forgot, and called out crossly,—

"Do hurry and go away. Don't wait to hang up my clothes, you slow old thing! Go, go!"

That hurt Nurse's feelings, and she went away without her good-night kiss. But May didn't care, and felt under her pillow the minute the door was shut. A lamp was always left burning; so she could see the little gold box she drew out.

"How pretty! I hope there is some candy in it," she said, opening it very carefully.

Oh, dear! what *do* you think happened? A wasp flew out and stung her lips; then both wasp and box vanished, and May was left to cry alone, with a sharp pain in the lips that said the unkind words.

"What a dreadful present! I don't like that spiteful fairy who sends such horrid things," she sobbed.

Then she lay still and thought about it; for she dared not call any one, because nobody must guess the secret. She knew in her own little heart that the cross words hurt Nursey as the sting did her lips, and she felt sorry. At once the smart got better, and by the time she had resolved to ask the good old woman to forgive her, it was all gone.

Next morning she kissed Nursey and begged pardon, and tried hard to be good till tea-time; then she ran to see what nice things they were going to have to eat, though she had often been told not to go into the dining-room. No one was there; and on the table stood a dish of delicious little cakes, all white like snowballs.

"I must have just a taste, and I'll tell mamma afterward," she said; and before she knew it one little cake was eaten all up.

"Nobody will miss it, and I can have another at tea. Now, a lump of sugar and a sip of cream before mamma comes, I so like to pick round."

Having done one wrong thing, May felt like going on; so she nibbled and meddled with all sorts of forbidden things till she heard a step, then she ran away; and by and by, when the bell rang, came in with the rest as prim and proper as if she did not know how to play pranks. No one missed the cake, and her mother gave her another, saying,—

"There, dear, is a nice plummy one for my good child."

May turned red, and wanted to tell what she had done, but was ashamed because there was company; and people thought she blushed like a modest little girl at being praised.

But when she went to bed she was almost afraid to look under the pillow, knowing that she had done wrong. At last she slowly drew out the box, and slowly opened it, expecting something to fly at her. All she saw was a tiny black bag, that began at once to grow larger, till it was big enough to hold her two hands. Then it tied itself tight round her wrists, as if to keep these meddlesome hands out of mischief.

"Well, this is very queer, but not so dreadful as the wasp. I hope no one will see it when I'm asleep. I do wish I'd let those cakes and things alone," sighed May, looking at the black bag, and vainly trying to get her hands free.

She cried herself to sleep, and when she woke the bag was gone. No one had seen it; but she told her mamma about the cake, and promised not to do so any more.

"Now this shall be a *truly* good day, every bit of it," she said, as she skipped away, feeling as light as a feather after she had confessed her little sins.

But, alas! it is so easy to forget and do wrong, that May spoilt her day before dinner by going to the river and playing with the boats, in spite of many orders not to do it. She did not tell of it, and went to a party in the afternoon, where she was so merry she never remembered the naughty thing till she was in bed and opened the fairy box. A little chain appeared, which in a flash grew long and large, and fastened round her ankles as if she were a prisoner. May liked to tumble about, and was much disgusted to be chained in this way; but there was no help for it, so she lay very still and had plenty of time to be sorry.

"It is a good punishment for me, and I deserve it. I won't cry, but I will— I *will* remember." And May said her prayers very soberly, really meaning to keep her word this time.

All the next day she was very careful to keep her lips from cross words, her hands from forbidden things, and her feet from going wrong. Nothing spoilt this day, she watched so well; and when mamma gave the good-night kiss, she said,—

"What shall I give my good little daughter, who has been gentle, obedient, and busy all day?"

"I want a white kitty, with blue eyes, and a pink ribbon on its neck," answered May.

"I'll try and find one. Now go to bed, deary, and happy dreams!" said mamma, with many kisses on the rosy cheeks, and the smile that was a reward.

May was so busy thinking about the kitty and the good day that she forgot the box till she heard a little "Mew, mew!" under her pillow.

"Mercy me! what's that?" And she popped up her head to see.

Out came the box; off flew the lid, and there, on a red cushion, lay a white kit about two inches long. May couldn't believe that it was alive till it jumped out of its nest, stretched itself, and grew all at once just the right size to play with and be pretty. Its eyes were blue, its tail like a white plume, and a sweet pink bow was on its neck. It danced all over the bed, ran up the curtains, hid under the clothes, nipped May's toes, licked her face, patted her nose with its soft paw, and winked at her in such a funny way that she laughed for joy at having such a dear kitty. Presently, as if it knew that bed was the place to lie quiet in, puss cuddled down in a little bunch and purred May to sleep.

"I suppose that darling kit will be gone like all the other things," said May, as she waked up and looked round for her first pretty gift.

No; there was the lovely thing sitting in the sun among the flower-pots, washing her face and getting ready for play. What a fine frolic they had; and how surprised every one was to see just the pussy May wanted! They supposed it came as kitties often come; and May never told them it was a fairy present, because she had promised not to. She was so happy with little puss that she was good all day; and when she went to bed she thought,—

"I wish I had a dog to play with darling Snowdrop, and run with me when I go to walk."

"Bow, wow, wow!" came from under the pillow; and out of the box trotted a curly black dog, with long ears, a silver collar, and such bright, kind eyes May was not a bit afraid of him, but loved him at once, and named him Floss, he was so soft and silky. Pussy liked him too; and when May was sleepy they both snuggled down in the same basket like two good babies, and went to by-low.

"Well, I never! What shall we find next?" said Nurse, when she saw the dog in the morning.

"Perhaps it will be an elephant, to fill the whole house, and scare you out of your wits," laughed May, dancing about with Snowdrop chasing her bare toes, while Floss shook and growled over her shoes as if they were rats.

"If your cousin John wants to give you any more animals, I wish he'd send a pony to take you to school, and save my old legs the pain of trotting after you," said Nurse; for May did have a rich cousin who was very fond of her, and often gave her nice things.

"Perhaps he will," laughed May, much tickled with the idea that it was a fairy, and not Cousin John, who sent the cunning little creatures to her.

But she didn't get the pony that night; for in the afternoon her mother told her not to sit on the lawn, because it was damp, and May did not mind, being busy with a nice story. So when she took up her box, a loud sneeze seemed to blow the lid off, and all she saw was a bit of red flannel.

"What is this for?" she asked, much disappointed; and as if to answer, the strip of flannel wrapped itself round her neck.

"There! my throat *is* sore, and I *am* hoarse. I wonder how that fairy knew I sat on the damp grass. I'm so sorry; for I did want a pony, and might have had it if I'd only minded," said May, angry with herself for spoiling all her fun.

It *was* spoilt; for she had such a cold next day she couldn't go out at all, but had to take medicine and keep by the fire, while the other children had a lovely picnic.

"I won't wish for anything to-night; I don't deserve a present, I was so disobedient. But I *have* tried to be patient," said May, feeling for the box.

The fairy had not forgotten her, and there was a beautiful picture-book, full of new, nice stories printed in colored ink.

"How splendid to read to-morrow while I'm shut up!" she said, and went to sleep very happily.

All the next day she enjoyed the pretty pictures and funny tales, and never complained or fretted at all, but was so much better the doctor said she could go out to-morrow, if it was fine.

"Now I will wish for the pony," said May, in her bed. But there was nothing in the box except a little red-silk rope, like a halter. She did not know what to do with it that night, but she did the next morning; for just as she was dressed her brother called from the garden,—

"May, look out and see what we found in the stable. None of us can catch him, so do come and see if you can; your name is on the card tied to his mane."

May looked, and there was a snow-white pony racing about the yard as if he was having a fine frolic. Then she knew the halter was for him, and ran down to catch him. The minute she appeared, the pony went to her and put his nose in her hand, neighing, as if he said,—

"This is my little mistress; I will mind her and serve her well."

May was delighted, and very proud when the pony let her put on the saddle and bridle that lay in the barn all ready to use. She jumped up and rode gayly down the road; and Will and mamma and all the maids and Floss and Snowdrop ran to see the pretty sight. The children at school were much excited when she came trotting up, and all wanted to ride Prince. He was very gentle, and every one had a ride; but May had the best fun, for she could go every day for long trots by the carriage when mamma and Will drove out. A blue habit and a hat with a long feather were bought that afternoon; and May was so happy and contented at night that she said to herself as she lay in bed,—

"I'll wish for something for Will now, and see if I get it. I don't want any more presents yet; I've had my share, and I'd love to give away to other people who have no fairy box."

So she wished for a nice boat, and in the box lay a key with the name "Water Lily" on it. She guessed what it meant, and in the morning told her brother to come to the river and see what she had for him. There lay a pretty green and white boat, with cushioned seats, a sail all spread, and at the mast-head a little flag flying in the wind, with the words "Water Lily" on it in gold letters.

Will was so surprised and pleased to find that it was his, he turned heels over head on the grass, kissed May, and skipped into his boat, crying, "All aboard!" as if eager to try it at once.

May followed, and they sailed away down the lovely river, white with real lilies, while the blackbirds sang in the green meadows on either side, and boys and girls stopped on the bridges to see them pass.

After that May kept on trying to be good, and wishing for things for herself and other people, till she forgot how to be naughty, and was the sweetest little girl in the world. Then there was no need of fairies to help her; and one night the box was not under the pillow.

"Well, I've had my share of pretty things, and must learn to do without. I'm glad I tried; for now it is easy to be good, and I don't need to be rewarded," said May, as she fell asleep, quite happy and contented, though she did wish she could have seen the fairy just once.

Next morning the first thing she saw was a beautiful bracelet, shining on the table; and while she stood admiring it, she heard the little voice sing,—

> "Here is the bracelet
>     For good little May
> To wear on her arm
>     By night and by day.
> When it shines like the sun,
>     All's going well;
> But when you are bad,
>     A sharp prick will tell.
> Farewell, little girl,
>     For now we must part.
> Make a fairy-box, dear,
>     Of your own happy heart;
> And take out for all
>     Sweet gifts every day,
> Till all the year round
>     Is like beautiful May."

As the last words were sung, right before her eyes she saw a tiny creature swinging on the rose that stood there in a vase,—a lovely elf, with wings like a butterfly, a gauzy dress, and a star on her forehead. She smiled, and waved her hand as she slowly rose and fluttered away into the sunshine, till she vanished from sight, leaving May with the magic bracelet on her arm, and the happy thought that at last she had *really* seen a fairy.

# The Three Frogs

HOP, CROAK, AND SPLASH were three little frogs who lived in a pleasant river, and had merry times swimming about or hopping on the green grass. At night they sat on the bank and sung together, very sweetly *they* thought; and if boats came by they skipped into the water, heels over head, with a great splashing and noise.

Hop was not contented with this quiet life; he wanted to see the world, and kept asking his brother Croak to go and travel with him.

"I'm tired of poking about in this stupid river, with no fun but leap-frog and singing. I want to know what is over that hill, and I'm going to find out. You can stay and doze in the mud if you please. I've got more spirit than that, and I'm off."

So away went Hop, singing gayly,—

> "A frog he would a-wooing go,
> Whether his mammy would let him or no,
> With a roly-poly, gammon and spinach,
> Heigh-ho, said Anthony Rowley."

His good little sister Splash begged him to stay, for the world was full of danger and he was too young to go alone. But Hop told her not to worry. Girls ought to keep at home, for they couldn't take care of themselves; but fine young fellows should see something of life before they settled down. His friend Turtle had invited him to go; and if such a slow chap as Creeper could start on a journey, of course the best jumper in the river would get on all right.

While he was saying good-by, the turtle had crept up the bank and was well on his way to the road beyond. Hop skipped after him; and when they had got to the hill-top they stopped to rest,—Creeper in the road on the warm sand, and Hop among some daisies close by.

"How big the world is!" he said, staring with his great eyes; for he had never seen houses before, and the village looked as grand to him as London would to us. "I like it, and I know I shall have a splendid time. Come on, slow coach! I see fountains over there, and want a good drink."

Just as he spoke a cart came by; and before poor Creeper could get out of the way, a wheel crushed him to death.

"Mercy on us! what horrid monsters those are!" cried Hop, leaping as fast as his legs could take him into a garden near by, where he lay trembling and scared half out of his wits. He thought the cart was a creature; and every time he heard the rumble of wheels his heart beat and he clasped his hands in fear as he sat under the burdock leaves. At last it seemed so quiet he ventured out, and had a lovely time in the nasturtium-bed, catching flies and playing bopeep with a little bird. Then he hopped to the grass-plot, where the sprinkler was whizzing round, and took a refreshing bath. He was just puffing his skin out and winking with pleasure when a fat toad, who lived under the piazza, told him very crossly to "clear out."

"You are a very rude old person, and I shall do as I like. This is not your garden; so you needn't goggle at me," answered saucy Hop, opening his wide mouth to laugh at the toad, who was so fat he couldn't take long leaps like the lively frog.

"Very well, dandiprat, I shall call the cat; and she will make you skip, unless you want that fine green jacket torn off your back by her sharp claws," said the toad, hopping slowly away to the sunny corner where a gray cat lay dozing.

"Pooh! I'm not afraid," said Hop; for he had never seen a cat, and thought the toad made it all up.

So he took a leisurely stroll down the walk, looking about him as if he owned the whole garden. Presently he saw a pretty little creature playing with leaves, and hurried on to speak to it, being eager to find friends in this pleasant place. You see, when the toad told the cat about the stranger, pussy only gaped and went to sleep again, not caring to play with any one. But the kitten who lay beside her was curious to see a frog, and ran off at once to find him. Hop did not know that this was the cat's daughter, till kitty pounced on him as if he had been a mouse, and instead of playing some nice game and telling all about the new world, as Hop expected, she clawed and bit him, tossed him up, and let him bump down again on the hard ground. He tried to get away, but she let him hop a little and then pounced again, cuffing him with her paws, and dragging him about till he was half dead.

He believed the old toad now, and thought the end of the world had come. It would have been the end of the world for him, if a dog had not bounced into the garden and made kitty fly up a tree, spitting and glaring like a little dragon. Poor Hop crept under a gooseberry bush, and lay there longing for gentle Splash to tie up his wounds and comfort his pain with spearmint from the river side and a cool lily-pad for a wet sheet to pack him in.

"It is an awful world, and I wish I was safe at home," he sighed, as the sun grew hot, the water was turned off, and the wind stopped blowing.

But he was too feeble to hop away, and lay there panting till night, when a shower saved his life; and early in the morning he started to find the river before he got into any more troubles.

He went very slowly, being lame and sore; but got out of the garden and was just planning to give one tremendous leap over the road, for fear he should get crushed as Creeper did, when he heard a soft rustling behind him, and saw a long, slender gray thing, with very bright eyes and a little tongue that darted out and in like a flash.

"I see no cruel claws; so it can't be a cat," thought Hop, feeling timid now about making new friends.

"Pretty fellow, come here and talk to me," hissed the snake, longing to eat the nice little froggie.

Hop felt rather nervous, but wished to be polite; so he let the stranger coil lovingly round him and look right into his face while listening to the tale of woe he gladly told. Presently he found he could not stir at all, nor move his eyes from the fiery eyes before him, and the darting tongue seemed ready to sting. Then he was frightened, and tried to escape; but he only gave one leap, for the snake caught him by the hind legs and held him fast, while swallowing him slowly down.

"Help, help!" cried Hop, in despair. "Croak! Splash! oh, come and save me, save me!"

But there was no help; and in a few moments there was no frog, for the last leg had vanished down the snake's throat. Poor little Hop!

Croak was a noisy fellow, and kept up a great racket trying to sing louder than any of the other frogs; for he was very proud of his voice, and sat on a log at night saying, "Ker honk! ker honk!" till every one was tired of hearing him.

The old ones told him not to wear his throat out till his voice was stronger; but he thought they envied him its power and sweetness, and croaked away louder than ever.

The boys who came to the river to bathe used to mock him, and try to see which frog sung so loud. This pleased him; and instead of keeping still and staying among his friends, silly Croak went and sat on a rock alone, that all might see and hear the great singer.

"Now," said the boys, "we can catch him and keep him in a tub; and when we are tired of his noise we can rap him on the head and make him be still."

So while the vain frog sat croaking at the top of his voice, two of the boys swam up to the rock and threw a net over him. He kicked and struggled; but they had him fast, and tied him up in a bundle till they got to the tub, and there they left him with a little grass, saying,—

"Now sing away, old fellow, and make yourself comfortable."

But Croak could not sing, he was so frightened and unhappy; for he was hungry and tired, and they didn't give him the right things to eat, nor any mossy log to rest on. They poked him with sticks, took him up to look at his funny toes, opened his big mouth, and held him by one leg to see him kick. He tried to climb out; but the sides of the tub were slippery, and he had to give it up. He kept swimming and floating till he was tired out, and ate bread-crumbs and grass to keep from starving; but he was very miserable, though children came to hear him sing, and he had nothing else to do.

"This isn't what I meant," sighed Croak, "and if ever I get out of this old tub, I'll keep very still and never try to make a noise in the world again."

Among the children was one kind little girl who pitied the poor frog, and one day when she was alone took him up carefully and put him on the grass, saying,—

"Run away, froggie, home to your mamma, and don't tell the boys I set you free."

"Thank you, my dear; those bad boys will never see or hear me again," answered Croak, hopping off as fast as he could go, never minding in his hurry that he was not taking the road to the river.

After he had gone a long way he came to a tank where a great many frogs seemed to be having a very nice time; for there was plenty of food, stones to sit on, and fresh water flowing in all the time.

"Ah! these must be very elegant people to live in this luxurious way. They sing pretty well, but not one has a splendid deep voice like mine. I'll jump in and astonish them with my best song," said Croak, after he had watched and listened for a while.

If he had only known that these frogs were kept there to be fattened for an old French gentleman to eat, he would have skipped away and saved his life; but he was so anxious to show off his voice, that he gave a jump and went splash into the tank, startling the others and making a great commotion. He liked that; and getting up on the highest stone, gave them his favorite "Ker honk" song, till the air rang with the sound.

The other frogs were much impressed, for *they* thought it fine music; so they gathered round, and shook hands and welcomed the stranger, sure that he must be a distinguished musician, he put on such airs. Now Croak was in his glory, and puffed himself out, and goggled at the lady-frogs till they put up their fans of green flag to hide their smiles. The young fellows tried to imitate him, till the tank was such a noisy place the old gentleman said to his cook,—

"Kill off a dozen of the fattest for dinner, and stop that din out there."

The frogs had told Croak that every now and then some of them were chosen to go and live in the great house; and all were eager to find out what good fortune had happened to their friends, for none ever came back to tell the sad truth. So when they saw the man in the white cap and apron come to the tank and look down at them, they all began to skip and prance, hoping to be chosen.

With a long-handled net the cook picked out the fattest and put them in a covered pail till he had his dozen. Croak had not been there long enough to get very plump, so he would have escaped that time if he had held his tongue. But he couldn't keep still, and made such a terrible noise the cook said,—

"I must catch and quiet that rascal, or my master will go distracted." So he held the net open; and that silly frog hopped in, little dreaming that he had sung his last song.

"Now we shall see fine things. Good-by, you poor dears! Be patient till your turn comes," he cried, as the bucket was carried away to the kitchen.

Croak was disappointed when he saw nothing but pots and pans and a great fire; for the vain fellow really thought he was chosen to sing before some fine people. But his disappointment turned to horror when he saw his friends taken out one by one and their poor little legs cut off to fry for dinner. That was the only part the cook used, and the rest he threw away. Croak was left to the last, as he was not to be eaten; and while he waited his turn, he dashed distractedly round and round the pail, trying to get away, and croaking so dismally it was a wonder the cook did not take pity on him. But he did not, and was just going toward the pail with the big knife in his hand, when the old gentleman came down to see if his orders were obeyed, for he thought a great deal of his dinner. All the poor little legs lay in the pan ready to cook; and he was so pleased that he said, looking at the thin frog swimming about in that lively way,—

"Ah! this is a very brisk fellow. I will put him in my aquarium; the gold-fish and the crab will like a little society, I think."

Then, catching Croak by one leg, he carried him upstairs and threw him into the great glass box where several pretty gold-fish and one cross crab lived together. Croak was so glad to escape frying that he was very quiet, humble, and good; and though his new home was a prison, he tried to be contented, and never complained when the lovely fish called him ugly and the cross crab nipped his toes. He was homesick, and longed sadly for the pleasant river, the jolly games he used to have, and his dear little sister. He never sang now, fearing to be killed if he did; but when the windows stood open through the summer night and he heard the music of his friends, he put his hands before his face and cried such bitter tears that the water grew quite salt. He bore it as long as he could; but his heart broke at last, and one day poor Croak was found floating on the top of the tank quite dead. So that was the end of him.

Good little Splash lived at home all safe and happy, and was so kind to every one that her neighbors loved her dearly and sung her praises at their evening concerts.

Now, the Frog Prince wished to marry, and was looking about for a wife, as he was very particular. So he wrapped himself up in a dead-leaf cloak, put an empty nut-shell on his head for a hood, and leaning on a bulrush staff, went hobbling along by the river like a poor old woman, begging at the different houses, that he might see how the lady-frogs behaved at home.

When he rode out as the Prince on a field-mouse, with flags flying, and all his court about him, the young lady-frogs stood modestly by their mammas, all in their best, and curtsied sweetly as he went by. But now he came to the back doors, a poor beggar, and it was very different. Some were lazy and lay late in their beds of river weeds, while the mothers did the work; some were greedy and ate all the best flies themselves; others slapped and scolded their little brothers and sisters instead of taking care of them; and nearly all were vain. The Prince caught many looking at their bright eyes in still pools, or putting on crowns of water flowers, or bathing in dew to keep the freckles from their faces. They were always ready to dance at balls, to go boating, or sing at the concerts where all could hear them; but few were busy, sweet, and dutiful at home, and the Prince nowhere found the bride he wanted. He was very fond of music; so he listened to the concerts, and soon began to wonder why they all sang a song with this chorus,—

> "Who is the fairest that swims in our river?
> Who is the dearest frog under the sun?
> Whose life is full of the sweetest endeavor?
> Who is our busiest, happiest one?

> Splash, Splash, darling thing!
> All delight her praise to sing."

"I must find this lovely creature and see if she is all they say, because if she is I'll make a Princess of her in the twinkling of an eye," said the Prince; and he set off to look for Splash, for he was a very energetic frog.

He soon found her, for she was always busy doing something for her neighbors; and he watched her teaching the little tadpoles to swim, helping the old frogs out to sit in the sun when damp weather gave them rheumatism, or taking care of the sick ones, or feeding the poor, or running errands for busy mammas with large families and lazy daughters.

In her own little home all was as neat as wax, but so lonely she did not like to stay there much. All day she helped others, and at evening sat at her door and thought sadly of her lost brothers. She was very pretty in her neat, gray gown and white apron, with her bright eyes, gentle face, and sweet voice; though she seldom sung, except lullabies to the little frogs and the sick folks.

She was rocking a small tadpole to sleep in this way one day, when the disguised Prince came hobbling along, and asked for a bit to eat. Putting little Wiggle in his cobweb hammock, Splash said kindly,—

"Yes, old mother, come in and rest while I get you some dinner. Here's a soft cushion of moss, and a leaf of water fresh from the spring."

The Prince sat a long time talking with her, and hearing about her brothers, and seeing how sweet she was. He made up his mind to marry at once; for frogs don't spend a long time and much money getting ready,— they just wash up their green and gray suits, and invite their friends to the wedding. The bride can always find a delicate cobweb on the grass for a veil, and that is all she needs.

The Prince thought he would try one thing more; so he said to her,—

"I'm very lame; will you take me to the palace? I want to see the Prince. Do you know him?"

"No; I'm only a humble creature, and he wouldn't care to know me," said Splash, modestly. "But I admire him very much, he is so brave and just and good. I love to see him go by, and always peep behind my curtain, he is such a splendid sight."

The Prince blushed under the nut-shell cap at such praise, and was sure, from the way Splash spoke, that she loved him a little bit. So he was very happy and wanted to dance, but kept quiet and leaned on her arm as she led him down the bank, put him nicely on a lily-pad, and rowed away, smiling

"The Three Frogs." From *Lulu's Library, Vol. 1:*
*A Christmas Dream,* 1886.

at him and talking so sweetly he got fonder and fonder of her every moment.

At last they came to the palace, all made of white water-lilies, with red cardinal-flowers for flags, floors of green moss, and pink toadstool tables spread with acorn cups of honey, berries, and all the dainties frogs love; for the Prince had sent a telegram by the wind to have a feast ready.

"Come in. I have something for you in return for your kindness to me. I'm not what I seem, and in a moment you shall see who your new friend is," said the Prince, leading her into the great hall where the throne was.

Then he left her, wondering what was to happen, while he hurried to throw off his old things and to put on his green velvet suit, his crown of cowslip, and the tall rush that was his sceptre. He looked very splendid, with white silk stockings on his long legs, his fine eyes shining, and his speckled waistcoat puffed out with the joy of his heart.

The trumpets sounded; all the frogs of the court came marching in, with the Prince at the head; and when they were seated at the tables, he took astonished Splash by the hand, and said in a loud voice,—

"This is your Queen,—the best, the loveliest in the land! Bring the wedding veil; let the bells ring, and shout with me, 'Hurrah! hurrah for Queen Splash!'"

# Sunshine, and Her Brothers and Sisters

ONCE UPON A TIME there was a very wise old spirit called Mother Nature, who lived in a beautiful place, and had a large family of children, whom she found it rather hard to manage. When they obeyed her, all went well; but when they played pranks or quarrelled, everything was in confusion, and all sorts of trouble came.

Sunshine, the eldest girl, was a sweet creature, always good, and a great comfort to her mother at all seasons. So were South and West Winds nice little girls; but Lightning, Thunder's twin sister, was very naughty, and liked to do mischief. Snow, the fourth daughter, was a cold, quiet spirit, fond of covering up the world with the nice white sheets she kept folded away in the sky. Rain was always crying, East Wind sulking, Thunder and Hail scolding and growling, and North Wind, the biggest of the boys, went roaring and blustering about so fiercely that every one ran before him, though his wholesome breath freshened the world, and blew away much rubbish, which his gentle sisters could not manage as they kept house.

"Now, my dears, I'm very tired and going to take a nap, so be good children; do your tasks nicely, and wake me in March," said Mother Nature, one November day, when her summer work was over, and her time for rest had come.

"Yes, mamma," said Sunshine, as she tucked her up with a kiss. "I will do my best to keep the girls busy and the boys in order. Have a good sleep, and I'll call you in time for the spring work."

Then the old lady tied her night-cap over her ears, and dozed off quite comfortably, while her good daughter, after a last smile at the frosty world, sent to her spinning, that there might be plenty of sunshine for the next summer.

"It's my turn now, and I'll cry as much as I like, for mother isn't here to stop me, and Sunny can't," said Rain; and down came floods of tears, while his brother, East Wind, began to blow till every one shivered, and coughs and colds and fog and mud made the world a dismal place. Sunny begged them to stop and give her a chance now and then, but they would not; and everybody said what a dreadful month November was that year.

Fortunately it was soon time for North Wind and his favorite sister Snow to come back from Iceland; and the moment the older brother's loud voice was heard, Rain and East ran and hid, for they were rather afraid of him.

"Ha, what a mess those rascals have made! Never mind, we'll soon have it all nice and tidy for Christmas," said North, as he dried up the mud, blew away the fog, and got the world ready for Snow to cover with her beautiful down quilt. In a day or two it looked like a fairy world, and Sunshine peeped out to do her part, making the ice on the trees glitter like diamonds, the snowy drifts shine like silver, and fill the blue sky full of light.

Then every one rejoiced, bells jingled merrily, children coasted and snow-balled; Christmas trees began to grow, and all faces to glow as they never do at any other time.

"The holydays shall be pleasant if I can only keep those bad boys in a good humor," said Sunny; and to make sure of them she fed Rain and East Wind on plum-cake with poppy-seeds in it, so they slept like dormice till the New Year was born.

Snow had her frolics, and no one minded, because she was so pretty; and North was so amiable just then that the white storms only made fine sleighing, and the fresh air kept cheeks rosy, eyes sparkling, lips laughing, and hearts happy as they should be at that blessed season.

Sunshine was so pleased that she came out to see the fun, and smiled so warmly that a January thaw set in.

"Dear me, I forgot that I must not be too generous at this season, or it makes trouble; for, though people enjoy my pleasant days, they leave off their furs and get cold. I'll go back to my spinning and only smile through the window; then no harm will be done."

Thunder and Lightning had been in Italy all this time, and they too got into mischief. Their mother had shut the twins up in a volcano to keep them out of the way till summer, when they were useful. Down there they found playmates to suit them, and had fine times rumbling and boiling, and sending out hot lava and showers of ashes to scare the people who lived near by. Growing tired of this, they at last planned to get up an earthquake and escape. So they kicked and shook the world like children tumbling about under the bed-clothes; and the fire roared, and Thunder growled, and Lightning flew about trying to get the lid of the volcano off. At last she did, and out they all burst with such a dreadful noise that the poor people thought the end of the world had come. Towns fell down, hills moved, the sea came up on the shore, ashes and stones covered up a whole city, and destruction and despair were everywhere.

"There! wasn't that a fine frolic? Mother won't dare to shut us up again, I fancy, when she sees what a piece of work we make for her," said naughty

Lightning, dashing about to peep through the smoke at the sad scene below.

"Grand fun! but if Sunshine wakes mother we shall wish we had not done it. Let's run away to Africa and hide till this is all forgotten," answered Thunder, rather ashamed of such a dreadful prank.

So they flew off, leaving great sorrow behind them; but Sunshine did not wake mamma, though West Wind came home from Italy to tell her all about it. There was trouble here also, for Rain and East Wind had waked up, and were very angry to find they had been dosed with poppy-seeds.

"Now we'll pay Sunny for that, and turn everything topsy-turvy," they said; and calling Hail, they went to work.

Rain emptied all his water-buckets till the rivers rose and flooded the towns; the snow on the hills melted and covered the fields, washed away the railroads, carried off houses, and drowned many poor animals; Hail pelted with his stones, and East Wind blew cold and shrill till there was no comfort anywhere.

Poor Sunny was at her wits' end with all these troubles; but she would not wake her mother, and tried to manage her unruly brothers alone. West helped her, for while Sunny shone, and shone so sweetly that Rain had to stop crying, West tugged at the weather-cocks till she made East give way, and let her blow for a while. He was out of breath and had to yield; so the "bad spell of weather" was over, and the poor, half-drowned people could get dry and fish their furniture out of the flood, and moor their floating houses at last. Sunny kept on smiling till she dried up the ground. West sent fresh gales to help her, and by March things looked much better.

"Now do be good children, and let us get ready for the spring-cleaning before mother wakes. I don't know what she *will* say to the boys, but I've done my best, and I hope she will be pleased with me," said Sunshine, when at last she sat down to rest a moment, tired out.

All the brothers and sisters except the naughty twins, gathered about her, and promised to be very good, for they loved her and were sorry for their pranks. Each tried to help her, and March was a very busy month, for all the winds blew in turn; even gentle South from far away came home to do her part. Snow folded up her down quilts and packed them away; Rain dropped a few quiet showers to swell the buds and green the grass, and Sunny began to shake out the golden webs of light she had been spinning all winter. Every one worked so well that April found that part of the world in fine order; and when South Wind blew open the first hyacinths, Mother Nature smelt them, began to rub her eyes and wake up.

"Bless me, how I've slept. Why didn't you rouse me sooner, dear? Ah, my good child, I see you've tried to do my work and get all ready for me," said the old lady, throwing away her night-cap, and peeping out of window at the spring world budding everywhere.

Then sitting in her mother's lap, Sunny told her trials and tribulations. At some Mamma Nature laughed, at others she frowned; and when it came to the earthquake and the flood, she looked very sober, saying, as she stroked her daughter's bright hair,—

"My darling, I can't explain these things to you, and I don't always understand why they happen; but you know we have only to obey the King's orders and leave the rest to him. He will punish my naughty children if he sees fit, and reward my good ones; so I shall leave them to him, and go cheerfully on with my own work. That is the only way to keep our lovely world in order and be happy. Now, call your brothers and sisters and we will have our spring frolic together."

They all came, and had a merry time; for as every one knows, April has every kind of weather; so each had a turn to show what he or she could do, and by May-day things were in fine trim, though East would nip the May queen's little nose, and all Sunny's efforts could only coax out a few hardy dandelions for the eager hands to pick.

But the children were happy, for spring had come; Mother Nature was awake again, and now all would be well with the world.

# The Fairy Spring

ONE SUMMER MORNING a party of little wood-people were talking together about something which interested them very much. The fruit-fairy was eating her breakfast as she swung on a long spray of the raspberry-vines that waved in the wind; a blue-bird was taking his bath in the pool below, looking as if a bit of the sky had fallen into the water as he splashed and shook the drops from his wings; Skip, the squirrel, was resting on the mossy wall, after clearing out his hole of last year's nuts, to be ready for a new supply; Spin, the spider, was busily spreading her webs to bleach, and Brownie, the little bear, was warming his fuzzy back in the sunshine, for his den was rather dark and cold.

"It is such a pity that no one understands what the brook is trying to tell them. If they only knew about the fairy spring as we do, this is just the day to set out and find it," said Iris, the elf, as she took the last sip of raspberry shrub from the pretty red cup, and wiped her lips on a napkin Spin had made for her.

"Ah, if they only did! how glad I should be to show them the way," answered the blue-bird, as he dried his feathers on a mossy stone, while the caddis-worms all popped their heads out of sight in their little stone houses for fear he might eat them up.

"I have called every child I see, and done my best to lead them up the mountain; but they won't come, and I cannot make them understand the sweet words the brook keeps singing. How dull human creatures are! Even Brownie knows this song, though he is a dear, clumsy thing, always going to sleep when he is not eating," said Skip, with a twinkle in his bright eye; for he and the little bear were good friends, though one was so brisk and the other so big and awkward.

"Of course I do; I've heard it ever since I was born, and the first long walk I took was up the mountain to find the wonderful spring. I drank of it, and have been the happiest creature alive ever since," answered Brownie, with a comfortable roll on the green grass.

"I am too busy to go, but my cousin Velvet-back often comes down and tells me about the splendid life he leads up there, where no foot ever treads on him, no hand ever breaks his webs, and everything is so still and bright that he always is in a hurry to get home again. When my weaving and bleaching are all done I am going up to see for myself;" and Spin shook off the tiny drops of dew which shone like diamonds on her largest web.

"There is one child who comes every day to look at the brook and listen to its babble as it runs under the little bridge over there. I think *she* will soon hear what it says, and then we will lead her along higher and higher till she finds the spring, and is able to tell every one the happy secret," said Iris, shaking out her many-colored robe before she skimmed away to float over the pool, so like a glittering dragon-fly few guessed that she was a fairy.

"Yes, she is a sweet child," said the bluebird, hopping to the wall to look along the lane to see if she was coming. "She never throws pebbles in the water to disturb the minnows, nor breaks the ferns only to let them die, nor troubles us as we work and play as most children do. She leans there and watches us as if she loved us, and sings to herself as if she were half a bird. I like her, and I hope she will be the first to find the spring."

"So do I," said Skip, going to sit by his friend and watch for the child, while Brownie peeped through a chink in the wall that she might not be frightened at sight of him, small as he was.

"She is coming! she is coming!" called Iris, who had flown to the railing of the rustic bridge, and danced for joy as a little figure came slowly down the winding lane.

A pretty child, with hair like sunshine, eyes blue as the sky, cheeks like the wild roses nodding to her on either side of the way, and a voice as sweet as the babbling brook she loved to sing with. May was never happier than when alone in the woods; and every morning, with her cup, and a little roll of bread in her basket, she wandered away to some of her favorite nooks, to feast on berries, play with the flowers, talk to the birds, and make friends with all the harmless wood-creatures who soon knew and welcomed her.

She had often wondered what the brook sang, and tried to catch the words it seemed to be calling to her. But she never quite understood till this day, for when she came to the bridge and saw her friends—blue-bird, squirrel, and dragon-fly—waiting for her, she smiled, and waved her hand to them, and just at that moment she heard the song of the brook quite plainly,—

> "I am calling, I am calling,
>     As I ripple, run, and sing,
> Come up higher, come up higher,
>     Come and find the fairy spring.
> Who will listen, who will listen
>     To the wonders I can tell,

Of a palace built of sunshine,
    Where the sweetest spirits dwell?—
Singing winds, and magic waters,
    Golden shadows, silver rain,
Spells that make the sad heart happy,
    Sleep that cures the deepest pain.
Cheeks that bloom like summer roses,
    Smiling lips and eyes that shine,
Come to those who climb the mountain,
    Find and taste the fairy wine.
I am calling, I am calling,
    As I ripple, run, and sing;
Who will listen, who will listen,
    To the story of the spring?"

"Where is it; oh, where is it?" cried May, when the song ended; for she longed to see this lovely place and enjoy these beautiful things.

"Go up higher, go up higher,
    Far beyond the waterfall.
Follow Echo up the mountain,
    She will answer to your call.
Bird and butterfly and blossom,
    All will help to show the way;
Lose no time, the day is going,
    Find the spring, dear little May,"

sung the brook; and the child was enchanted to hear the sweet voice talking to her of this pleasant journey.

"Yes, I will go at once. I am ready, and have no fear, for the woods are full of friends, and I long to see the mountain top; it must be so lovely up there," she said, looking through the green arches where the brook came dancing down over the rocks, far away to the gray peak, hidden in clouds.

There lay the fairy spring, and she was going to find it. No one would miss her, for she often played all day in the forest and went home with the lambs at night. The brook said, "Make haste!" so away she went over the wall, with Skip leaping before her, as if to show the safest stones to set her little feet on. Iris waved the raspberry-sprays, to attract her with the ripe fruit, and when the basket was nearly full, Blue-bird flew from tree to tree to lead her on further into the wood. Brownie dodged behind the rocks and fallen logs, waiting for his turn to come, as he had a fine surprise for the little traveller by and by.

It was a lovely road, and May went happily on, with thick moss underneath, shady boughs overhead, flowers to nod and smile at her, and friends to guard, guide, and amuse her. Every ant stopped work to see her pass; every mosquito piped his little song in her ear; birds leaned out of their nests to bid her good-day, and the bright-eyed snakes, fearing to alarm her, hid under the leaves. But lovely butterflies flew round her in clouds; and she looked like a pretty one herself, with her blue gown and sunny hair blowing in the wind.

So she came at last to the waterfall. Here the brook took a long leap over some high rocks, to fall foaming into a basin fringed with ferns; out of which it flowed again, to run faster than ever down to join the river rolling through the valley, to flow at last into the mighty ocean and learn a grander song.

"I never can get up there without wings," said May, as she looked at the high rocks with a tangle of vines all over them. Then she remembered what the brook told her, and called out,—

"Echo, are you here?"

"Here!" answered an airy voice.

"How can I climb up?"

"Climb up."

"Yes; but can I get through the vines?"

"Through the vines."

"It is very high, but I can try it."

"Try it, try it," answered the voice so clearly that May could not doubt what to do.

"Well, if I'm brave I shall be helped."

"Be helped," answered Echo.

"Now I'm coming, and I hope I shall find you, sweet Echo."

"Find sweet Echo," sung the voice; and when May laughed, a softer laugh answered her so gayly that she forgot her fear in eagerness to see this new friend, hiding above the waterfall.

Up she went, and as if fairy hands cleared the way for her, the tangled vines made a green ladder for her feet, while every time she stopped for breath and called, as she peeped into the shadowy nooks or looked at the dashing water, "Are you here?" the mocking voice always answered from above,—

"Here!"

So she climbed safely up and sat to rest at the top, looking down the valley where the brook danced and sparkled as if glad to see her on her way. The air blew freshly, and the sun shone more warmly here, for the trees were not so thick, and lovely glimpses of far-off hills and plains, like pictures set in green frames, made one eager to go on and see more.

Skip and Blue-bird kept her company, so she did not feel lonely, and followed these sure guides higher and higher, till she came out among the great bare cliffs, where rocks lay piled as if giants had been throwing them about in their rough play.

"Oh, how large the world is! and what a little thing I am!" said May, as she looked out over miles of country so far below that the towns looked like toy villages, and people like ants at work. A strong wind blew, all was very still, for no bird sang, and no flowers bloomed; only green moss grew on the rocks, and tiny pines no longer than her finger carpeted the narrow bits of ground here and there. An eagle flew high overhead, and great white clouds sailed by, so near that May could feel their damp breath as they passed.

The child felt a little fear, all was so vast and strange and wonderful; and she seemed so weak and small for a moment she half wished she had not come. She was hungry and tired, but her basket was empty, and no water appeared. She sighed, and looked from the mountain top, hidden in mist, to the sunny valley where mother was, and a tear was about to fall, when Iris came floating to her like a blue and silver butterfly, and alighting on her hand let May see her lovely little face, and hear her small voice as she smiled and sung,—

> "Have no fear,
> Friends are here,
> To help you on your way.
> The mountain's breast
> Will give you rest,
> And we a feast, dear May.
> Here at your feet
> Is honey sweet,
> And water fresh to sip.
> Fruit I bring
> On Blue-bird's wing,
> And nuts sends merry Skip.
> Rough and wild,
> To you, dear child,

Seems the lonely mountain way;
But have no fear,
For friends are near,
To guard and guide, sweet May."

Then at the tap of the fairy's wand up gushed fresh water from the rock; Blue-bird dropped a long stalk of grass strung with raspberries like red beads; Skip scattered his best nuts; and Brownie came lumbering up with a great piece of honey-comb, folded in vine-leaves. He had found a wild-bees' nest, and this was his surprise. He was so small and gentle, and his little eyes twinkled so kindly, that May could not be afraid, and gladly sat down on the crisp moss to eat and drink with her friends about her.

It was a merry lunch, for all told tales, and each amused the little pilgrim in his or her pretty way. The bird let her hold him on her hand and admire his lovely blue plumes. Skip chattered and pranced till there seemed to be a dozen squirrels there instead of one. Brownie stood on his head, tried to dance, and was so funny in his clumsy attempts to outdo the others that May laughed till many echoes joined in her merriment. Iris told her splendid stories of the fairy spring, and begged her to go on, for no one ever had so good a chance as she to find out the secret and see the spirit who lived on the mountain top.

"I am strong and brave now, and will not turn back. Come with me, dear creatures, and help me over these great rocks, for I have no wings," said May, trudging on again, much refreshed by her rest.

"I'll carry you like a feather, my dear; step up and hold fast, and see me climb," cried Brownie, glad to be of use.

So May sat on his fuzzy back as on a soft cushion, and his strong legs and sharp claws carried him finely over the rough, steep places, while Blue-bird and Skip went beside her, and Iris flew in front to show the way. It was a very hard journey, and poor fat Brownie panted and puffed, and often stopped to rest. But May was so surprised and charmed with the lovely clouds all about her that she never thought of being tired. She forgot the world below, and soon the mist hid it from her, and she was in a world of sunshine, sky, and white clouds floating about like ships in a sea of blue air. She seemed to be riding on them when one wrapped her in its soft arms; and more than once a tiny cloud came and sat in her lap, like a downy lamb, which melted when she tried to hold it.

"Now we are nearly there, and Velvet comes to meet us. These fine fellows are the only creatures who live up here, and these tiny star-flowers the only green things that grow," said Iris, at last, when all the clouds were underneath, and the sky overhead was purple and gold, as the sun was going down.

Velvet ran nimbly to give May a silver thread which would lead her straight to the spring; and the path before her was carpeted with the pretty white stars, that seemed to smile at her as if glad to welcome her. She was so eager that she forgot her weariness, and hurried on till she came at last to the mountain top, and there like a beautiful blue eye looking up to heaven lay the fairy spring.

May ran to look into it, thinking she would see only the rock below and the clouds above; but to her wonder there was a lovely palace reflected in the clear water, and shining as if made of silver, with crystal bells chiming with a sound like water-drops set to music.

"Oh, how beautiful! Is it real? Who lives there? Can I go to it?" cried May, longing to sink down and find herself in that charming palace, and know to whom it belonged.

"You cannot go till you have drunk of the water and slept by the spring; then the spirit will appear, and you will know the secret," answered Iris, filling a pearly shell that lay on the brim of the spring.

"Must I stay here all alone? I shall be cold and afraid so far from my own little bed and my dear mother," said May, looking anxiously about her, for the sky was growing dim and night coming on.

"We will stay with you, and no harm can come to you, for the spirit will be here while you sleep. Drink and dream, and in the morning you will be in a new world."

While Iris spoke Brownie had piled up a bed of star-flowers in a little crevice of the rock; Velvet had spun a silken curtain over it to keep the dew off; Blue-bird perched on the tallest stone to keep watch; and when May had drunk a cup of the fairy water, and lay down, with Skip rolled up for a pillow, and Brownie at her feet for a warm rug, Iris waved her wand and sung a lullaby so sweet that the child was in dreamland at once.

When she woke it was day, but she had no time to see the rosy sky, the mist rolling away, or the sunshine dazzling down upon the world, for there before her rising from the spring, was the spirit, so beautiful and smiling, May could only clasp her hands and look. As softly as a cloud the spirit floated toward her, and with a kiss as cool as a dew-drop, she said in a voice like a fresh wind,—

"Dear child, you are the first to come and find me. Welcome to the mountain and the secret of the spring. It is this: whoever climbs up and drinks this water will leave all pain and weariness behind, and grow healthy in body, happy in heart, and learn to see and love all the simple

"The Fairy Spring." From *Lulu's Library, Vol. 2:
The Frost King,* 1887.

wholesome things that help to keep us good and gay. Do you feel tired now, or lonely, or afraid? Has the charm begun to work?"

"Yes," cried May, "I think it has, for I feel so happy, light, and well, I could fly like a bird. It is so lovely here I could stay all my life if I only had mamma to enjoy it with me."

"She will come, and many others. Little children often are wiser than grown people, and lead them up without knowing it. Look and see what you have done by this longing of yours for the mountain top, and the brave journey that brought you here."

Then the spirit touched May's eyes, and looking down she saw the little path by which she had come grow wider and smoother, till it wound round and round the mountain like a broad white ribbon, and up this pleasant path came many people. Some were pale and sad; some lame, some ill; some were children in their mothers' arms; some old and bent, but were climbing eagerly up toward the fairy spring,—sure of help and health when they arrived.

"Can you cure them all?" asked May, delighted to see what hope and comfort her journey had given others.

"Not all; but every one will be the better for coming, even the oldest, the saddest, and the sickest; for my four servants, Sunshine, Fresh-air, Water, and Rest, can work miracles, as you will see. Souls and bodies need their help, and they never fail to do good if people will only come to them and believe in their power."

"I am so glad, for mamma is often ill, and loves to come to the hills and rest. Shall I see her soon? Can I go and tell her all I have learned, or must I stay till she comes?" asked May, longing to run and skip, she felt so well with the fairy water bubbling in her veins.

"Go and tell the news, and lead the others up. You will not see me, but I am here; and my servants will do their work faithfully, for all who are patient and brave. Farewell, dear child, no harm will come to you, and your friends are waiting to help you down. But do not forget when you are in the valley, or you will never find the fairy spring again."

Then the spirit vanished like mist, and May ran away, singing like a bird, and skipping like a little goat, so proud and happy she felt as if she could fly like a thistle-down. The path seemed very easy now, and her feet were never tired. Her good friends joined her by the way, and they had a merry journey back to the valley. There May thanked them and hastened to tell all she had seen and heard and done. Few believed her; most people said, "The child fell asleep and dreamed it." A few invalids looked up and sighed to be there, but had no courage to climb so far. A poet said he would go at once, and set off; so did a man who had lost his wife and little children, and was very sad. May's mother believed every word, and went hand in hand with the happy child along the path that grew wider and smoother with every pair of feet that passed.

The wood-creatures nodded at May, and rejoiced to see the party go; but there was no need of them now, so they kept out of sight, and only the child and the poet saw them. Every one enjoyed the journey, for each hour they felt better; and when at last they reached the spring, and May filled her little cup for them to drink the sweet water, every one tasted and believed, for health and happiness came to them with a single draught.

The sad man smiled, and said he felt so near to heaven and his lost children up there that he should stay. The poet began to sing the loveliest songs he ever made, and pale mamma looked like a rose, as she lay on the star-flowers, breathing the pure air, and basking in the sunshine. May was the spirit of the spring for them, and washed away the tears, the wrinkles, and the lines of pain with the blessed water, while the old mountain did its best to welcome them with mild air, cloud pictures, and the peace that lies above the world.

That was the beginning of the great cure; for when this party came down all so beautifully changed, every one began to hurry away to try their fortune also. Soon the wide road wound round and round, and up it journeyed pilgrims from all parts of the world, till the spirit and her servants had hundreds of visitors each day. People tried to build a great house up there, and make money out of the spring; but every building put up blew away, the water vanished, and no one was cured till the mountain top was free again to all.

Then the spring gushed up more freshly than before; the little star-flowers bloomed again, and all who came felt the beauty of the quiet place, and were healed of all their troubles by the magic of the hills where the spirit of health still lives to welcome and bless whoever go to find her.

# Queen Aster

FOR MANY SEASONS the Golden-rods had reigned over the meadow, and no one thought of choosing a king from any other family, for they were strong and handsome, and loved to rule.

But one autumn something happened which caused great excitement among the flowers. It was proposed to have a queen, and such a thing had never been heard of before. It began among the Asters; for some of them grew outside the wall beside the road, and saw and heard what went on in the great world. These sturdy plants told the news to their relations inside; and so the Asters were unusually wise and energetic flowers, from the little white stars in the grass to the tall sprays tossing their purple plumes above the mossy wall.

"Things are moving in the great world, and it is time we made a change in our little one," said one of the roadside Asters, after a long talk with a wandering wind. "Matters are not going well in the meadow; for the Golden-rods rule, and they care only for money and power, as their name shows. Now, *we* are descended from the stars, and are both wise and good, and our tribe is even larger than the Golden-rod tribe; so it is but fair that we should take our turn at governing. It will soon be time to choose, and I propose our stately cousin, Violet Aster, for queen this year. Whoever agrees with me, say Aye."

Quite a shout went up from all the Asters; and the late Clovers and But-tercups joined in it, for they were honest, sensible flowers, and liked fair play. To their great delight the Pitcher-plant, or Forefathers' Cup, said "Aye" most decidedly, and that impressed all the other plants; for this fine family came over in the "Mayflower," and was much honored every where.

But the proud Cardinals by the brook blushed with shame at the idea of a queen; the Fringed Gentians shut their blue eyes that they might not see the bold Asters; and Clematis fainted away in the grass, she was so shocked. The Golden-rods laughed scornfully, and were much amused at the suggestion to put them off the throne where they had ruled so long.

"Let those discontented Asters try it," they said. "No one will vote for that foolish Violet, and things will go on as they always have done; so, dear friends, don't be troubled, but help us elect our handsome cousin who was born in the palace this year."

In the middle of the meadow stood a beautiful maple, and at its foot lay a large rock overgrown by a wild grape-vine. All kinds of flowers sprung up here; and this autumn a tall spray of Golden-rod and a lovely violet Aster grew almost side by side, with only a screen of ferns between them. This was called the palace; and seeing their cousin there made the Asters feel that their turn had come, and many of the other flowers agreed with them that a change of rulers ought to be made for the good of the kingdom.

So when the day came to choose, there was great excitement as the wind went about collecting the votes. The Golden-rods, Cardinals, Gentians, Clematis, and Bitter-sweet voted for the Prince, as they called the handsome fellow by the rock. All the Asters, Buttercups, Clovers, and Pitcher-plants voted for Violet; and to the surprise of the meadow the Maple dropped a leaf, and the Rock gave a bit of lichen for her also. They seldom took part in the affairs of the flower people,—the tree living so high above them, busy with its own music, and the rock being so old that it seemed lost in meditation most of the time; but they liked the idea of a queen (for one was a poet, the other a philosopher), and both believed in gentle Violet.

Their votes won the day, and with loud rejoicing by her friends she was proclaimed queen of the meadow and welcomed to her throne.

"We will never go to Court or notice her in any way," cried the haughty Cardinals, red with anger.

"Nor we! Dreadful, unfeminine creature! Let us turn our backs and be grateful that the brook flows between us," added the Gentians, shaking their fringes as if the mere idea soiled them.

Clematis hid her face among the vine leaves, feeling that the palace was no longer a fit home for a delicate, high-born flower like herself. All the Golden-rods raged at this dreadful disappointment, and said many untrue and disrespectful things of Violet. The Prince tossed his yellow head behind the screen, and laughed as if he did not mind, saying carelessly,—

"Let her try; she never can do it, and will soon be glad to give up and let me take my proper place."

So the meadow was divided: one half turned its back on the new queen; the other half loved, admired, and believed in her; and all waited to see how the experiment would succeed. The wise Asters helped her with advice; the Pitcher-plant refreshed her with the history of the brave Puritans who loved liberty and justice and suffered to win them; the honest Clovers sweetened life with their sincere friendship, and the cheerful Buttercups brightened her days with kindly words and deeds. But her best help came from the rock and the tree,—for when she needed strength she leaned her delicate head against the rough breast of the rock, and courage seemed to come to her from the wise old stone that had borne the storms of a hundred years; when her heart was heavy with care or wounded by unkindness, she looked up to the beautiful tree, always full of soft music, always pointing heavenward, and was comforted by these glimpses of a world above her.

The first thing she did was to banish the evil snakes from her kingdom; for they lured the innocent birds to death, and filled many a happy nest with grief. Then she stopped the bees from getting tipsy on the wild grapes and going about stupid, lazy, and cross, a disgrace to their family and a terror to the flowers. She ordered the field-mice to nibble all the stems of the clusters before they were ripe; so they fell and withered, and did no harm. The vine was very angry, and the bees and wasps scolded and stung; but the Queen was not afraid, and all her good subjects thanked her. The Pitcher-plant offered pure water from its green and russet cups to the busy workers, and the wise bees were heartily glad to see the Grape-vine saloon shut up.

The next task was to stop the red and black ants from constantly fighting; for they were always at war, to the great dismay of more peaceful insects. She bade each tribe keep in its own country, and if any dispute came up, to bring it to her, and she would decide it fairly. This was a hard task; for the ants loved to fight, and would go on struggling after their bodies were separated from their heads, so fierce were they. But she made them friends at last, and every one was glad.

Another reform was to purify the news that came to the meadow. The wind was telegraph-messenger; but the birds were reporters, and some of them very bad ones. The larks brought tidings from the clouds, and were always welcome; the thrushes from the wood, and all loved to hear their pretty romances; the robins had domestic news, and the lively wrens bits of gossip and witty jokes to relate. But the magpies made much mischief with their ill-natured tattle and evil tales, and the crows criticised and condemned every one who did not believe and do just as they did; so the magpies were forbidden to go gossiping about the meadow, and the gloomy black crows were ordered off the fence where they liked to sit cawing dismally for hours at a time.

Every one felt safe and comfortable when this was done, except the Cardinals, who liked to hear their splendid dresses and fine feasts talked about, and the Golden-rods, who were so used to living in public that they missed the excitement, as well as the scandal of the magpies and the political and religious arguments and quarrels of the crows.

A hospital for sick and homeless creatures was opened under the big burdock leaves; and there several belated butterflies were tucked up in their silken hammocks to sleep till spring, a sad lady-bug who had lost all her children found comfort in her loneliness, and many crippled ants sat talking over their battles, like old soldiers, in the sunshine.

It took a long time to do all this, and it was a hard task, for the rich and powerful flowers gave no help. But the Asters worked bravely, so did the Clovers and Buttercups; and the Pitcher-plant kept open house with the old-fashioned hospitality one so seldom sees now-a-days. Everything seemed to prosper, and the meadow grew more beautiful day by day. Safe from their enemies the snakes, birds came to build in all the trees and bushes, singing their gratitude so sweetly that there was always music in the air. Sunshine and shower seemed to love to freshen the thirsty flowers and keep the grass green, till every plant grew strong and fair, and passersby stopped to look, saying with a smile,—

"What a pretty little spot this is!"

The wind carried tidings of these things to other colonies, and brought back messages of praise and good-will from other rulers, glad to know that the experiment worked so well.

This made a deep impression on the Golden-rods and their friends, for they could not deny that Violet had succeeded better than any one dared to hope; and the proud flowers began to see that they would have to give in, own they were wrong, and become loyal subjects of this wise and gentle queen.

"We shall have to go to Court if ambassadors keep coming with such gifts and honors to her Majesty; for they wonder not to see us there, and will tell that we are sulking at home instead of shining as *we* only can," said the Cardinals, longing to display their red velvet robes at the feasts which Violet was obliged to give in the palace when kings came to visit her.

"Our time will soon be over, and I'm afraid we must humble ourselves or lose all the gayety of the season. It is hard to see the good old ways changed; but if they must be, we can only gracefully submit," answered the Gentians, smoothing their delicate blue fringes, eager to be again the belles of the ball.

Clematis astonished every one by suddenly beginning to climb the maple-tree and shake her silvery tassels like a canopy over the Queen's head.

"I cannot live so near her and not begin to grow. Since I must cling to something, I choose the noblest I can find, and look up, not down, forevermore," she said; for like many weak and timid creatures, she was easily guided, and it was well for her that Violet's example had been a brave one.

Prince Golden-rod had found it impossible to turn his back entirely upon her Majesty, for he was a gentleman with a really noble heart under his yellow cloak; so he was among the first to see, admire, and love the modest faithful flower who grew so near him. He could not help hearing her words of comfort or reproof to those who came to her for advice. He saw the daily acts of charity which no one else discovered; he knew how many trials came to her, and how bravely she bore them; how humbly she asked help, and how sweetly she confessed her shortcomings to the wise rock and the stately tree.

"She has done more than ever we did to make the kingdom beautiful and safe and happy, and I'll be the first to own it, to thank her and offer my allegiance," he said to himself, and waited for a chance.

One night when the September moon was shining over the meadow, and the air was balmy with the last breath of summer, the Prince ventured to serenade the Queen on his wind-harp. He knew she was awake; for he had peeped through the ferns and seen her looking at the stars with her violet eyes full of dew, as if something troubled her. So he sung his sweetest song, and her Majesty leaned nearer to hear it; for she much longed to be friends with the gallant Prince, and only waited for him to speak to own how dear he was to her, because both were born in the palace and grew up together very happily till coronation time came.

As he ended she sighed, wondering how long it would be before he told her what she knew was in his heart.

Golden-rod heard the soft sigh, and being in a tender mood, forgot his pride, pushed away the screen, and whispered, while his face shone and his voice showed how much he felt,—

"What troubles you, sweet neighbor? Forget and forgive my unkindness, and let me help you if I can,—I dare not say as Prince Consort, though I love you dearly; but as a friend and faithful subject, for I confess that you are fitter to rule than I."

As he spoke the leaves that hid Violet's golden heart opened wide and let him see how glad she was, as she bent her stately head and answered softly,—

"There is room upon the throne for two: share it with me as King, and let us rule together; for it is lonely without love, and each needs the other."

What the Prince answered only the moon knows; but when morning came all the meadow was surprised and rejoiced to see the gold and purple flowers standing side by side, while the maple showered its rosy leaves over them, and the old rock waved his crown of vine-leaves as he said,—

"This is as it should be; love and strength going hand in hand, and justice making the earth glad."

# The Brownie and the Princess

SHE WAS NOT A REAL BROWNIE, but a little girl named Betty, who lived with her father in a cottage near a great forest. They were poor; so Betty always wore a brown frock, a big brown hat, and, being out in the sun a great deal, her face was as brown as a berry, though very pretty with its rosy cheeks, dark eyes, and curly hair blowing in the wind. She was a lively little creature, and having no neighbors she made friends with the birds and flowers, rabbits and squirrels, and had fine frolics with them, for they knew and loved her dearly. Many people drove through the beautiful wood, which was not far from the King's palace; and when they saw the little girl dancing with the daisies in the meadow, chasing squirrels up the trees, splashing in the brook, or sitting under her big hat like an elf under a mushroom, they would say, "There is the Brownie."

Betty was wild and shy, and always tried to hide if any one called to her; and it was funny to see her vanish in a hollow tree, drop down in the tall grass, or skip away into the ferns like a timid rabbit. She was afraid of the fine lords and ladies, who laughed at her and called her names, but never thought to bring a book or a toy or say a kind word to the lonely little girl.

Her father took care of the deer in the King's park and was away all day, leaving Betty to sweep the little house, bake the brown bread, and milk Daisy the white cow, who lived in the shed behind the cottage and was Betty's dearest friend. They had no pasture for her to feed in; so, when the work was done, Betty would take her knitting and drive Daisy along the road where she could eat the grass on either side till she had had enough and lay down to rest under some shady tree. While the cow chewed her cud and took naps, the little girl would have fine games among her playmates, the wood creatures, or lie watching the clouds, or swing on the branches of the trees, or sail leaf boats in the brook. She was happy; but she longed for some one to talk to, and tried vainly to learn what the birds sang all day long. There were a great many about the cottage, for no one troubled them, and they were so tame they would eat out of her hand and sit on her head. A stork family lived on the roof, swallows built their clay nests under the eaves, and wrens chirped in their little homes among the red and white roses that climbed up to peep in at Betty's window. Wood-pigeons came to pick up the grain she scattered for them, larks went singing up from the grass close by, and nightingales sang her to sleep.

"If I only knew what they said, we could have such happy times together. How can I ever learn?" sighed Betty, as she was driving Daisy home one day at sunset.

She was in the wood, and as she spoke she saw a great gray owl fluttering on the ground as if he was hurt. She ran at once to see what ailed the bird, and was not afraid, though his round eyes stared at her, and he snapped his hooked beak as if very angry.

"Poor thing! its leg is broken," she said, wondering how she could help it.

"No, it is n't; it's my wing. I leaned out of my nest up there to watch a field mouse, and a ray of sunshine dazzled me so I tumbled down. Pick me up, child, and put me back, and I shall be all right."

Betty was so surprised to hear the owl speak that she did not stir; and thinking she was frightened at his cross tone, the gray bird said more gently, with a blink of its yellow eyes and a wise nod,—

"I shouldn't speak to every one, nor trust any other child; but I know you never hurt anything. I've watched you a long time, and I like you; so I'm going to reward you by giving you the last wish you made, whatever it is. I can: I'm a wizard, and I know all sorts of magic charms. Put me in my nest, tell me your wish, and you shall have it."

"Oh, thank you!" cried Betty, joyfully. "I wished to understand what birds say."

"Dear me, that's a wish that may make trouble; but I'll grant it if you won't tell any one how you learned the secret. I can't have people coming to me, and my neighbors won't want their gossip heard by many ears. They won't mind you, and it will amuse you, poor thing!" said the owl, after a pause.

Betty promised, and, holding the fat bird carefully in her arm, she climbed up the old oak and put him safely in his hole, where he settled himself with a great ruffling of feathers and a hoot of pleasure at being home again.

"Now, pull the tallest bit of down off my right ear and put it in your own; then you will hear what the birds say. Good-night; I'm used up and want to rest," said the owl, with a gape.

"Thank you," said Betty, and ran after Daisy, who was slowly eating her way home.

The bit of down lay snugly in Betty's ear, and in a moment she heard many sweet voices called to one another,—"Good-night!" "Happy dreams!" "A bright to-morrow;" "Lie still, my darlings;" "Hush, my birdie, sleep till day,"–and all sorts of pretty things, as the wood-birds were going to bed with the sun. When she came to the cottage the papa stork was standing on one leg, while the mamma tucked the little ones under her wings, scolding now and then as a red bill or a long leg popped out. The doves were cooing tenderly in the pine that rustled near by, the swallows, skimming over the ground to catch and bring their babies a few more gnats for supper, and the wrens were twittering among the roses like the little gossips they were.

"Now I shall know what they all are saying," cried Betty, trying to hear the different voices; for there were so many going at once it was difficult to understand the sweet new language.

So she milked Daisy, set the table, and made ready for her father, who was often late, then took her bowl of bread and milk and sat on the door-step listening with all her might. She always strewed crumbs for the wrens, and they flew down to eat without fear. To-night they came, and as they pecked they talked, and Betty understood every word.

"Here's a fine soft bit, my love," said the papa, as he hopped briskly about, with his bright eye on the little girl. "Have a good supper while I feed the children. The child never forgets us, and saves me many a long journey by giving us these nice crumbs. I wish we could do something for her."

"So do I, and quite tire my wits trying to make some plan to give her pleasure. I often wonder why the little Princess up at the palace has so much and our dear Betty so little. A few of the books and toys that lie about up there would make this child so happy. It is a pity no one thinks of it;" and the kind Mamma Wren sighed as she ate a nice bit close to Betty's bare foot.

"If she was not so shy and would let people speak to her, I think she would soon make friends, she is so pretty and gay," answered the papa, coming back for another load for the hungry babies in the nest.

"The Princess has heard of her and wants to see her. I heard the maids talking about it to-day when I went to call on Cousin Tomtit in the palace garden. They said her Highness was to drive through the pine wood early tomorrow morning to breathe the fresh air, and hoped to see the Brownie and the pretty white cow. Now, if Betty only knew it, she might gather a posy of cowslips, and when the little lady comes give them to her. That would please her very much and bring Betty some pretty gift; for her Highness is generous, though sadly spoilt, I'm afraid."

This fine plan of Mamma Wren's pleased Betty so much that she clapped her hands and startled the birds away.

"I'll do it! I'll do it!" she cried. "I always wanted to see the little Princess father has told me about. She is ill, and cannot run and play as I do, so I should love to please her, and the cowslips are all out. I'll go early and get a hat full, and not run away if she comes."

Betty was so full of this delightful plan that she went early to bed, but did not forget to lean out of her window and peep through the roses into the nest where Mamma Wren brooded over her babies while the papa roosted near by with his head under his wing.

"Good-night, dear birds; thank you very much," whispered Betty; but they did not mind her, and only twittered sleepily as if a dream disturbed them.

> "Up, up, little maid;
>     Day has begun.
> Welcome with us
>     Our father, the sun!"

sang the larks, as they rose from the grass and waked Betty with their sweet voices.

> "Tweet, tweet, it is morning;
>     Please get up, mamma.
> Do bring us some breakfast,
>     Our dearest papa,"

twittered the young wrens, with their mouths wide open.

> "Click, clack, here's another day;
> Stretch our wings and fly away
> Over the wood and over the hills,
> Seeking food for our babies' bills;"

and away went the storks with their long legs trailing out behind, while the little ones popped up their heads and stared at the sun.

> "Cluck! cluck!
> Here's good luck:
> Old yellow-legs
> Has laid two eggs,
> All fresh and sweet,
> For our girl to eat,"

cackled the gray hens, picking about the shed where the cock stood crowing loudly.

> "Coo! coo! coo!
> Come, bathe in the dew;
> For the rosy dawn shines
> Through our beautiful pines.
> So kiss, every one,
> For a new day's begun,"

called the doves softly to one another as they billed and cooed and tripped about on their little pink feet.

Betty looked and listened at her window, and was so happy she kissed the roses nodding at her, then ran down to make the porridge, singing like a bird herself. When her father had gone away to work she made haste to milk Daisy, sweep the floor, and make all tidy for the day before she went to wait for the Princess.

"Now, you eat your breakfast here while I get the cowslips; for this is a pretty place to be in, and I want you to look very nice when the fine people come," said Betty, as she left the cow to feed in a little shady nook by the road where the grass was green and an old oak made pleasant shade.

The cowslips were all open and as yellow as gold, so Betty made a great nosegay of some and a splendid cowslip-ball of the rest; then she put them in her hat, well sprinkled with water, and sat on a fallen log knitting busily, while Daisy lay down to chew her cud, with a green wreath of oak leaves round her neck for full dress.

They did not have to wait long. Soon the tramp of horses was heard, and along the wood-road came the white ponies tossing their heads, the pretty carriage with coachman and footman in blue and silver coats, and inside the little Princess, with white plumes waving from her hat as she sat by her nurse, wrapt in a soft silken cloak, for the summer air seemed cold to her.

"Oh, there's the Brownie and her pretty white cow! Tell her not to run away, I want to see her and hear her sing," cried the little Princess, eagerly, as they came nearer.

Betty was rather scared, but did not run away; for the nurse was a kind-looking old woman in a high peasant cap, who smiled and nodded at her with a motherly look, and seemed much pleased when she held up the cowslips, saying,—

"Will the little lady have them?"

"Oh yes, I wanted some; I never had a cowslip ball before. How pretty it is! Thank you, Brownie," cried the Princess, with both hands full of flowers as she laughed with pleasure.

"I picked them all for you. I have so many, and I heard you cried for some," said Betty, very glad that she had not run away and spoiled the little lady's drive.

"How did you know?" asked the Princess, staring at her.

"The birds told me," said Betty.

"Oh yes! brownies are fairies, and understand bird-talk; I forgot that. I know what parrots say, but not my other birds. Could you tell me?" asked the Princess, leaning down very earnestly, for any new thing pleased her.

"I think so, if tame ones sing like the wild ones," answered Betty, proud to know more than the fine child did.

"Come to the palace and tell me; come now, I can't wait! My canary sings all day, but I never understand a word, and I must. Tell her to come, Nurse," commanded the Princess, who always had her own way.

"Can you?" asked the old woman. "We will bring you back at night. Her Highness has a fancy to see you, and she will pay you for coming."

"I can't leave Daisy; we have no field to put her in, and if I shut her up in the shed all day she will be hungry and call for me," answered Betty, longing to go, but not liking to leave her dear cow to suffer.

"Put her in that field till you come back; I give you leave. All this land is mine, so no one will blame you. Do it! said the Princess, waving her hand to the footman, who jumped down and had Daisy in the great clover-field before Betty could say a word.

"She will like that; and now I can go if you don't mind my old gown and hat,—I have no other clothes," she said, as the cow began to eat, and the footman opened the carriage door for her.

"I like it. Come in.—Now, go home at once," said the Princess; and there was poor little Betty rolling away in the grand carriage, feeling as if it was all a fairy tale.

The Princess asked a great many questions, and liked her new friend more and more; for she had never spoken to a poor child before, or known how they live. Betty was excited by this fine adventure, and was so gay and charming in her little ways that the old nurse soon forgot to watch lest she should do or say something amiss.

When they drove up to the great marble palace shining in the sun, with green lawns and terraces and blooming gardens all about it, Betty could only hold her breath and look with all her eyes as she was led through splendid halls and up wide stairs into a room full of pretty things, where six gayly dressed maids sewed and chattered together.

The Princess went away to rest, but Betty was told to stay there and be dressed before she went to play with her Highness. The room was full of closets and chests and boxes and baskets, and as the doors opened and the covers flew off, Betty saw piles of pretty frocks, hats, cloaks, and all manner of dainty things for little girls to wear. Never had she dreamed of such splendid clothes, all lace and ribbons, silk and velvet. Hats with flowers and feathers, pretty pink and blue shoes with gold and silver buckles, silk stockings like cobwebs, and muslin and linen petticoats and nightgowns and little caps all embroidered as if by fairy fingers.

She could only stand and look like one in a dream while the maids very kindly took away her poor brown dress and hat, and after much gossip over what looked best, at last put on a rosy muslin frock, a straw hat with roses in it, and some neat shoes and stockings. Then when her hair was smoothed in thick brown curls, they told her to look in the tall mirror and tell what she saw there.

"Oh, what a pretty little girl!" cried Betty, smiling and nodding at the other child, who smiled and nodded back at her. She did not know herself, never having had any glass but a quiet pool in the wood or the brook in the meadow.

The maids laughed, and then she saw who it was, and laughed with them, and danced and courtesied and was very merry till a bell rang and she was ordered to go to her Highness.

It was a lovely room, all hung with blue silk and lace, with a silver bed, and chairs and couches of blue damask, pictures on the walls, flowers in all the windows, and golden cages full of birds. A white cat slept on its cushion, a tiny dog ran about with a golden collar hung with bells, and books and toys were heaped on the tables. The Princess was scolding her nurse because she wanted her to rest longer after the drive; but when Betty came in looking so pretty and gay, the frown changed to a smile, and she cried,—

"How nice you look! Not like a Brownie now; but I hope you have not forgotten about the birds."

"No," said Betty; "let me listen a minute and I'll tell you what they say."

So both were silent, and the maid and nurse kept as still as mice while the canary sang his shrill, sweet song, and Betty's face grew sad as she heard it.

"He says he is tired of his cage and longs to be free among the other birds; for a tree is a better home than a golden palace, and a crumb in the wood sweeter than all the sugar in his silver cup. 'Let me go! let me go! or my heart will break!' That is what he says, and the bulfinch sings the same song; so do the love birds and the beautiful gay one whom I don't know."

"What does Polly say? I understand him when he talks, but not when he scolds and chatters to himself as he is doing now," said the Princess, looking much surprised at what she heard; for she thought her birds must be happy in such fine cages.

Betty listened to the great red and green and blue parrot, who sat on a perch wagging his head and chuckling to himself as if he were enjoying some good joke. Presently Betty blushed and laughed, and looked both troubled and amused at what she heard; for the bird was gabbling away and nodding his head at her in a very funny manner.

"What does he say?" asked the Princess, impatiently.

"Please don't ask. You will not like it. I could n't tell," said Betty, still laughing and blushing.

"You *must* tell, or I'll have Polly's neck wrung. I *will* know every word, and I won't be angry with *you,* no matter what that saucy bird says," commanded the Princess.

"He says this," began Betty, not liking to obey, but afraid poor Polly would be hurt if she did not: "'Now here's a new pet for her Highness to torment. Nice, pretty little girl! Pity she came, to be made much of for a day or two and then thrown away or knocked about like an old doll. She thinks it all very fine here, poor thing! But if she knew all I know she would run away and never come back; for a crosser, more spoilt child than her Highness never lived.'"

Betty dared not go on, for the Princess looked angry; and the maid went to slap the parrot, who gave a queer laugh and snapped at her fingers, squalling out,—

"She is! she is! and you all say it behind her back. *I* know your sly ways. You praise and pet her, and pretend that she is the sweetest darling in the word, when you know that this nice, rosy, good little girl out of the wood is worth a dozen silly, tyrannical princesses. Ha! ha! I'm not afraid to speak the truth, am I, Betty?"

Betty was frightened, but could not help laughing when the naughty bird winked at her as he hung upside down, with his hooked beak wide open and his splendid wings flapping.

"Tell me! tell me!" cried the Princess, forgetting her anger in curiosity.

Betty had to tell, and was very glad when Bonnibelle laughed also, and seemed to enjoy the truth told in this funny way.

"Tell him you know what he says, and ask him, since he is so wise, what I shall do to be as good as you are," said the Princess, who really had a kind little heart and knew that she was petted far too much.

Betty told the parrot she understood his language, and he was so surprised that he got on his perch at once and stared at her, as he said eagerly,—

"Don't let me be punished for telling truth, there's a dear child. I can't take it back, and since you ask my advice, I think the best thing you can do for her Highness is to let her change places with you and learn to be contented and useful and happy. Tell her so, with my compliments."

Betty found this a hard message to give; but it pleased Bonnibelle, for she clapped her hands and cried,—

"I'll ask mamma. Would you like to do it, Brownie, and be a princess?"

"No, thank you," said Betty; "I could n't leave my father and Daisy, and I'm not fit to live in a palace. It's very splendid, but I think I love the little house and the wood and my birds better."

The nurse and the maid held up their hands, amazed at such a fancy; but Bonnibelle seemed to understand, and said kindly,—

"Yes; I think it is very dull here, and much pleasanter in the fields to do as one likes. May I come and play with you, and learn to be like you, dear Betty?"

She looked a little sad as she spoke, and Betty pitied her; so she smiled and answered gladly,—

"Yes, that will be lovely. Come and stay with me, and I will show you all my playmates, and you shall milk Daisy, and feed the hens, and see the rabbits and the tame fawn, and run in the daisy field, and pull cowslips, and eat bread and milk out of my best blue bowl."

"Yes, and have a little brown gown and a big hat like yours, and wooden shoes that clatter, and learn how to knit, and climb trees, and what the birds say!" added Bonnibelle, so charmed at the plan that she jumped off the couch and began to skip about as she had not done for days before.

"Now come and see my toys, and choose any you like; for I'm fond of you, dear, because you tell me new things and are not like the silly little lords and ladies who come to see me, and only quarrel and strut about like peacocks till I'm tired of them."

Bonnibelle put her arm round Betty, and led her away to a long hall so full of playthings that it looked like a splendid toy-shop. Dolls by the dozen were there,—dolls that talked and sang and walked and went to sleep, fine dolls, funny dolls, big and little doll queens and babies, dolls of all nations. Never was there such a glorious party of these dear creatures seen before; and Betty had no eyes for anything else, being a real little girl, full of love for dollies, and never yet had she owned one.

"Take as many as you like," said Bonnibelle. "I'm tired of them."

It nearly took Betty's breath away to think that she might have a dozen dolls if she chose. But she wisely decided that one was enough, and picked out a darling baby-doll in its pretty cradle, with blue eyes shut, and flaxen curls under the dainty cap. It would fill her motherly little soul with joy to have this lovely thing to lie in her arms by day, sleep by her side at night, and live with her in the lonely cottage; for baby could say "Mamma" quite naturally, and Betty felt that she would never be tired of hearing the voice call her by that sweet name.

It was hard to tear herself from the cradle to see the other treasures; but she went to and fro with Bonnibelle, admiring all she saw, till Nurse came to tell them that lunch was ready and her Highness must play no more.

Betty hardly knew how to behave when she found herself sitting at a fine table with a footman behind her chair and all sorts of curious glass and china and silver things before her. But she watched what Bonnibelle did, and so got on pretty well, and ate peaches and cream and cake and dainty white rolls and bonbons with a good appetite. She would not touch the little birds in the silver dish, though they smelt very nice, but said sadly,—

"No, thank you, sir; I couldn't eat my friends."

The footman tried not to laugh; but the Princess pushed away her own plate with a frown, saying,—

"Neither will I. Give me some apricot jelly and a bit of angel cake. Now that I know more about birds and what they think of me, I shall be careful how I treat them. Don't bring any more to my table."

After lunch the children went to the library, where all the best picture-books ever printed were ranged on the shelves, and cosey little chairs stood about where one could sit and read delicious fairy tales all day long. Betty skipped for joy when her new friend picked out a pile of the gayest and best for her to take home; and then they went to the music-room, where a band played beautifully and the Princess danced with her master in a stately way that Betty thought very stupid.

"Now you must dance. I've heard how finely you do it; for some lords and ladies saw you dancing with the daisies, and said it was the prettiest ballet they ever looked at. You *must!* No, please do, dear Betty," said Bonnibelle, commanding at first; then, remembering what the parrot said, she spoke more gently.

"I cannot here before these people. I don't know any steps, and need flowers to dance with me," said Betty.

"Then come on the terrace; there are plenty of flowers in the garden, and I am tired of this," answered Bonnibelle, going through one of the long windows to the wide marble walk where Betty had been longing to go.

Several peacocks were sitting on the steps, and they at once spread their splendid tails and began to strut before the children, making a harsh noise as they tossed the crowns of shining feathers on their heads.

"What do they say?" asked the Princess.

"'Here comes the vain little creature who thinks her fine clothes handsomer than ours, and likes to show them off to poorer people and put on proud airs. We don't admire her; for we know how silly she is, for all her fine feathers.'"

"I won't listen to any more rude words from these bad birds, and I won't praise their splendid tails as I meant to. Go along, you vain things! no one wants you here," cried Betty, chasing the peacocks off the terrace, while the Princess laughed to see them drop their gorgeous trains and go scurrying away with loud squawks of fear.

"It was true. I *am* vain and silly; but no one ever dared to tell me so, and I shall try to do better now I see how foolish those birds look and how sweet you are," she said, when Betty came skipping back to her.

"I'll make a peacock dance for you. See how well I do it!" and Betty began to prance, with her full pink skirt held up, and her head tossed, and her toes turned out, so like the birds that old Nurse and the maid, who had followed, began to laugh as well as Bonnibelle.

It was very funny; and when she had imitated the vain strutting and fluttering of the peacocks, Betty suddenly dropped her skirt, and went hurrying away, flapping her arms like wings and squawking dismally.

She wanted to please the Princess and make her forget the rude things she had been forced to tell; so when she came running back she was glad to find her very merry, and anxious for more fun.

"Now I'll do the tulip dance," said Betty, and began to bow and courtesy to a bed full of splendid flowers, all gold and scarlet, white and purple; and the tulips seemed to bow and courtesy back again like stately lords and ladies at a ball. Such dainty steps, such graceful sweeps and elegant wavings of the arms one never saw before; for Betty imitated the tall blossoms waving in the wind, and danced a prettier minuet with them than any ever seen at court.

"It is wonderful!" said the maid.

"Bless the dear! she must be a real fairy to do all that," said the old nurse.

"Dance again! oh, please dance again, it is so pretty!" cried the Princess, clapping her hands as Betty rose from her farewell courtesy and came smiling toward her.

"I'll give you the wind dance; that is very gay, and this fine floor is so smooth I feel as if my feet had wings."

With that Betty began to flutter to and fro like a leaf blown by the wind; now she went down the terrace as if swept by a strong gust, now she stood still, swaying a little in the soft breath of air, then off she spun as if caught in a storm, eddying round and round till she looked like a stray rose-leaf whisked over the ground. Sometimes she whirled close to the Princess, then blew up against the stout old nurse, but was gone before she could be caught. Once she went down the marble steps at a bound and came flying over the railing as if in truth she did have wings on her nimble feet. Then the gale seemed to die away, and slowly the leaf floated to the ground at Bonnibelle's feet, to lie there rosy, breathless, and tired.

Bonnibelle clapped her hands again; but before she could tell half her delight, a beautiful lady came from the window, where she had seen the pretty ballet. Two little pages carried her long train of silvery silk; two ladies walked beside her, one holding a rose-colored parasol over her head, the other with a fan and cushion; jewels shone on her white hands and neck and in her hair, and she was very splendid, for this was the Queen. But her face was sweet and lovely, her voice very soft, and her smile so kind that Betty was not afraid, and made her best courtesy prettily.

When the red damask cushion was laid on one of the carved stone seats, and the pages had dropped the train, and the maids had shut the parasol and handed the golden fan, they stepped back, and only the Queen and nurse and little girls were left together.

"Does the new toy please you, darling?" asked the shining lady, as Bonnibelle ran to climb into her lap and pour out a long story of the pleasant time she had been having with the Brownie. "Indeed I think she is a fairy, to make you so rosy, gay, and satisfied."

"Who taught you to dance so wonderfully, child?" asked the Queen, when she had kissed her little daughter, glad to see her look so unlike the sad, cross, or listless creature she usually found.

"The wind, Lady Queen," answered Betty, smiling.

"And where did you get the fine tales you tell?"

"From the birds, Lady Queen."

"And what do you do to have such rosy cheeks?"

"Eat brown bread and milk, Lady Queen."

"And how is it that a lonely child like you is so happy and good?"

"My father takes care of me, and my mother in heaven keeps me good, Lady Queen."

When Betty said that, the Queen put out her hand and drew the little girl closer, as if her tender heart pitied the motherless child and longed to help if she only knew how.

Just then the sound of horses' feet was heard in the great courtyard below, trumpets sounded, and every one knew that the king had come home from hunting. Presently, with a jingling of spurs and trampling of boots, he came along the terrace with some of his lords behind him.

Every one began to bow except the Queen, who sat still with the Princess on her knee, for Bonnibelle did not run to meet her father as Betty always did when he came home. Betty thought she would be afraid of the King, and so she would perhaps, if he had worn his crown and ermine cloak and jewels everywhere; but now he was dressed very like her father, in hunter's green, with a silver horn over his shoulder, and no sign of splendor about him but the feather in his hat and the great-ring that glittered when he pulled off his glove to kiss the Queen's hand; so Betty smiled and bobbed her little courtesy, looking boldly up in his face.

He liked that, and knew her, for he had often seen her when he rode through the wood.

"Come hither, Brownie, I have a story you will like to hear," he said, sitting down beside the Queen and beckoning to Betty with a friendly nod.

She went and stood at his knee, eager to hear, while all the lords and ladies bent forward to listen, for it was plain that something had happened beside the killing of a stag that day.

"I was hunting in the great oak wood two hours ago, and had knelt down to aim at a splendid stag," began the King, stroking Betty's brown head, "when a wild boar, very fierce and large, burst out of the ferns behind me just as I fired at the deer. I had only my dagger left to use, but I sprang up to face him, when a root tripped my foot, and there I lay quite helpless, as the furious old fellow rushed at me. I think this little maid here would have been Queen Bonnibelle to-morrow if a brave woodman had not darted from behind a tree and with one blow of his axe killed the beast as he bent his head to gore me. It was your father, Brownie, and I owe my life to him."

As the King ended, a murmur rose, and all the lords and ladies looked as if they would like to give a cheer; but the Queen turned pale and old Nurse ran to fan her, while Bonnibelle put out her arms to her father, crying,—

"No, I will never be a queen if you die, dear papa!"

The King took her on one knee and set Betty on the other, saying gayly,—

"Now what shall we do for this brave man who saved me?"

"Give him a palace to live in, and millions of money," said the Princess, who could think of nothing better.

"I offered him a house and money, but he wanted neither, for he loved his little cottage and had no need of gold, he said. Think again, little maids, and find something he *will* like," said the King, looking at Betty.

"A nice field for Daisy is all he wants, Lord King," she answered boldly; for the handsome brown face with the kind eyes was very like her father's, she thought.

"He shall have it. Now wish three wishes for yourself, my child, and I will grant them if I can."

Betty showed all her little white teeth as she laughed for joy at his splendid offer. Then she said slowly,—

"I have but one wish now, for the Princess has given me a dear doll and many books; so I am the happiest creature in all the kingdom, and have no wants."

"Contented little lass! Who of us can say the same?" said the King, looking at the people round him, who dropped their eyes and looked foolish, for they were always asking favors of the good King. "Well, now let us know the one thing I can do to please brave woodman John's little daughter."

"Please let the Princess come and play with me," said Betty, eagerly.

The lords looked horrified, and the ladies as if they would faint away at the mere idea of such a dreadful thing. But the Queen nodded, Bonnibelle cried, "Oh, do!" and the King laughed as he asked in a surprised tone,—

"But why not come and play with her here? What is there at the cottage that we have not at the palace?"

"Many things, Lord King," answered Betty. "She is tired of the palace and everything in it, she says, and longs to run about in the wood, and be well and gay and busy all day long, as I am. She wants to bake and milk and sweep and knit, and hear the wind blow, and dance with the daisies, and talk with my birds, and dream happy dreams, and love to be alive, as I do."

"Upon my word, here's a bold Brownie! But she is right, I think; and if my Princess can get a pair of cheeks like these down at the cottage, she shall go as often as she likes," said the King, amused at Betty's free words, and struck by the contrast between the two faces before him, one like a pale garden lily and the other like a fresh wild rose.

Then Bonnibelle burst out and told all the story of the day, talking as she had never talked before; and every one listened, amazed to see how lively and sweet her Highness could be, and wondered what had made such a sudden change. But the old nurse went about, saying in a whisper,—

"She is a real Brownie, I know it; for no mortal child would be so bold and bright, and do what she has done,—bewitched both King and Queen, and made her Highness a new child."

So all looked at Betty with great respect; and when at last the talk was over and the King rose to go, with a kiss for each little girl, every one bowed and made way for the Brownie, as if she too were a Princess.

But Betty was not proud; for she remembered the peacocks as she walked hand in hand with Bonnibelle after the royal papa and mamma over the terrace to the great hall, where the feast was spread and music sounding splendidly.

"You shall sit by me and have my golden cup," said Bonnibelle, when the silver horns were still, and all waited for the King to hand the Queen to her place.

"No, I must go home. It is sunset; Daisy must be milked, and father's supper ready when he comes. Let me run away and get my old clothes; these are too fine to wear in the cottage," answered Betty, longing to stay, but so faithful to her duty that even the King's command could not keep her.

"Tell her to stay, papa; I want her," cried Bonnibelle, going to the great gilded chair where her father sat.

"Stay, child," said the King, with a wave of the hand where the great jewel shone like a star.

But Betty shook her head and answered sweetly,—

"Please do not make me, dear Lord King. Daisy needs me, and father will miss me sadly if I do not run to meet him when he comes home."

Then the King smiled, and said heartily,—

"Good child! we will not keep you. Woodman John gave me my life, and I will not take away the comfort of his. Run home, little Brownie, and God bless you!"

Betty tripped upstairs, and put on her old frock and hat, took one of the finest books and the dear doll, leaving the rest to be sent next day, and then tried to slip away by some back door; but there were so many halls and steps she got lost, and came at last into the great hall again. All were eating now; and the meat and wine and spicy pies and piles of fruit smelt very nice, and Betty would have only brown bread and milk for supper; but she did not stay, and no one but the pages saw her as she ran down the steps to the courtyard, like Cinderella hurrying from the hall when the clock struck twelve and all her fine clothes vanished.

She had a very happy walk through the cool green wood, however, and a happy hour telling her father all about this wonderful day; but the happiest time of all was when she went to bed in her little room, with the darling baby fast asleep on her arm, and the wrens talking together among the roses of how much good their wise Brownie would do the Princess in the days to come.

Then Betty fell asleep and dreamed such lovely dreams of the moon with a sweet face like the Queen's smiling at her, of her father looking as proud and handsome as the King, with his axe on his shoulder and the great boar dead at his feet; and Bonnibelle, rosy, gay, and strong, working and playing with her like a little sister in the cottage, while all the birds sang gayly:—

"Bonnibelle! Bonnibelle!
Listen, listen, while we tell
A sweet secret all may know,
How a little child may grow
Like a happy wayside flower,
Warmed by sun, fed by shower,
Rocked by wind, loved by elf,
Quite forgetful of itself;
Full of honey for the bee,
Beautiful for all to see,
Nodding to the passers-by,
Smiling at the summer sky,
Sweetening all the balmy air,
Happy, innocent, and fair.
Flowers like these blossom may
In a palace garden gay;
Lilies tall or roses red,
For a royal hand or head.
But be they low, or be they high,
Under the soft leaves must lie
A true little heart of gold,
Never proud or hard or cold,
But brave and tender, just and free,
Whether it Queen or beggar be;
Else its beauty is in vain,
And never will it bloom again.
This the secret we would tell,
Bonnibelle! Bonnibelle!"

# Mermaids

"I WISH I WERE A SEA-GULL or a fish or a mermaid; then I could swim as much as I like, and not have to stay on this stupid dry land all day," said Nelly, as she sat frowning and punching holes in the sand one summer morning, while the waves came murmuring up on the beach, and a fresh wind sang its pleasant song.

The little girl loved to bathe so well that she wanted to be in the water all the time, and had been forbidden to go into the sea for a day or two because she had a cold. So she was in a pet, and ran away from her playmates to sit and sulk in a lonely spot among the rocks. She had been watching the gulls fly and float, with their white wings shining as they dipped down or soared away in the sunshine. As she wished her wish a very large one swept down upon the sand before her, and startled her by saying in a hoarse tone, as she stared at its bright eyes, the red ring round its neck, and the little tuft on its head,—

"I am the King of the gulls, and I can grant any one of your wishes. Which will you be,—a fish, a bird, or a mermaid?"

"People say there are no mermaids," stammered Nelly.

"There are; only mortals cannot see them unless I give the power. Be quick! I don't like the sand. Choose, and let me be off!" commanded the Great Gull, with an impatient flutter of its wide wings.

"Then I'll be a mermaid, please. I always wanted to see one, and it must be very nice to live always in the water."

"Done!" said the gull, and was gone like a flash.

Nelly rubbed her eyes, and looked about her rather scared; but nothing had happened to her yet, and she was just going to complain that the bird had cheated her, when the sound of soft voices made her climb the rock behind her to see who was singing down there.

She nearly fell off again when she spied two pretty little creatures floating to and fro on the rocking waves. Both had long brown hair, green eyes as clear as crystal, pale faces, and the sweetest voices Nelly had ever heard. But the strange thing was that each little body ended in a shining tail,—one all golden, the other all silver scales. Their little breasts and arms were white as foam, and they wore bracelets of pearls, strings of rosy shells about their necks, and garlands of gay sea-weed in their hair. They were

355

singing as they rocked, and throwing bubbles to and fro as if playing ball. They saw Nelly in a moment, and tossing a great rainbow-colored bubble toward her, cried gayly,—

"Come and play, little friend. We know you, and have often tried to make you see us when you float and dive so bravely in our sea."

"I long to come; but it is so deep there and the waves are so rough that I should be dashed on the rocks," answered Nelly, charmed to see real mermaids at last, and eager to go to them.

"We came for you. The King-gull told us to call you. Slip off your clothes and spring down to us; then we will change you, and you can have your wish," said the mermaids, holding up their arms to her.

"My mother said I must not go into the sea," began Nelly, sadly.

"What is a mother?" asked one little seamaid, while the other laughed as if the word amused her.

"Why, don't you know? Don't you have fathers and mothers down there?" cried Nelly, so surprised that she forgot her wish for a moment.

"No; we are born of the moon and the sea, and we have no other parents," said Goldfin, the shining one.

"How dreadful!" exclaimed Nelly. "Who takes care of you, and where do you live? Without fathers and mothers you cannot have any home."

"We take care of ourselves. All the sea is our home, and we do as we please. Come, come, and see how gay it is!" called Silver-tail, the other mermaid, tossing bubbles like a juggler till the air was full of them as they sailed away on the wind.

Now, if Nelly had not been angry with her good mamma just then, and ready for any disobedience, she would never have been so naughty, or have gone to play with such strange friends. She was very curious to see how they lived, and be able to relate her adventures when she came back, as she was sure she would, all safe and sound. So she dropped her clothes on the rock and splashed into the green pool below, glad to show off her fine swimming. But Goldfin and Silver-tail caught her and bade her drink the spray they held in their hands.

"Sea water is salt and bitter; I don't like it," said Nelly, holding back.

"Then you cannot be like us. Drink, and in a moment see what will happen!" cried Goldfin.

Nelly swallowed the cold drops and caught her breath, for a dreadful pain shot through her from her head to her feet, while the mermaids chanted some strange words and waved their hands over her. It was gone in an instant, and she felt like a cork floating on the water. She wondered, till glancing down she saw that her little white legs were changed to a fish's tail of many colors, which gently steered her along as the waves rippled against her breast.

"Now I am a mermaid," she cried, and looked into the pool to see if her eyes were green, her face pale, and her hair like curly brown sea-weed.

No; she had her child's face still, with rosy cheeks, blue eyes, and yellow curls. She was not disappointed, however, for she thought it a prettier face than the moony ones of her new playmates; so she laughed and said gayly,—

"Now you will play with me and love me, wont' you?"

"What is love?" asked Silver-tail, staring at her.

"Why, when people love they put their arms round one another and kiss, and feel happy in their hearts," answered Nelly, trying to explain the beautiful word.

"How do you kiss?" asked Goldfin, curiously.

Nelly put an arm round the neck of each, and softly kissed them on their cold wet lips.

"Don't you like it? Is it sweet?" she asked.

"I feel that you are warmer than I, but I think oysters taste better," said one; and the other added,—

"Mermaids have no hearts, so that does not make us happier."

"No hearts?" cried Nelly, in dismay. "Can't you love? Don't you know about souls and being good, and all that?"

"No," laughed the mermaids, shaking their heads till the drops flew about like pearls. "We have no souls, and don't trouble about being good. We sing and swim and eat and sleep; is not that enough to make us happy?"

"Dear me, how queer they are!" thought Nelly, half afraid, yet very anxious to go with them and see more of this curious sea-life of which they had spoken. "Don't you care about me at all, and don't you want me to stay with you a little while?" she asked, wondering how she should get on with creatures who could not love her.

"Oh yes, we like you as a new playmate, and are glad you came to see us. You shall have our bracelets to wear, and we will show you all kinds of pretty things down below, if you are not afraid to come," answered the mermaids, dressing her in their garlands and necklaces, and smiling at her so sweetly that she was ready to follow as they swam away with her far out on the great billows that tossed them to and fro but could not drown or harm them now.

Nelly enjoyed it very much, and wondered why the fishermen in their boats did not try to catch them, till she learned that mermaids were invisible and were never caught. This made her feel very safe, and after a fine game of play she let her friends take her by the hand and sink down to the new world below. She expected to find it very gay and splendid, with sea-coral trees growing everywhere, palaces of pearl, and the ground covered with jewels; but it was dim and quiet. Great weeds fanned to and fro as the water stirred them; shells lay about on the sand, and queer creatures crawled or swam everywhere.

The green sea-water was the sky, and ships cast their shadows like clouds over the twilight world below. Several gray-bearded old mermen sat meditating in nooks among the rocks, and a few mermaids lay asleep in the great oyster-shells that opened to receive them and their beds of sea-weed. A soft murmur was in the air like the sound one hears in shells, and no-where did Nelly see any toys or food or fun of any sort.

"Is this the way you live?" she asked, trying not to show how disap-pointed she was.

"Isn't it lovely?" answered Goldfin. "This is my bed, and you shall have the shell between Silver-tail and me. See! it is lined with mother-of-pearl, and has a soft cushion of our best sea-weeds to lie on."

"Are you hungry?" asked Silver-tail. "Come and have some shrimps for dinner,—I know a fine place for them,—or oysters if you like them bet-ter."

Nelly was ready to eat anything, the sea air had given her such a fine appetite; so they swam away to gather the pretty pink shrimps in scallop shells, as little girls gather strawberries in baskets; then they sat down to eat them, and Nelly longed for bread and butter, but dared not say so. She was so surprised at all she saw, that this queer, cold lunch was soon forgot-ten in the wonderful tales the mermaids told her, as they cracked snails and ate them like nuts, or pulled the green sea-apples tasting like pickled limes from the vines that climbed up the rocks.

"You don't seem to have a very large family, or have the others gone to a party somewhere?" asked Nelly, rather tired of the quiet.

"No; there never are many of us. A new brood will be out soon, and then there will be some little mer-babies to play with. We will show you the Wonder-tree, if you are done eating, and tell you all about it," answered Silver-tail, floating away with a wave of the hand.

Nelly and Goldfin followed to a lonely place, where a tall plant grew up from the sand till its branches reached the air above and spread out like floating weeds covered with little pods like those we often snap under our feet as they lie dry upon the beach.

"Only a few of these will bloom; for there never are many mermaids in the sea, you know. It takes long for the tree to reach the light, and it cannot blossom unless the full moon shines on it at midnight; then these buds open, and the water-babies swim away to grow up like us," said Silver-tail.

"Without any nurses to take care of them, or mothers to pet them?" asked Nelly, thinking of the pretty baby at home with whom she was so fond of playing.

"They take care of themselves, and when there are too many in one place the old mermen send away some to another ocean; so we get on quietly, and there is room for all," said Goldfin, contentedly.

"And when you die, what happens?" asked Nelly, much interested in these queer creatures.

"Oh, we grow older and grayer and sit still in a corner till we turn to stone and help make these rocks. I've been told by Barnacle, the old one yonder, that people sometimes find marks of our hands or heads or fins in the stone, and are very much puzzled to know what kind of fish or animal made the prints; that is one of our jokes;" and both the mermaids laughed as if they enjoyed bewildering the wits of the people who were so much wiser than they.

"Well, I think it is much nicer to be buried under grass and flowers when our souls have flown away to heaven," said Nelly, beginning to be glad she was not a "truly" mermaid.

"What is heaven?" asked Silver-tail, stupidly.

"You would not understand if I tried to tell you. I can only say it is a lovely place where we go when we die, and the angels don't puzzle over us at all, but love us and are glad to see us come," said Nelly, soberly.

Both little maids stared at her with their green eyes as if they wanted to understand, but gave it up, and with a whisk of their shining tails darted away, calling to her,—

"Come and play with the crabs; it's great fun."

Nelly was rather afraid of crabs, they nipped her toes so when she went among them; but having no feet now, she felt braver, and was soon having a gay time chasing them over the rocks, and laughing to see them go scrambling sidewise into their holes. The green lobsters amused her very much by the queer way they hitched along, with their great claws ready to grasp and hold whatever they wanted. It was funny to see them wipe their bulging eyes with their feelers and roll them about on all sides. The hermit crabs in their shells were curious, and the great snails popping out their horns; the sea-spiders were very ugly, and she shook with fear when the horrible Octopus went by, with his eight long arms waving about like snakes and his hooked beak snapping.

"Show me something pretty," she begged; "I don't like these ugly things. Haven't you any flowers or birds or animals here to play with?"

"Oh yes, here are our sea anemones, yellow, red, and white, all blooming in their beds; and these lovely plants of every color which you call weeds. Then there are the coral trees, far away, which we will show you some day, and the sponges on the rocks, and many other curious things," answered Goldfin, leading Nelly up and down to see the only flowers they had. Then Silver-tail said,—

"She will like the nautilus boats and the flying fish, and a ride on the dolphins and whales. Come and let her see that we have birds and animals as well as she."

Up they went; and when Nelly saw the lovely red and blue creatures like a fleet of fairy boats floating over the waves, she clapped her hands and cried,—

"We have nothing so beautiful on the land! How delicate and fair they are! Won't the wind tear them to pieces and the storms wreck them?"

"Watch and see!" answered the mermaids, well pleased at her delight; and as a gust blew by every silken sail was furled, the lovely colors vanished, and the fairy boats sank out of sight safely to the bottom of the sea.

"Our sailors can't do that," said Nelly; "and when our ships go down they never come up again."

Just then some fish flew over their heads and splashed down again, while the gulls snapped at them in vain.

"Those are our birds, and here are our horses. People call them porpoises, but we call them dolphins, and have many a fine gallop on their backs," said Goldfin, as a school of great creatures came gambolling by.

Up sprang the mermaids, and went swiftly dashing through the water with high leaps now and then, as their sea-horses reared and plunged, tossing their tails and waving their fins as if they enjoyed the frolic. Nelly did, and wished to ride longer; but a whale appeared, and her playmates went to climb on his back and hear the news from the North Sea. It was like a moving island, and they sat under the fountain as he spouted water and rolled about lazily basking in the sun after his cold voyage.

"Don't we have good times?" asked Silver-tail, when they slid down the slippery sides of the monster and climbed up again as if coasting.

"Splendid! I like to be a mermaid and have no lessons to study, no work to sew, no nurse to scold me, and no mamma to forbid my swimming as much as I choose," said naughty Nelly; but as she spoke and looked toward the land now far away, a little pain went through her heart to remind her that she was not a real mermaid, and still had a conscience, though she would not listen to it.

They played all the afternoon, had an oyster supper, and went early to bed to get a good nap before midnight, because the moon was full and they hoped the Wonder-tree would bloom before morning.

Nelly liked the quiet now; and the soft song of the sea lulled her to sleep, to dream of sailing in a nautilus boat till a dreadful cuttle-fish came after her and she woke in a fright, wondering to find herself lying on a bed of wet weeds in a great shell.

"Come away; it is time, and a lovely night," called the mermaids, and with several new friends they all hurried up to watch the buds open when the moon kissed them.

The sea shone like silver; the stars seemed to float there as well as in the sky, and the wind blew off the shore bringing the sweet smell of hay-fields and gardens. All the sea people sang as they lay rocking on the quiet waves, and Nelly felt as if this were the strangest, loveliest dream she had ever dreamed.

By and by the moon shone full upon the Wonder-tree, and one by one out popped the water-babies, looking like polliwogs, only they had little faces and arms instead of fins. Lively mites they were, swimming away at once in a shoal like minnows, while the older mermaids welcomed them and gave them pretty names as the tiny things came to peep at them and dart between the hands that tried to grasp them. Till dawn they kept in the moonlight, growing fast as they learned to use their little tails and talk in small, sweet voices; but when day came they all sank down to the bottom of the sea, and went to sleep in the shell cradles made ready for them. That was all the care they needed, and after that they had no nursing, but did what they liked, and let the older ones play with them like dolls.

Nelly had several pets, and tried to make them love and mind her; but the queer little creatures laughed in her face when she talked to them, darted away when she wanted to kiss them, and stood on their heads and waggled their bits of tails when she told them to be good. So she let them alone, and amused herself as well as she could with other things; but soon she grew very tired of this strange, idle life, and began to long for some of the dear old plays and people and places she used to like so much.

Every one was kind to her; but nobody seemed to love her, to care when she was good, or wish to make her better when she was selfish or angry. She felt hungry for something all the time, and often sad, though she hardly knew why. She dreamed about her mother, and sometimes woke up feeling for baby, who used to creep into her bed and kiss her eyes open in the morning. But now it was only a water-baby, who would squirm away like a little eel and leave her to think about home and wonder if they missed her there.

"I can't go back, so I must forget," she said, and tried to do it; but it was very hard, and she half wished she was a real mermaid with no heart at all.

"Show me something new; I'm tired of all these plays and sights and toys," she said one day, as she and her two playmates sat stringing little silver and rosy shells for necklaces.

"We are never tired," said Goldfin.

"You haven't any minds, and don't think much or care to know things. I do, and I want to learn a little or make some one happy if I can," said Nelly, soberly, as she looked about the curious world she lived in and saw what a dim, cold, quiet place it was, with the old mermen turning to stone in their nooks, the lazy mermaids rocking in their shells or combing their hair, and the young ones playing like so many stupid little fishes in the sun.

"We can't go to the South Sea yet, and we have nothing more to show you unless a great storm comes up," said Silver-tail.

"Perhaps she would like a wreck; there is a new one not far off," proposed Goldfin. "A big ship went over a small one, and it sank very soon. One of Mother Carey's chickens told me about it this morning, and I thought we might go and see it before it is all spoiled. Things that men make never last very long in our sea."

"Yes, let us go; I long to see and touch something my people made. Your world is wonderful, but I begin to think my own is the best, for me at least," said Nelly, as they left their pearls and swam away to the wreck, which lay down among the rocks, fast going to pieces. "Where are the people?" she asked, as they were about to float in at the broken windows and doors. She was very much afraid that she might see some poor drowned creature, and it would trouble *her,* though the mermaids might not care.

"Little Chick said they were all saved. It was a fruit-ship, and there were only a few passengers. One lady and child and some men went away in the boats to the shore, but left everything else behind."

"I'm so glad!" cried Nelly, feeling her heart warm in her breast at the good news about the mother and little child.

The ship had been loaded with oranges, and the sand was covered with boxes of them broken open, and letting the fruit float to the top of the water. Much was spoiled, but some was still good, and Nelly told the mermaids to taste and see if oranges were not better than salt sea-apples. They did not like them, but played ball with the golden things till Nelly proposed that they should toss some on the shore for the fishermen's children. That suited them; and soon the beach was covered with oranges, and the poor little people were running and screaming with delight to pick up this splendid feast.

"I wish there were some pretty things to give them; but there are only the sailors' bags of clothes all wet, and those are not nice," said Nelly, enjoying this game very much; for she was homesick and longed to hear human voices and see faces like her own. She wanted to do something for some one, and be loved a little. So she peeped all about the ship, and at last, in one cabin better than the others, she found the toys and clothes of the little child and its mother. She was very glad of that, and, knowing how children love their own things and cry when they are lost, she gathered up all that were not spoiled, and made Goldfin and Silver-tail help her carry them to the shore, where people had gathered to save whatever came from the wreck.

There was great rejoicing when these small treasures came ashore, and they were carried to the house where the lady and the child were. This pleased Nelly very much, and even the lazy mermaids found the new game pleasant; so they went on floating things to the beach, even the heavy bags with the poor sailors' clothes, wet books, and boxes, which otherwise would have been lost. No one could see Goldfin and Silver-tail, but now and then some child would cry out, when Nelly lingered to look and listen through the foam and spray,—

"Oh, I saw a face over there,—a dear little face, very pretty but sad, and a hand waved at me! Could it be a mermaid?"

Then some older person would say,—

"Nonsense, child! there are no mermaids. It is only the reflection of your own face in the water. Come away, or the tide will catch you."

If Nelly had not been partly human this could not have happened; and though no one believed in her, she took comfort in the thought that she was not all a fish, and loved to linger where she could see the children at play long after Goldfin and Silver-tail had grown tired of them and gone back to their own affairs.

The longer she stayed the more sad she grew; for the land seemed pleasanter now than the sea,—the green, dry, warm land, with the flowers and trees, birds and lambs, and dear people to love and care for her. Even school looked like a happy place; and when she thought of her own home, where mother and Baby were, her heart was so full of longing for them that her tears dropped into the sea, and she held out her arms, crying sadly,—

"Oh, mamma, dear mamma, forgive me, love me, and help me to come back to you!"

No one answered, no one came; and poor Nelly sank sobbing down to cry herself to sleep in her pearl-lined bed, with no good night kiss to comfort her.

Every day she longed more and more to go home, and grew more and more tired of the sea and all in it. The mermaids could not amuse her nor understand her sorrow; so she went to wise old Barnacle and asked him what she should do to be a child again.

"No one but the King of the gulls can change you, my Periwinkle," said the merman, kindly. "You must wait and watch for him patiently. He is not seen very often; so it may be years before he comes again. Meantime be happy with us, and don't fret for that very dry land in which we see no beauty."

This comforted Nelly a good deal, and she spent half her time floating on the waves, calling the gulls, feeding them, and making them her friends, so that they might be sure to tell her when the King came. Other kind things she did, trying to be good; for *she* knew, though even the wise old merman did not, that naughty people *cannot* be happy. She gathered all the curious shells she could find, and strewed them on the beach for the children playing there. She popped the cross crabs and lobsters into the nets let down for them, and helped the fishermen to many a good load for market. She sat and sang among the rocks where lonely people could hear the faint sweet music and enjoy it. She watched over the little people when they went bathing, and loved to catch and kiss the rosy babies as they splashed about, and send quiet ripples to refresh the sick ones when their nurses dipped them in the wholesome sea.

She was good to all the wounded fishes who got hurt by the many enemies that haunt the great ocean, and tried to teach the cruel sharks, the ugly octopus, and the lazy snails to be kinder and more industrious. They did not mind her; but it kept her busy, and made her heart tender to try to help all who came near her, and every night when she went to her lonely bed she said hopefully,—

"Perhaps to-morrow the King will come and let me go home. When I do, mamma must find a better Nelly than the naughty, wilful one who ran away."

She supposed her mother would think her drowned when the clothes were found on the rock, and often mourned over the sorrow she had given those at home. But she cheered herself with imagining the joy her wonderful return would bring, and could hardly wait for that happy time.

The mermaids were soon going far away to the South Sea for the winter, and begged her to come with them, telling how lovely everything was there,—all about the pearl-divers, the Spice Islands, the coral trees, and the many wonders of that summer world. But Nelly no longer cared for any place but the pretty cottage on the cliff that overlooked the sea, and she was not tempted by any of the fine tales they told.

"No; I'd rather live here all alone where I can see my own people and home, even if I wait years and years before the King comes. I know now what a silly child I was to leave everything that I was made to use and enjoy, and try to be a creature without any soul. I don't care if my heart does ache; I'd rather be as I am than like you, without any love in you or any wish to be good and wise and happy as we are."

Goldfin and Silver-tail thought her very ungrateful after she said that, and left her alone. But she did not care; for Father Barnacle was to stay and "stone up," as they called their queer way of dying. So when all had gone she was very kind to the old merman, who never stirred out of his nook, but sat meditating on the hundred years of his life and wondering what would become of the rock he was slowly to grow a part of.

Nelly did not want him to die yet; so she brought him nice things to eat, sang to him, and asked so many questions that he was forced to keep awake and answer them. Oh, such wonderful stories as he told her! Such interesting histories of sea flowers, fishes, and monsters, such wise lessons in tides and stars, and the mysteries of the great ocean! Nelly would sit on a conch shell and listen for hours, never tired of these new fairy tales.

But she did not forget to watch for the Great Gull, and every day floated near the shore, beckoning every white-winged bird that flew by and asking for tidings of the King. At last he came! Nelly was lying on the waves idly singing to herself, with one hand held up for her pet sandpiper to light upon, when, instead of little Peep, a great silvery bird perched there, and looking up she saw the fiery eye, the red ring about the neck, the crest on the head, and with a joyful splash she cried out,—

"He's come! he's come! Oh, dear King, give me another wish, a better wish, and let me be a little girl again."

"Done!" said the Great Gull, waving his wings over her. "Will you be contented now?"

"I will! I will! answered Nelly, eagerly.

"Never wilful and disobedient?"

"Never, never!"

"Sure you won't want to be a bird, a fish, or a mermaid again?"

"Yes, yes; for nothing is so lovely as to be a child."

"Good!" and suddenly clutching her in his strong claws the gull flew high up in the air as if he were going to take her to his nest and eat her like a fish.

Poor Nelly was sadly frightened; but before she could catch her breath to ask what was to happen, the King said, in a loud voice, "Remember!" and let her drop.

She expected to be dashed on the rocks below, and thought that was to be her punishment, perhaps; but to her great surprise she floated down like a feather, and found herself lying on the sand in her own shape and the very clothes she wore when she went away. She lay a moment enjoying the comfort of being warm and dry, and feeling the dear earth under her.

"Why, darling, how long you have been asleep!" said a voice close by; and starting up Nelly saw her mother stooping over her, while Baby was creeping nearer to laugh and crow as he peeped into her face to see if she was awake.

"Oh, mamma, dear mamma, I am so glad to have you again! I was very naughty, but I've learned a lesson, and I'm going to be your good child now," cried Nelly, holding her mother tight with many kisses.

"Bless the dear! she has been dreaming, and wakes up in a lovely mood," said mamma, laughing.

"Didn't you think I was drowned? How long have I been away?" asked Nelly, looking about her as if bewildered.

"About an hour. I was not troubled, for I knew you would not break your promise, dear."

"Then it *was* a dream, and I haven't been a mermaid?" said Nelly.

"I hope not; for I like my little girl just as she is. Tell me the dream while I smooth away these tangles before we go home."

So, sitting on her mother's knee, while Baby dug holes in the sand, Nelly told her adventures as well as she could; for now it all seemed dim and far away, and nothing remained clear in her mind but the thought that it was indeed a lovely and a happy thing to be a little child with a heart to feel, a mother to love, and a home to live in till we go to find that other one, fairer than any on the earth or in the sea.

# The Flower's Story

MARION HAD BEEN ILL, and was still so weak that she had to lie on her bed many hours each day trying to sleep and rest. One winter afternoon when the snow fell quietly outside and the room was very still, with Nurse dozing in her chair, the kitten purring on the rug, and nothing new or pretty to look at but a bunch of pansies in a glass beside the bed, Marion said to herself with a sigh,—

"If I only had some one to tell me a story I should be able to get through this long day without fretting. But Mamma is away, Nurse is tired, and I know all my books by heart; so what can I do, since I'm too tired to play with my dolls?"

No one answered this important question; and Marion sighed again as she turned to look at the other side of the room, hoping to discover some help or amusement in that direction. The queer ladies on the great Japanese fan over the glass stared at her with their small eyes, but seemed too busy drinking tea out of red and yellow teapots to take any interest in the pale little girl on the bed. The pins sat primly in the blue satin cushion as usual; but neither the pearl fly, the golden rose-headed one, nor the funny mourning brooch Nurse was so fond of,—with hair in it, and a picture of a fat baby at the back,—could amuse Marion now. The dolls lay piled up in the cradle, with their poor arms and legs sticking out in all directions, sadly neglected by their little mamma; while the dear books upon the shelves had been read so often lately that they had nothing new and pleasant to offer now.

"Oh dear! I wish the birds on the wall-paper or the children in the pictures hanging round my room could sing and talk to me. I've been so good and patient I really think some one *ought* to take pity on a poor little sick girl and do something to please her," said Marion, with a third sigh, heavier than the others.

It made such a breeze that it blew one of the flowers out of the glass. Marion took it up and looked at it, ready for any playmate, even a ladies'-delight.

It was a very pretty one, and showed such a smiling face among its dark and bright petals that the child felt as if she had found a friend, and kissed it softly, being rather tender-hearted just then as well as lonely.

To her great surprise the flower nodded at her, and then a faint, sweet voice said, as she still held it close to her face,—

"Now I can speak, and am very glad to come and amuse you; for we have been pitying you very much, because we also are lonely and home-sick so far from our own people."

"Why, you dear little thing, how lovely it is to hear you talk and see you smile at me! Please tell me all about yourself. I'm fond of flowers, and was so pleased when one of my schoolmates sent me this pretty nosegay of pansies," said Marion, charmed with this surprise.

"I have no story; for I was born in a green-house, and have lived in a little flower-pot all my life, with many sisters, who are carried away when they bloom, and never come back again. We only sat for a few hours in a shop before we were pinned in paper, and brought here by a dreadful boy, who left us at your door. We were much pleased to find ourselves in this pretty vase of fresh water in a quiet, warm room, with a gentle mistress to look at us. Now, if you want a story about our people, I will tell you an old one that all our family know and like very much."

"Do!" cried Marion; and then, with kitty asleep on her arm, she lay and listened with the deepest interest to this little history of—

### THE PRINCES AND THE PANSIES: A FAIRY TALE

ONCE UPON A TIME there was a King who had two little sons, named Purple and Plush because they always wore mourning for their mother, who died when they were born. The King would not wear purple, which is the proper color for royal sorrow. He was a very selfish man, and cared only for his own comfort; so he lived in his splendid rooms, and amused himself among his books, quite lazy and contented in his green velvet dressing-gown and red cap, sleeping a great deal, reading, and drinking wine so that he might forget the loss of his beautiful queen.

He did not care about his little sons, and left them to the nurses and then the tutors, as they grew up from babies to pretty boys, so sweet and wise and good that people said the spirit of their dead mother must watch over them; and perhaps it did. They were always together, always busy, always kind and gentle, but rather sad, because their father did not love them; and all the affection of the many friends they made could not make up for the loss of father and mother love.

His subjects wanted the King to marry again, so that the court might be gay with feasts and balls and splendid games as it used to be; but he was too selfish and lazy to disturb himself, till a certain beautiful lady came to see him. She was a widow, with two little daughters, named Primrose and Daffodil because they always wore yellow gowns. Their mother was the Princess Jonquil, and dressed in cloth of gold. She was very proud, and wished to be queen; so she put on a purple velvet cloak, and made the little girls wear purple hats to look as if they mourned like the rest of the kingdom, and went to court to marry the King. They were all so pretty and charming that every one admired and welcomed them; and while the Princess played chess and read poetry to amuse his Majesty, the children played together and tried to be friends.

But Primrose and Daffodil were vain and selfish and wilful; and the little Princes soon found that they expected to have their own way about everything, and flew into sad passions if any one dared to reprove them. So the little boys were more unhappy than ever when they were told that their father was to marry the Princess, and these disagreeable girls were to be their half-sisters.

There was a splendid wedding, and the bells rang, and the trumpets sounded, and every one feasted and danced; for the fountains were filled with wine, and tables were spread in the marketplace, so that all the poor people could have a good time as well as the rich. The new Queen was very anxious to please her subjects, and made things so gay that at first every one praised her; and the King gladly let her rule, as it left him quiet with his books and bottles. Now the little girls were prouder than ever, and shone like the sun in their fine new gowns. But the Princes would not change their purple velvet suits, though they put on gold belts and set jonquils in their caps in honor of the Queen. They tried to enjoy the gayety, but soon found that they were neglected by every one; for people saw who was to have the power, and hastened to pet and flatter the young Princesses in order to please their mother. She showed how she meant to rule the first time she took the throne; for the King was not there, and she sat alone in her cloth-of-gold robes very splendid to see. She put her daughters one at each side on the green satin chairs set for the Princes, and ordered the poor boys to share her footstool between them.

Some people were very angry at this, and told the King. But he only said: "Don't trouble me. Her Majesty will do as she thinks best; and my sons will obey her as if they were her own." So nothing could be done; and the gentle boys sat at the Queen's feet, while the vain little girls rustled and smiled and tossed their heads on the high seats where they did not belong.

This was the beginning of sad times for the Princes; for the new mother wanted them out of the way that she might reign when the King died. She dared not send them away so soon; but she ordered them to live quietly with their tutors and servants in a lonely part of the palace, and never allowed them to come to the feasts, the hunting-parties, or any of the splendid shows with which she amused the people. Since their father did not object, the boys obeyed, and amused themselves by working among the flowers with old Adam, the gardener, who taught them many curious, useful, and beautiful things about trees and plants. They also learned to play and sing, and often sat in the summer evenings making music with their little lutes sweeter than that of the nightingales in the rose-bushes, or the court concerts, where the bad Queen and the proud Princesses sat in all their splendor. The boys studied and grew wise with the teachers, who loved them; but as time went by they began to long for more freedom and pleasure, when the horns blew and all the great people rode away to hunt the deer or fly their falcons. They begged the Queen to let them see their father; but when she saw what handsome, tall lads they were growing she was more anxious than ever to get rid of them, and in the night she sent her soldiers to take them to the tower, where they were shut up in a high room, with only bread and water to live on,—no books, no friends, no freedom; for no one knew where they were, because the Queen told the father that they had run away, and when he had sent some people to look for them he troubled himself no more about the matter.

So they lived for a year all alone in the tower; but they were not very unhappy, for the sun smiled in at them, birds built nests in the ivy that covered the gray walls, and the wind sang them to sleep as it roared or whispered round their high room. They loved and cheered each other, and kept up their courage till one day no bread and water was put in at the little wicket of the door. For three days no food came, and then they knew that the wicked Queen meant to starve them to death. People thought them lost; and all but the few who were faithful forgot the Princes and obeyed the Queen, who now ruled over them like a tyrant, while her daughters grew more proud and selfish every day, and the old King slept most of the time, careless of everything but his ease.

"Now, brother, we must escape, for it is plain that no one will help us; so we will help ourselves," said Purple bravely, resolving not to starve to death to please a cruel stepmother.

"We will," cried Plush; "but how can we get out of this high tower with no ladder?"

"We will make one. I've often planned it all, but thought it our duty to

obey. Now it is right to take care of ourselves, and try to reach our father if
we can. Let us braid ropes of the straw of our beds, the blankets and sheets,
and as many of our clothes as we can spare. All these will not make a ladder
long enough to reach the ground; but it will carry us down to where the ivy
branches are strong, and from there we can climb safely to the bottom. We
will go by night and find good old Adam. He will feed and help us and tell
us what to do."

"A splendid plan! Let us set to work while our strength holds out or it
will be too late," answered Plush, who was very white and weak with hunger.

Busily flew the fingers, and soon long coils of cord were made; while the
poor lads chewed leaves and drank the rain to keep themselves alive. At last
they had enough to reach a long way down; and when night came Purple
made his brother go first,—for he was an hour younger, and rather lighter,
and he wanted to be sure he was safe before he escaped himself. Down
climbed Plush, while the other lad leaned out, with his hands on the frail
ladder, holding his breath till the dark figure was out of sight in the gloom,
and a soft whistle told him that all was safe with the dear boy. Then he
followed, and Plush caught him in his arms as he came climbing down;
while all the little birds sat silent in their nests among the ivy, and not a
stout branch broke under the clinging hands and feet,—for birds and
plants loved them, and were faithful friends, as we shall see.

In the darkness the Princes found their way to Adam's house in the great
garden, and were welcomed joyfully; for the old man thought them dead.
When he heard their story he told them that they could never reach their
father, and that they were in danger of their lives if they tried to do so; for
the Queen was very cruel and powerful, and would not let them live if she
could help it.

"Go away till you are grown, my dear little masters; then come back as
men and take the kingdom that belongs to you."

"But how can we live? What can we do, since we have no money or
friends to help us?" asked the boys, as they rested after a good supper.

"Here are your lutes," said old Adam; "I took care of them for you; and
you can go singing through the world, and so earn money for your bread. I
will give you some magic seeds which my father left me, saying that they
would not grow unless royal hands planted them, when they would bring
fortune to the happy owner for whom they bloomed. I taught you how to
garden; so when you are safely out of the kingdom sow the seed in some
wild spot, and see if the story is true. I have nothing else to give you but

bread and wine and all good wishes, my dear wronged Princes. God be with you, and bring you safely home again to reign over us long and happily."

The brothers thanked him heartily, and at dawn stole out of the city with their lutes at their backs, wallets of food at their sides, and each wrapped in a russet mantle made out of Adam's old cloak. Freedom and fresh air soon gave them back their strength and courage, and when they were at a safe distance from home they began to sing and play in the villages as they travelled along. With their faded suits, bonny faces, and gentle manners, they were a charming pair of young troubadours, and every one was glad to listen to the sweet music they made. Rich people threw silver into the caps they held up when the songs were done, and poor people gladly gave them food and beds since they had no money to give. In this way they got on very pleasantly through the winter, for in that country there was no snow; and the lads grew strong and brave trudging over hill and dale, with no enemies but wind and rain to fear, and leaving many friends behind them. They liked the free life, though it was hard; but they never forgot that they were princes, even when their purple suits were in rags and the russet cloaks worn out. Nothing mean or selfish, cruel or unjust, ever disturbed the peace of their honest hearts and clean consciences; and many generous acts, gentle words, and brave thoughts made the beggar lads kings of themselves at least, and very rich in the blessings of those whom they so kindly helped and comforted.

When spring came they were far from home, and felt that it was time to try the fairy flowers. So they chose a sunny spot on a lonely moor, where the earth was rich, and a brook kept it moist, and no one cared what they did, and there they planted the seeds and tended them carefully. While waiting for the blossoms they built a hut of green branches, and lived on wild berries, the rabbits they snared, the fish they caught, and the black bread they bought of an old woman who came to look for herbs. They had saved a little money, and when that was gone one of them would wander off for a few days singing some more into the bag, while the other watched over the bed of tender plants fast growing green and strong.

They wondered what the magic flowers would be, and often feared that they would never bloom, it was so long before any buds appeared.

"If no flowers come we shall know that we are not the right gardeners, though we *are* royal," said Purple, as he watered the bed one day.

"Then we will go on singing till we get round the world brother. By that time we shall be men and can fight for our kingdom," answered Plush, weeding busily in among the low plants that spread far and wide with large tightly folded buds on all of them.

"Our old neighbor, the herb-woman, is very curious about this plot of ours, and wants to know what we are going to raise here. I told her we did not know, but when the flowers came she might see them, because she is very wise and this may be some new herb which will cure the sick. That would be a pleasant thing to do, even if we never made a fortune."

"Indeed it would! I'd rather make people happy than be a king, and so would you, brother."

As the boys spoke a very sweet perfume filled the air, and all the leaves rustled softly as if the south wind stirred them. Then everything was still again, and the larks twittered high above their heads as if they were telling some good news to the beautiful blue world far above the clouds.

Next morning, when the Princes went to their garden, lo! it was all in bloom, and lay there like a gold and purple carpet fit for a king. The flowers were pansies, but such as were never seen before; for these were very large and all alike, looking like little faces, half sad, half cheerful, as the yellow and the dark leaves framed them in. They were very sweet, and as they nodded in the wind seemed to be whispering something to one another so interesting that the lads longed to know the pretty story they were telling.

"What can we do with them, and how can they bring us good luck?" said the elder brother, looking seriously down at the lovely things.

"Enjoy them first, then sell them in little posies, and so make money; for they are the finest ever seen, and people will be glad to buy them," answered the younger, as he began to gather the great beauties at his feet.

"So we can, and keep the seed, and go on planting and selling till we are rich. It is slow work, but we learned to be patient in the tower, and will wait to see what fortune heart's-ease is to bring us," said Prince Purple, going down on his knees before a group of lovely flowers, who bent as if glad to be gathered by such gentle hands.

"Heyday! what have we here? Surely you are fairy gardeners, my sons, to bring such splendid blossoms out of this wild moor," said a cracked voice behind them, as the old herb-woman came hobbling up with her apron full of mushrooms and her basket of sweet smelling roots and leaves.

"Only pansies, mother, for the market," answered Plush, looking up with a smile.

"See how sweet they are! You shall have the first because you are so kind to us," added Purple, offering her a bunch of them as gallantly as if he were kneeling to a queen instead of an old woman as brown and wrinkled as a withered leaf.

"Good lads! I'll be still kinder and read the story these fine flowers are trying to tell," she said, as her eyes shone and her skinny hands turned the pansies to and fro. "I can read all plants, and so I learn many strange things. See if you understand this sad tale, for this is what is written on these flowers, and it must be true, for they cannot lie."

The Princes drew nearer and watched curiously as a trembling finger pointed out the different parts while the old woman spoke, glancing into their tell-tale faces now and then.

"There are five leaves. This great golden one sits alone on her green seat at the top. These two smaller yellow ones, with a touch of purple in them, sit on either side; but these two purple ones have only one seat between them, though they are the handsomest of all. Now look here in the middle, and see this little image like a man in a green gown and a red cap hiding away in the warmest, safest place with a bag of seeds which will ripen by-and-by if he will let the sun in. Come now, do you see any meaning to that, my sons?" asked the old soul, with a sharp look at the boys, who blushed and smiled and sighed, but could not speak, for here was their own sad story truly told in the magic flower.

The herb-woman nodded wisely, but only said in a kind tone, as she put the posy in her bosom,—

"Heart's-ease won't grow for every one, but all the world wants it and will pay well for it; so sell your pansies, lads, and earn a fortune worth having. I'll be in the market-place when you come, and say a good word for you, though you don't need it with such bonny faces and gentle ways of your own."

Then she went away, and the wondering Princes made haste to pick all the flowers that were in bloom, tying the bunches up with sweet-scented grass, and laying them in baskets of green rushes which they had made. A pretty sight it was; for the little pansy faces seemed to smile up at whoever looked, the sweet breath called out, "Come and buy us!" and the dew sparkled on the leaves like diamonds on the gold and purple robes of some queen.

When the Princes came to the town they stood in the market-place and cried their wares like the other people with fruit and vegetables; but their faces were so noble, their voices so clear, their flowers so large and beautiful, that in spite of their poor clothes and humble work every one who saw and heard them felt that there was something strange and interesting about the fine boys who called so sweetly,—

"Heart's-ease! here's fresh heart's-ease! Who'll buy? Who'll buy?"

All who passed were charmed with the great pansies, for the like had never been seen in that country; so the baskets were soon empty, and more than one bit of gold shone among the copper and silver coins in their pockets, because the rich as well as the poor hastened to buy heart's-ease. Much pleased with their day's work, the lads went gayly home to water the bed and rejoice over the buds that were thicker than ever. After that they sold flowers all summer long; for the magic pansies kept on blooming till the frost came, and every one who bought them discovered that they really did bring comfort and happy thoughts, and this made high and low eager to get them. Doctors sent for them for the sick; sad people ordered many to cheer them up; even bad people loved them because the bright faces, half grave, half gay, never reproached them, but smiled so pleasantly, that they woke better feelings in the evil minds. Far and wide flew the fame of this new herb, as they called it; and kings and queens begged for the seed, since they especially needed heart's-ease. Several plants even reached the lazy King as he sat in his luxurious room drinking his wine, studying, and sleeping; and the sight of the flowers woke him up, for his beautiful dead wife's name was Pansy, and he began to wonder where his sons could be and to ask about them.

The Queen also needed the wonderful herb, for she was troubled by the disorder of her kingdom. Her subjects did not love her, and grew tired of being taxed to pay for her splendor. They began to rebel, especially the poor, of whom she took no care, but left them to starve and suffer while she enjoyed herself. Even the rich and noble people became discontented and wanted to be still richer and nobler, and quarrelled among themselves, and hinted that she had killed or banished the Princes, who ought to be ruling, and would now do it better than she did.

Primrose and Daffodil had sent for the magic flowers because they wanted everything new and pretty that they heard of, no matter what it cost. When the lovely things arrived in beautiful china urns, the young Princesses were charmed with them and forbade any one else to have them.

"These are our colors, and these flowers shall be our royal badge, and no one must wear them under pain of death," they said; and they put their servants as well as themselves into new suits of purple velvet and gold, very splendid to see, with pansies everywhere,—on carriages and clothes, banners and furniture,—very proud of the graceful coat-of-arms.

But they, like their mother, soon found that the name meant something more than a pretty flower; for *pensée* is the French for "a thought," and into their careless minds came thoughts of all the harm they had done, as if the breath of the new-fashioned violet reproached them, while the sweet little faces recalled the sad ones of the banished boys whose places they had unjustly taken.

So all were ill at ease, and the spell of the flower began to work at home as well as abroad, helping to make things ready for the wanderers when they should return.

Meantime the Princes were travelling round the world, learning much and growing wise and good as well as tall and brave, and handsomer than ever. In the winter time they sang and played, and no Christmas feast was merry without the lute-players, no peasant's wedding quite perfect till they came, and often in palaces they made music for lords and ladies to dance by, and were generously paid. But what they liked better was to sing in prisons, hospitals, or poor places, where they not only gave pleasure but money, and then stole away without stopping to be thanked, so happy to be able to help the sad and sick and suffering.

In summer they rested in some pleasant spot, and planted the magic seed which would grow in any soil and was admired everywhere. So they went on their way busily and happily, leaving music and flowers behind them, and making the world brighter and better by sweet sounds and happy thoughts, till they were called "The Blessed Boys," and were waited for and welcomed and loved east and west and north and south.

Summers and winters passed, and they were tall youths when they came again to their father's kingdom in their journey round the world. But though old and wise enough now to rule, and sure to be gladly received by the discontented people, they found that they no longer felt bitter and angry with those who had wronged them. Time had taught them to forgive and forget; their peaceful, happy life made war distasteful, and they loved freedom so well that they had no heart to force others to obey.

"We reign over a larger and lovelier kingdom than this, our subjects love us dearly, and we are not tied to a throne, but are as free as the wind; let us be content with this, and ask for nothing more," said Prince Purple to his brother, as they looked down on the familiar city while resting on a hill outside the gates.

"I don't care to be shut up in a palace and obliged to live by rule any more. But if what we heard is true, there is plenty of work to do for the poor here, and we have saved so much we can at least begin to help those who suffer most. No one need know us, and we can be at work while waiting for our father to remember and recall us," answered Plush, who was as princely yet as delicate as the soft silken stuff he loved to wear.

So they disguised themselves as young Brothers of Mercy in black hoods and gowns, and went into the city looking about them for a home. Old Adam was still alive, but very poor now; for the Queen had sent him away when the Princes escaped, and the King had forgotten him. The boys found him out and told him who they were, and lived with him, making the old man very happy, proud, and comfortable. All day they went about among the poor, helping them in many ways; for the money they had earned never seemed to give out, no matter how generous they were. Heart's-ease sprang up where they walked, as if the magic seeds fell out of their pockets unseen; and soon they could be traced all over the city by happy faces, and the pots of pansies in humble windows where no flowers would ever grow before. No one knew them by any name but that of "The Brothers;" and many sick, sad souls blessed them for the good they did so quietly.

Before long, tidings of these wonderful young men reached the palace, where the old King now lay ill, and the Queen lived in fear of her life, for the people hated her and might break out at any moment. She sent for the Brothers; and they came at once, hoping to do some good. Nobody recognized the pretty Princes in the tall young monks, half hidden in their hoods and gowns; but comfort and courage seemed to come with them, for the sick King grew stronger when they prayed or sang beside him, and the sad Queen took heart, and confessed her sins to them, begging them to tell her what to do, since selfish splendor brought neither happiness, love, nor honor.

"Repent, and undo the wrong you have done," answered one Brother, boldly.

"But the Princes are lost or dead, and my people hate me," sighed the poor Queen.

"God has taken better care of the motherless boys than you did, and they will come back when it is time. Do you pity and help your people. Make them love and trust you; then you will be safe and happy, and your kingdom glorious," said the other Brother in his gentle voice.

"I will, I will!" cried the Queen, while repentant tears fell on her cloth-of-gold mantle, which was not dimmed by the salt drops, but seemed to shine the brighter for them.

The she took counsel with the Brothers; and while Plush nursed and cheered the old father, Purple helped his stepmother to win the confidence of her people by giving bread and money generously, building better houses for them, making wiser laws, and ruling with mercy and justice, till peace came back and the danger of rebellion was over,—for kindness conquers all things.

The Princesses at first objected to these changes, and were angry with the new-comers for preaching self-denial, humility, and simplicity; but the monks made them so beautiful by their persuasive words and lovely lives that soon these royal girls, as well as all their ladies, began to see how selfish and frivolous their days had been and to long for better things.

It took time to teach them to freely put away their fine clothes, forget their luxurious habits, and heartily enjoy good books, wise society, real charity, and all the sweet, simple duties, pleasures, and lessons which make life happy and death peaceful when it comes to kings as well as beggars.

Slowly the beautiful work went on. The old father seemed to wake up and wonder why he had been wasting time in dreams. It was too late now for him to rule; he had not strength enough, and he vainly longed for his brave boys. The Queen sat alone on the throne, forgiven and loved, and might have been happy if the thought of the lost Princes had not haunted her till she was so full of remorse and sorrow she resolved to go into a convent and do penance for her sins. But who should reign in her place? The King was too old and feeble, the Princesses too young, and the rightful heirs were lost or dead.

"Now is the time!" said Purple. "We are needed, and must enter into our kingdom before some usurper comes to take it."

"I am ready, brother; and we both are fitter to rule as princes for having learned to work, wait, and be happy as beggars," answered Plush.

There was to be a grand council of all the wise men, great lords, and good people to decide about a new king; for the Queen wanted to abdicate, being tired of her splendor. When all were gathered together, and the beautiful ladies looked down from the gallery at the knights in armor, the gray-headed ministers, and the sturdy citizens, every one was glad to see the beloved Brothers come in and stand humbly at the lower end of the council board. They were welcome everywhere; for though so young, they seemed to understand the hearts of people better than the old men who studied books all their long lives. After much debate the Queen said, as she left the great golden chair empty,—

"Let us leave it to our good friends who have helped us so much, and taught us to see what is needed on a throne. Dear Brothers, come up hither, and tell us who shall sit here, for I am not worthy."

Without a word the two young monks went to the high place, and, standing on either side of the Queen, dropped off their disguises. There, brave in purple velvet suits, with the golden heads and handsome faces of the royal boys, older and graver, but still the same,—there were the lost Princes, come to their own at last!

People were so startled that for a moment no one spoke or stirred; all stood up and stared silently while Purple said, with a smile and gesture that won their hearts,—

"We are ready to take our rightful places, if you need us, glad to forget the past, forgive our wrongs, and try to make the future happier for all. We have been prisoners, beggars, gardeners, minstrels, and monks in our long wanderings. Now we are princes again, more fit to rule because of the hard lessons we have learned; while time and poverty and pain have taught us the value of patience, justice, courage, and mercy."

As he ended a great shout greeted them, and the Queen fell at their feet praying for pardon; while Primrose and Daffodil hid their faces, remembering the cruel things they had said and done. There could be no doubt that the Princes were welcome home and well beloved, for soon all over the city flew the glad news. Bells rang, bonfires blazed, people danced and sang, and feasts were spread in palaces and cottages in honor of the Blessed Boys.

The old King was startled wide awake, and so delighted that he got straight out of his bed, cured of all his ills but age, as if by magic. The Queen smiled again, and felt that she was forgiven; penitent Primrose and Daffodil grew as sweet and gay as the flowers they were named for, and the Princes fell in love with them in the good old fairy-tale fashion. Everything was all right now, and the kingdom soon looked like a great garden of pansies; for the chosen flower blossomed everywhere, and rich and poor loved it.

Before long two splendid weddings were seen at court, and a new throne was made,—a double one, for on it sat the twin kings with their young wives beside them. The old King abdicated at once; and the Queen was so tired of reigning that she gladly devoted herself to her husband, both enjoying the happiness of their children, who ruled long and well over Pansyland,—for they gave that name to their country out of gratitude to the flower that brought them friends and fortune, wisdom and heart's-ease.

"That is a pleasant story, and I shall remember it," said Marion, as the teller leaned down to refresh itself with a sip of water after the long tale.

"Remember also what it means, my dear," said the flower in its sweet voice. "Learn to rule yourself; make your own little kingdom a peaceful, happy one, and find nothing too humble to teach you a lesson,—not even a Ladies'-Delight."

# The Silver Party

"SUCH A LONG MORNING! Seems as if dinner-time would *never* come!" sighed Tony, as he wandered into the dining-room for a third pick at the nuts and raisins to beguile his weariness with a little mischief.

It was Thanksgiving Day. All the family were at church, all the servants busy preparing for the great dinner; and so poor Tony, who had a cold, had not only to stay at home, but to amuse himself while the rest said their prayers, made calls, or took a brisk walk to get an appetite. If he had been allowed in the kitchen, he would have been quite happy; but cook was busy and cross, and rapped him on the head with a poker when he ventured near the door. Peeping through the slide was also forbidden, and John, the man, bribed him with an orange to keep out of the way till the table was set.

That was now done. The dining-room was empty and quiet, and poor Tony lay down on the sofa to eat his nuts and admire the fine sight before him. All the best damask, china, glass, and silver was set forth with great care. A basket of flowers hung from the chandelier, and the sideboard was beautiful to behold with piled-up fruit, dishes of cake, and many-colored finger-bowls and glasses.

"That's all very nice, but the eating part is what *I* care for. Don't believe I'll get my share to-day, because mamma found out about this horrid cold. A fellow can't help sneezing, though he *can* hide a sore throat. Oh hum! nearly two more hours to wait;" and with a long sigh Tony closed his eyes for a luxurious yawn.

When he opened them, the strange sight he beheld kept him staring without a thought of sleep. The big soup-ladle stood straight up at the head of the table with a face plainly to be seen in the bright bowl. It was a very heavy, handsome old ladle, so the face was old, but round and jolly; and the long handle stood very erect, like a tall thin gentleman with a big head.

"Well, upon my word that's queer!" said Tony, sitting up also, and wondering what would happen next.

To his great amazement the ladle began to address the assembled forks and spoons in a silvery tone very pleasant to hear:—

"Ladies and gentlemen, at this festive season it is proper that we should

380

enjoy ourselves. As we shall be tired after dinner, we will at once begin our sports by a grand promenade. Take partners and fall in!"

At these words a general uprising took place; and before Tony could get his breath a long procession of forks and spoons stood ready. The finger-bowls struck up an airy tune as if invisible wet fingers were making music on their rims, and led by the stately ladle like a drum-major, the grand march began. The forks were the gentlemen, tall, slender, and with a fine curve to their backs; the spoons were the ladies, with full skirts, and the scallops on the handles stood up like silver combs; the large ones were the mammas, the teaspoons were the young ladies, and the little salts the children. It was sweet to see the small things walk at the end of the procession, with the two silver rests for the carving knife and fork trotting behind like pet dogs. The mustard-spoon and pickle-fork went together, and quarrelled all the way, both being hot-tempered and sharp-tongued. The steel knives looked on, for this was a very aristocratic party, and only the silver people could join in it.

"Here's fun!" thought Tony, staring with all his might, and so much interested in this remarkable state of things that he forgot hunger and time altogether.

Round and round went the glittering train, to the soft music of the many-toned finger-bowls, till three turns about the long oval table had been made; then all fell into line for a contra-dance, as in the good old times before every one took to spinning like tops. Grandpa Ladle led off with his oldest daughter, Madam Gravy Ladle, and the little salts stood at the bottom prancing like real children impatient for their turn. When it came, they went down the middle in fine style, with a cling! clang! that made Tony's legs quiver with a longing to join in.

It was beautiful to see the older ones twirl round in a stately way, with bows and courtesies at the end, while the teaspoons and small forks romped a good deal, and Mr. Pickle and Miss Mustard kept every one laughing at their smart speeches. The silver butter-knife, who was an invalid, having broken her back and been mended, lay in the rack and smiled sweetly down upon her friends, while the little Cupid on the lid of the butter-dish pirouetted on one toe in the most delightful manner.

When every one had gone through the dance, the napkins were arranged as sofas and the spoons rested, while the polite forks brought sprigs of celery to fan them with. The little salts got into grandpa's lap; and the silver dogs lay down panting, for they had frisked with the children. They all talked; and Tony could not help wondering if real ladies said such things when they put *their* heads together and nodded and whispered, for some of the remarks were so personal that he was much confused. Fortunately they took no notice of him, so he listened and learned something in this queer way.

"I have been in this family a hundred years," began the soup-ladle; "and it seems to me that each generation is worst than the last. My first master was punctual to a minute, and madam was always down beforehand to see that all was ready. Now master comes at all hours; mistress lets the servants do as they like; and the manners of the children are very bad. Sad state of things, very sad!"

"Dear me, yes!" sighed one of the large spoons; "we don't see such nice housekeeping now as we did when we were young. Girls were taught all about it then; but now it is all books or parties, and few of them know a skimmer from a gridiron."

"Well, I'm sure the poor things are much happier than if they were messing about in kitchens as girls used to do in your day. It is much better for them to be dancing, skating, and studying than wasting their young lives darning and preserving, and sitting by their mammas as prim as dishes. *I* prefer the present way of doing things, though the girls in this family *do* sit up too late, and wear too high heels to their boots."

The mustard-spoon spoke in a pert tone, and the pickle-fork answered sharply,—

"I agree with you, cousin. The boys also sit up too late. I'm tired of being waked to fish out olives or pickles for those fellows when they come in from the theatre or some dance; and as for that Tony, he is a real pig,—eats everything he can lay hands on, and is the torment of the maid's life."

"Yes," cried one little salt-spoon, "we saw him steal cake out of the sideboard, and he never told when his mother scolded Norah."

"So mean!" added the other; and both the round faces were so full of disgust that Tony fell flat and shut his eyes as if asleep to hide his confusion. Some one laughed; but he dared not look, and lay blushing and listening to remarks which plainly proved how careful we should be of our acts and words even when alone, for who knows what apparently dumb thing may be watching us.

"I have observed that Mr. Murry reads the paper at table instead of talking to his family; that Mrs. Murry worries about the servants; the girls gossip and giggle; the boys eat, and plague one another; and that small child Nelly teases for all she sees, and is never quiet till she gets the sugar-bowl," said Grandpa Ladle, in a tone of regret. "Now, useful and pleasant chat at table would make meals delightful, instead of being scenes of confusion and discomfort."

"I bite their tongues when I get a chance, hoping to make them witty or to check unkind words; but they only sputter, and get a lecture from Aunt Maria, who is a sour old spinster, always criticising her neighbors."

As the mustard-spoon spoke, the teaspoons laughed as if they thought *her* rather like Aunt Maria in that respect.

"I gave the baby a fit of colic to teach her to let pickles alone, but no one thanked me," said the pickle-fork.

"Perhaps if we keep ourselves so bright that those who use us can see their faces in us, we shall be able to help them a little; for no one likes to see an ugly face or a dull spoon. The art of changing frowns to smiles is never old-fashioned; and lovely manners smooth away the little worries of life beautifully." A silvery voice spoke, and all looked respectfully at Madam Gravy Ladle, who was a very fine old spoon, with a coat of arms on it, and a polish that all envied.

"People can't always be remembering how old and valuable and bright they are. Here in America we just go ahead and make manners and money for ourselves. *I* don't stop to ask what dish I'm going to help to; I just pitch in and take all I can hold, and don't care a bit whether I shine or not. My grandfather was a kitchen spoon; but I'm smarter than he was, thanks to my plating, and look and feel as good as any one, though I haven't got stags' heads and big letters on my handle."

No one answered these impertinent remarks of the sauce-spoon, for all knew that she was not pure silver, and was only used on occasions when many spoons were needed. Tony was ashamed to hear her talk in that rude way to the fine old silver he was so proud of, and resolved he'd give the saucy spoon a good rap when he helped himself to the cranberry.

An impressive silence lasted till a lively fork exclaimed, as the clock struck, "Every one is coasting out-of-doors. Why not have our share of the fun inside? It is very fashionable this winter, and ladies and gentlemen of the best families do it, I assure you."

"We will!" cried the other forks; and as the dowagers did not object, all fell to work to arrange the table for this agreeable sport. Tony sat up to see how they would manage, and was astonished at the ingenuity of the silver people. With a great clinking and rattling they ran to and fro; dragging the stiff white mats about; the largest they leaned up against the tall caster, and laid the rest in a long slope to the edge of the table, where a pile of napkins made a nice snowdrift to tumble into.

"What *will* they do for sleds?" thought Tony; and the next minute chuckled when he saw them take the slices of bread laid at each place, pile on, and spin away, with a great scattering of crumbs like snowflakes, and much laughter as they landed in the white pile at the end of the coast.

"Won't John give it to 'em if he comes in and catches 'em turning his nice table topsy-turvy!" said the boy to himself, hoping nothing would happen to end this jolly frolic. So he kept very still, and watched the gay forks and spoons climb up and whiz down till they were tired. The little salts got Baby Nell's own small slice, and had lovely times on a short coast of their own made of one mat held up by grandpa, who smiled benevolently at the fun, being too old and heavy to join in it.

They kept it up until the slices were worn thin, and one or two upsets alarmed the ladies; then they rested and conversed again. The mammas talked about their children, how sadly the silver basket needed a new lining, and what there was to be for dinner. The teaspoons whispered sweetly together, as young ladies do,—one declaring that rouge powder was not as good as it used to be, another lamenting the sad effect of eggs upon her complexion, and all smiled amiably upon the forks, who stood about discussing wines and cigars, for both lived in the sideboard, and were brought out after dinner, so the forks knew a great deal about such matters, and found them very interesting, as all gentlemen seem to do.

Presently some one mentioned bicycles, and what fine rides the boys of the family told about. The other fellows proposed a race; and before Tony could grasp the possibility of such a thing, it was done. Nothing easier, for there stood a pile of plates, and just turning them on their edges, the forks got astride, and the big wheels spun away as if a whole bicycle club had suddenly arrived.

Old Pickle took the baby's plate, as better suited to his size. The little salts made a tricycle of napkin-rings, and rode gayly off, with the dogs barking after them. Even the carving-fork, though not invited, could not resist the exciting sport, and tipping up the wooden bread-platter, went whizzing off at a great pace, for his two prongs were better than four, and his wheel was lighter than the china ones. Grandpapa Ladle cheered them on, like a fine old gentleman as he was, for though the new craze rather astonished him, he liked manly sports, and would have taken a turn if his dignity and age had allowed. The ladies chimed their applause, for it really was immensely exciting to see fourteen plates with forks astride racing round the large table with cries of, "Go it, Pickle! Now, then, Prongs! Steady, Silver-top! Hurray for the twins!"

The fun was at its height when young Prongs ran against Pickle, who did not steer well, and both went off the table with a crash. All stopped at once, and crowded to the edge to see who was killed. The plates lay in pieces, old Pickle had a bend in his back that made him groan dismally, and Prongs had fallen down the register.

Wails of despair arose at that awful sight, for he was a favorite with every one, and such a tragic death was too much for some of the tender-hearted spoons, who fainted at the idea of that gallant fork's destruction in what to them was a fiery volcano.

"Serves Pickle right! He ought to know he was too old for such wild games," scolded Miss Mustard, peering anxiously over at her friend, for they were fond of one another in spite of their tiffs.

"Now let us see what these fine folks will do when they get off the damask and come to grief. A helpless lot, I fancy, and those fellows deserve what they've got," said the sauce-spoon, nearly upsetting the twins as she elbowed her way to the front to jeer over the fallen.

"I think you will see that gentle people are as brave as those who make a noise," answered Madam Gravy, and leaning over the edge of the table she added in her sweet voice, "Dear Mr. Pickle, we will let down a napkin and pull you up if you have strength to take hold."

"Pull away, ma'am," groaned Pickle, who well deserved his name just then, and soon, thanks to Madam's presence of mind, he was safely laid on a pile of mats, while Miss Mustard put a plaster on his injured back.

Meanwhile brave Grandpapa Ladle had slipped from the table to a chair, and so to the floor without too great a jar to his aged frame; then sliding along the carpet, he reached the register. Peering down that dark, hot abyss he cried, while all listened breathlessly for a reply, "Prongs, my boy, are you there?"

"Ay, ay, sir; I'm caught in the wire screen. Ask some of the fellows to lend a hand and get me out before I'm melted," answered the fork, with a gasp of agony.

Instantly the long handle of the patriarchal Ladle was put down to his rescue, and after a moment of suspense, while Prongs caught firmly hold, up he came, hot and dusty, but otherwise unharmed by that dreadful fall. Cheers greeted them, and every one lent a hand at the napkin as they were hoisted to the table to be embraced by their joyful relatives and friends.

"What did you think about down in that horrid place?" asked one of the twins.

"I thought of a story I once heard master tell, about a child who was found one cold day sitting with his feet on a newspaper, and when asked what he was doing, answered, 'Warming my feet on the "Christian Register.'" I hoped my register would be Christian enough not to melt me before help came. Ha! ha! See the joke, my dears?" and Prongs laughed as gayly as if he never had taken a header into a volcano.

"What did you see down there?" asked the other twin, curious, as all small people are.

"Lots of dust and pins, a doll's head baby put there, Norah's thimble, and the big red marble that boy Tony was raging about the other day. It's a regular catch-all, and shows how the work is shirked in this house," answered Prongs, stretching his legs, which were a little damaged by the fall.

"What shall we do about the plates?" asked Pickle, from his bed.

"Let them lie, for we can't mend them. John will think the boy broke them, and he'll get punished, as he deserves, for he broke a tumbler yesterday, and put it slyly in the ash-barrel," said Miss Mustard, spitefully.

"Oh! I say, that's mean," began Tony; but no one listened, and in a minute Prongs answered bravely,—

"I'm a gentleman, and I don't let other people take the blame of my scrapes. Tony has enough of his own to answer for."

"I'll have that bent fork for mine, and make John keep it as bright as a new dollar to pay for this. Prongs is a trump, and I wish I could tell him so," thought Tony, much gratified at this handsome behavior.

"Right, grandson. I am pleased with you; but allow me to suggest that the Chinese Mandarin on the chimney-piece be politely requested to mend the plates. He can do that sort of thing nicely, and will be charmed to oblige us, I am sure."

Grandpapa's suggestion was a good one; and Yam Ki Lo consented at once, skipped to the floor, tapped the bits of china with his fan, and in the twinkling of an eye was back on his perch, leaving two whole plates behind him, for he was a wizard, and knew all about blue china.

Just as the silver people were rejoicing over this fine escape from discovery, the clock struck, a bell rang, voices were heard upstairs, and it was very evident that the family had arrived.

At these sounds a great flurry arose in the dining-room, as every spoon, fork, plate, and napkin flew back to its place. Pickle rushed to the jar, and plunged in head first, regardless of his back; Miss Mustard retired to the caster; the twins scrambled into the salt-cellar; and the silver dogs lay down by the carving knife and fork as quietly as if they had never stirred a leg; Grandpapa slowly reposed in his usual place; Madam followed his example with dignity; the teaspoons climbed into the holder, uttering little cries of alarm; and Prongs stayed to help them till he had barely time to drop down at Tony's place, and lie there with his bent leg in the air, the only sign of the great fall, about which he talked for a long time afterward. All was in order but the sauce-spoon, who had stopped to laugh at the Mandarin till it was too late to get to her corner; and before she could find any place of concealment, John came in and caught her lying in the middle of the table, looking very common and shabby among all the bright silver.

"What in the world is that old plated thing here for? Missis told Norah to put it in the kitchen, as she had a new one for a present to-day—real silver—so out you go;" and as he spoke, John threw the spoon through the slide,—an exile forevermore from the good society which she did not value as she should.

Tony saw the glimmer of a smile in Grandpapa Ladle's face; but it was gone like a flash, and by the time the boy reached the table nothing was to be seen in the silver bowl but his own round rosy countenance, full of wonder.

"I don't think any one will believe what I've seen, but I mean to tell, it was so *very* curious," he said, as he surveyed the scene of the late frolic, now so neat and quiet that not a wrinkle or a crumb betrayed what larks had been going on.

Hastily fishing up his long-lost marble, the doll's head, and Norah's thimble, he went thoughtfully upstairs to welcome his cousins, still much absorbed by this very singular affair.

Dinner was soon announced; and while it lasted every one was too busy eating the good things before them to observe how quiet the usually riotous Tony was. His appetite for turkey and cranberries seemed to have lost its sharp edge, and the mince-pie must have felt itself sadly slighted by his lack of appreciation of its substance and flavor. He seemed in a brown-study, and kept staring about as if he saw more than other people did. He examined Nelly's plate as if looking for a crack, smiled at the little spoon when he took salt, refused pickles and mustard with a frown, kept a certain bent fork by him as long as possible, and tried to make music with a wet finger on the rim of his bowl at dessert.

But in the evening, when the young people sat around the fire, he amused them by telling the queer story of the silver party; but he very widely left out the remarks made upon himself and family, remembering how disagreeable the sauce-spoon had seemed, and he privately resolved to follow Madam Gravy Ladle's advice to keep his own face bright, manners polite, and speech kindly, that he might prove himself to be pure silver, and be stamped a gentleman.

# *Bibliography*

## Louisa M. Alcott's Fairy Tales and Fantasy Stories

"Flower Fables." *Flower Fables*. Boston, George W. Briggs and Co., 1855.

"The Frost-King; or, the Power of Love." *Flower Fables*. Boston: George W. Briggs and Co., 1855. Rpt. with changes in *Lulu's Library. Vol. 2. The Frost King*. Boston: Roberts Brothers, 1887.

"Eva's Visit to Fairy-Land." *Flower Fables*. Boston: George W. Briggs and Co., 1855. Rpt. with changes in *Lulu's Library. Vol. 2*.

"Lily-Bell and Thistledown." *Flower Fables*. Boston: George W. Briggs and Co., 1855. Rpt. with changes in *Lulu's Library. Vol. 2*.

"Little Bud." *Flower Fables*. Boston: George W. Briggs and Co., 1855. Rpt. with changes in *Lulu's Library. Vol. 2*.

"Little Annie's Dream; or, the Fairy Flower." *Flower Fables*. Boston: George W. Briggs and Co., 1855.

"Ripple, the Water-Spirit." *Flower Fables*. Boston: George W. Briggs and Co., 1855. Rpt. in *Merry's Museum* 3, no. 5 (May 1870). Rpt. with changes in *Lulu's Library. Vol. 2*.

*The Rose Family. A Fairy Tale*. Boston: James Redpath, 1864. Rpt. in *Morning-Glories, and Other Stories*. Boston: Horace B. Fuller, 1868.

"What the Bells Saw and Said." *Saturday Evening Gazette* 53, no. 51 (21 Dec. 1867). Rpt. in *Proverb Stories*. Boston: Roberts Brothers, 1882.

"Shadow-Children." *Morning-Glories, and Other Stories*. Boston: Horace B. Fuller, 1868. Rpt. in *Aunt Jo's Scrap-Bag: An Old-Fashioned Thanksgiving*. Boston: Roberts Brothers, 1882.

"What the Swallows Did." *Morning-Glories, and Other Stories*. Boston: Horace B. Fuller, 1868. Rpt. in *Aunt Jo's Scrap-Bag: An Old-Fashioned Thanksgiving*.

"Little Gulliver." *Morning-Glories, and Other Stories*. Boston: Horace B. Fuller, 1868. Rpt. in *Aunt Jo's Scrap-Bag: An Old-Fashioned Thanksgiving*.

"The Whale's Story." *Morning-Glories, and Other Stories*. Boston: Horace B. Fuller, 1868. Rpt. in *Aunt Jo's Scrap-Bag: An Old-Fashioned Thanksgiving*.

"A Strange Island." *Morning-Glories, and Other Stories*. Boston: Horace B. Fuller, 1868. Rpt. in *Aunt Jo's Scrap-Bag: An Old-Fashioned Thanksgiving*.

"Fancy's Friend." *Morning-Glories, and Other Stories*. Boston: Horace B. Fuller, 1868. Rpt. in *Aunt Jo's Scrap-Bag: An Old-Fashioned Thanksgiving*.

"Madam Cluck, and Her Family." *Merry's Museum* 2, no. 8 (Aug. 1869). Rpt. in *Aunt Jo's Scrap-Bag: My Boys*. Boston: Roberts Brothers, 1872.

"A Curious Call." *Merry's Museum* 2, no. 2 (Feb. 1869). Rpt. in *Aunt Jo's Scrap-Bag: My Boys*.

"What Fanny Heard." *The Youth's Companion* 42, no. 19 (13 May 1869). Rpt. in *Aunt Jo's Scrap-Bag: Cupid and Chow-Chow*.

"A Marine Merry-Making." *Merry's Museum* 2, no. 10 (Oct. 1869). Rpt. in *Aunt Jo's Scrap-Bag: Cupid and Chow-Chow*.

"Fairy Pinafores." *Aunt Jo's Scrap-Bag: Cupid and Chow-Chow*. Boston: Roberts Brothers, 1874.

"The Moss People." *Aunt Jo's Scrap-Bag: Cupid and Chow-Chow*. Boston: Roberts Brothers, 1874.

"The Autobiography of an Omnibus." *St. Nicholas* 1, no. 12 (Oct. 1874). Rpt. in *Aunt Jo's Scrap-Bag: My Girls*. Boston: Roberts Brothers, 1878.

"Rosa's Tale." *Aunt Jo's Scrap-Bag: Jimmy's Cruise in the Pinafore*. Boston: Roberts Brothers, 1879.

"What Becomes of the Pins." *Aunt Jo's Scrap-Bag: Jimmy's Cruise in the Pinafore*. Boston: Roberts Brothers, 1879.

"The Dolls' Journey from Minnesota to Maine." *Aunt Jo's Scrap-Bag: An Old-Fashioned Thanksgiving*. Boston: Roberts Brothers, 1882. Rpt. as *The Dolls' Journey*. Boston: Little, Brown, 1902.

"A Christmas Dream, and How It Came True." *Harper's Young People* 4, nos. 162 and 163 (5, 12 Dec. 1882). Rpt. in *Lulu's Library. Vol. 1. A Christmas Dream*. Boston: Roberts Brothers, 1886, and rpt. as *A Christmas Dream*. Boston: Little, Brown, 1901.

"The Candy Country." *St. Nicholas* 13 (Nov. 1885): 1. Rpt. in *Lulu's Library. Vol. 1. A Christmas Dream* and rpt. as *The Candy Country*. Boston: Little Brown, 1900.

"The Skipping Shoes." *Lulu's Library. Vol. 1. A Christmas Dream*. Boston: Roberts Brothers, 1886.

"Cockyloo." *Lulu's Library. Vol. 1. A Christmas Dream*. Boston: Roberts Brothers, 1886.

"Rosy's Journey." *Lulu's Library. Vol. 1. A Christmas Dream*. Boston: Roberts Brothers, 1886.

"The Fairy Box." *Lulu's Library. Vol. 1. A Christmas Dream*. Boston: Roberts Brothers, 1886.

"The Three Frogs." *Lulu's Library. Vol. 1. A Christmas Dream*. Boston: Roberts Brothers, 1886.

"Sunshine, and Her Brothers and Sisters." *Lulu's Library. Vol. 2. The Frost King*. Boston: Roberts Brothers, 1887.

"The Fairy Spring." *Lulu's Library. Vol. 2. The Frost King*. Boston: Roberts Brothers, 1887.

"A Flower Fable." ["Queen Aster."] *The Woman's Journal* 18, no. 9 (26 Feb. 1887). Rpt. in *The Union Signal* 13, no. 10 (10 Mar. 1887). Rpt. as "Queen Aster" in

*Lulu's Library.* Vol. 2. *The Frost King* and rpt. as *Morning-Glories and Queen Aster.* Boston, Little, Brown, 1903.

"The Brownie and the Princess." *Lulu's Library.* Vol. 2. *The Frost King.* Boston: Roberts Brothers, 1887.

"Mermaids." *Lulu's Library's.* Vol. 2. *The Frost King.* Boston: Roberts Brothers, 1887.

"The Flower's Story." *Lulu's Library.* Vol. 2. *The Frost King.* Boston: Roberts Brothers, 1887.

"The Silver Party." *Harper's Young People* 9, no. 421 (22 Nov. 1887). Rpt. in *Lulu's Library.* Vol. 3. *Recollections.* Boston: Roberts Brothers, 1889.


## Secondary Sources


Attebery, Brian. *The Fantasy Tradition in American Literature: From Irving to Le Guin.* Bloomington: Indiana Univ. Press, 1980.

Bettelheim, Bruno. *The Uses of Enchantment: The Meaning and Importance of Fairy Tales.* New York: Random House, 1976.

Blount, Margaret. *Animal Land: The Creatures of Children's Fiction.* New York: Avon, 1974.

Bottigheimer, Ruth B., ed. *Fairy Tales and Society: Illusion, Allusion, and Paradigm.* Philadelphia: Univ. of Pennsylvania Press, 1986.

―――. *Grimms' Bad Girls and Bold Boys: The Moral and Social Vision of the Tales.* New Haven: Yale Univ. Press, 1987.

Briggs, Katherine. *The Fairies in English Tradition and Literature.* Chicago: Univ. of Chicago Press, 1965.

Cameron, Eleanor. *The Green and Burning Tree.* Boston: Little, Brown, 1969.

Carter, Lin. *Imaginary Worlds.* New York: Ballantine Books, 1973.

Chase, Richard. *The Jack Tales.* Boston: Houghton Mifflin, 1943.

Cook, Elizabeth. *The Ordinary and the Fabulous: An Introduction to Myths, Legends, and Fairy Tales for Teachers and Storytellers.* Cambridge: Cambridge Univ. Press, 1969.

Cott, Jonathan, ed. *Beyond the Looking Glass: Extraordinary Works of Fairy Tale and Fantasy.* New York: Stonehill Publishing, 1973.

Franz, Marie-Louise von. *An Introduction to the Interpretation of Fairy Tales.* New York: Spring, 1970.

Heuscher, Julius E. *A Psychiatric Study of Fairy Tales.* Springfield, Ill.: Thomas, 1963.

Jackson, Rosemary. *Fantasy: The Literature of Subversion.* London: Methuen, 1981.

Lochhead, Marion. *The Renaissance of Wonder in Children's Literature.* Edinburgh: Canongate, 1977.

Manlove, C. N. *Modern Fantasy: Five Studies.* Cambridge: Cambridge Univ. Press, 1975.

Opie, Iona and Peter. *The Classic Fairy Tales.* New York: Oxford Univ. Press, 1974.

Sale, Roger. *Fairy Tales and After: From Snow White to E. B. White.* Cambridge: Harvard Univ. Press, 1978.

Sax, Boria. *The Frog King: On Legends, Fables, Fairy Tales and Anecdotes of Animals.* New York: Pace Univ. Press, 1990.

Tatar, Maria M. *The Hard Facts of the Grimms' Fairy Tales.* Princeton: Princeton Univ. Press, 1987.

Thalmann, Marianne. *The Romantic Fairy Tale: Seeds of Surrealism.* Trans. Mary B. Corcoran. Ann Arbor: Univ. of Michigan Press, 1964.

Thompson, Stith. *The Folktale.* New York: Holt, Rinehart and Winston, 1946.

Waggoner, Diana. *The Hills of Faraway: A Guide to Fantasy.* New York: Atheneum, 1978.

West, Mark I., ed. *Before Oz: Juvenile Fantasy Stories from Nineteenth-Century America.* Hamden, Conn.: Archon Books, 1989.

Yolen, Jane. *Touch Magic: Fantasy, Faerie and Folklore in the Literature of Childhood.* New York: Philomel Books, 1981.

Zipes, Jack. *Breaking the Magic Spell: Radical Theories of Folk and Fairy Tales.* London: Heinemann, 1979.

———. *The Brothers Grimm: From Enchanted Forests to the Modern World.* New York and London: Routledge, 1988.

———. *Fairy Tales and the Art of Subversion: The Classical Genre for Children and the Process of Civilization.* London: Heinemann, 1983.